LUCIUS ANNAEUS SENECA was born some time between 1 BCE and 4 CE, in Corduba in southern Spain, to a Roman equestrian family. Seneca's father ('Seneca the Elder') had a successful rhetorical career, and educated his sons in Rome, in rhetoric and philosophy. Seneca was a lifelong adherent to Stoic philosophy.

Accused of committing adultery with Caligula's sister Julia Livilla, Seneca was exiled by Claudius in 41 CE and sent to Corsica, where he spent the next eight years. Several of Seneca's philosophical treatises were probably written in exile, along with many or most of his dramatic tragedies. He was brought back to Rome in 49 CE, through the intercession of Agrippina, who wanted a tutor for her son, Nero.

On the accession of Nero, in 54 CE, Seneca became Nero's tutor and adviser, together with the praetorian prefect Burrus. Their power diminished after 59 CE, when they refused to help Nero kill his mother, Agrippina. In the early 60s Seneca officially retired from public life, and wrote his *Epistulae Morales*, the *Letters on Morality*.

In 65 CE Nero accused Seneca of involvement in the plot to kill him, and forced him to commit suicide.

ELAINE FANTHAM taught at Princeton University from 1986 to 2000. Her most recent books include *Roman Literary Culture* (1996), *Ovid's 'Metamorphoses'* (Oxford Approaches to Literature, 2004), and *The Roman World of Cicero's 'De Oratore'* (2004). She has introduced and annotated Virgil's *Georgics* and introduced the *Aeneid* for Oxford World's Classics.

OXFORD WORLD'S CLASSICS

===

SENECA

Selected Letters

===

Translated with an Introduction and Notes by
ELAINE FANTHAM

8 9 16 18 48 84 90

. What does it mean
to "keep well"?

. How does seneca
vie w love?
vs. friendship.

. what does it mean to
live happily. what is
necessary.

OXFORD
UNIVERSITY PRESS

OXFORD
UNIVERSITY PRESS

Great Clarendon Street, Oxford OX2 6DP

Oxford University Press is a department of the University of Oxford.
It furthers the University's objective of excellence in research, scholarship,
and education by publishing worldwide in

Oxford New York

Auckland Cape Town Dar es Salaam Hong Kong Karachi
Kuala Lumpur Madrid Melbourne Mexico City Nairobi
New Delhi Shanghai Taipei Toronto

With offices in

Argentina Austria Brazil Chile Czech Republic France Greece
Guatemala Hungary Italy Japan Poland Portugal Singapore
South Korea Switzerland Thailand Turkey Ukraine Vietnam

Oxford is a registered trade mark of Oxford University Press
in the UK and in certain other countries

Published in the United States
by Oxford University Press Inc., New York

British Library Cataloguing in Publication Data

Data available

Library of Congress Cataloging in Publication Data

Data available

Typeset by Glyph International, Bangalore, India
Printed in Great Britain
on acid-free paper by
Clays Ltd, St Ives plc

ISBN 978-0-19-953321-3

1 3 5 7 9 10 8 6 4 2

CONTENTS

INTRODUCTION

Seneca's Home and Family

We often speak of Seneca as the most distinguished of the many Spanish writers and poets of Rome's imperial age, starting from his own father of the same name, and his nephew Lucan, and including Columella, Martial, and Quintilian. But although all of these writers came from Spain, they were Roman (or Italian) in descent, culture, and tradition. Scipio Africanus had taken eastern and southern Spain from the Carthaginians during the Hannibalic war, and most of the Spanish peninsula had been Roman since the second century BCE. The cities of Baetica (the region of southern Spain around the River Baetis) boasted elites of predominantly Roman or Italian origin.

We know Seneca's father from the reminiscences of the Roman declamatory schools during the Augustan age which he assembled for publication towards the end of his long life:[1] he also wrote an unpublished history of the Roman civil wars. However, despite possessing a very personal work full of his opinions, we can neither date his birth precisely nor the years in which he was living on his estates in Spain or visiting Rome. Father Seneca came from the city of Corduba (Cordova in Andalucia), which had been settled with Roman citizens as early as 152 BCE. It had ties of loyalty to both Pompey and Caesar, and must have found it difficult to stay on good terms with both sides in the civil war, but did not suffer any loss of status, becoming a formal Roman colony either under Caesar or Augustus. Its culture was clearly somewhat colonial, and we should assume that once the civil wars were over its leading men travelled freely and frequently between Corduba and Rome, whether on financial or political business. The elder Seneca told his sons, in the preface to his reminiscences, that only civil war stopped him going as a boy to Rome

---

[1] The title *Oratorum et Rhetorum Sententiae Divisiones Colores* is difficult to translate without paraphrase or supplement. I would suggest 'The aphorisms, argumentative analyses and psychological turns of speakers and teachers of rhetoric'. My chief modern source on Seneca the Elder is the fine study of Janet Fairweather, *Seneca the Elder* (Cambridge: Cambridge UP, 1981). References to this work in the text will be given as *Contr.* = *Controversiae*, a simplified version of the title.

where he might have heard Cicero—that is, before Cicero's murder in 43 BCE. This suggests that he was born well before 50 BCE. He probably reached Rome soon after 40 BCE, and we know that he enjoyed the patronage of the former Caesarian Asinius Pollio, consul in that year. Pollio had celebrated his triumph in 39, but after the breach between Octavian and Antony he held aloof from their growing conflict and devoted himself to civilian activities, founding Rome's first public library in the Atrium Libertatis, and acting as host for private recitations and rhetorical declamations.[2] Seneca apparently stayed in Rome most of the next twenty years or more until his late marriage (in around 10 BCE?) to Helvia, the only child of a prominent Roman family from his own part of Spain. They had three sons: Novatus, subsequently adopted by the consul Junius Gallio,[3] born in or soon after 8 BCE; our Lucius Annaeus Seneca, born between 4 and 1 BCE; and M. Annaeus Mela, who would become the father of the poet Annaeus Lucanus (Lucan).

When father Seneca dedicated his reminiscences to his sons almost forty years later, he would have been over 80 years old, about the age of his wife Helvia's father—who was still alive a few years later (*Dialogues*, XII.18.9). Given his advanced years, it is not surprising that the preface dedicating his work to his three sons reflects stern moral disapproval of the ways of modern youth (now two generations his junior); the sons themselves, already in their thirties, were presumably old enough to have passed through the youthful debaucheries father Seneca denounces:

Now our discipline is growing worse daily, whether from the luxury of this generation—for nothing is so deadly to intellects as luxury—or because when the rewards were lost of this most noble art, all competition was transferred to shameful activities that thrived with great honour and profit, or by that malicious law of fate that matters brought to their highest level of achievement slip back to their lowest, faster indeed than they rose.

For now the minds of our idle youth are sluggish, and men do not keep awake in toil over a single honourable achievement; sleep and apathy and worse than sleep and apathy, a perverted energy for bad behaviour, has seized their minds, and the disgusting passion for singing and dancing keeps them effeminate: to crimp their hair and strain their voices to the

---

[2] The elder Seneca reports attending these on several occasions.
[3] He took on the name of his adoptive father: Gallio was proconsul of Achaea, and one of the suffect consuls of 56 CE.

endearments of women, to compete with women in the softness of their bodies and grooming themselves with the most unclean of cleansing, is the model of behaviour for our young men. Who of your contemporaries is, should I say, talented enough, dedicated enough, or need I say it, enough of a man? Softened and gutless, they remain as they were born through their lives, taking others' virtue by storm but indifferent to their own. (*Contr.* Pref., 7–9)

Romans of this period were trained in composing such denunciations of fashionable amusements, but one can only hope that the old man recognized the difference between his rhetoric and the more ordinary weaknesses of the new generation. Diatribes like this should perhaps increase our sympathy for young Seneca and appreciation for the respect he always shows for his father's views.

From the writings of our Seneca, dated from approximately 37 CE to his death in 65, we can more or less reconstruct his troubled early life.[4] He was brought to Rome as a child by his maternal aunt (*Consolation to Helvia*, 19: perhaps his mother was detained by being pregnant with his younger brother) and educated there, but he was delicate (he describes his own attacks of asthma) and would later spend many years for the sake of his health with his aunt in Egypt, where her husband Galerius was imperial prefect. His aunt was important in promoting Seneca's political career and his quaestorship, but we do not know how he spent his early adult years. If he was still delicate he may have delayed entry into public life, which made severe physical demands on orators in the courts. Or he may have found the later years of Tiberius an unfavourable climate for starting his career.

No doubt father Seneca hoped that his sons, or at least the two eldest, would make a name in the lawcourts and be considered for public office, but by the time he composed his reminiscences (probably during the reign of Caligula, 37–41 CE) he speaks quite clearly of the dangers of a political career. To his youngest son, Mela, he says: 'since your brothers are preoccupied with ambition and preparing themselves for public life and public offices, in which the very honours hoped for are to be feared, being eager to encourage and praise their efforts, dangerous as they may be, so long as they are

---

[4] Apart from the writings of Seneca himself my primary guide has been Miriam Griffin's *Seneca: A Philosopher in Politics* (Oxford: Oxford UP, 1976). Where no ancient or modern source is credited my account is shaped by hers.

honourable; while they are on their voyage I am happy to keep you in harbour' (*Contr.* 2, Pref. 4). By this time Seneca had held the junior magistracy of the quaestorship, but his family seems to have been compromised by association with Tiberius' controversial praetorian prefect Sejanus, and will have come under suspicion after the latter's fall in 30 CE.[5]

We do not know whether Seneca held his quaestorship before the fall of Sejanus, but he offended Gaius Caesar (Caligula), possibly for the same reason which was to lead to his exile under Claudius in 41 CE—his friendship with Gaius' dangerously power-hungry sisters Agrippina and Livilla.[6] It is rather earlier that we should place Seneca's serious interest in philosophy. He tells us on separate occasions that as a young man he studied with the philosophers of the school of Sextius (such as Papirius Fabianus) and developed an enthusiasm for moral philosophy, but was discouraged by his father, partly because students of philosophy were suspected by the emperor (Tiberius) and associated with dissidence (letter 104). Probably the father was happy to let his delicate son spend some time listening to the lectures of philosophers, but became alarmed when young Seneca began to take this pursuit too seriously.

The family's wealth might seem to have made it unnecessary for Seneca to enrich himself further through public life, but it may equally have led father Seneca to regard a life spent in practising philosophy with as little favour as a modern father would consider his expensively educated son entering the church or becoming an underpaid academic. Certainly, by the time he composed the preface to his reminiscences the old man had acquiesced, not without regret, in the apolitical life of his youngest son Mela: in a passage which seems unkind to his older sons, he says:

I am glad to report this [critical appraisal of Papirius' spoken eloquence] dearest Mela, because I see that your spirit is alien to public duties and averse to any kind of ambition, eager for one thing only—to be eager for nothing. But do devote yourself to eloquence, it is easy to pass from this into

---

[5] There is evidence for this at *Annals*, VI.3, where Tacitus resumes his narrative after the fall of Sejanus in 30: Tiberius rebukes Gallio as a junior senator, for proposing privileged seating for members of the praetorian guard (which Sejanus commanded) at the theatre.

[6] On Gaius' attitude to Seneca and his jealousy of Seneca's eloquence see Suetonius, *Caligula*, 51.

every kind of art; it trains even those whom it does not prepare for itself . . . continue where your spirit leads you, and content with your father's rank (as a knight) remove a great part of your life from the risk of Fortune. You had a greater talent than your brothers, capable of every kind of virtuous skill: but it is even a pledge of a superior nature not to be corrupted by its own excellence into putting it to bad use. (*Contr.* 2, Pref. 3)

We have no evidence of his attitude to Seneca, and can only hope he treated all his sons with the same sympathy and respect.

Probably soon after his father's death Seneca was accused by political supporters of Claudius' wife Messalina of adultery with Livilla. He was found guilty and exiled to the island of Corsica in 41, where he stayed for eight years. Any political career he might have aspired to was on hold. From his essay of consolation to his mother Helvia (*Dialogues*, XII.2–3), we know that Seneca was married and had recently lost a baby son. The *Consolation* itself was no doubt partly an act of self-justification aimed at a wider public, but offers a sympathetic portrait of Helvia as both mother and grandmother: his tactful description of his father's *antiquus rigor* and fondness for ancestral tradition suggests a degree of complicity with his (much younger, perhaps 60-year-old) mother, who had been discouraged by her husband from pursuing philosophy out of his distaste for women who used learning for social display (*Dialogues*, XII.17.4). But Seneca takes pains to stress his mother's sober and chaste life, and to reassure her that he will spend his exile in a fashion worthy of her virtuous standards.

Seneca would be approaching 50 when Messalina's disgrace and suicide led Claudius to remarry: under various pressures the emperor chose Agrippina, great-grand-daughter of Augustus and of Mark Antony, already twice married, and mother by her first husband of a young teenage son Domitius Ahenobarbus.

Agrippina's previous acquaintance with Seneca led her to have him recalled in 49 CE and made tutor to the boy. The end of Seneca's exile was the beginning of his moral enslavement—but this was not immediately apparent. Both Seneca and his brother Gallio were now marked out for consulships, Gallio as a suffect[7] in 55, while Seneca apparently was one of the suffects of 56. But Seneca was faced with

---

[7] 'Suffects' were men elected consul during the year to replace the primary consuls (Ordinarii) who opened the year and gave its name in the public records.

the progressively more impossible task of guiding this overgrown boy: once adopted by his stepfather Claudius, young Domitius, now with the adoptive name Ti. Claudius Nero, was ready to marry his stepsister Octavia and displace his younger stepbrother Britannicus. Agrippina made sure that Claudius died prematurely in 54. Nero became emperor in his place. The public face of things was apparently calm during five years in which Nero's policies were guided by Seneca and the praetorian prefect Burrus—the so-called *Quinquennium Neronis*—but privately there began a power–struggle which led to the sudden deaths of first Britannicus and then Agrippina. Seneca was in no position to prevent these acts, and was mocked after Agrippina's death for composing for Nero a speech of intolerable hypocrisy in which the young emperor congratulated himself on escaping the murderous intrigues of his mother. Naturally, given his wealth and influence with the young emperor, Seneca had powerful enemies, but even the most ruthless of these, the professional accuser Suillius, had no lasting effect when he launched his attack in 58 CE.[8] Seneca was still useful to Nero. But by 62 CE the emperor had become infatuated with his friend Otho's wife Poppaea, and repudiated Octavia, bringing false charges of adultery against her: despite (or because of?) public protests, she was first exiled from Rome then exiled to an island, where she was murdered.

Seneca's ally in guiding Nero, the praetorian prefect Burrhus, died at about this time, and Seneca's enemies were muttering that it was time for the young emperor to dispose of his teacher. Knowing this, Seneca desperately sought to withdraw from the hazards of court life and to shed the private wealth which Nero was eager to claim for himself. Tacitus turns the interview which Seneca sought with the emperor into a black comedy, in which Nero left his former tutor no escape (*Annals*, XIV.52).[9]

When Nero increasingly rejected his friendship, Seneca begged for an interview, and when this was granted began to speak: 'This is the fourteenth year, Caesar, since I was brought into contact with your prospects,

[8] Tacitus, *Annals*, XIII.42, cf. other accusations of extortionate provincial usury in XIII.43.

[9] On his narrative at *Annals*, XIV.52–5, and the speech he puts into Seneca's mouth, Griffin, *Seneca* (p. 281, n. 4), notes that its convincing authenticity reflects Tacitus' familiarity with Seneca's public speeches indicated elsewhere.

and the eighth that you have been in imperial power; in the intervening time you have heaped so great a quantity of honours and wealth upon me that nothing is lacking to my happiness except its moderation. I shall use great models, not of my fortune but your own. Your great-grandfather Augustus permitted Marcus Agrippa seclusion at Mytilene, and Gaius Maecenas retirement in the city itself as if travelling abroad. One of these as his partner in warfare, the other after being wearied by many toils at Rome, had received rewards generous indeed but in proportion to their great services. What else have I been able to offer your generosity than studies reared in the shadow, which have acquired glory because I seemed to be a supporter in the early training of your youth, a great reward for this action. But you have enveloped me in vast influence and money beyond counting, so much that I usually wonder to myself: Am I, born in equestrian rank in the provinces, being counted among the city's leading men? Has my new birth shone forth among nobles displaying their long-lived honours? Where is that spirit once content with moderate circumstances? Does it lay out these parklands and stroll through these suburban estates and overflow with such expanses of land and such widespread interest? Only one defence has occurred to me, that I ought not to resist your gifts.

But each of us has reached his limit, you of as much generosity as any leader should bestow on a friend, and I as much as a friend should accept from his leader: any more simply increases resentment. This indeed, like all mortal things, lies beneath your greatness, but it is weighing upon me and I need succour. Just as I would ask for a support if I were weary in warfare or on a journey, so in this journey of life as an old man, unequal to the lightest of anxieties, now that I can support my wealth no further, I am asking for help. Have your business administered by your agents, and taken into your private portfolio. I will not thrust myself down to actual poverty, but after handing over the resources whose splendour blinds me, I will recall to spiritual concerns whatever time is set aside for the care of my parks and villas. You have abundant strength and control of the highest level of achievement seen over so many years; we older friends can request our repose. And this too will redound to your glory, to have raised to the heights men who would also be content with a moderate fortune.'

Nero's answer is clever and cruelly insincere. He begins by claiming that his ability to refute Seneca's protests is itself a debt to Seneca's teaching, and leads into the claim that he still needs Seneca's wisdom to save him from backsliding. Besides, if Seneca returned his wealth and property people would talk not of Seneca's nobility but of his, Nero's, covetousness and cruelty: 'it would not be becoming for a

wise man to win glory for himself from something that begets dishon-
our for his friend.' Tacitus adds that Nero ended with an embrace
and kisses, being an expert in concealing his hatred in treacherous
blandishment. 'So Seneca, as was the outcome of every conversation with a master, gave him thanks; but he changed the habits of his
former powerful position, banning gatherings of clients to greet him,
avoiding escorts, seldom coming to the city, as if he were kept at home
by adverse health or the pursuit of philosophy' (*Annals*, XIV.53–6).

   The interview is the product of Tacitus' literary art, but it con-
veys with bloodcurdling vividness the claustrophobic world in which
Seneca now had to operate. Tacitus confirms Seneca's fearful position
incidentally at *Annals*, XV.45.3: he avoided even leaving his *cubiculum*
(more like a study than a bedroom), and after Nero attempted to have
him poisoned by a freedman, kept to a very simple diet, varied only
with country-grown fruit and running water. So let us take refuge, as
Seneca did, in his writings.

Seneca's Writings

The major problem for would-be critics is that there is no external evidence and surprisingly little internal evidence to guide us in
dating his works either relatively, to each other, or absolutely. Seneca
was both poet and prose writer, and one's instinct is to look for work
that he might have produced to occupy himself in exile; he actually claims to divert himself not only with philosophical speculation
but with 'less serious writings' (*levioribus studiis*, *Dialogues*, XX.1).
A body of his tragedies has survived,[10] which cannot be dated by
internal allusions but have been given relative datings by various
stylistic features. The first in the oldest manuscript of this group of
plays, *Hercules Furens*, contains a lament which is closely parodied
in the satirical account of Claudius' deification, *Ludus de Morte
Claudi* or *Apocolocyntosis* (*Pumpkinification of Claudius*), written in
55 CE, the year after Claudius' death. Stylistic features have been

---

[10] There are two manuscript traditions: editors usually follow the order of the plays
in the Codex Etruscus: this contains *Hercules*, *Medea*, *Troades*, *Phaedra*, *Agamemnon*,
Oedipus, *Thyestes*, *Phoenissae*, and *Hercules Oetaeus*. The other family of manuscripts
presents a different order, uses some different titles, and includes the post-Senecan tragedy *Octavia* about Nero's divorce and relegation of his wife. On the *Octavia* see now
A. J. Boyle's edition and translation (Oxford: Oxford UP, 2008).

used to classify three tragedies, *Agamemnon*, *Phaedra*, and *Oedipus*, as having been written earlier than *Hercules Furens*: two others, *Medea* and *Trojan Women*, are close to *Hercules* in technique and so probably come from the same few years; and two more, *Thyestes* and *Phoenissae* (the latter without choral odes, so incomplete), have been seen as composed after 59 under an increasingly tyrannical Nero.

It is true that the plots of both *Phoenissae* and *Thyestes* are concerned with sibling hatred—the expulsion of Polynices from Thebes by Eteocles, and the exile of Thyestes by Atreus. The latter play in particular is saturated with the tyrannical boasts of Atreus, and an atmosphere of evil in his court which may remind us strongly of Tacitus' portrait of Nero. But these boasts were inherent in the traditional presentation of the myth, from Accius' version late in the second century BCE if not earlier. Critics have also tried to see Agrippina in the Jocasta of Seneca's *Oedipus*, who dies cursing her womb for conceiving an abomination,[11] but such gestures were known to educated Romans from Greek tragedy and did not need to wait for Nero's birth or Agrippina's last words.

Seneca's prose writings begin with the *Consolation to Marcia* (one of a series of philosophical writings collected under the rather misleading title of *Dialogues*), composed under Gaius, then further *Consolations* to his mother Helvia (41 CE) and to Polybius, the emperor's freedman in charge of petitions (probably written in 43 after Claudius' successful campaign against Britain): the three books *On Anger* (*Dialogues* III–V) are full of resentment against Gaius, and also seem to be early. The other dialogues are harder to date. *On Providence* and *The Constancy of the Wise Man* are placed first and second in the collected dialogues, but *On Providence* is addressed to Lucilius, the younger friend who is also the addressee of the *Letters on Morality* (*Epistulae Morales*) and *Natural Questions* (*Quaestiones Naturales*). Does this mean that it was composed in the same period as those late works? There is nothing in its content to suggest that it could not have been written early in Seneca's career, but the common addressee and overlap of themes with several of the letters encourage us to think that *On Providence* could be a later composition, placed first within the corpus of *Dialogues* because of its fundamental topic—'Why do

---

[11] This is the reference of her last exclamation to Nero's assassins: 'strike me in the belly' (*ventrem feri*, Tacitus, *Annals*, XIV.8.6).

bad things happen to good men?'—vindicating divine providence
by reinterpreting misfortunes, rather than because of its date of
composition.

I have passed over four of the essays collected among the *Dialogues*,
but they invite closer attention because they share a number of elements with the *Letters on Morality*, including a number of veiled allusions to the hazards of public life: these are *De Vita Beata* (VII, *On
the Happy Life*, to his brother Gallio); *De Otio* (VIII, *On Leisure*, to
Annaeus Serenus); *De Tranquillitate* (IX, *On the Tranquillity of the
Mind*, to Serenus); and *De Brevitate Vitae* (X, *On the Shortness of
Life*, to his father-in-law Paulinus). Thus *De Vita Beata* opens with
a warning against the corrupting influence of public opinion: 'we
shape ourselves too much to respond to gossip . . . the mass of
people are opposed to the demands of reason'. It moves through a
re-examination of Epicureanism which repudiates living for pleasure,
but affirms that the teachings of Epicurus himself have been mis-
understood, and were chaste and upright (13.1). But one ingredient
which may suggest that this was an early dialogue is Seneca's extended
defence of the wise man who enjoys wealth, balanced by insistence on
its proper use (21–6); this anticipates his later analysis of the liberality
of conferring benefits (*On Benefits*); to this add Seneca's arguments
for the rightness of showing one can live without wealth—something
treated in several letters.[12]

On Leisure is mutilated; we have neither its beginning nor
its end, but the first surviving sentences again advocate withdrawal:
'it will be good for a man to withdraw into himself; we do better
acting as individuals'. Seneca divides modes of life into living for
contemplation, living for pleasure, and living for action. The last
was always the most esteemed course for Romans, but Seneca recognizes that this may not be possible. A man is required to benefit other
men—if possible, many men; if not, then a few; if not a few, then
the men closest to us; if not them, then oneself (3.2). But partici-
pating in civic life depends on the condition of the community, and
after reviewing various states Seneca concludes (8.3) that he is able

---

[12] The argument echoes attitudes shown by Panaetius and Poseidonius (who did not
want to offend wealthy patrons) but is at variance with other writings. There is no simple
explanation, as is shown by Griffin, *Seneca*, ch. 9.

to think of no state which can tolerate a wise man, or which he in turn can tolerate.[13]

On the Tranquillity of the Mind is complete, and is the only dialogue in which Seneca includes a speech for his interlocutor; this is his friend Annaeus Serenus, who had risen to be one of the two prefects of the praetorian guard, and would suffer poisoning from mushrooms at a banquet along with many other guests.[14] Serenus asks Seneca what he should do in his state of anxiety and discontent; Seneca in reply quotes the philosopher Athenodorus: the best remedy for this discontent would have been to keep oneself busy with administering public life and citizen obligations (the latter could be individual services in the courts); but given the prevalence of slanderers it will be best to avoid public life altogether. 'If a man cannot be a soldier, let him seek office. If he must live without office, let him be an orator. If silence is imposed on him, let him help a fellow citizen by silent recommendation. If even entering the Forum is dangerous, let him play the good companion, faithful friend, and abstemious guest in private homes, at shows and parties. If he has lost the citizen's duties, let him perform those of a man' (4.3–6). Later Seneca seems to come closer to his own condition in the later years under Nero, claiming that 'many men of necessity must cling to their high position (*fastigium*) since they cannot step down without falling' (10.6). But his recommendation to Serenus is retirement, a retirement well spent in serious study of virtue, together with cultivation of one's family estate and judicious relaxation.

How early did Seneca begin longing to withdraw from Nero's intolerable court? Did he write this before 55, when he would irrevocably be in the position that the ancient proverb called holding a wolf by the ears, where one can neither hold on nor let go? The last of these dialogues, placed in the manuscripts before the two *Consolations* from 41 and 43, is *On the Shortness of Life*, dedicated to his father-in-law Paulinus, who held the responsible position of *curator annonae*, supervisor of the public grain supply. Its message is again the shortness of life and hazards of postponing *otium* (leisure), as otherwise

---

[13] For arguments for and against positing a late, Neronian dating for *On Leisure*, see Griffin, *Seneca*, 317, 355, and G. D. Williams (ed., *Seneca: De Otio; De Brevitate Vitae* (Cambridge: Cambridge UP, 2003), 16.

[14] Our source is Pliny, *Natural History*, XII.96, writing about this type of mushroom. It is not clear whether deliberate poisoning was suspected.

admirable men like Augustus and Cicero had done. But *otium* must be wisely used. As for Paulinus, Seneca reminds him of the strains of a political position and the quest for office (17.5–6): he has given enough of his life to service and should now give what is left to studious leisure. Miriam Griffin argued some years ago[15] that the dialogue was intended to provide a public justification for Paulinus, who was probably aged around 65 in 55 CE, to step down from this onerous job. But we should also take into account the arguments advanced for an earlier date of 49, or one as late as 62. Most recently, G. D. Williams's introduction to the dialogue[16] has left the date open between 49 and 55.

Perhaps, then, the preference for leisure explicit and implicit in several of these dialogues, along with some themes in common with the letters—avoidance of the crowd, finding wisdom in Epicurus, learning to do without riches—favours a later composition, when Seneca himself had begun to long for withdrawal, but there is nothing to determine a clear dating.

On Mercy was written for the new emperor Nero, and its praise for his merciful nature has to do the job of an exhortation or 'Mirror for the Prince'. It almost certainly belongs in the emperor's first year, but it seems unfinished—Book 2 is truncated. The seven books *On Benefits* also seem to have been written to advocate generosity and discrimination to the emperor, whose role entailed enormous disbursements to cities (after disasters) and individuals, but to modern eyes its length is out of proportion to its theme.

I have left to last the works we know Seneca was writing after 62 CE. In his *Consolation to Helvia* Seneca declared that there were two things which exile and temporal powers could not take away from anyone: the laws and forces of nature (chiefly the heavenly bodies, which could be seen from all over the Roman world), and the improvement of one's own soul. He could have added that these topics were both safe from provoking political suspicion. Now withdrawn to his own rooms in his villa, Seneca devoted himself to the seven books of *Natural Questions* comparing and to some extent evaluating theories of cosmology and meteorology, on the behaviour of thunder and comets, earthquakes and volcanoes, and rivers. These were not

---

[15] *Journal of Roman Studies*, 52 (1962), 104 f.
[16] pp. 19–20.

original research but based on the works of Greek scientists up to and including Posidonius, and Seneca is content to state the problem and offer a choice of solutions without hoping to settle on a reply. As the preface to what is called Book IV of the *Natural Questions* shows, this work is dedicated to Lucilius:

As you say, Lucilius, best of men, Sicily and the service of your leisured administration delights you and will continue to delight you if you are willing to control it within its limits and not turn an administrative task into a governor's command. I don't doubt you will do this, because I know how foreign you are to ambition and how attached to leisure and culture. Let men who can't stand themselves hanker after a crowd of tasks and people, but you are on the best terms with yourself . . . so *do as you have been accustomed to, dear Lucilius*, and detach yourself as much as you can from crowds.

Note that the italicized phrase coincides with the opening of the *Letters*. But a lot of the advice which follows in this preface is very specific, and probably familiar to readers of manuals for governors, even the most judicious, like Cicero's carefully personalized letter to his brother Quintus as governor of Asia ('Letters to his Brother' 1.1). The *Letters*, by contrast, are not concerned with Lucilius' administrative task, his staff, or his social relations with Romans or provincials. Their themes are far more personal and need separate consideration. In what sense is this a correspondence?

The Letters on Morality

As Personal Communication

We naturally want to know something about Lucilius Iunior, Seneca's partner in this correspondence. But we know only what Seneca himself tells us (or tells Iunior!) in the letters and *Natural Questions*, which he was also composing in these years between 63 and his death.[17] The Preface to *Natural Questions*, Book IV, shares with some of the early letters the recommendation to Lucilius to shun the worldly crowd around him, even to seek retirement from his privileged position as

---

[17] Lucilius is also the dedicatee of the dialogue *On Providence* (*De Providentia*), but it cannot be dated, and contains no personal information about him. We cannot assume from its relative simplicity of theme, or its position first in the collection of *Dialogues*, that it was written early.

procurator (senior financial officer) of the emperor's huge estates in Sicily. Along with a powerful invective against the flatterers who lobbied and molested Roman officials Seneca puts into Lucilius' mouth proud statements that he had faced the risk of tortures threatened by Gaius (Caligula) without resorting to escape by suicide, and had maintained his loyalty to Gaetulicus against the slanders of Messalina, wife to Claudius when he was made emperor in 41. The same preface stresses Lucilius' humble origin and indifference to wealth as well as his devotion to composing poetry.[18] If he was genuinely of humble origin he may not have known the elite figures like Passienus Crispus or Gallio whom Seneca mentions in the preface, or even the cynic teacher Demetrius. But if he was implicated, as Seneca seems to have been, in the alleged conspiracy of Gaetulicus around 40 CE Lucilius cannot have been much younger than Seneca. It is simply the premiss of these *Letters on Morality* that Seneca as spiritual trainer is senior to Iunior.

Why are they called *Morales*? Because their purpose and dominant theme is to reinforce Lucilius' struggle to achieve the wisdom and serenity of a man uninfluenced by worldly emotions — desires and fears, and angry or envious reactions to others. While many of the letters open with lively vignettes of Seneca's day-to-day experience and expand into literary critical or social comment, the letters are, as it were, a course of moral therapy, designed to sustain Lucilius' integrity.

It is part of this continuing moral programme that Seneca's first letter is styled as a reply. 'Yes, do just that, dear Lucilius' means that we are to imagine Lucilius having written to report some new moral initiative he has taken up for Seneca's approval. And this is supported by the key passage in letter 118: 'You are demanding more frequent letters from me, so let us compare our accounts; you will find you cannot pay off your debt. In fact *we had agreed that your letters would come first*: you would write and I would write back. But I am not going to be difficult; I know that it is safe to be your creditor. So I will give you a letter in advance . . .' This would imply that Seneca usually waited for an enquiry from Lucilius (and many of his letters actually begin with the words 'You ask me what . . . ; You would

---

[18] For Lucilius' poetic ambitions see letter 79 in this selection: fragments of his poetry are quoted by Seneca in letters 8.10 and 24.21.

like to know; You are curious whether . . .') before sending his next letter. But this carries the fictive assumption of the correspondence too far.[19]

As an imperial procurator Lucilius would certainly have the use of the fast imperial post, at least to Rome itself, from where Seneca's servants could retrieve missives — but this would take, say, three days at best to reach Rome, and Seneca himself, as Tacitus indicates and as is confirmed by several letters, stayed out of Rome and kept continually on the move. (Lucilius too was often on the move within Sicily as part of his administrative duties.) So we should assume anything from four to eight days for a letter to reach either correspondent. Many of the earlier letters open by reacting to something Lucilius has said, and some letters style themselves as replies: one at least (letter 46) thanks him for sending Seneca a treatise, and the next in the series speaks of talking to Lucilius' 'people', seemingly the slave messengers. The uncertainties of delivery are represented as a real problem: so letters 59 and 74 open by thanking Lucilius for a letter which has just been delivered. But letter 50 speaks of receiving a letter many months after it was written.

If we consider 124 letters (not to mention the lost letters deduced from Gellius' quotation from 'Book XXII', reproduced here in the Appendix) written in just over two years, this averages a letter every six or seven days, but once we abandon the hypothesis of a reciprocal exchange of letters it is clear that Seneca wrote whenever he wanted to discuss a new topic or revive an old one. He may well have written several letters within a few days, or taken some time in order to complete a longer missive, like the dialogue-length letters 66, 90, 94, and 95.[20] The letters confine themselves to personal moral concerns, often introduced by some relevant anecdote. But there are very few — perhaps only half-a-dozen — indications of where Seneca

---

[19] Griffin, *Seneca*, appendix B4: 'The Fictional Character of Seneca's Correspondence with Lucilius', lists opening gambits which either mention a letter from Lucilius or imply one by mentioning Lucilius' requests. For a balanced presentation of the distinctive nature of this correspondence see Donald Russell's chapter, 'Letters to Lucilius', in C. D. N. Costa (ed.), *Seneca* (London and Boston: Routledge & Kegan Paul, 1974) and two essays by Marcus Wilson, 'Seneca's Epistles . . . A Revaluation', in *Imperial Muse = Ramus*, 16 (1987), and 'Seneca's Epistles Reclassified', in S. J. Harrison (ed.), *Texts, Ideas and the Classics: Scholarship, Theory and Classical Literature* (Oxford: Oxford UP, 2001).

[20] Only letters 90 and 95 are included in this selection.

is writing from,[21] and in contrast with conventional letters (which tended to bear exact dates in order to alert the recipient to the time consumed in delivery) slightly fewer and certainly vaguer chronological markers, limited only to the time of year.[22]

The correspondence seems most likely to have been a one-sided initiative by Seneca, with Lucilius' consent, even gratitude. The pose of response to Lucilius' requests was in the tradition of treatises dedicated to trusted friends and often claiming to be answering their requests. Thus Cicero addressed his *Orator* to Brutus in order to satisfy Brutus' protests at his previous arguments. Poetry too adopted this pose, as in the anecdote told by Pliny of the absent-minded Iavolenus Priscus, in the audience when his friend began an epigram 'Priscus, you bid me . . .' Perhaps half-asleep, Priscus leapt up and said: 'I certainly am not bidding you' (Pliny, *Letters*, VI.15.2).

Given the contexts in which Seneca composed his correspondence, and his desire to keep a close focus on timeless moral issues, it is interesting to see his discreet attempts at circumstantiality to achieve verisimilitude. Thus letter 15 takes up the traditional opening 'If you are well that is good; I am well', and offers his own variant: 'If you are practising philosophy, it is good . . .' Other early letters also pay some general attention to Lucilius' official position, which exposed him to flatterers, busybodies, and slanderers, and intermittently mention his official travel in Sicily. One letter (24) shows Lucilius apparently frightened of an impending lawsuit—a situation repeated in one of Pliny's letters to Suetonius; another responds to Lucilius' passing sickness; a letter about half-way through the sequence (64) speaks of regret for their long separation. But although the early letters (such as 7) reflect Seneca's own frequent concerns by urging Lucilius to resign from official duties and withdraw from society, there is no sense even in the last few letters that Lucilius' tour of duty is coming to an end or that Seneca has reached the end of his programme

[21] The clearest cases are the letters from Campania.

[22] Letter 18 notes that it is December, and the Saturnalia; letter 23 claims winter has been short and is nearly over, but in letter 67 it is still only spring, presumably of the same year (63?). Letter 91 can be dated by the great fire of Lyons (Sept. 63?), and 122 marks the shrinking daylight of autumn. We might also expect that the Campanian letters would come from either the April vacations of senate and courts, or August, when the summer heat made Rome unbearable.

of therapy. Perhaps he was intending to continue when the aftermath of the abortive conspiracy led to Seneca's imposed suicide.

Adapting the Epistolary Tradition to a Moral Purpose

As Russell ('*Letters to Lucilius*') points out, the Hellenistic manual *On Style* attributed to Demetrius of Phalerum singles out letters for their effectiveness in representing a personality: 'The letter, like the dialogue, should abound in glimpses of character (*ethos*). It may be said that everybody writes a letter as the image of his soul. In every other genre of writing we can discern the writer's character, but in none so clearly as the epistolary' (*On style*, §227, tr. Rhys Roberts, modified). Is this how Seneca saw his own correspondence? Besides the all-important personal relationship we need to put the letters in the context of the literary and philosophical traditions. The same letter 21 which promises Lucilius immortality quotes from Cicero's letters to Atticus, and from a letter of Epicurus to Idomeneus which claimed that his own letters would make Idomeneus more famous than all his other activities (compare also letter 79).

Seneca himself ends most of the first thirty letters with sayings from Epicurus, and will cite him at length in later letters.[23] Brad Inwood has rightly stressed the importance of Epicurus' letters as a precedent,[24] but what remains of his correspondence are three long treatises with little actual epistolary setting, and some significant excerpts from letters to other friends. There is a certain inconsistency in Seneca's insistence on doing one's own thinking rather than quoting moral tags from the great names of Stoicism given his free quotation of these excerpts from Epicurus.

Cicero's letters to Atticus are another matter. Atticus outlived Cicero by some fifteen years, and it is assumed that he edited and circulated Cicero's letters to himself (we do not know how many letters

---

[23] See in this selection the last paragraphs of letters 2, 7, 8, 9, 11, 14, 21, 24, 27, 28; the comments in 33 on why Seneca had left off adding these maxims, and from later letters 67, 79 (like 21, preoccupied with posterity), 89, and 97. For the surviving letters and excerpts of Epicurus see B. Inwood and L. P. Gerson, *Hellenistic Philosophy: Introductory Readings* (Indianapolis: Hackett, 1988).

[24] See *Reading Seneca* (Oxford: Oxford UP, 2005), esp. ch. 1 on Seneca's cultural background: also Inwood's annotated translation of *Seneca's Philosophical Letters*, and his paper 'The Importance of Form in Seneca's Philosophical Letters' in R. Morello and A. Morrison (eds.), *Ancient Letters: Classical and Late Antique Epistolography* (Oxford: Oxford UP, 2007).

he suppressed). In letter 21 Seneca claims that it is Cicero's letters, not his connections with the imperial house, which do not permit Atticus' name to fade. There is no critical assessment here, but two later letters quote from the first book of the *Letters to Atticus*: letter 97 uses it as evidence for the moral corruption of Clodius' bribery in the time of Cato the Stoic saint; letter 118, with which we began above, quotes Cicero's request to Atticus to write him 'whatever comes into his mouth' in terms of political gossip, in order to repudiate this kind of material in favour of one's own moral needs. The fact that Seneca only quotes Cicero in these later letters, and only from Book I of the *Letters to Atticus*, suggests that he knew of the letters as early as letter 21 but had some difficulty in getting to read them; he is in fact one of the earliest sources.

Seneca himself insists that the purpose of his writing is to encourage or compel Lucilius to act for the best interests of his own mind, taking moral initiatives.[25] This is why certain themes, like the importance of honourable behaviour (Greek *to kalon*, Latin *pulchrum*), are reiterated; this is why Seneca constantly appeals to his own experience and his day-to-day moral successes and lapses to keep Lucilius striving for moral improvement. Almost every letter carries its own measure of encouragement, and any letter which concerns itself with explanation, whether of physics or psychology or ethics, explicitly moves forward to what Lucilius must do to benefit from this knowledge.

Seneca was a highly committed philosopher, impatient with logical puzzles but ready to argue in detail important points of doctrine. Nonetheless, he was writing for Lucilius and for an amateur public. It is important to keep in mind that Seneca put moral impact before intellectual debate: he called these philosophical essays by an entirely new title, *Epistulae Morales*, and wrote them with a moral purpose to promote moral behaviour in their readers.

Seneca thought of himself as following and occasionally modifying Stoic teaching, and yet as we saw, he repeatedly quotes and interprets sayings of Epicurus, founder of the rival school, in his early

---

[25] Until twenty years ago most students of ancient philosophy did not recognize the value of any philosophical discussion not aimed at logically cohesive systems and a Platonic search for truth. Martha Nussbaum should be credited for reaffirming the value of protreptic, and moral therapy—that is, arguments aimed at healing the disturbed mind and activating moral behaviour.

letters, and echoes Epicurus sometimes without acknowledgement in a number of later letters. One obvious incentive to quote Epicurus would be that Stoic teachers do not seem to have communicated through personal letters. But it only makes sense for Seneca to use Epicurus' writings because the two philosophical schools had so much in common: so it is helpful to approach the main Stoic ethical doctrines through comparison with the rival school.[26]

Both schools were founded at the turn of the fourth to third centuries BCE, when the empires of Alexander's successors gave little scope for principled citizens to influence government; this is partly reflected in their stance towards what had been essential to city-state Greeks, participation in governing their city. But while Epicurus advocated abstinence from public life, Zeno and subsequent Stoics saw participation as a duty wherever a man was free to do so. It was also part of Epicurean quietism that they believed in detached gods, living apart from a purely material physical universe, serenely perfect but unconcerned with men's needs or prayers, neither punishing nor rewarding. The Stoic thinkers, by contrast, saw the universe as activated by divine purpose; the divinity might be called God, or Nature, or Providence, but this being had designed the geocentric universe and all its creatures in the interests of mankind, which alone shared in the divine gift of Reason. Reason was what distinguished humans from beasts, and their purpose in turn was to eliminate all emotional disturbance which might obstruct the development of their reason[27] or weaken its control. The best way to eliminate disturbing emotions, whether hope and fear for the future or joy and grief in the present, was to desire nothing that was external, outside a person's control.

But this brings up the chief problem of Stoic eschatology. If the universe was governed by a providence which was wise, benevolent

[26] On both Epicureanism and Stoicism see A. A. Long and D. Sedley (eds.), *The Hellenistic Philosophers* (Cambridge: Cambridge UP, 1987); Inwood and Gerson, *Hellenistic Philosophy*. On Stoicism see A. A. Long (ed.), *Problems in Stoicism* (Cambridge: Cambridge UP, 1971), and J. M. Rist, *Stoic Philosophy* (Cambridge: Cambridge UP, 1969).

[27] This may be the best place to set out the problem of translating Latin *animus*. I have avoided 'soul' because of its Christian associations. Instead I usually translate it as 'mind' or 'intellect', and sometimes, where it is seen as a motivator, as 'spirit'. Plato had posited a tripartite 'soul' in which reason (*logistikon*) ought to be in control of the passionate *thumos* and the brutish appetites (*epithumetikon*). But to Stoics the *animus* was a single entity whose function was reasoning, but which also potentially contained the passions.

and omnipotent, how did one explain individual and collective misfortune? This is a larger version of the modern problem: why do bad
things happen to good people? Stoicism offered as one answer (an
answer Seneca himself sets out in his dialogue *On Providence* dedicated to Lucilius) that misfortune was sent by providence to test and
strengthen the human as s/he strove towards goodness: being tested,
like Socrates condemned to death or Cato forced to choose suicide
rather than live under Caesar, was a demonstration of divine respect.
But clearly this is no answer to collective misfortunes, so-called
'acts of God' like earthquakes. A less satisfactory answer was to reify
Misfortune, adapting the pagan goddess Tychē/Fortuna, and set her
up as a kind of Satan responsible for accidental or undeserved misfortunes. This was a common rhetorical trope among pagans of all kinds,
and Seneca uses this concept somewhat uncritically.

Much of Seneca's persuasion is aimed at warning Lucilius against
fears and desires, and arguing that health, strength, beauty, wealth,
prosperity, and recognition were morally neutral or indifferent; not
to be rejected but not to be sought for either. Thus, poverty, exile,
disrepute, and sickness were not really bad; only dishonourable and
vicious behaviour was truly bad. In its simplest form this features
in Seneca's correspondence as learning to do without what is superfluous: not just to make do without it, but to avoid any preoccupation with external and superfluous things. Where this breaks down
for many of us is in its inclusion of other humans—wife, children,
friends—as external and optional. Thus, in letter 9 Seneca claims
that if a friend dies you should look for a new one; yet friendship is
not purely selfish, since the wise man will want friends in order to
help them in trouble and do them kindnesses.

It is not surprising, then, that so many of these letters counsel withdrawal, avoiding the company of worldly people (letter 7), and avoiding the damage done to one's *animus* by ambition and greed or sheer
assimilation to crude and mistaken popular opinion. Seneca's own
exposed position at court prevented him from coming any closer to
discussing moral freedom, but he does find space to encourage maintaining one's principles in privacy. Under Nero it was not enough
to be silent. Paetus Thrasea had absented himself from the senate
rather than voice his dissent, but Nero still treated this as defiance
and had him executed. Under Nero a self-imposed death might be
the only expression of liberty. This brings us to suicide, an increasing

preoccupation of Seneca's letters, but a step for which Plato and the Greek Stoics made allowance under strict limitations. One's life belonged to God, and it was not right to take it unless he gave a sign, such as an ulcer that refused to heal, that one should be ready to die. The good Stoic would die rather than commit or suffer a disgraceful act; he would die if his ill-health rendered him unfit to perform his moral or social duties. Roman tradition, even more than Greek, was full of public figures who took their own lives after defeat or condemnation, or brought a terminal illness to an end by starving themselves. Nero took advantage of this tradition when he sent his last messengers to Seneca and Petronius and Thrasea and Barea Soranus, ordering their deaths. (Such enforced suicides usually preserved the victim's property for his family to inherit.) Tacitus voices disgust at the numbers of unmemorable deaths he has to record in *Annals*, XVI.15–16, but the Romans of his own age created a new and edifying genre, the 'death scenes of distinguished men'. These are as Roman in spirit as they are Stoic (indeed Petronius was far from Stoic), but it had never been difficult for Romans to reconcile the traditional morality of their class with the moral imperatives of Stoicism.

To the modern reader, secular or devout, the letters display an alarming imbalance between preoccupation with perfecting the self [28] and a much slighter concern with helping others.[29] But if we stress not the self as beneficiary but the self as agent, and the constant message that he who would be good must trust himself, help himself, be content with himself (that is, not reaching out for external benefits) and be consistent with himself, then the call to action is not self-satisfied or even self-centred, but extremely demanding. These are not letters one can receive comfortably.

This may be the best place to mention certain formal features of Seneca's philosophical argumentation noted by Erasmus in the expansive dedication of his second and most thorough edition of *Seneca*[30] to Bishop Tomicki in 1529. Erasmus notes two weaknesses

---

[28] See Catharine Edwards, 'Self-scrutiny and Self-transformation in Seneca's Letters', *Greece & Rome*, 44 (1997), 23–38, repr. as Ch. 3 of the Oxford Readings in Classical Studies, *Seneca*, ed. John G. Fitch (Oxford: Oxford UP, 2008).

[29] This can be found in e.g. letter 95.51–3.

[30] This is letter 2091 in Erasmus' *Opus Epistularum* (ed. P. S. Allen), which I quote here from the forthcoming translation of Alexander Dalzell for the *Collected Works of Erasmus*. The *Seneca* of 1529 combined all the verse and prose writings of Seneca the Younger

common to Seneca's letters and other philosophical writings: the first is Seneca's curious flexibility in assigning objections and other speeches to adversaries (often introduced only by 'he says'), and ending without marking where the arguments resume after speech:

Occasionally he introduces a new speaker or changes speakers without warning the reader, which is another reason for the obscurity of his work. Sometimes you cannot tell whether the speaker is the author himself, or his adversary in the debate or a third person . . . he is much given to the use of dialogue in which he puts words of his own into the mouths of various characters . . . it is not that he does this badly but he does it too often and in too rhetorical a style, that is, he aims more at pleasing the reader than advancing the serious business in hand. (442–51)

He also complains that Seneca:

likes to poke fun at sophistic cleverness and at the subtle but unimportant questions that philosophers raise. Often he wastes the reader's time with silliness of this sort, and in the process confirms the truth of Quintilian's criticism that he is not well-grounded in philosophy . . . but what is the point of filling page after page with niggling questions of the sort which Chrysippus asked? . . . from time to time however we find him condemning it. What need is there to do something simply in order to denounce what one has done? (501–13 with omissions)

Only towards the end of his critique, after noting Seneca's tendency to an impulsive disorganization that neglects headings and jumps categories, and after comparing him unfavourably with Aristotle (455–71), does Erasmus turn specifically to the letters:

Seneca seems to have chosen this genre in order to give full rein to his talents; for no other offers the same scope. Anything you hear or read or anything that appears to you in a dream is matter for a letter. Moreover you can begin and end and change direction wherever you wish. But one misses in Seneca that quality that lends other letters their greatest charm, that is that they are a true reflection of a real situation. (564–9)

It seems, then, that Erasmus too was a sceptic about the letters as half of a literal correspondence, and read each letter as a spontaneous and independent text.

with his father's *Controversiae* and *Suasoriae*, attributing all these works to the same man, 'L. Annaeus Seneca'.

The Social and Cultural Aspects of the Letters

Like other Roman letter-writers Seneca is reticent about his private life; these letters do not include family news of his brothers or his precocious young nephew, or mention his wife Pompeia Paulina except twice: incidentally when he is using Paulina's pet clown Harpaste to illustrate human delusions in letter 50.2, and more explicitly in letter 104, with comments which allows us to feel the mutual affection of husband and wife. Letter 104 is also one of the very few letters which refer to his properties outside Rome. The place at Nomentum (mentioned in letters 104 and 110) was only acquired under Nero, and cannot be the same as the old family villa outside town (*suburbanum*) of letter 12. But his Nomentan estate became famous for the immensely prized vineyard which Seneca bought at an inflated price from Remmius Palaemon, according to Pliny.[31] Seneca, who himself later gave up drinking wine (see letter 104), was a known connoisseur of viticulture, and is singled out for praise on this score by both Pliny and Columella. Pliny adds to his tale of the vineyard that Seneca was 'the most learned man of his day, eminent in power which subsequently grew to excess and fell upon him, though he was no admirer of hollow luxury'. Columella (III.3.3) too reports the productivity of the Nomentan estate, as well as calling Seneca 'a man of exceptional talent and learning'. A late letter (123) is written from his 'place at Alba' only a half-day's journey from Rome, where he can call on a bailiff, a steward, and at least one tenant to help with emergency supplies. A number of Seneca's letters, starting with letter 49, are written from Campania, and mention recent arrivals or imminent departures—from Baiae or Puteoli or Naples.[32] Perhaps the strangest of these letters is 56, written when Seneca has taken an apartment over a public bath-house to test his ability to concentrate despite distractions from urban noise, and it too ends by speaking of imminent departure (56.15). But he could not stay away from Campania, and Seneca was

---

[31] *Natural History*, XIV.50. Pliny devotes a chapter to Seneca's skill in increasing the returns from his vineyard, and quotes the equally famous expertise of Aegialus, the owner of Scipio's old villa at Liternum whose methods Seneca quotes extensively in letter 86.

[32] It was customary for Roman writers to warn their correspondents if they were moving on, so that later messages would be directed to the next stopping-place. Compare in this selection letters 51, 53, 56, 57, 70, and 77. But Seneca seems unusually restless, perhaps for fear of Nero's plotting: letter 72 reports that he could not remain long enough in any place to compose a more substantial discussion.

returning from there to Rome when the centurion sent with Nero's
order to commit suicide found him where he would die, in the suburban villa four miles from the city (Tacitus, *Annals*, XV.60).

Readers of any Latin literature from the first century CE (from
declamatory excerpts to Petronius to Juvenal) will first think of the
favourite denunciations of luxury: of levelling hills and extending
promontories to create private harbours; of creating channels for
fish ponds and sowing woodlands on rooftops; these were the cli-
chés taught in the schools under the heading 'the passage on luxury',
'the passage on current degeneration'.[33] Denunciation of gluttony
and extravagant dining is another commonplace, but not as part of
Seneca's own direct experiences. We do meet various aspects of the
urban and rural slave 'families', from the superannuated pet-slave of
Seneca's childhood, the bailiff's son in letter 12, to the fancy pages
and footmen of the urban wealthy (letter 122), and letter 47 has long
been a favourite source for the only partly liberal attitudes Seneca
offers.[34] The letters illustrate every level of travelling, from the parade
of outrunners and wagonloads of equipment of the wealthy (letter
123) to Seneca's own idea of austerity, riding on mule-back with only
one cartload of slaves (letter 87). And several letters, like 87, reveal a
cult of poverty and fasting or plain diet practised by Seneca himself,
in which a wealthy man would keep one room almost bare of furniture
to simulate the poor man's hut—the *cella pauperis* of letters 18.7 and
100.6: 'let us do without the variety of marble veneers and conjunc-
tion of waters flowing between bedchambers, and the poor man's cell
and whatever else luxury, not content with simple elegance, mixes up;
as people often say, "the house is in good shape" '.

It is not surprising that Seneca makes few allusions to attending
entertainments. We would not expect a man of his age and education
to enjoy them. Apart from the early diatribe against the off-peak killing exercises of the arena (letter 7), Seneca uses tragedy (80.7–8) to
mark the ironic discrepancy between the buskin and cloak of the stage
hero and his shabby offstage existence, and surprisingly cites mime
(108.7–11, cf. 115.14–15) to illustrate the power of wise sentiments

---

[33] These are the *locus de luxuria* and *locus de saeculo* mentioned by Seneca's father: the
architectural feats violating nature on land and sea were already a favourite theme in the
last decades BCE; see e.g. Sallust, *Catiline*, 55 and Horace, *Odes*, II.15.

[34] On Seneca and slavery see now K. R. Bradley in Fitch (ed.), *Seneca*.

when they are cast in memorable verse. Occasionally, too, he alludes to the declamatory world his father loved (e.g. letter 122).

What we miss — vignettes of senatorial debate or financial business in the forum and litigation in the courts — are absent from the letters partly because of Seneca's purpose in composing this extended sequence (which was to stay focused on the inner man), but also because of his now deliberately withdrawn mode of living. He has made a virtue of necessity and counsels Lucilius to shun the common crowd and avoid sharing in ordinary gossip (7.6–9, cf. 10.1) because he himself is stepping back not just from public life but from living in public. At Lucilius' urgent request (or so he would have us believe) Seneca does supply some brief details of his daily routine in letter 83. On a day uninterrupted by business, he divides his time between his couch for resting and his reading, with only a small concession to exercise. His personal trainer is a slave-boy Pharius, with whom Seneca used to be able to keep up in running, but now Pharius is growing up and he needs a younger or smaller pacemaker. This is followed by a cold bath, then some dry bread and a snack (*sine mensa prandium*), and a very short siesta, more like a cat-nap, until he is roused by the shouts of the audience at the circus games.

Instead of popular entertainments Seneca prefers study, and not just moral philosophy. At least two letters advise against reading too broad a selection of books (e.g. letters 27, 45). Unlike Cicero, Seneca tells us nothing about his library, but his quotations from Zeno and later Stoics such as the polymath Poseidonius and Hecato suggest he had texts to hand. There are a number of rewarding letters that touch on listening to philosophers' lectures (cf. especially letter 40), and Seneca himself describes attending the almost deserted philosophy lectures of Metronax at Naples while crowds pour into the theatre (76.4); he includes many reminiscences of moral teachers, Papirius Fabianus, Attalus, and Demetrius.[35] Seneca is not just reading but writing, and not just the works which have come down to us. His book on moral philosophy, mentioned in letters 106, 108, and 109, probably remained unfinished at his death, but we know he also wrote on geography and the anthropology of India and Egypt, and on meteorology.

[35] Papirius Fabianus: 11.4, 40.12 (also 52.11, 58.6, and an extended appreciation at 100.1–6, not in this selection); Attalus: 67.15, and 108.13 and 23; Demetrius: 20.9, 62.3 (both stressing his simple dress in a plain tunic), 67.14 and 91.19).

The study of language and art of composition were pre-eminent in Roman education and adult leisure: so the long letters 88 and 108 criticize from different points of view the 'take' of various kinds of grammarian or antiquarian which bypasses the moral purpose and function of both poetry (Virgil in particular, used to provide an allegorical parallel to the good man's progress) and prose (surprisingly, the only detailed example is Cicero's *On the Republic*, in letter 88).[36] Seneca was extraordinarily interested in style, as is shown by his letter 46, written in apparent excitement at receiving Lucilius' latest work; its stylistic merits are discussed at length, but there is no hint of its topic. Other letters offer stylistic appraisals of, for example, Papirius, and letters 114 and 115 deal primarily with questions of style as a reflection of moral strength or weakness: letter 114 is famous for its systematic criticism of Maecenas' diction.

Within any but the shortest letters the common pattern seems to be the hook — the curious anecdote — catching the reader's interest in the first four sections, followed (often in section 5) by the more abstract moral theme; but many letters run through as many as three distinct, and sometimes only loosely related, topics.

If we expect a sense of moral victory in the last surviving book of letters, or of bringing the race towards virtue to its finishing-post, I have not found one. And there are Gellius' quotations criticizing earlier authors for their style, quoted from a later book, presumably lost. Did the letters continue into Seneca's last months? The surviving books leave the impression that the correspondence was going to continue, or would have done so if Seneca had been allowed to stay out of the crisis of suspicion spreading in ever-wider circles around the Pisonian conspiracy, discovered early in 65 before it was brought to birth. Nero wanted to find Seneca complicit and duly ordered him to end his life; allowing him, at least, to do it in private at home, with his beloved wife, in the company of two close philosophical friends and his doctor. Tacitus' detailed narrative reflects some of the loyal bias of his source, Seneca's follower Fabius Rusticus, and Seneca's mode of death was clearly shaped by his admiration for Socrates and Cato of Utica: it contains recognizable elements from both the *Phaedo* and the Catonian legend known to us from Plutarch, writing a generation or more after Seneca. Dio's version (LXII.25) obviously derives from

---

[36] For Seneca's negative judgments of Ennius and Cicero see the Appendix.

a hostile source, but there is no reason to give it credit, nor, as some recent scholars have done, to read hypocrisy into the behaviour of Seneca and his wife as Tacitus reports it. If their behaviour in this final crisis was motivated by an aspiration to glory, this was a motive respected among elite Romans.

When Nero's centurion refused to let Seneca take up tablets to compose a new will in favour of the loyal friends who had not forsaken him (62), Seneca turned to them:

He bore witness that since he was prevented from thanking them for their services to him, he was leaving them the one best thing he had, the likeness of his life; [37] and if they kept it in mind they would harvest the fruit of their loyal friendship as reputation for noble behaviour. Controlling their tears now by argument, now more rigorously like one imposing discipline, he called them back to a resolute attitude, asking where were their rules of wisdom and their method rehearsed over so many years of responding to impending misfortune. Who was unaware of Nero's cruelty? Nothing else was left after killing his mother and brother except to add the death of the man who reared and taught him.

(63) When he had conducted this discussion with them all in common, he embraced his wife, and softening a little the courage he was showing he begged and besought her to restrain her grief and not maintain it for ever, but tolerate her loss of her husband with honourable solaces by contemplating his virtuous life. She in reply declared she had resolved on death for herself, and demanded the services of an executioner. Then Seneca, sympathizing with her aspiration and from love, because he did not want to leave her who was so dear to him to suffer abuse, said: 'I had shown you the beguilements of life but you prefer the glory of death; I will not begrudge you your role as model. Let the courage of this brave end be equal in us both, but there will be more distinction in your death.' (Tacitus, *Annals*, XV.62–3)

For all Seneca's moral determination, it proved much less easy for him to achieve physical death. Although husband and wife cut open their veins simultaneously, Seneca's ageing body, starved by his meagre diet, would not bleed, and he urged his wife to withdraw to another room so as to avoid distressing her further. There he had additional veins in his legs cut and waited for this to take effect. At this last moment he called in secretaries and dictated 'the writings which

---

[37] Latin *imago vitae suae*, the title of Griffin's analysis of Seneca's character and self-representation in Fitch (ed.), *Seneca*; see also Edwards, 'Self-scrutiny'.

are now published for the crowd to read' (Tacitus does not quote or summarize them but it is generally thought that these discussed the nature of death and the soul, on which we have Seneca's views in several of the *Letters on Morality*, e.g. 67, 70). But even the next remedy, the hemlock Seneca had procured in emulation of Socrates, had no effect, and he resorted to a bath of extremely hot water, some of which he poured, like Socrates, as a libation to Jupiter the Liberator. This third attempt succeeded, and he managed to lose consciousness and pass out of life overcome by the steam. His death was followed by a quick cremation, 'as he had ordered long before when still supreme in power and wealth'. But Paulina was revived on Nero's orders, against her will, and not allowed to die with him.

Seneca's wealth and the responsibility of his power while it lasted lost him the sympathy of many contemporaries, but the letters show he was conscious of his shortcomings, and however self-conscious, their genuine motive is to benefit, through Lucilius their explicit reader, his contemporaries and his posterity, which now includes us. We have lost the art of exhortation and, worse, the willingness to learn from exhortation. But at least these letters represent encouragement to good behaviour without the bribe of either human or divine approval; if their power consists in denying the reader easy comfort, they are also fascinating in the variety of their topics and illustrations, and often brilliant in their compelling and immediate personal voice.

NOTE ON THE TEXT

There is an authoritative account of the manuscript history of all
Seneca's works, including the *Epistulae Morales*, by L. D. Reynolds,
editor of the Oxford Classical Texts editions of the *Dialogues* and
Letters in *The Medieval Tradition of Seneca's Letters* (Oxford: Oxford
UP, 1965); compare his Latin introduction to the Oxford Classical
Text (1965), which is the basis of my translation, and the relevant
pages of *Texts and Transmissions* (of which he is also the editor, 1983),
on Seneca's works (pp. 357–60) and on the *Letters* (pp. 369–75).

Some time after the fourth century of our era the body of these
letters was divided into three parts which were preserved separately
from each other. The last part, of unknown size, was quickly lost, but
a passage from the second-century writer Aulus Gellius (included
below as an Appendix) quotes from Book XXII. Letters 1–88 (Books
I to XIII) seem to have been more popular than letters 89–124 (Books
XIV to XX), and survive in more manuscripts from the ninth to
twelfth centuries, when they begin to appear together. They were
increasingly popular with scholars, and by 1475 or around that year
four editions had appeared from Paris, Rome, Naples, and Strasburg.
The separate preservation of the two segments, as with a less common
division between letters 1–52 and 53–88, need not represent an original articulation by Seneca, although they do coincide with the book
units attested in the manuscripts, in which letters 1–52 are contained
in Books I–V, letters 53–88 in Books VI–XIII, and letters 89–124 in
Books XIV–XX. There was probably another unit equal in length,
from which a letter in Book XXII is excerpted by Aulus Gellius, *Attic
Nights*, XII.2 (see the Appendix). But these divisions do not match
the change of form between Books I–III and IV–V, or of locality to
Campania at letter 49 in Book V, ending with letter 57 in Book VI.
Not all the book units are marked, and there are no headings or letter
numbering for Books XI–XIII and XVII–XVIII; nor are the books of
consistent length, either in number of letters or, more surprisingly,
in actual pages.

The scientifically edited text that has come down to us has essen-
tially the form which it was given by Erasmus in his edition of all
Seneca's works in 1529. The present selection of 80 letters comprises

nearly two-thirds of the collection. They have been chosen to represent Seneca's world, the breadth of his interests in life as well as his doctrine (for example, aspects of death, the consciousness of animals and infants, men's perverse reversal of night and day), and the vivid variety of both his illustrative examples and moral exhortations. The following letters are included:

BOOK I (1–12): complete
BOOK II (13–21): letters 14, 15, 16, 18, 19, 21
BOOK III (22–9): letters 24, 26, 27, 28
BOOK IV (30–41): letters 31, 33, 34, 35, 36, 37, 38, 39, 40, 41
BOOK V (42–52): letters 44, 46, 47, 48, 51
BOOK VI (53–62): letters 53, 54, 55, 56, 57, 60, 61, 62
BOOK VII (63–9): letters 63, 64, 65, 67, 68
BOOK VIII (70–4): letters 72, 73
BOOK IX (75–80): letters 76, 77, 78, 79
BOOK X (81–3): letters 82, 83
BOOKS XI–XIII (84–8): letters 84, 86, 87, 88 (no book divisions transmitted)
BOOK XIV (89–92): letters 90, 91
BOOK XV (93–5): letter 95
BOOK XVI (96–100): letters 97, 99
BOOKS XVII–XVIII (101–9): letters 101, 104, 105, 107, 108 (no book divisions)
BOOK XIX (110–17): letters 110, 114, 116
BOOK XX (118–24): letters 118, 121, 122, 123, 124

SELECT BIBLIOGRAPHY

Bibliographical Note

There is less literature on Senecan prose in English than by French, German, and Italian authors, but much recent work is not relevant to our translations: it is more concerned with Seneca's form and his style than with his thought. On Seneca's political and moral role Griffin, *Seneca: A Philosopher in Politics*, is superb; add Rawson, 'Roman Rulers and the Philosophic Adviser', in Griffin and Barnes (eds.), *Philosophia Togata I*. On Seneca's philosophical background and contemporaries see Brad Inwood, *Reading Seneca*, and note chapter 6, 'Seneca and his Contemporaries', in M. P. O. Morford, *The Roman Philosophers*. On Hellenistic and Roman Stoics see Inwood, *A Stoic Reader*. On Roman Stoicism see A. A. Long, *Problems in Stoicism*, and the collection by Long and David Sedley, *The Hellenistic Philosophers*. On Posidonius and Seneca's use of his work see I. G. Kidd, 'Posidonius as Philosopher-Historian', pp. 38–50, in Griffin and Barnes, *Philosophia Togata I*, and Kidd's complete translation of the fragments in *Posidonius*, Vol. 3. On Seneca as a literary critic see Donald M. Russell and M. Winterbottom, *Ancient Literary Criticism*.

On Seneca's family, see Griffin, 'The Elder Seneca and Spain', *JRS* (1972); on his social milieu, S. Dill, *Roman Society from Nero to Marcus Aurelius*; on Campania, J. D. Arms, *Romans on the Bay of Naples and Other Essays*. Among biographies are V. Sorensen, *Seneca: The Humanist at the Court of Nero*, and P. Veyne, *Seneca: The Life of a Stoic*.

Besides the Oxford World's Classics translation of seven dialogues, note John Cooper and J. F. Procope, *Seneca: Moral and Political Essays* (*On Anger, On Mercy, On the Private Life*, and Books I–IV of *On Favours*) (Cambridge: Cambridge UP, 1995); also Susanna Braund's new edition of *Seneca: De Clementia*, edited with text, translation, and commentary (Oxford: Oxford UP, 2009). The University of Chicago Press has commissioned a complete translation of all Seneca's works, some of which have already appeared.

Readers with a predominantly philosophical interest should consult the selection of letters and discussion in B. Inwood, *Seneca's Philosophical Letters* (Oxford: Oxford UP, 2007).

Costa, C. D. N. (ed.), *Seneca* (London and Boston: Routledge & Kegan Paul, 1974).

Bowersock, G. W., 'Seneca's Greek', in De Vivo and Lo Cascio (eds.), *Seneca*.

Bradley, K. R., 'Seneca on Slavery', in Fitch (ed.), *Seneca*.

Brunt, P. A., *Roman Imperial Themes* (Oxford: Oxford UP, 1990).

Champlin, E., *Nero* (Princeton: Princeton UP, 2003).

D'Arms, J., *Romans on the Bay of Naples and Other Essays on Roman Campania* (Edipuglia, 2003).

De Vivo, A., and Lo Cascio, E. (eds.), *Seneca uomo politico e l'eta di Claudio e di Nerone* (Bari: Edipuglia, 2003).

Dill, S., *Roman Society from Nero to Marcus Aurelius* (London: Macmillan, 1925).

Edwards, C., *Death in Ancient Rome* (New Haven and London: Yale UP, 2007).

—— 'Epistolography', in *A Companion to Latin Literature*, ed. S. J. Harrison (Oxford: Blackwells, 2005).

—— 'Self-scrutiny and Self-Transformation in Seneca's Letters', in Fitch (ed.), *Seneca*.

Erskine, A., 'Money Loving Romans', *Papers of the Leeds Latin Seminar*, 9, ARCA (Liverpool, 1996).

Fairweather, J., *The Elder Seneca* (Cambridge: Cambridge UP, 1981).

Fitch, J. G. (ed.), *Seneca*, Oxford Readings in Classical Texts (Oxford: Oxford UP, 2008).

Griffin, M. T., 'The Elder Seneca and Spain', *JRS* 62 (1972), 1–19.

—— '*Imago vitae suae*', in Costa (ed.), *Seneca,* and Fitch (ed.), *Seneca*.

—— *Seneca: A Philosopher in Politics* (Oxford: Oxford UP, 1976).

—— 'Philosophy, Cato and Roman Suicide, I and II', *Greece & Rome*, 33 (1976), 64–75, 192–202.

Habinek, T. N.,'An Aristocracy of Virtue: Seneca on the Beginnings of Wisdom', *Yale Classical Studies*, 29, 187–203.

Inwood, B., *Reading Seneca* (Oxford: Oxford UP, 2005).

—— *Seneca's Philosophical Letters* (Oxford: Oxford UP, 2007).

—— 'The Importance of Form in Seneca's Philosophical Letters', in Morello and Morrison (eds.), *Ancient Letters*.

—— *The Stoic Reader* (Indianapolis: Hackett, 2008).

—— and Gerson, L. P., *Hellenistic Philosophy: Introductory Readings*, Epicurus and Epicureans, pp. 4–77; Stoicism, pp. 77–158 (Indianapolis: Hackett, 1988).

Ker, J., 'Seneca, Man of Many Genres', in K.Volk and G. D. Williams (eds.), *Seeing Seneca Whole: Perspectives on Philosophy, Poetry and Politics* (New York: Columbia UP, 2006).

—— *The Deaths of Seneca* (New York: Oxford UP, 2009).

Kidd, I. G., 'Posidonius as Philosopher-Historian', in Miriam T. Griffin and Jonathan Barnes (eds.), *Philosophia Togata I: Essays on Philosophy and Roman Society* (Oxford: Oxford UP, 1989).

Kidd, I. G., *Posidonius*, Vol. 3, *The Translation of the Fragments* (Cambridge: Cambridge UP, 1999).

Levick, B. M., 'Seneca and Money', in De Vivo and Lo Cascio (eds.), *Seneca*.

Long, A. A. (ed.), *Problems in Stoicism* (London: Athlone, 1971).

—— and Sedley, D., *The Hellenistic Philosophers* (Berkeley: University of California Press, 1987).

Morello, R., and Morrison, A. D. (eds.), *Ancient Letters: Classical and Late Antique Epistolography* (Oxford: Oxford UP, 2007).

Morford, M. P. O., *The Roman Philosophers, from the Time of Cato the Elder to Marcus Aurelius* (London: Routledge, 2002).

Motto, A. L., *Seneca: A Sourcebook. Guide to the Thought of L. Annaeus Seneca in the Extant Prose Works: Ep. Mor., Dialogi, Ben., Clem. and Quaestiones Naturales* (Indianapolis: Hackett, 1970).

—— *Essays on Seneca* (Heidelberg: Peter Lang, 1993).

—— *Further Essays on Seneca* (Heidelberg: Peter Lang, 2001).

Nussbaum. M., *The Therapy of Desire: Theory and Practice in Hellenistic Ethics* (Princeton: Princeton UP, 1994).

Rawson, E., 'Roman Rulers and the Philosophic Adviser', in Griffin and Barnes (eds.), *Philosophia Togata I* (Oxford: Oxford UP, 1989).

Reynolds, L. D., *The Medieval Tradition of Seneca's Letters* (Oxford: Oxford UP, 1965).

—— (ed.), *Texts and Transmissions* (Oxford: Oxford UP, 1983).

Roller, M. B., *Constructing Autocracy: Aristocrats and Emperors in Julio-Claudian Rome* (Princeton: Princeton UP, 2001).

Russell, D. A., '*Letters to Lucilius*', in Costa (ed.), *Seneca*.

—— and Winterbottom, M., *Ancient Literary Criticism* (Oxford: Oxford UP, 1975).

Sorensen, V., *Seneca: The Humanist at the Court of Nero* (Chicago: Chicago UP, 1929).

Veyne, P., *Seneca: The Life of a Stoic* (London: Routledge, 2003).

Williams, G. D. (ed.), *Seneca: De Brevitate Vitae, De Otio* (Cambridge: Cambridge UP, 2003).

Wilson, M., 'Seneca's *Letters to Lucilius*: a Revaluation', in *Imperial Muse = Ramus*, 16 (1987).

—— 'Seneca's Epistles Reclassified', in S. J. Harrison (ed.), *Texts, Ideas and the Classics: Scholarship, Theory and Classical Literature* (Oxford: Oxford UP, 2001).

Wirszubski, C., *Libertas as a Political Idea in the Late Roman Republic and Early Principate* (Cambridge: Cambridge UP, 1950).

Wistrand, M., *Entertainment and Violence in Ancient Rome: The Attitudes of Roman Writers in the First Century AD* (Oxford: Oxford UP, 1978).

Further Reading in Oxford World's Classics

Cicero, *Selected Letters*, trans. P. G. Walsh.
Pliny the Younger, *Complete Letters*, trans. P. G. Walsh.
Seneca, *Dialogues and Essays*, trans. John Davie, ed. Tobias Reinhardt.
—— *Six Tragedies*, trans. Emily Wilson.
Tacitus, *The Annals: the Reigns of Tiberius, Claudius, and Nero*, trans. J. C. Yardley, ed. Anthony A. Barrett.

A CHRONOLOGY OF
LUCIUS ANNAEUS SENECA

49–45 BCE	Civil war between Julius Caesar and the republicans commanded by Pompey. After the defeat of Pharsalus (48) republicans regroup in Africa, but are again defeated by Caesar at Thapsus; Cato 'of Utica' earns his position as a Stoic hero by his suicide immediately after Utica (46). Pompey's sons rally support in southern Spain, but are finally defeated at Munda in 45; Seneca's father's birth-date is disputed, but he was a child at the time.
44 BCE	Assassination of Julius Caesar.
31 BCE	Victory of Caesar's 'son' Octavian over Antony and Cleopatra. Occupation of Egypt.
27 BCE	Octavian restores senatorial control of non-militarized provinces, receives title 'Augustus'.
27 BCE–14 CE	Principate of Augustus.
?1 BCE–4 CE	Birth of Seneca.
14–37 CE	Principate of Tiberius.
37–41 CE	Principate of Gaius (Caligula).
41 CE	Claudius becomes emperor; under the influence of his wife Messalina he relegates Seneca to exile in Corsica.
49 CE	After Messalina's disgrace and suicide Claudius marries his niece Agrippina, who has Seneca recalled to serve as tutor to her son Domitius Ahenobarbus, adopted the following year as Claudius Nero.
54 CE	Death of Claudius; Nero becomes emperor. Seneca composes the *Apocolcyntosis* ('Pumpkinification') mocking the deification of Claudius.
55 CE	Nero has his stepbrother Britannicus poisoned.
59 CE	Nero has his mother murdered. Between 55 and 62 Seneca composes *De Clementia* (*On Mercy*) and *De Beneficiis* (*On Benefits*).

SELECTED LETTERS

Letter 1 (Book I.1) *In answer to Lucilius, who has declared himself determined to make the best use of his time.*

Yes, do just that, dear Lucilius:* liberate yourself, and gather and save   1
up the time which until now was being taken from you by force or
stealth or simply slipping away unnoticed. Convince yourself that the
situation is as I describe it; some periods of time are snatched from
us, some are stolen, and some simply seep away. Yet the most shameful loss is the loss due to carelessness. Indeed, if you consider things
attentively, the greatest part* of life slips away in failure, a great part
in futility, and all of it in distraction.

Name anyone to me who puts a price on time, who values the day,   2
who understands that he is dying each and every day. For we deceive
ourselves by looking for death ahead of us, whereas a great part of
death has already taken place. Whatever part of life is behind us is
possessed by death. So, dear Lucilius, do what you say you are doing
and embrace every hour; in this way you will have to depend less on
tomorrow if you seize hold of today. While life is being postponed, it
rushes past.

Everything else is beyond our grasp, only time is ours. Nature pro-   3
duced us to claim ownership only of this one fleeting and slippery
property, from which anyone who chooses may dispossess us. And
men's stupidity is so great that they allow the most trivial cheap
objects, ones easy to replace, to be charged against their credit once
they have obtained them. But no one thinks he owes anything when
he has received a gift of time. And yet this is the only thing that even
a grateful person cannot return. You may wonder how I myself am   4
dealing with this, since I am making these recommendations to you.
I will confess honestly that the sum of my expenses is accounted for,
as happens to anyone indulgent but careful. I cannot say I am not
making any losses, but I can say what I am losing and why and how.
I will be able to explain the reasons for my poverty. But the same thing
has happened to me as to most people reduced to lack of resources
through no fault of their own: everyone pardons me but no one comes
to my aid. So what should we say? I don't think of anyone as poor if   5
he finds whatever little is left over is enough. But I prefer that you
should keep your own resources safe, and you will be starting at a
good time. For, as our ancestors realized, 'thrift comes too late at the

bottom of the barrel',* for what is left at the bottom is not only miserably little but miserably poor in quality. Keep well.

Letter 2 (Book I.2) *On restlessness, whether in physical travel or indiscriminate reading.*

1 I have formed good expectations of you, both from what you write and from what I hear of your activities. You are not rushing around or letting a change of place upset you. That is the disturbance of a sick spirit. I think it is the first proof of a stable mind to be able to pause
2 and spend time with oneself. But now make sure that reading many authors and every kind of book-roll does not represent a kind of unsettled drifting. You should linger over and feed yourself upon a chosen few intellects if you want to take in anything that will stay faithfully in your mind. The man who is everywhere is nowhere. When men spend their life in travelling around, they have many hosts but no real friendships. The same thing must happen to those who do not devote themselves intimately to any one intellect but take in
3 everything at speed and in haste. Food that is evacuated as soon as it is consumed gives no benefit and does not add its strength to the body.* Nothing delays healing as much as a constant change of remedies. A wound on which medications are tried out does not knit into a scar. A seedling that is constantly transplanted does not build up strength. Indeed, nothing is so beneficial that it can do good on the run; hence a great number of books slackens the mind. So, since you cannot read as much as you possess, it is enough to have the amount
4 you can read. 'But', you will say, 'sometimes I want to open this book, and sometimes that.' It shows a fussy appetite to sample many foodstuffs: when they are assorted and ill-matched they corrupt rather than nourish the tissues. So constantly read the approved texts, and when you fancy turning aside to others, return to the originals; get yourself some daily support against poverty, against death, and equally against other plagues. When you have surveyed many writ-
5 ings, choose one idea to digest that day. I do this too, and take hold of one thought from the many I have read. This is the thought for today, which I got from Epicurus (for it is my custom to visit the opposite camp, not as a deserter but as a spy). 'Happy poverty is an honourable condition.'* For if it is happy, it is not poverty; a man on good terms with poverty is rich. It is not the man with too little property, but the

one who wants more, who is a pauper. What does it matter how much is stored in his strongbox or his granaries, how large the scale of his pasturing or moneylending, if he is hovering over other men's property and calculating not what he has acquired but what is to be acquired? You ask what is the proper measure of wealth? The best measure is to have what is necessary, and next best, to have enough. Keep well.

Letter 3 (Book I.3) *On the proper basis of real friendship. Seneca warns Lucilius against making a man into a friend before he knows the man's character. But once someone has become a friend, he should be trusted and should share one's anxieties. (See also letter 9 on the wise man's friendships.)*

You gave a friend, as you write, letters to pass on to me. But then you 1 warn me not to share with him everything that concerns you, since you do not usually do this yourself either. So in one and the same letter you call him a friend and then take back the name. Now, if you used the earlier phrase in the common fashion and called him a friend in the same way we call all competitors for office 'good men' or as we call those we meet 'sir', if their name does not occur to us, then let it pass! But if you call anyone a friend whom you do not trust as much 2 as you do yourself, you are seriously mistaken, and do not know the meaning of true friendship. Certainly take counsel over everything with your friend, but take counsel over him first. You must give trust once you have formed a friendship, but form judgement beforehand. Men confuse the proper order of behaviour when they go against the recommendations of Theophrastus* and judge after they have given their love, instead of giving love after they have passed judgement. Think long whether someone should be taken into your friendship. When you have decided on it, welcome him with your whole heart; speak as confidently with him as with yourself. And as for yourself, 3 live so that you trust nothing to yourself that you would not trust even to an enemy. But since some issues will arise that custom keeps private, share with your friend all your cares and deliberations. You will make him loyal if you think him so. For some people have taught others to cheat them by fearing to be cheated, and by their suspicions have given others the right to offend. Why should I hold back any words in my friend's company? Why should I not think of myself

4 as alone when enjoying his company? Some people tell strangers what should only be entrusted to friends, and unburden whatever is bothering them on random ears. On the other hand, some are frightened of even their dearest friends knowing; they would not even trust themselves, if they could avoid it, and keep everything bottled up in their hearts. But we should not follow either course; for it is equally a
5 fault to trust everyone and to trust no one. However, I would call the first fault more honourable, the second more safe. In this way you would criticize both those who are always ill at ease, and those who are always at ease. For the kind of activity that delights in bustle is not activity, but the fretting of a harassed mind. And it is not ease that judges all movement to be a nuisance, but slackness and languishing.
6 So the saying I read in Pomponius* will be committed to your mind: 'some men have retreated so far into the shadows that they think whatever is in the daylight is in dazzling confusion.' Those attitudes should be blended: the man at ease should take action, and the man of action should take ease. Take counsel with Nature: she will say that she made both day and night for you. Keep well.

Letter 4 (Book I.4) *On cultivating tranquillity of mind and rejecting fear of death. Seneca starts from the comparison of a man becoming wise to a boy coming of age. It is equally foolish to scorn life and to fear death, and calmness can be achieved by learning that there is no reason to fear death, which is always with us.*

1 Keep on as you have begun, and press on as quickly as possible so that you can enjoy a calm and correct state of mind for as long as possible. In fact you will enjoy it while you are correcting it and even while you are making it calm. It is a different kind of pleasure we receive from
2 contemplating a mind pure and shining, free of every stain. You must surely remember the great joy you felt when you set aside your child's toga to put on your toga of manhood and were escorted to the forum:* expect a greater joy when you put aside a child's state of mind and philosophy has enrolled you among grown men. For it is not childhood, but childishness, a much more serious defect, that still persists. And this is all the worse because we have the authority of older men
3 but the failings of children, and not just children but babies. Children are afraid of trivial things, but babies fear imaginary ones, while we are afraid of everything. Only make progress and you will realize that

there are some things we should not fear just because they bring so much fear with them. No suffering is great if it has an end. Death is coming to you: it would have been worth fearing if it could coexist with you. But it must either not reach you, or pass you by. You will 4 say, 'it is hard to induce the mind to scorn life itself'. But don't you see what foolish reasons lead men to scorn life? One man hanged himself in front of his girlfriend's door, another threw himself from the roof to avoid listening to his master's rage, another drove a knife into his body to avoid being recaptured when a fugitive.* Don't you think virtue could achieve what excessive fear achieves? No man can have a carefree life if he devotes too much concern to prolonging it, count-ing a number of consular years among important blessings. Practise 5 thinking this over* each day, so that you can calmly leave life, which so many men clutch at and hold on to as someone swept away by the current clutches at thornbushes and jagged objects. Most people are buffeted between fear of death and the agony of living; they don't want to live and they don't know how to die.

So make life pleasant for yourself by casting away all anxiety about 6 it. No good thing helps its possessor unless his mind is ready to lose it. And no loss is easier than losing something if its loss cannot be missed. So harden yourself against these troubles which can befall even the most powerful among men. It was a minor and a eunuch who 7 determined Pompey's fate, and a cruel and arrogant Parthian who decided the fate of Crassus. Gaius Caesar ordered Lepidus to offer his neck to the tribune Dexter, and himself lost his life to Chaerea:* there is no one whom Fortune promoted so high that she could not threaten him with evils as great as her promises. Don't trust this calm: the sea will be churned up in a mere moment. Boats are engulfed on the same day that they have played on the waters. Think that a robber 8 or an enemy can hold his sword to your throat. Even in the absence of higher authority there is no slave that does not have power of life and death over you.

What I am saying is that anyone who scorns his life is the master of yours. Review the precedents of men who died from household vio-lence, whether open or treacherous, and you will realize that as many men died from the anger of slaves as of kings. So what does it matter how powerful is the man you fear, when anyone at all can do the deed which causes your fear? But if you happen to fall into the hands of 9 the enemy, as victor he will order you to be taken away to the death

which is already your destination. So why deceive yourself and realize
only now what you have long since been suffering? What I am saying
is that you have been on the way to death since you were born. We
should consider these and similar thoughts in our hearts if we want to
wait calmly for that last hour, given that this fear torments all our
remaining hours.

10   But to put an end to this letter, read what won my approval today—
this too is taken from other men's gardens:* 'poverty reconciled by
the law of nature is great wealth.' Now do you know what limits the
law of Nature imposes on us? Not to suffer starvation or thirst or
cold. To drive off hunger and thirst you do not have to sit at arrogant
doorways or endure a painful frown and condescending courtesy; you
do not have to risk the seas or follow armies on the move: what nature
11 needs is available and set before you. Men only sweat over superfluous things; these are what wear out our toga* and force us to grow old
under canvas, or drive us onto foreign shores; what is enough is in our
reach. Keep well.

Letter 5 (Book I.5) *On avoiding conspicuous austerity and the meaning of 'living according to Nature.' Adopting a severe lifestyle is one
aspect of the wider issue of shunning the crowd, and actually withdrawing
or retiring from public life raised in letters 7 and 8.*

1 I heartily approve and rejoice that you are studying with perseverance
and abandoning all else for this one thing, to make yourself a better
man each day; in fact I am not just urging you to persevere, but
encouraging you. But I would warn you not to behave like men who
are indifferent to progress but want to attract notice, or to adopt
2 behaviour that is conspicuous in your dress or way of life. Avoid rough
dress and an unshorn head and a straggling beard, and a declaration
of loathing for money, and the practice of sleeping on the ground,
and any other perverse affectation. The name of philosophy is enough,
even if it were bandied in moderation, to provoke resentment; what
will happen if we begin to exclude ourselves from everyday practices?
Let everything in our hearts be different, but let our appearance suit
3 our fellow men. Our toga should not dazzle, nor should it be drab.
We should not have silverware chased with solid gold, but we should
not think it a mark of thrift to go without silver and gold; let our aim
be to follow a better life than the crowd, but not one opposed to it;

otherwise we simply drive off and turn away the men we are trying to correct. This way we also make sure that they avoid trying to imitate any aspect of our behaviour for fear that they will have to imitate it completely. This is the first promise of philosophy, a feeling for all, 4 human courtesy and sociability. But stressing difference will keep us away from this policy. We should make sure that the actions we take in order to win admiration are not absurd and offensive. Now our objective is to live according to Nature, and it is contrary to Nature to torment one's body and shun easy forms of cleanliness and aspire to shabbiness and follow a diet that is not just cheap but loathsome and horrible. Just as it is typical of luxury to hanker after fancy delicacies, 5 so it is a mark of madness to shun normal foods available at a low cost. Philosophy demands thrift, not self-punishment, and thrift need not be unadorned. This is the measure I choose, that our life should be a compromise between virtuous behaviour and public practice: let everyone admire our life, but also see it as familiar. 'What shall we do 6 then? Behave like everyone else? Will there be no difference between us and them?' Yes, a great difference. Let the man who examines us more closely recognize that we are not like the common crowd. Let the man who enters our house admire us rather than our furnishings. The man is truly great who uses earthenware in the same way as silver, but another man is not inferior for using his silver as if it were earthenware. It is the mark of a weak mind not to be able to tolerate wealth.

But to share with you today's little bit of profit, I found in our 7 Hecato* that a limit to desires also contributes to curing fear. He says, 'you will cease to fear if you also cease to hope.' You will ask: 'How are such opposite things on equal terms?' That's the way it is, Lucilius, although they seem in conflict, they are bound together. Just as the same chain links the prisoner and the soldier, so these emotions which seem so opposed advance together; fear goes along with hope. And I 8 am not surprised that they proceed like this; each emotion comes from a mind in suspense, each is troubled by expectation of what is to come. But the chief cause of each is that we do not adapt ourselves to present circumstances but send our thoughts running ahead. So foresight, the greatest good of our human condition, is turned into an evil. Wild 9 beasts run away from dangers when they see them. Once they have escaped, they are free of anxiety. But we are tormented by both the future and the past. Our own good qualities do us a great deal of harm, for memory recalls and foresight anticipates the torment of fear. No one is wretched only about what is at hand. Keep well.

Letter 6 (Book I.6) *Seneca offers Lucilius evidence of his own gradual advance in virtue.*

1 I realize, Lucilius, that I am not just being improved but transformed. Not that I can yet promise or hope that nothing is left in me that needs to be changed. Of course I have many faults that should be corrected, reduced, abolished. And even this is proof of a mind transformed for the better, that it sees the faults which it had not noticed until now. Some sick men are congratulated when they realize that
2 they are sick. So I would have liked to share with you this sudden change in me; then I would begin to have a surer confidence in our friendship, the true friendship which neither hope nor fear nor self-interest can sever, the friendship with which men die and for which
3 they die. I will cite many men to you who did not lack a friend, but lacked friendship. This cannot happen when a similar will draws spirits into a partnership in desiring what is honourable. How could it not fail to happen? For friends know they have everything in common, indeed they share their misfortunes more closely.

   You cannot conceive how much power I see each day bringing
4 to me. 'So pass on to me', you say, 'these techniques which you have found so effective.' Truly, I want to pour everything into you and I am glad to learn something so that I may teach it. In fact nothing will give me pleasure, however exceptional and beneficial, if I am to know it for myself alone. If wisdom is bestowed with this proviso, that I keep it locked up without uttering it, I shall refuse it. There is no
5 pleasure in possessing any good thing without a partner. So I shall send you the actual books, and to prevent you wasting a lot of effort in chasing the scattered recommendations that will benefit you, I will mark these so that you can immediately reach what has my approval and admiration. But the living voice and conversation will do you more good than the text. You must come to witness the real thing, first because men trust their eyes more than their ears; next, because the approach through recommendations is long, but that of examples is short and effective.
6   Cleanthes would not have reproduced Zeno's thought if he had only heard him. He shared in Zeno's life and saw his private actions,

he watched him to see whether he lived according to his own code.*
Plato and Aristotle and the whole crowd of philosophers each following his different path derived more from Socrates' behaviour than his
words. It was not Epicurus' teaching but his company that made
Metrodorus and Hermarchus and Polyaenus into great men. And
I am not summoning you just so that you will make your own progress,
but to promote it: for we will contribute greatly to each other.

Until then, since I owe you the daily instalment of pay, I will tell 7
you what delighted me in Hecato. He says: 'You ask what progress
I have made? I have begun to be a friend to myself.' He did indeed
make great progress; he will never be alone. You should know that this
man is now everyone's friend. Keep well.

Letter 7 (Book I.7) *On the gratuitous cruelty of public executions in
the arena and the moral harm done by contact with the crowd of spectators and their vicious relish for human suffering. But any contact with
vicious men will only corrupt (§6). One has to avoid either imitating
common attitudes or hating them, and teach only those ready to learn,
not trying to convert a general audience. Even a single listener, or none
at all, is good enough for the man behaving rightly. It is important to
distinguish the enforced combats of batches of condemned criminals sent to
fight until one of their opponents should kill them, from the skilled combat
of trained gladiators in appropriate defensive armour. See M. Wistrand,*
Entertainment and Violence in Rome in the First Century AD
(Oxford: Oxford UP, 1978).

You ask what I think you should take special care to avoid: the crowd.* 1
You cannot yet trust yourself safely to it. I at least will admit my weakness; I never bring back the same character which I took from home.
Something has been upset from the state of calm I had achieved:
something of the faults I had put to flight returns. It is like the experience of the sick, who have been so affected by long weakness that
they cannot go out anywhere without being shaken up; this is what
happens to us as our minds are being restored from a long sickness.
Association with a large group is harmful; there is no one who does 2
not either recommend some fault to us or impose it upon us or smear
it on us when we are unaware. At any rate, the bigger the gathering
with which we are mingling, the greater the danger. But nothing is
so harmful to good character as to sit idly at a show; it is then that

3 faults sneak up on us more easily because of pleasure. What do you think I mean? I come back more miserly, more ambitious, more self-indulgent, worse, more cruel and inhuman, because I was among human beings. I happened upon the midday show expecting entertainment and wit and some relaxation, to rest men's eyes from the sight of human blood. It was quite the opposite. Whatever combat there was before was an act of mercy. Now they have dropped fooling and it is pure murder. The men have no protective armour. Since their whole bodies are exposed to the blows they never strike a blow in

4 vain. This is what most people prefer to regular pairings and pairings on request. Why wouldn't they prefer such easy game? The steel is not fended off by helmet or shield. What is the point of protective devices or techniques? All such things are a mere obstacle to death. In the morning men are thrown to lions and bears, at noon to the spectators. They order the killers to be thrown to others who will kill them, and keep back the victor for another slaughter; the outcome for the fighters is death. It is a total war of steel and fire. This is what happens with an empty arena.

5 'But maybe he committed a robbery, or killed a man!' Just because he killed, did he deserve to suffer this? What did you do, you wretch, to deserve watching this display? 'Kill him, beat him, burn him!' 'Why is he so timid in hurling himself on the steel? Why is he not falling more bravely? Why is he dying so apathetically? Let them battle it out with slashing blows that make open wounds, so that the fighters suffer mutual death strokes while exposing their bare breasts.' The show is interrupted. 'Have some men throttled in the interval so there is something to watch.' Come, don't you even realize that bad examples fall back on those who make them happen? Thank the immortal gods that you are teaching a man to be cruel who cannot

6 learn. An unformed spirit, one not sufficiently firm in its grasp of morality, must be rescued from the people. It is so easy otherwise to cross over to the majority. The alien crowd could have shaken the moral purpose of Socrates or Cato or Laelius:* so true is it that none of us, even when we try hardest to shape and trim our mind, can with-

7 stand the onset of faults escorted by such a great retinue. A single example of self-indulgence or avarice does a great deal of harm; a fussy dinner companion gradually weakens and softens our manhood. A rich neighbour rouses our greed, a malicious companion rubs off his envy on the most open and spotless fellow; what do you think happens

to a character on whom a communal assault has been mounted? You 8
must either imitate men or loathe them. In fact you should avoid
either course. You should not become like evil men because they are
many, or be hostile to the many because they are unlike you. Withdraw
into yourself as far as you can, and associate with those who will make
you better. Invite those whom you can make better. This benefits both
sides, and men learn while they are teaching. There is no reason for 9
pride in displaying your character to push you into the public eye, to
recite or debate, as I might have wished you to do, if your wares were
suitable for the people: there is no one who can understand you.
Perhaps some person, one man or another, will come upon you, and
even he will need to be shaped and trained to understand you. 'Then
for whom did I learn these teachings?' You need not be afraid of
having wasted your effort if you have learned them for yourself.

But so that I have not learned this just for my own good, I shall 10
share with you three magnificent sayings that came my way to the
same effect: this letter will pay out what is due to you as a debt; accept
the other two as advance payment. Democritus* said: 'one man is as
good as a whole city for me, and the city is as good as one man.' And 11
that other man, whoever it was (the author is disputed), made a good
point, when he was asked why he observed so carefully an art that
would reach only a few. He said: 'a few are enough for me, one is
enough, or even no one is enough.' Epicurus made the third, quite
splendid, comment when he was writing to one of his fellow students.
'I am not saying this for many, but for you. For one of us is a good
enough audience for the other.' You must bury these thoughts deep in 12
your mind, Lucilius, so that you condemn the pleasure that comes
from the agreement of a majority.

Many men praise you, but what reason do you have to be pleased
with yourself, if you are the kind of man whom the common crowd
can understand? Let your virtues look inwards. Keep well.

Letter 8 (Book I.8) *On withdrawal (*secedere*): Seneca continues
the theme of withdrawal from letter 7, but adds that his withdrawal is a
positive retirement in order to write for the future enlightenment of posterity. Lucilius should shun the tastes and indulgences of the crowd. Instead
Seneca turns to recommendations (based on his own example) for a life
spent in withdrawal even from accepted social obligations.*

1   You say: 'are you ordering me to shun the crowd and go into retreat and
    be content with my good conscience? Where are those recommenda-
    tions of yours that order me to die in action?' As to what I seem to be
    urging for the time being, I have withdrawn myself for this purpose
    and shut the door so as to be helpful to a greater number. No day ends
    for me in leisure. I claim part of the night for study. I am not inclined
    to sleep, but I am vulnerable to it and hold to their task my eyes worn
2   out and drooping with keeping watch. I have not just withdrawn from
    men but from business, especially my own; I am doing the business
    of our descendants. I am writing some works that can benefit them.
    I commit to writing beneficial warnings like the prescriptions of useful
    medications, because I have found them effective on my sores, which
3   even if they have not been quite healed, have ceased to spread. I show
    others the right path, which I myself only discovered late on when
    weary with straying. I cry out: 'shun whatever pleases the common
    herd, what chance has allocated. Halt with suspicion and fear before
    every benefit that comes by chance: both wild beasts and fish get caught
    when some hope entices them. Do you think these are gifts of Fortune?*
    They are traps. Whoever among you wants to live a safe life should
    avoid as best he can presents smeared with birdlime, which cheat us
    poor fools with this belief: we think we have taken hold of them, but we
4   are stuck fast to them. That course leads to downfall. The outcome of
    this life lived on high is to fall, and we cannot even resist when success
    begins to force us off the track,* either by managing to stay upright or
    by a single instant crash. Fortune does not overturn us but pierces and
5   crushes us. So hold fast to this sound and healthy way of life, to indulge
    your body only as much as is sufficient for good health. You must treat
    it more harshly so that it obeys the mind; let food abate hunger and
    drink quench thirst, your clothing ward off the cold and your house be
    just a barrier against hostile weather. It makes no difference whether it
    is built of turf or the polychrome marbles of a foreign race: be sure a
    man is as well protected by thatch as by gold. Despise everything which
    unnecessary toil presents as ornament and decoration. Think that
    nothing deserves admiration except the mind, which being itself great
    counts nothing else as great.'
6   If I say this to myself and to our descendants, don't I seem to you
    to be doing more good than when I go into court as sponsor for bail,
    or press my seal-ring on the tablets of a will, or offer my voice and
    service to a candidate in the senate? Believe me, men who seem to

do no public business are doing more important things: they are handling the business of gods and men at the same time.

But now I must come to an end, and follow my own custom of paying something for this letter. It won't come from my resources. We are still plundering Epicurus, from whom I read this remark today. 'You should be a slave to philosophy in order to obtain true liberty.'* The man who submits and surrenders himself to philosophy is not being put off to a later day; he is turned around on the instant. For the mere fact of being the slave of philosophy is liberty. You may perhaps ask me why I take so many fine sayings from Epicurus rather than our own school. But why do you think these sayings belong to Epicurus and are not common to us all? How many things the poets say which either have been said or should be said by philosophers? I will not touch on our tragic writers or the toga dramas:* yes, even these have an element of severity and are halfway between tragedies and comedies. What a great number of eloquent lines lie neglected in the mimes! How many sayings of Publilius* ought to be voiced by actors not in comic slippers but tragic buskins! I will repeat one line of his which is relevant to philosophy and the topic which was just now in my hands; it declares that we should not include the gifts of chance among our possessions:

> Everything that comes from wishing is foreign to us.

And I remember you expressed this line quite a bit more elegantly but more briefly:

> That is not yours which fortune has made yours.

Nor will I pass over that other saying expressed by you even better:

> The good that can be given can be removed.

I am not debiting this as payment, since it has been offered to you from your own pocket. Keep well.

Letter 9 (Book I.9) *On self-sufficiency and the value of friendship. Seneca returns to the theme of friendship from a new point of view; the wise man should not need friends. But he does need them to be objects of his kindness, and Seneca distinguishes between self-interested and altruistic friendship.*

1 You want to know whether Epicurus is right to criticize in one of his letters those who say the wise man contents himself with himself and so does not need friends. This is made a reproach to Stilbo* by Epicurus and others who think a mind immune to feeling is the chief
2 good. But we have to fall into ambiguity if we want to express *apatheia* briefly in one word and call it unfeelingness,* since this can be taken as the opposite of what we mean. We mean the man who spurns every feeling of distress, but it will be understood as the man who cannot endure any distress. So consider whether it is not better to speak of an
3 invulnerable spirit, or a spirit set beyond all suffering. This is the difference between us Stoics and the Epicureans; our wise man overcomes every discomfort but feels it, theirs does not even feel it. What they and we have in common is that the wise man is contented with himself.* But he still wants to have a friend and a neighbour and a
4 housemate, although he is able to satisfy his own needs. See just how well he is contented with himself; sometimes even with a part of himself. If disease or the enemy destroys his hand, if any accident puts out his eye or eyes, what is left of his body will satisfy him and he will be as happy with a damaged or mutilated body as when it was intact. But if he does not miss what he has lost this does not mean he prefers to have lost them.*

5 The wise man is contented, not so that he wants to go without a friend, but so that he is able to go without: and the word 'able' means accepting the loss of a friend calmly. For he will never be without a friend; he has it in his power to provide a new one instantly. If Pheidias* has lost a statue he will quickly make another; just so, this craftsman in making friendships will substitute another friend in
6 place of one he lost. You ask how he will make one quickly? I'll tell you, if we agree that I can pay my debt to you immediately and we call it even as far as this letter is concerned. Hecaton says: 'I will show you a love-charm free of any drug or herb or any witch's spell. If you want to be loved, then love!' For the familiarity of an old and trusty friendship not only gives great pleasure, it also offers the beginning and the
7 formation of a new friendship. The difference between the man who has formed a friendship and someone just starting to form it is the same as between reaping and sowing. The philosopher Attalus* used to say that it was more pleasing to make a friend than to have one, 'just as it is more pleasing for an artist to paint than to have completed the painting'. That preoccupation with the work under way derives

[handwritten annotation: yet again, play with creating / friend — not / valuing as equal]

an immense enjoyment simply from being occupied; the man who has raised his hand from the finished work does not feel the same delight. Now he is enjoying the result of his art, but when he was painting he was enjoying the art itself. The youth of children is more rewarding but their infancy is sweeter. *[handwritten: complexity?]*

Now let us return to our theme. For even if the wise man is contented with himself he still wants to have a friend, if for no other reason then to practise friendship, not to let such a great merit lie inert, and not for the reason Epicurus mentioned in that letter, to have someone to sit with him when he is sick, or to come to his aid when he is in prison or in need. Rather, it is so that he may have someone whose sickbed he can visit, a man to set free when he is surrounded by an enemy guard. The man who looks to his own needs and approaches friendship with this motive has the wrong idea. As he began so will he end; he provided himself with a friend to bring him help against imprisonment, and as soon as the chains have fallen he will leave. These are what people call friendships of convenience; a man adopted from self-interest will please only as long as he is useful. This is why a crowd of friends surrounds men in time of success but there is a desert around their ruin, and friends flee when they are put to the test. This is why there are so many wicked examples of men either abandoning or betraying others out of fear. The beginnings and ends inevitably match. The man who began to be a friend from his own interest will also cease when it is in his interest; he will choose some reward at the expense of friendship, if he has chosen any aspect of it except itself. 'So why are you providing yourself with a friend?' To have someone for whom I can die, someone to follow into exile, so that I can put myself in the path of his death and sacrifice myself. The other attitude you describe is a business agreement, not friendship, if it develops for advantage and looks to what it will gain. No doubt the emotions of lovers have something similar to friendship; you could say it was a crazy kind of friendship. So does anyone fall in love for profit? Or for the sake of ambition or glory? Love in itself, disregarding all else, inflames hearts in desire for beauty but also with some hope of reciprocal affection. Well, then, does a shameful passion arise for a more honourable reason? You will say: 'the issue is not whether friendship is to be desired for its own sake.' On the contrary; nothing is more in need of proof. For if friendship is desirable on its own account, a man who is contented with himself can still seek it.

[margin numbers: 8, 9, 10, 11, 12]

[handwritten margin note: + Amount / aren't those mentioned in 8 tests?]

'Then how will he approach it?' As he would approach the most
beautiful of all things, not beguiled by profit nor terrified by the vicissitudes of fortune; a man who forms friendship for happy circumstances is stripping it of its dignity.

13   'The wise man is contented with himself.' Most men misinterpret
this, dear Lucilius; they push aside the wise man everywhere and
force him to withdraw into his own skin. Now we must distinguish
what that phrase promises and to what extent; the wise man is contented with himself for living happily, not just for living: indeed,
living requires many things, but living happily needs only a sound
14   and upright mind that holds fortune in contempt. I would like to
demonstrate another distinction, this time made by Chrysippus.* He
says the wise man needs nothing, and yet he has use for many things:
'on the other hand the fool has use for nothing (for he does not know
how to use anything) but needs everything.' The wise man has use for
his hands and eyes and many things necessary for daily use, but needs
nothing: for need is a matter of necessity, and nothing is necessary to
15   the wise man. So although he is contented with himself he has use for
friends: he wants to have as many as possible, not so as to live happily,
since he will live happily even without friends. The highest form of
good does not seek external tools: it is cherished at home and entirely
formed from its own resources: it begins to be vulnerable to fortune
16   if it seeks any part of itself from outside. 'Then what will the wise
man's life be like if he is left without friends when thrown into prison
or penniless in a foreign country or delayed on a long voyage or shipwrecked on a deserted shore?' It will be like that of Jupiter when the
universe has dissolved* and the gods have been piled into a mass, and
as Nature lapses he reposes in himself, briefly surrendering to his
own thoughts. The wise man does the same: he retreats into himself
17   and stays with himself. As long as he is free to arrange his affairs
under his own control he is contented with himself and yet marries
a wife; contented, and yet he rears children; contented, and yet he
would not live if he had to live without another person. It is no personal advantage that takes him to friendship but a natural stimulus.
For just as there is an innate sweetness in other things, so there is with
friendship. Just as we feel a distaste for isolation and quest for com-
panionship, as Nature brings man close to man, so there is a stimulus
18   in this too that make us desirous of friendship. All the same, although
he is most devoted to friends he will match himself with them and

often put himself first; he will limit every good within himself and
say what Stilbo said—the same Stilbo whom Epicurus' letter attacks.
For when his city was taken by siege and he had lost his children and
lost his wife, when he emerged alone and yet happy from that nationwide fire, Demetrius, who took his name Poliorketes from the sacking
of cities, asked him whether he had lost anything. 'No,' said Stilbo,
'I have all my goods with me.' Here is a brave and gallant man! He   19
conquered his enemy's conquest. 'I have lost nothing,' he said and
forced the other to wonder whether he had conquered. 'All my goods
are with me,' justice, virtue, prudence, this very art of thinking nothing good that could be taken away. We marvel at some creatures which
pass through fires without harm. How much more marvellous is the
man who has emerged unharmed and without loss through weapons
and ruins and fires. You see how much more easy it is to conquer a
whole tribe than one man? This claim of his is something shared with
a Stoic; he too carries his goods undamaged through burned-out
cities, since he is contented with himself; it is by this limit that he
measures his happiness. So that you don't think we Stoics are the   20
only ones to utter noble sayings, note that Epicurus, who rebuked
Stilbo, voiced a saying rather like his, which you must take in good
part, even if I have already crossed out today's debt. He said: 'If any
man does not see his own possessions as abundant, even if he is master
of the whole world he is still wretched.' Or, if you think it is better
expressed like this (for our purpose should be to consider not sayings
but meanings): 'a man is wretched who does not think himself perfectly happy, though he may rule the world.' To show you that these   21
sentiments are universal, since Nature has dictated them, you will
find in the comic poet:

> No man is blest who does not think it so.

What difference does it make what your condition is, if you think it
bad? 'So what', you say, 'are we to think? If a shamefully rich man   22
calls himself happy, shall this fellow who is master of many but slave
of more, become happy on his own vote?' What matters is not what
he says but what he feels, and not what he feels one day but what he
continues to feel. But you have no reason to fear that so great a blessing will befall an unworthy fellow: unless a man is wise his own circumstances will not please him; every kind of folly is plagued with
self-disgust. Keep well.

Letter 10 (Book I.10) *On the potential harm from bad company and the need to address only honest prayers to God even away from other men.*

1 That's it: I haven't changed my mind. Shun the crowd, shun the few, shun even a single man. I don't have anyone with whom I would want to share you. And see what a favourable judgement you have from me; I am daring to trust you to yourself. As the story goes, Crates, the disciple of the same Stilbo* whom I mentioned in the previous letter, once saw a young man walking in isolation on the shore and asked what he was doing by himself. The youth said: 'I am talking to myself.' Then Crates said: 'Watch out, I beg you, and pay careful attention;

2 you are talking with a bad man.' We usually watch over someone mourning or in a state of fear in case he misuses his time alone. There is really no one among the unwise who ought to be left alone; that is when they make bad decisions, that is when they devise future hazards for others or themselves, that is when they draft wicked desires; that is when the mind lays open whatever it concealed out of fear or shame, that is when it puts an edge on boldness, rouses desire, and provokes anger. In short, the one advantage of solitude, entrusting nothing to anyone, and not being afraid of an informer, is wasted on the fool; he betrays himself.

So see what I am hoping from you, indeed promising myself (for hope is the name of an undefined good thing); there is no one I would

3 rather have you consort with than yourself. I go over in my memory the noble spirit in which you threw out some claims, filled with such great strength; I instantly congratulated myself and said, 'those words did not come from the lips, those sayings have a basis; that man is not

4 just one of the common people, but is aiming for salvation'. Speak like that, live like that; see that nothing discourages you. You can decline with thanks to the gods your old prayers and take up different ones anew; ask for good sense and good health, first of the mind then of the body. Why not make those prayers often? Ask God boldly; you will not be asking him for anything that is not your due.

5 But to send the letter in my usual way with some small gift, what I found in Athenodorus* is right: 'Know that you have been set free from all desires when you reach the point of asking nothing from God except what you can ask for openly.' As it is, how great is human folly! Men whisper the most shameful prayers to the gods, and if anyone bends an ear they fall silent, and tell the God what they do not want a

man to know. So consider whether this cannot be a beneficial principle: live with men as if God sees you, and talk with God as if men
were listening. Keep well.

Letter 11 (Book I.11) *On physical blushing and moral bashfulness.*
Seneca argues that there are physical reactions a man cannot control and
should not be blamed for. In §8 he uses his 'Epicurean' envoi to change to
a different theme; the recommendation to imagine one's actions under the
observation of a respected and virtuous man.

Your friend has spoken with me, a young man of good character whose   1
first words showed me how well endowed he was with spirit and intelligence and even moral progress. He gave us a sample which he will
match, since he did not speak after rehearsing but when taken by surprise. When he had pulled himself together he could scarcely shake
off his bashfulness, a good sign in a young man; so deeply was he
covered with blushes. This, as far as I can guess, will stay with him
even when he has gained strength and shed all failings, even when he
is wise. But the natural failings of the body and mind are not cast off
by any degree of wisdom; whatever is inherent and inborn may be
softened by skill but is not overcome. Even on some of the most   2
courageous speakers sweat breaks out in front of the people just as
if they were weary or fevered; some men's knees tremble when they
are about to speak, some grind their teeth, their tongue stumbles and
their lips stick fast; neither training nor experience ever shakes this
off, but nature imposes her power and by this failing reminds even
the toughest men of her claims. I know that blushing is one of these   3
failings which suddenly suffuses the most authoritative men. But
it is more apparent in young men, who have both more natural heat
and a delicate brow; but it affects old hands and elderly men just the
same. Some men should most be feared when they blush, as if they
had poured out all their shame. Sulla was most violent when blood   4
rushed to his face. Nothing was more vulnerable than Pompey's face;
he never failed to blush in front of a large group, at least in public
assemblies. I remember Fabianus* blushed when he was brought into
the senate as a witness, and this modesty suited him marvellously. It   5
didn't arise from weakness of mind but from the unfamiliarity of the
situation which, even if it does not shatter unpractised speakers, disturbs them, inclined as they are to this by a natural tendency. For just

as some men have good blood, some have hasty and mobile blood that
6 quickly rushes into the face. As I said, no wisdom drives this away;
otherwise a man would have the world under his command if he
brushed off all failings. Whatever the circumstances of birth and constitution of the body have assigned to him will cling even when the
mind has calmed itself intensely and often. None of these traits can
7 be forbidden any more than they can be induced. These are the signs
by which actors who imitate the emotions, when they are expressing
the fear and trembling that stands for sadness, simulate bashfulness:
they cast down their gaze, mute their speech, fix their eyes on the
earth and keep them down; but they cannot create blushing: it is
neither to be inhibited nor induced. Wisdom promises no remedy
against this, it achieves nothing; these traits are independent of us:
they appear unbidden and vanish unbidden.

8　　　Now the letter is demanding proper closure. Read this saying,
which is useful and beneficial, and which I want you to plant fast in
your mind. 'We ought to cherish some good man and keep him always
before our eyes, so that we will live as if he were watching and do
9 everything as if he could see us.' This was Epicurus' recommendation, dear Lucilius; he gave us a guardian and attendant,* and quite
rightly: a lot of offences are averted if men have a witness when they
are about to offend. His mind should have someone to respect, on
whose authority he makes even his secret thoughts more pure. Happy
the man who sets others right not only in person but even when he is
imagined! Happy too the man who can so respect another that he
calms and controls himself even at the memory of this person. For
the man who can respect someone so greatly will soon become worthy
10 of respect himself. So choose Cato, or if he seems to you too severe,
choose Laelius, a man of milder disposition. Choose the man who has
won your approval by his life and speech and the features which display his character; constantly show him to yourself as either a guardian or an example. I mean that we need someone to whose standards
our behaviour may steer itself; you will not correct what is distorted
except by a straight ruler. Keep well.

Letter 12 (Book I.12) *Seneca uses a visit to his childhood home to
illustrate how the decay in his country villa, the decline of the plane trees
he himself planted, and finally the ageing of his childhood playmate have*

*convinced him of his advanced age. This leads to consideration (§6) of
each day as a fraction of a larger unit of natural time and the span of life,
and the proper way to look forward to death, not like the maudlin Pacuvius
(§8) who staged a performance of his own funeral every evening.*

Wherever I turn I see proofs of my old age. I came to my villa outside   1
town and began to complain about the cost of maintaining the building, which was falling apart. My overseer said it was not due to
any neglect on his part; he was doing everything he could, but the
building was old. This villa was formed beneath my hands. What will
happen to me if stones of my age are already crumbling? I was angry   2
with him and seized the next excuse for grumbling. I said: 'These
plane trees are obviously being neglected; they have no foliage. How
knotty and parched the branches are, and how shabby and rough their
trunks! This wouldn't be so if anyone was digging around them and
irrigating them.' He swore by my guardian spirit* that he was doing
everything he could, not letting his care lapse in any respect, but they
were getting old. Between you and me, I had planted them, I had seen
their first leaf. Then I turned to the doorway and said: 'Who is that   3
fellow—that shabby old creature put outside the door, and quite
rightly, since he is ready to be discarded? Where did you find him?
What fancy took you to rescue another man's corpse?' But the fellow
said: 'Don't you recognize me? I am Felicio, whom you used to make
little presents to; I am the son of the overseer Philositus, your old
pet.'* I said: 'The fellow is quite crazy; was he once a little lad and my
favourite? It's certainly possible; for he is losing his teeth this very
moment.'

So I owe it to my villa outside town that my old age was displayed   4
wherever I turned my eyes. Let us embrace it and appreciate it: it
is full of pleasure, if you know how to enjoy it. Apples are sweetest
when they are beginning to shrivel; the greatest beauty of boyhood
comes at its end; wine-bibbers get most pleasure from the last drink,
the one that puts them under and gives the last touch to drunkenness.
Every pleasure saves its sweetest moment for its end. So one's age is   5
most pleasant when it is beginning to go downhill, but not yet headlong, and I judge that even the moment on the brink of collapse has
its pleasures, or else in place of pleasures comes the very fact of needing nothing. How sweet it is to have worn out one's desires and left
them behind! You say: 'It is disagreeable to have death in full sight.'

6 But first of all, that should be as much in prospect for an old man as a young (for we are not summoned according to our order of registration), then again, no man is so old that he does not greedily hope for another day. And each single day is a step in life. Our entire life is made up of fractions and has greater cycles set around smaller ones; there is one that encompasses them all and encloses them (this is from one's day of birth to one's last); there is another which omits the years of youth; there is one which draws all boyhood into its area, and then there is the year including in itself all seasons that are repeated to make up life; the month is surrounded with a narrower circle, and the day has the smallest circuit, but this too comes from its beginning to

7 its end, from sunrise to sunset. So Heraclitus,* who was called after the obscurity of his speech, says: 'One day is like every day.' And different men understood this in different ways. He said that *a day was equal in its hours, and he is not lying; for if a day is the period of twenty-four hours, then all days must be equal to each other, since the night claims what the day has lost. Another interpreter said one day is equal to all the others by resemblance; since even the longest lapse of time contains nothing you would not find in one day; there is light then darkness, and in the alternating sequence of the universe that makes them more in number but not different: the daylight** is sometimes shortened and sometimes

8 more prolonged. So every day should be arranged as if it were bringing up the rear and rounding off and filling out life. Pacuvius, who made the Syrian command his own by continual occupation, used to pay himself the rites of the dead with wine and funeral offerings, before being carried out from dinner to his bedchamber with this refrain chanted by his eunuch slaves to an accompanying band: *il a*

9 *vécu, il a vécu.** There was no day when he did not have himself carried out for burial. And we ought to do with a good conscience what he did out of a bad one, saying as we go to sleep:

> I have lived and run the course that Fortune gave.*

If God adds a morrow, let us accept it gladly. That man is happiest and most firmly in charge of himself who waits for the next day without anxiety: anyone who says 'I have lived my life' gets up each day to some profit.

10 But now I should round off the letter. 'What?' you say. 'Is it coming to me like this without any daily allowance?' Don't be afraid; it is bringing something. Why did I say 'something?' It is bringing

something important. What can I give it to convey to you more glorious than this saying: 'It is bad to live in necessity, but there is no need
to live in necessity.'* Of course there is no need. There are many
paths to liberty all around us, short and easy ones. Let us thank God
that no one can be detained in life; we can trample on necessities. You 11
say, 'Epicurus said that: what claim have you on borrowed thoughts?'
Anything true is mine; I shall persist in loading you with Epicurus, so
that those who swear allegiance to his words but do not value what is
said but by whom will know that the best sayings are always true.
Keep well.

Letter 14 (Book II.2) *Seneca discusses human concern for one's own
body, and fear of suffering physical pain, especially pain imposed upon
us by an oppressor or tyrant figure. (By listing as potential oppressor the
common people or a faction of the senate before mentioning a single auto-
crat, Seneca comes as near as he dare approach to his own situation under
the power of Nero.) The wise man will never provoke the anger of the
crowd or the powerful individual, yet (§12) Cato in his wisdom opposed
Pompey and Caesar both during and before the outbreak of civil war. For
Seneca, as for his nephew Lucan (especially in Book II of the Civil War),
Cato serves as a safely removed model for the wise man's attitude, enabling
Seneca to postpone indefinitely (§14) the larger issue of whether the wise
man should even participate in public life.*

I acknowledge that affection for our body is innate in us, and I 1
acknowledge that we are its guardians and protectors. I don't deny
that I should indulge it, only that I should be enslaved to it. For the
man who is a slave to his body, who is too afraid for it, who relates all
actions to its needs, will also be a slave to many people. But we should 2
behave not as though we are obliged to live for the sake of our body,
but bearing in mind that we cannot live without it. It is excessive love
for it that disturbs us with fears, burdens us with anxieties, and
exposes us to insults: honour is cheap to the man for whom his body
is dear. Let us take good care of it, but on these terms, that when
reason and self-respect and integrity demand, it should be dispatched
to the pyre. Still, as far as we may let us avoid discomforts as well 3
as dangers, and steer ourselves back to safety by devising means to
escape what we should fear. Unless I am mistaken there are three
kinds of dread: we fear poverty, we fear diseases, and we fear what

4   may be inflicted on us at the hands of a more powerful figure. None
    of all these misfortunes distresses us more than what is threatened by
    another man's power, for this comes with a mighty din and disturb-
    ance. The natural woes which I mentioned, poverty and disease, sneak
    up in silence and do not inflict any terror on the eye or ear; the other
    evil makes a huge parade; it surrounds itself with steel and fire and
5   chains and the horde of wild beasts launched against human flesh. In
    this context think of prison and crosses, the rack and the hook and the
    stake driven right through a man's body to project from his throat,
    and limbs torn apart by driving chariots, and the tunic woven and
    smeared with fiery substances, and whatever else cruelty has devised.
6   So it is not surprising if this causes the worst fear, since it has enor-
    mous variety and terrifying equipment. For just as the torturer
    achieves more by displaying a greater number of instruments of pain
    (since the sight of them overwhelms men who would have resisted the
    actual suffering), so of all the terrors that overcome and break our
    spirits the ones with something to display are more effective. Those
    other plagues are not less severe—I mean hunger and thirst and
    stomach ulcers and fever that burns up the flesh—but they are
    unseen, they have nothing to brandish or thrust in front of us; like
    great wars, these campaigns of terror have triumphed by their appear-
    ance and display of instruments.
7   So let us take pains to avoid causing offence. Sometimes it is the
    people we must fear, sometimes, if the constitution of the state is one
    where most business is transacted by the senate, we must fear influen-
    tial men; sometimes we must fear autocrats to whom the power has
    been given over the people and by the people. To keep all these as
    friends is hard work; it is enough not to have them as enemies. So the
    wise man will never provoke the anger of the powerful, but avoid it
    just like a hurricane on his voyage.
8   When you were making for Sicily you crossed the straits. The rash
    pilot despised the bluster of the south-west wind (for this is the wind
    that roughens up the Sicilian sea and raises it in breakers); he did not
    aim for the left shore, but the one nearer to where Charybdis churns
    up the waters.* But a more cautious pilot asks those familiar with the
    region what the current is like, what signs the clouds show; he steers
    his course far from that area notorious for its eddies. The wise man
    does the same thing; he shuns the power that will bring him harm,
    making it his first care not to seem to shun it; for a part of being

safe from care lies in not explicitly seeking safety, since a man is condemning whatever he shuns.

So we must look around to see how we can be safe from the crowd. 9 First we should not desire the same prizes as they do: quarrels arise between competitors. Then we should not possess anything that can be stolen at great profit to the trickster; let there be the least possible amount of spoils on your body. Nobody seeks human blood for its own sake, or very few: more men calculate than feel hatred. The brigand passes over the man stripped of possessions. Even on a road beset with highwaymen the poor man is left in peace. Then 10 there are three things we should contrive to avoid according to the old rule: hatred, envy, and contempt. Only wisdom will show how this is done; for the calculation is difficult, and we must be afraid lest fear of envy drives us into contempt, and while we are reluctant to trample we may seem ready to be trampled on. Yet being an object of fear has given many people reason to feel fear themselves. We must pull back from all sides; it is no less harmful to be held in contempt than to be respected. So we should take refuge in philosophy; this 11 kind of study will be like a badge of sanctity not only with good men but even those moderately bad. For public eloquence and any other things that stir up the people make enemies, whereas this calm occupation intent on its own business cannot be held in contempt, since of all the arts it is honoured even among the worst villains. Wickedness will never gain so much strength or conspire against the virtues, that the name of philosophy does not remain sacred and worthy of reverence. But even philosophy must be practised calmly and with moderation.

'Well, then,' you say, 'does Cato seem to you to practise philosophy 12 with moderation, since he quelled civil war by his verdict? As mediator he stepped between the arms of the frenzied war-leaders. When some men opposed Pompey and others Caesar, he challenged both at the same time.'* Someone may well dispute whether at that time any 13 wise man should have taken part in politics. What are you thinking of, M. Cato? It is no longer a matter of freedom: that was ruined long since. The issue is whether Caesar or Pompey shall possess the state. What business of yours is that contest? There is no part for you to play. They are choosing a master. What does it matter to you which man wins? The better man may win, but the man who wins cannot avoid becoming worse. I have touched on the last role played by Cato,

but not even his earlier years were such that they allowed the wise
man a role, surrounded as he was by the plundering of the state. What
else did Cato do than shout and utter futile protests, when he was at
one time hauled by the hands of the common people and dragged
smothered in spittle to be carted out of the Forum, and at another
time escorted from the senate into jail?

14   But we will consider later whether the wise man should devote
himself to public life. Just now I am summoning you to join the Stoics
who were shut out of public life and withdrew to cultivate their lives
and establish rights for humanity without causing any offence to the
more powerful. The wise man will not disturb the customs of the
people nor attract the people's attention to himself by the novelty of

15 his way of life. 'Well then, will he at least be safe if he adheres to this
intention?' I can no more promise you this than good health in a man
of abstinent habits, and yet abstinence does make for good health.
A ship may meet its doom in harbour, but what do you think happens
in open sea? How much more readily would doom have befallen our
abstinent man, if he was occupied in pursuing serious policies, since
even his leisure is not safe! Innocent men have sometimes been ruined
(who denies it), but guilty men much more often. A man's skill has

16 proved itself if he is struck down while fully armed. In short, the wise
man looks to the purpose of all actions, not their consequences;
beginnings are in our power, but Fortune judges the outcome, and
I do not grant her a verdict upon me. 'But she will bring some form
of harassment and failure.' The brigand may kill, but he is not passing condemnation.

17   Now you are holding your hand out for the daily alms. I will fill it
with a golden contribution, and since we have mentioned gold, listen
to how its use and income can be more welcome to you. 'He makes
best use of wealth who needs it least.' 'Tell me the author,' you say.
To show you how generous I am I resolved to cite precepts from other
schools. It comes from Epicurus or Metrodorus or someone from

18 that workshop. And what does it matter who said it? He said it for
everyone. The man who needs wealth is afraid for it, and no man
enjoys an asset that is a source of trouble. He is eager to add something to it, and while he is concentrating on the increase he has forgotten to use it. He makes up his accounts, treads the marketplace,
and keeps turning over his calendar: instead of a master he has become
an accountant. Keep well.

Letter 15 (Book II.3) *This letter too starts from concern with the body. Seneca deplores modern forms of physical training, but recognizes the value of fitness, and suggests simpler substitutes. (See also letter 83, §§1–5 on his own health regime.)*

Men of old had a custom preserved into my lifetime of adding to 1 the first words of a letter: 'If you are well that is good; I am well.'* We are right to say: 'If you are practising philosophy, it is good', for ultimately this is to be well. Without it the mind is sick, and the body too, even if it is very strong, is only well like that of a madman or lunatic. So take special care of this kind of well-being, and then 2 physical well-being in second place: it will not cost you much if you want to be in good health. For the activity of developing the biceps and stretching the neck and strengthening the lungs is foolish, dear Lucilius, and ill-fitted to an educated man: even when your diet has worked out well and your muscles have built up you will never match the strength or weight of a fattened ox. Add to this that the spirit is crushed by too great a bodily bulk and becomes less nimble. So, as best you can, check your body and make free space for your mind.   3

Many disadvantages follow for men devoted to physical health; first exercises, whose effort exhausts the spirit and makes it unfit for concentration and more demanding studies; then the refinement of one's thought is encumbered by the surfeit of food. Add the problem of the lowest class of slaves as instructors, men obsessed by oil and wine,* who have spent the day to their satisfaction if they have sweated well and if they have gulped down to replace the lost moisture a great amount of drink that will penetrate a hungry man more deeply. To drink and sweat is the life of a dyspeptic. There are easy and quick 4 exercises which tire the body out quickly and save time, which we should particularly keep in mind; running and moving the arms with weights, and jumping, either the high jump that lifts the body or the long jump which thrusts it forward, or the leaping of the Salii or to speak more insultingly, of a fuller:* choose any of these, *a simple and easy exercise.** Whatever you do, come back quickly from the body to 5 the mind; exercise the mind night and day. It is nourished by a moderate effort; neither cold nor heat will prevent this kind of exercise, not even old age. Cherish the kind of good which improves with old age. Nor am I ordering you to be constantly bent over a book or note- 6 book: you have to give some respite to the mind, but such that it is not slackened but relaxed. Riding in a litter* shakes up the body and does not get in the way of study; you could read or dictate, you could speak

7 or listen, in fact not even walking prevents any of these activities. And do not despise exercising the voice, although I forbid you to raise and lower it through pitches and fixed rhythms.* Supposing the next thing you fancied was to learn how to walk? Invite those whom hunger has taught new skills; there will be someone to control your steps and watch your cheeks as you eat and go as far as your patience and gullibility will extend his shamelessness. What then? Shall your voice begin immediately with shouting and extreme urgency? It is so natural to build excitement gradually that even men quarrelling begin with talk and then pass on to shouting; no one starts instantly with a

8 hue and cry. So however your mental impulse urges you on, make your rebuke of vices now more passionately, now more calmly, as your voice itself encourages you *in that direction; let it sink moderately,** not collapse when you withdraw and hold it back; *let it not have the violence of an attendant or* work off its rage as if you were an uneducated countryman. For we are aiming, not to give the voice exercise, but for it to exercise power over others.

9   I have relieved you of not a little trouble; one small reward and one Greek comment will join these favours. Here is a remarkable recommendation: 'A foolish life is thankless and anxious; it is entirely directed towards the future.' You ask: 'Who said this?' The same man as before. Now what do you think is meant by a foolish life? That of the clowns Baba and Ision? No! It is our own life driven headlong by blind desire towards things that will harm us, and at best never satisfy us. For if anything could be enough for us it would have been, but we do not think how pleasant it is to demand nothing, how glorious to be sated

10 and not depend on Fortune. So remember here and now how much you have achieved: when you see how many have gone ahead of you, think of the number of men following you. If you want to be grateful to the gods and your life, think how many you are ahead of. Why compare

11 yourself with others? You have gone ahead of yourself. Set a limit which you could not exceed even if you wanted; away with those treacherous good things which are better in expectation than when you obtain them. If they had any solid merit they would sooner or later fill you, but as it is, they rouse the thirst of whoever drinks them. Let us reject showy displays: why should I persuade Fortune to give me what unpredictable chance offers for the future rather than persuade myself not to seek it?

And why should I seek it? Why should I heap up property, forgetting human frailty? What should I toil for? Imagine this is your last day of life; or if not, the next to last. Keep well.

Letter 16 (Book II.4) *Compliments to Lucilius lead to warnings that he is not yet secure in his moral stability. At §4 Seneca introduces the problematic issue of what is fated and cannot be averted. His injunction to obey fate gladly but fortune with resistance might have led to real confusion, so he relinquishes it (§6) for the simpler topic of living according to nature, not human opinions.*

I know that these things are quite obvious to you, Lucilius: that no $_1$ one can live happily, or even bearably, without the pursuit of wisdom, and that a happy life is achieved by refining that wisdom, but life can be bearable even when wisdom is only beginning to take shape. But this obvious maxim must be reinforced and more deeply rooted by daily review; there is more effort in keeping to your resolve than in resolving on an honourable course. You must persist and build up strength by constant diligence until what is now a good intention becomes a good state of mind. So you do not need further argument $_2$ from me or so long a declaration; I realize you have made great progress. I know where your words are coming from; they are not feigned or given an artificial complexion. But I will say what I feel, that I am already hopeful for you but not yet confident. I want you to do the same thing: you have no reason to feel a quick and self-confidence. Search yourself and examine and observe yourself in different ways: look first and foremost to see whether you have made progress in philosophy or in real life. Philosophy is not a skill shaped $_3$ for popular appeal or for display; it does not consist of words but deeds. It is not taken up to make sure the day passes with some enjoyment, to take the boredom out of leisure; it moulds and shapes the mind, arranges one's life, controls one's actions, points out what is to be done or avoided: it is seated at the helm and steers the course of those adrift among dangerous shoals. Without it no man can live without fear or anxiety; countless things occur each hour that need the advice which we must seek from philosophy. Someone will object: $_4$ 'What good is philosophy to me if something is fated? How does it help me if God is directing life, what does it help if chance is in command? For certainties cannot be changed and nothing can be devised

against what is uncertain: either God has anticipated my decision and determined what I should do or fortune makes no concession to my
5 planning.' Whichever of these is true, Lucilius, or if they all are, we must practise philosophy: whether the fates bind us in an inexorable law, or God as supreme judge of the universe has ordained everything, whether chance or order drives and buffets human affairs, it is philosophy that must protect us. It will urge us to obey God gladly but fortune with defiance; it will teach you to follow God but endure
6 chance. But I must not pass over now into the debate over what is in our power if providence is in control, or if the sequence of fates drags us in bonds, or if unforeseen and sudden events tyrannize; I am returning now to the point of warning and urging you not to let the zeal of your spirit ebb and lose heat. Control it and ensure that what is now an urge becomes a lasting disposition.

7   If I know you well you will have been looking round from the start to see what little gift this letter has brought: search it and you will find out. No reason to admire my generous spirit; so far I am being generous at others' expense. Now why did I say others? Whatever anyone has said well is mine. And this is another of Epicurus' sayings: 'If you live according to nature you will never be poor; if you live according to
8 men's opinions you will never be rich.'* Nature asks only for a little, but opinion wants something beyond measure. Let everything that many wealthy men possessed be piled upon you, let fortune sweep you beyond the scale of private money, let it cover you with gold and clothe you in purple and carry you to such a degree of luxury and wealth that you cover the earth in sheets of marble; suppose you not only possess but can trample on wealth; add statues and paintings and whatever luxury any craft has contrived; you will learn from these to long for
9 greater possessions. Natural desires are limited, but desires born of false beliefs have no way of ending; for there is no boundary to what is false. If you travel on the road there is a destination, but wandering from it has no measure. So draw back from empty pleasures, and when you want to know whether what you are aiming for entails a natural desire or a blind craving, consider whether it can stop at any point: if, when you have advanced some distance, there is always a more distant goal, know that this is not a natural desire. Keep well.

Letter 18 (Book II.6) *It is the holiday season of the Saturnalia. Seneca debates how far to go along with society's increasing frivolity, and suggests an exercise in self-imposed austerity.*

It is December now,* and yet the community is sweating most pro- 1
fusely. Public licence has been given to self-indulgence; every part of
town echoes with enormous preparations, as if there were any difference between the Saturnalia and business days; but there is so little
difference that I think the fellow was not mistaken who said that
December once used to be a month but now lasts the whole year. If I 2
had you here with me I would be glad to consult you about what you
thought we ought to do, whether we should make no change from our
daily routine, or dine more casually and discard our togas so as not to
seem in conflict with public behaviour. For, just for the sake of pleasure
and the holidays we have changed our dress,* a thing that only used to
happen in an emergency and a crisis of the state. If I know you well you 3
would play the role of a mediator and want us neither to be like the felt-
capped crowd* in all respects, nor completely unlike them, unless it is
precisely in these days that we need to discipline our spirit, so that it
holds aloof from all pleasures just when the whole crowd has thrown
itself into them; for the spirit gives the strongest proof of its resolve
by not being attracted or distracted by pleasures which lead to self-
indulgence. It is much more strong-willed to be sober and dry when the 4
people are drunk and throwing up, but the other course is more moderate, not to distinguish or mark oneself nor get involved with everything,
but to do the same things in a different way, since it is possible to observe
a holiday without self-indulgence.

In fact I am so determined to test your firmness of mind that I will 5
instruct you according to the instruction of great men; set aside a few
days in which you will content yourself with the smallest and poorest
diet and rough, shaggy clothing, and say to yourself: 'Is this what I
was afraid of?' Let your mind prepare itself for these difficult cir- 6
cumstances in freedom from care, and let it be strengthened against
the injustices of fortune while still enjoying her favours. The soldier
makes forced marches in the midst of peace and plants his stake without any enemy and wears himself out with superfluous toil so that he
will be strong enough for necessary toil: if you do not want a man to
tremble in action, exercise him beforehand. Men followed this principle when they imitated poverty each and every month, coming close
to starvation, so that they would never be afraid of what they had
often learned. You do not need to think that I am talking about the 7
dinners of Timon* and poor men's cells and all the other games which
luxury plays from boredom with riches; let it be a real straw mattress
and soldier's blanket and hard rough bread. Bear this for three or four

Test yourself.
Not God testing

days or sometimes more, so that it is not a game but a test; then,
believe me, Lucilius, you will delight in being full on a *dupundius** and
realize that you don't need Fortune's favour to be carefree: for even

8 when she is angry she will grant enough to meet necessity. However,
there is no reason for you to think you are doing a great deal (for you
are doing what many thousands of slaves and many thousand poor
men do). Respect yourself for doing so without duress, because it will
be as easy for you to experience this all the time as to suffer it from
time to time. Let us train ourselves for combat with the wooden post,
and make poverty familiar company so that fortune does not catch us
unawares. We will be more carefree as rich men if we know how far

9 from hard it is to be poor. Epicurus, that teacher of pleasure, had
certain days when he only grudgingly staved off his hunger, wanting
to see whether he would fall short of fully realized pleasure, or how
much it would fall short or whether it was worth compensating with
much effort. At least this is what he says in the letters to Polyaenus
when Charinus was in office;* in fact he boasts of feeding for less than
an *as*, whereas Metrodorus, who had not yet made so much progress,

10 needed a whole *as*. Do you think there could be real satisfaction with
this diet? There is even pleasure: I don't mean the trivial, fleeting
pleasure which has to be replenished, but a stable and reliable pleasure. For water and barley groats or a crust of barley bread* is not a
pleasant thing but it is the greatest pleasure to be able to find pleasure
even in these foods and to have brought oneself to the level which no

11 unjust act of fortune can snatch away. Prison diet is more generous,
but the man who is going to execute offenders set apart for capital
punishment does not feed them so meanly: what greatness of spirit it
is to stoop of one's own accord to what even men condemned to the

12 last penalty do not have to fear! So begin, dear Lucilius, to follow
their habit and mark down some days on which you retreat from your
possessions and become intimate with the most meagre diet; begin to
do business with poverty:

> Dare, my guest, to scorn wealth
> And make yourself worthy of the divine.*

13   No one is worthy of the God unless he despises possessions; I am
not forbidding you to own them, but I want to ensure that you own
them without fear, and you will only achieve this in one way, if you
persuade yourself that you will live happily even without them, if you
always look on them as if they were going to disappear.

But now let us begin to wrap up the letter. You will say: 'First pay 14
back your debt.' I will refer you to Epicurus, and he will pay out the
coin: 'Excessive anger leads to insanity.'* You must know how true
this is when you have either a slave or an enemy. This passion* will 15
burn up against all kinds of people; it springs as much from love as
from hatred, no less in serious matters than in sport and fun; nor does
the seriousness of its cause make any difference, only the nature of the
mind it affects. In the same way it makes no difference how big
a fire is, only where it occurs, for solid objects do not catch even
from a big fire, but dry material easily kindled will even nurse a spark
into a conflagration. That's how it is, dear Lucilius. The outcome of
immense anger is madness, and so anger should be avoided not for
the sake of moderation but of actual sanity. Keep well.

Letter 19 (Book II.7) *Seneca congratulates Lucilius on his moral
progress, and warns him against the distraction of his present public career
and of worldly ambition.*

My heart leaps whenever I receive your letters: they fill me with good 1
hope, and now they are not just making promises about you but guarantees. Do just that, I beg and beseech you—for what better request
can I make of a friend than I make for his own sake? If you can, slip
away from those distractions; if you can't slip away, tear yourself away.
We have wasted enough time; let us begin to gather our luggage in
our old age. Is this at all risky? We have lived on the high seas, let us 2
die in port. And I would not urge you to seek a reputation from your
withdrawal, something you should neither vaunt nor hide, for
I will never drive you so far away by condemning the madness of
mankind that I want you to prepare some hiding-place in which to
fade away forgotten: see to it that your withdrawal is not conspicuous
but visible. Then men whose decisions about retirement are still open 3
and being made for the first time will see whether they want to pass
their lives unseen; you do not have the choice. The energy of your
intellect, stylishness of your writings, your distinguished and noble
friendships, even fame, have now taken you over; even if you were
submerged at the outer edge of life or deeply buried, your former
achievements will point to you. You cannot choose darkness: much of 4
your former brilliance will follow you wherever you flee; but you can
claim repose without the hatred of any man, without any longing or
distress of your mind. For what will you leave behind that you can

regret its abandonment? Clients? None of them is seeking you for yourself, but to get something from you; once it was friendship, but now spoils: if childless old men change their wills the greeter will move to another man's doorway. A great thing cannot come cheap; calculate whether you would rather abandon yourself or some of your
5 possessions. If only you had been lucky enough to grow old within the limits of your birthright, and fortune had not sent you up aloft! Your swift success has carried you far from the sight of a healthy life, so has your province and official position and whatever is promised by them: then greater responsibilities will take hold of you and others following them; what escape will there be?
6 Why are you waiting until you cease to have what you want? The time will never come. Just as we say there is a sequence of causes from which fate is contrived, so there is of desires.* One is born out of another's ending. You have sunk into that life which will never spontaneously put an end to your miseries and enslavement: pull out your neck worn by the yoke: it is better for it to be cut once than always worn down.
7 If you retreat into your private affairs everything will be smaller but will still fill life up: but as it is, the very many chores heaped up from all sides do not satisfy you. So which do you prefer? To be sated instead of empty, or to suffer hunger amid abundance?

Success is greedy and exposed to the greed of others; as long as nothing is sufficient for you, you will not be enough for others. You
8 say: 'How shall I get out?' As best you can. Think how many undertakings you have risked for the sake of money, how many you have toiled over for the sake of honour: now you must dare some attempt on behalf of our retirement, or grow old in that desert of administrative positions and then duties in the city, surrounded by storms and ever-new waves which it is not possible to escape by any modesty of living or calmness. For what does it matter whether you want to stay calm? Your fortune doesn't want it. What if you allow it to grow even
9 now? Whatever increases your success will increase your fears. At this point I want to pass on to you a saying of Maecenas,* who spoke the truth even on the rack: 'For height itself thunder-strikes the high places.' If you ask in what book he said this, it is the one called *Prometheus*. What he meant was that 'height has its summit struck by thunder'. So is any influence worth so much that you should have such tipsy talk? He was a very talented man, and would have

provided a great example of Roman eloquence if success had not
sapped his sinews, in fact unmanned him. This is the end that awaits
you if you do not haul in your sails, unless—something he wanted too
late—you stick close to land.

I could provide an argument to match this opinion of Maecenas, 10
but you will raise a dispute against me, if I know you, and be unwilling to accept my debt except on harsh and upright terms.* As things
are, we must borrow from Epicurus. He says: 'You must take care
about the men with whom you eat and drink before worrying about
what you eat or drink; for feasting on meat without a friend is the
life of a lion or wolf.' 11

You will not have this freedom of choice unless you withdraw: otherwise you will have the guests your secretary has picked out from the
crowd of greeters. And a man goes astray if he looks for a friend in his
reception hall and tests him at dinner. A busy man beset by his own
possessions has no greater disadvantage than thinking men are his
friends when he himself is no friend, because he thinks his favours
are effective in winning over hearts, whereas some men hate him more
fiercely as they owe him more favours. A light indebtedness makes a
debtor, but a heavy one an enemy. Then don't favours produce friend- 12
ships? They would, if one was able to choose men to receive them, if
the favours are well placed, not randomly scattered. So until you
begin to live by your own judgement, use this advice from the wise, to
think it more relevant who is accepting your favours than what he has
accepted. Keep well.

Letter 21 (Book II.9) *Seneca uses the unspecified anxieties of Lucilius
to advise him about the triviality of external concerns and importance of
being at peace with oneself. This letter marks Seneca's adherence to the
two traditions of philosophical letters of advice (Epicurus) and personal
correspondence (Cicero), before moving on to Epicurus' precepts about
reducing desires (§§7–9) and praising the spirit of austerity symbolized
by both the inscription and the keeper of Epicurus' garden.*

Do you think you are having trouble with those fellows you wrote 1
about?* Your biggest trouble is with yourself, it is you who are bothering yourself. You don't know what you want, and are better at admiring the honourable course than following it; you see where happiness
lies but don't dare to make your way to it. But I will tell you what is

hindering you, since you cannot see it for yourself: you think the circumstances that you are going to leave behind are grand and glorious;
so when you imagine the carefree state which you are going to enjoy,
the glamour of this life from which you are retiring holds you back as
2 if you were going to sink into a shabby and humble condition. You are
wrong, dear Lucilius; from this life to that is a rise in your condition.
Imagine the difference between glitter and light, in which the light
has its own sure source but the shine of glitter comes from elsewhere:
that is the difference between this life and that. This life is struck by
a light coming from outside it, and whoever stands in its path will
instantly cast a thick shadow: the other shines with its own light. Your
own studies will make you glorious and renowned. Let me cite an
3 example from Epicurus. When he wrote to Idomeneus calling him
away from a glamorous life to reliable and lasting glory, for Idomeneus
was then a minister of royal power handling great affairs, Epicurus
said: 'If you are moved by glory, my letters will make you better known
than all the things you cherish and which make you cherished.'* And
4 did he lie? Who would know Idomeneus if Epicurus had not inscribed
him in his letters? Deep forgetfulness has buried all those grandees
and satraps and the king himself from whom men begged for
Idomeneus' office. It is Cicero's letters that do not allow Atticus'
name to be forgotten.* It would not have done Atticus any good to
have Agrippa as son-in-law and Tiberius as his granddaughter's husband and Drusus Caesar as his great-grandchild: he would have been
passed over in silence among such great names if Cicero had not
5 attached him to himself. The great depths of time will cover us up
and few talents will raise their heads and resist being forgotten, and
assert their claims for long before ultimately fading into the same
silence. I am promising you, Lucilius, what Epicurus was able to
promise his friend; I shall have influence with posterity and bring out
names that will persist along with me. Virgil promised eternal memory
to two young men and has kept his promise:

> Happy pair! If my songs have any power to praise,
> No day will ever steal you from a mindful age,
> While Aeneas' house stands on the unshakeable rock
> The Capitol, and Rome's great father rules.*

6 Whenever anyone has been promoted to distinction by Fortune,
whenever men were members and agents of another's power, their

influence has been strong and their house thronged as long as they
remained successful; after them the memory as quickly failed. The
respect for intellects grows, and not only are they honoured in themselves but whatever has been associated with their memory is taken
up and preserved.

To make sure that Idomeneus has not found his way into my letter   7
free of charge, he himself will pay for it from his pocket. It was to
him that Epicurus wrote that famous statement exhorting him to
make Pythocles rich but not in a public and vulnerable way. 'If you
want to make Pythocles rich,' he said, 'you should not add to his
money but subtract from his desire.' That statement is too obvious to 8
need interpretation, and too eloquent to need support. I would just
warn you not to think this was only a comment on riches: it will be
just as valid wherever you apply it. 'If you want to make Pythocles
honourable, you should not add to his honours, but subtract from his
desires; if you want him to enjoy continuous pleasure you should not
add to his pleasures, but subtract from his desires; if you want to
make Pythocles an old man and round out his life, you should not
add to his years but subtract from his desires.' You do not have to 9
assign these sayings to Epicurus: they are common property.* I think
we must follow in philosophy the same procedure as in the senate:
if someone makes a proposal which partly pleases me, I order him to
divide his proposal and follow what I approve of.

I am particularly glad to mention these excellent sayings of
Epicurus so that those who resort to him, led on by a misplaced hope,
who think they will have a cloak for their vices, may use them as proof
that wherever they go they will have to live honourably. When you 10
approach his little garden and its inscription—'Stranger, this is a
good place to stay: here pleasure is the highest good'*—the hospita-
ble and humane guardian of that household will be ready and welcome you with barley groats and offer you water in generous quantities
and say: 'Have you been well entertained?' He says: 'These gardens
do not provoke hunger but suppress it, and do not increase thirst with
their drinks, but quench it with a free and natural remedy; I have
grown old enjoying this pleasure.' I am talking to you of the desires 11
which don't respond to consolation, which must be given something
to make them cease. For as to the other extraordinary desires which
one may postpone, or check and suppress, I will give this one warning;
that pleasure is natural, but not necessary.* You owe it nothing: if you

pay it any heed, that is voluntary. Your stomach does not listen to advice; it demands and hails you. But it is not a tiresome creditor; it can be sent away with a little, if you only give it what you ought, not what you can. Keep well.

Letter 24 (Book III.3) _Seneca advises Lucilius not to waste his peace of mind worrying about everyday anxieties, or fearing loss and death. This letter (the longest in the correspondence up to this point) is one of his most impassioned, maximizing the rhetoric of death in order to inspire fearless courage. Seneca uses both the standard Stoic examples of constancy (§§7–11, including his fullest account of Cato's self-inflicted death) and the standard Epicurean denunciation of false beliefs about life after death (§§18–21) to reinforce his exhortations. On Seneca's use of moral examples see Roland G. Mayer, 'Roman Historical Exempla in Seneca', in J. G. Fitch (ed.),_ Seneca _(Oxford: Oxford UP), 299–315._

1 You say you are worried about the verdict of the court case which your enemy's frenzy is threatening against you: you think I will encourage you to anticipate a better outcome and relax in a beguiling hope. For why is it necessary to invite misfortunes, to anticipate what must be suffered soon enough when it occurs, and ruin the present with fear for the future? And it is undoubtedly foolish to be unhappy now 2 because you are going to be unhappy sooner or later. However, I will guide you to freedom from care by a different path: if you want to cast off all anxiety, imagine that whatever you fear will happen is going to happen anyway, and whatever that trouble is, measure it in your mind and examine your fear: you will surely realize that what you dread is 3 either not serious or not lasting. And you will not have to spend long collecting examples to support you; every age has produced them. Wherever you direct your memory in either domestic or foreign affairs you will think of intellects with great talent or great achievement. If the verdict goes against you, can anything happen to you more severe than being sent into exile or led off to prison? Does anyone ever have to fear anything worse than subjection to torture or death? Set up each of these misfortunes and summon as supporters those who scorned them: you do not have to search for these men, just take your pick. 4 Rutilius endured his condemnation as if nothing else distressed him except that there had been a mistaken verdict. Metellus* bore his exile bravely and Rutilius even gladly; the former served the state

by returning, the latter denied his return to Sulla, who could not be denied anything at that time. Socrates held discussions in prison and refused to leave, although he had friends who promised him exile: he stayed so as to remove the fear of the two most serious threats to men, death and imprisonment. Mucius* put his own hand into the fire. It is 5 cruel to be burned, how much more so if you suffer it by your own act. You see how an uneducated man not equipped by any instruction against death or pain, trained only in a soldiers' resolve, imposed on himself the penalty for his failed attempt. He stood there watching his right hand being consumed in the enemy's brazier and did not remove the hand when its bones were laid bare, until the fire was taken away by the enemy. He might have done something more successful in that camp, but nothing braver. See how much fiercer is courage in taking on dangers than cruelty in demanding them; Porsena was more ready to pardon Mucius for intending to kill him than Mucius pardoned himself for failing to kill.

You say, 'these are the stories repeated in all the schools; soon, 6 when we come to the contempt for death, you will be telling me about Cato'.* Why shouldn't I tell the story of him reading Plato's book on that last night, with his sword set by his head? He had taken thought for the two tools needed in the final crisis, one to make him willing to die, the other to make him able. So when public affairs were settled as best these shattered and desperate measures could be, he determined to make sure that no one was free to kill Cato or had the privilege of saving him: drawing the sword which he had kept pure of all slaughter 7 until that last day, he said: 'You have achieved nothing, Fortune, in resisting all my undertakings. Until now I did not fight for my liberty but that of my country, nor did I act with such determination in order to live free, but so as to live among free men: now that the affairs of mankind are beyond hope let Cato be escorted to safety.' Then he 8 inflicted a mortal wound on his body, and when it was bound up by the doctors, leaving him less blood and less strength but the same spirit, he was angry not just with Caesar but with himself and thrust his hands into the wound and cast out, rather than released, that noble spirit despising all power.

I am not piling up examples now to exercise my wits but to encour- 9 age you against what seems most fearful to you; and I shall encourage you more easily if I show that not only brave men despised this impulse to breathe out their soul, but that some men cowardly in

other respects matched the spirit of the bravest in this matter, like the
Scipio who was Pompey's father-in-law.* When he was carried back
to Africa by a contrary wind and saw his ship was being captured by
enemies, he drove his sword through his body and said to those seek-
10 ing the commander: 'The commander is in good hands.' This saying
made him the equal of his ancestors and did not let the fated glory of
the Scipios in Africa come to an end. It was great to defeat Carthage
but greater to defeat death. He said: 'The commander is in good
hands.' Is there any other way a commander, especially one com-
11 manding Cato, should have died? I am not going to take you back to
historical anecdotes or gather the despisers of death from all the centuries, many as they are. Just look back to our own times, whose lacka-
daisical self-indulgence we lament: these years will pile up cases from
all ranks, all conditions, and every age, who have cut short their misfortunes by death. Believe me, Lucilius, death is so far from fearful
12 that it is through its kindness we need fear nothing. So listen to your
enemy's threats without anxiety, and though your own good conscience gives you confidence, still, since there are many factors outside the case, hope for the fairest judgement, and prepare yourself for
what is most unfair. And remember this above all, to take away the
panic about the situation and see what each matter entails; you will
realize that there is nothing terrible in those circumstances except
13 fear itself. Something you see happen to children happens to us, who
are overgrown children: if they see the people they love, whom they
are used to and play with, wearing masks, they are terrified; but the
mask should be removed not just from persons but from things, and
their proper appearance restored.

14   Death, why do you show me swords and fires and a host of threatening executioners all around you?* Take away the parade which conceals you and enables you to intimidate the foolish: you are death,
which my slave and my maid just recently treated with contempt.
Why do you lay out whips and racks for torture with a great display?
Why do you set out individual contrivances designed to torture each
and every joint, and a thousand other tools to torment a man bit by
bit? Put away these things which strike us dumb; order the groans and
cries to be silent and the awfulness of screams forced out when men
are torn apart: why, you are just pain, which that gouty fellow despised,
which the dyspeptic puts up with while indulging himself, which the
girl endures in childbirth. You are trivial if I can bear you, and brief if
I cannot bear you.

Think over all this in your heart, ideas you have often heard and 15
often uttered, but then prove whether you have really heard and
uttered them by the result, since the most shameful failure men
reproach us with is to deal with the language of philosophy but not its
deeds. Well then, is this the first time you have felt death impending
upon you, or exile, or pain? You were born for these evils. Let us think
of anything that can happen as going to happen. I know you have
surely done what I warn you to do. Now I am reminding you not to let 16
your spirit drown in that anxiety, for it will grow blunt and have less
energy when you must rise up. Divert it from the private issue to the
public: say your poor body is mortal and brittle, and the prospect of
pain will not arise only from injustice or overweening power. Even
pleasures turn to torture, feasting brings indigestion, and drunkenness the stupor or tremor of the nerves, while lusts bring distortions
of the feet and arms and all the joints. I shall be impoverished: then 17
I will be among the majority of men. I shall be exiled: then I will think
that I was born where I am sent. I shall be chained: what then? Am I
unfettered now? Nature bound me to this burdensome weight of my
body. I shall die; what you are saying is: 'I shall no longer be vulnerable to sickness or being fettered or death.'

I am not so silly as to copy the Epicurean incantation at this point 18
and say that the fear of the underworld is baseless, that Ixion is not
turned on the wheel, nor is the rock pushed uphill on Sisyphus'
shoulders, nor can any man's flesh be reborn and eaten away each day;
no one is so childish as to fear Cerberus and the darkness and the
appearance of ghouls assembled from bare bones.* Death either consumes us or releases us; if we are released a better future awaits us
without the burden of the body; if we are consumed there is nothing
left and blessings and evils are cleared away together. Let me quote 19
your verse at this point, after first reminding you to judge that you
did not write it for others but for yourself. It is shameful to say
one thing and do another; how much more so to write one thing
and believe another. I remember you once expatiated on the theme
that we did not suddenly collapse in death but gradually advanced
towards it. We are dying every day, since a part of our life is sub- 20
tracted every day, and even when we are growing life is shrinking. We
lost our infancy, then our boyhood, then our youth. Right up to yesterday every moment of time past is lost; we are sharing with death
the day that we are spending now. Just as it is not the last drop that
stops the water-clock* but every drop that has previously fallen, so

the last hour when we cease to exist is not the only one to cause death but the only one to complete it: we reach death then but we have been 21 coming to it for a long time. When you described this with your customary style, you, who are always great but never more passionate than when you lend your words to truth, said:

Death does not come at once: what takes us is death's last phase.*

I would rather you read your own words than my letter; it will be manifest to you that the death we fear is the last and not the only moment.

22 I see what you are looking for; you are looking to see what I have used as a prop for this letter, some spirited saying of some thinker, some useful recommendation. So I shall send something from the actual material I had in hand. Epicurus scolds those who lust for death no less than those who fear it, and says: 'It is absurd to run to death out of weariness with life, when it is your way of living that has 23 made you run towards death.' And similarly he says in another place: 'What is so absurd as to seek death when you have made your life troubled by the fear of death?'* And you may add this comment to the same effect, that men's lack of foresight, even folly, is so great that 24 some men are driven towards death by fear of death. Whichever of these sayings you meditate on, you will strengthen your spirit to endurance, whether of death or life: we must be advised or given strength for both lots, so that we do not either love life or hate it too much. Even when reason urges us to put an end to ourselves, our 25 impulse must not be formed thoughtlessly or in a rush. A wise and courageous man should not flee from life but depart from it: above all, let him avoid that emotion which has overwhelmed so many, the lust for dying. For just as there is a heedless propensity of the mind for other things, so there is, dear Lucilius, for death. This often takes hold of noble men with keen spirits, but often takes the inert and 26 supine: the first group despises life, the second rejects it. There are some affected by the same surfeit of doing and seeing, not a hatred of life but a distaste for it, something we slip into even at the impulse of philosophy, when we say: 'How long will it always be the same? I shall wake up, and go to sleep, eat and feel hungry, shiver with cold and sweat from heat. There is no end of anything, but everything is linked in a cycle, things hasten past or follow on: night pursues day and day night, summer ends in autumn, autumn is hurried on by

winter, which in turn is subdued by spring: everything passes but so
as to return. I am not doing or seeing anything new. Boredom sets in
even at this business of living.' There are many who do not think
living is cruel but simply superfluous. Keep well.

Letter 26 (Book III.6) *On old age and its loss of powers as a gentle
approach towards death. More thoughts about facing death (to be continued in letter 27).*

I was telling you just recently that I was in sight of old age, but now   1
I am afraid I have left old age behind me. A different name would fit
these years, at any rate, this bodily condition, since old age is the name
for a weary age, not one broken down. Count me among those shattered and reaching their end. Yet with you as audience I am thankful   2
to myself; I do not feel the harm done by old age in my spirit, though
I do feel it in body. Only my faults and their supporting behaviour
have grown old; my spirit is thriving and glad to have little to do with
the body; it has set down most of its burden. It is rejoicing and disputing with me over old age, declaring that this is its prime. Let us
believe it and let the spirit enjoy its benefit. It is bidding me turn to   3
reflection and work out what I owe in the tranquillity and moderation
of my character to wisdom and what to old age: it bids me examine
what I am not able to do and what I do not wish to do, treating whatever I am glad I cannot do as if I had refused to do it. Indeed, what
grievance is there or inconvenience if whatever ought to have ended
has ebbed away?

   You say: 'It is a major inconvenience to shrink and fade or, to put it   4
precisely, to melt away. For we haven't suddenly been pushed over or
laid low, we are being eaten away, and the days take away something
from our strength one by one.' But is there any better finale than to
sink into one's end as nature releases us? Not because a stroke and
sudden departure from life is something bad, but because this stealthy
loss is a gentle way. At least while the testing moment is approaching
and the day comes that will cast the verdict over all of my years, I am
observing myself and consoling myself. 'So far,' I say, 'what we have   5
demonstrated in deeds or words is nothing. Those are trivial and
deceptive tokens of my spirit wrapped in many charming blandish-
ments: I will trust to death to judge what I have achieved. So I am
preparing myself without hesitation for the day when I will cast away

tricks and disguises and pass judgement on myself, whether
I am talking bravely or feel that way, whether the defiant phrases
6 I have tossed out against fortune are a pretence and a mime. Take
away men's assessment: it is always ambiguous and divides in both
directions. Take away the pursuits that have occupied all my life;
death will pass the verdict on you. This is what I have to say: debates
and cultured conversations and sayings gathered from the recommendations of the wise and learned speech do not show the true
strength of the spirit, since even the most cowardly are bold in speech.
What you have achieved will be made manifest when you give up the
7 ghost. I accept the terms and am not afraid of the judgement.' While
I am saying this to myself, consider that I have also said it to you. You
are younger. What difference does that make? It is not years that are
being counted up. It is not clear where death is waiting for you, so you
should wait for it everywhere.

8   I was ready to come to a close and my hand was reaching for the last
phrase, but I must complete my accounts and provide this letter with
its passage money. Imagine I am not telling you where I will borrow:
you know whose strongbox I employ. Just wait a little while and the
money will be counted out from my own purse; meanwhile I will take
a loan from Epicurus, who says: 'Practise death in advance,'* or if it is
easier to convey his meaning, something like this: 'It is a great thing to
9 learn how to die.' Perhaps you think it superfluous to learn something
that can only be implemented once. This is the very reason we have to
practise; we must always learn anything that we cannot test to see if we
10 know it. 'Practise death!' The man who says this is bidding us practise
liberty. The man who has learned to die has unlearned how to be a
slave; he is above all power, or at least beyond its reach. What do prison
and guards and locked doors mean to him? He has a free way out.
There is only one chain that keeps us bound, the love of life, and even
if this should not be rejected, it should be reduced so that if circumstances require nothing will hold us back or prevent us from being
ready instantly for whatever action is needed. Keep well.

Letter 27 (Book III.6) *Seneca acknowledges that while prescribing
behaviour to Lucilius he is merely a fellow patient, talking to his friend as
he would to himself. They should focus on lasting goods, particularly the
mind's own good, virtue. Virtue cannot be delegated, as one ignorant man*

tried to delegate his literary culture to his slaves. Men must practise virtue
for themselves.

'Are you giving me advice?' you say; 'Have you already advised and   1
corrected yourself? Is that why you are at leisure to set others straight?'
I am not so persistent that I will seek out cures while I am sick, but
I will talk to you about our common suffering and share remedies as
if I am lying in the same hospital. So listen to me as though I am talking to myself: I will let you into my intimate thoughts and reckon
up with myself in your company. I keep rebuking myself: 'Count your   2
years and you will be ashamed to want and plan the same things you
wanted as a boy. In short, furnish yourself with this defence approaching the day of death; let your faults die before you. Send off those
troubling pleasures which cost so dear; they are harmful not just as
they approach but when they are past. Just as anxiety does not fade
over crimes, even if they go undetected at the time, so regret for evil
pleasures lasts even after them. They are not firm and reliable; even if
they don't do harm they escape from you. Look around instead for   3
some lasting good thing; but there is none except what the mind finds
from and for itself. Only virtue guarantees continuing and carefree
joy: even if something gets in the way, it is like clouds which are
moved beneath the sky and never overcome the daylight.' When shall   4
it be my good luck to reach this joy? It is not lingering, but let it come
on fast. There is a great deal of the task ahead on which you must
spend your wakefulness and your effort if you want it to come about;
this business does not allow for using deputies. The nature of writing   5
allows for another kind of assistance. Within our memory there was
a wealthy man, Calvisius Sabinus, with the property and intellect
of a freedman; I never saw a man more unworthy of his riches. His
memory was so bad that he would forget the name sometimes of
Ulysses, at other times of Achilles or Priam, whom he knew as well
as we know our slave escorts. No ageing personal assistant who does
not give men their proper names but imposes others, ever greeted
men by their tribe as badly as Calvisius misnamed the Trojans and
Achaeans.*

But he still wanted to seem educated. So he dreamed up this short-   6
cut; he bought slaves for a high price, one of whom knew Homer and
another Hesiod, and besides, he allocated several others each to one
of the nine lyric poets. Don't be surprised that he paid a great deal for

them: he had not found them trained but commissioned their training. Once he had assembled this household he began to molest his
dinner guests. He kept these slaves at his side, and whenever he was
looking for the verses to quote he often dried up in the middle of a
7 phrase. Satellius Quadratus, that nibbler of wealthy fools and flatterer
to go along with it,* and mocker, a role associated with the other two,
urged him to hire grammarians to pick up the crumbs: when Sabinus
said that each slave cost him 100,000 sesterces, he said: 'You could
have bought as many book-cases of texts for less.' But Sabinus was of
8 the opinion that he knew whatever any one in his household knew. So
Satellius began to exhort him to take up wrestling, although he was
sick and pale and weedy. When Sabinus retorted: 'How can I, when
I can hardly stay alive?', Satellius answered: 'Don't say that, please,
don't you see how many stout slaves you have?' Good sense is not
borrowed or bought; indeed, I think that if it were for sale it would
not find a buyer; but bad sense is bought every day.
9   But now take my debt to you and fare well. 'Poverty adjusted to the
law of nature is wealth.'* Epicurus often says this in different ways,
but anything that is never properly learned is never said too often: you
need only show remedies to some men, but you have to force them
into the minds of others. Keep well.

Letter 28 (Book III.7) *Lucilius has supposedly complained that
travelling abroad has not relieved his discontent. Seneca tells him that his
mental condition is not dependent on his circumstances; no place is alien,
and yet nowhere is so disturbing as his regular haunt, the Forum. In a
partial answer to the problem posed in letter 14, he now claims the wise
man will choose peace rather than public involvement.*

1 Do you think you are the only man this happened to, and feel
amazed as if this was a new experience, that after such prolonged
travels and with such changes of scene you have not shaken off your
sadness and depression? You should change your attitude, not
your surroundings.* You may have crossed the expanse of sea, and as
our Virgil says, 'lands and cities may grow distant', but your faults
2 will follow you wherever you reach. This is what Socrates said to a
man who was complaining: 'Why are you surprised that travelling
does you no good, when you are carrying your own state of mind
around with you? The same cause is weighing you down now which

drove you from home.' How can the novelty of other lands please you,
or making acquaintance with cities and landscapes? That bustling
turns futile. You ask me why this flight is not helping you? Because
you are in your own company. You must cast off the burden of
your spirit; until then no place will please you. Think of your own   3
condition as our Virgil presented the state of the prophetess when
already roused and stimulated and possessed by a great rush of alien
inspiration:

> The prophetess raves frantic, struggling to shake the god
> Out of her breast.

You turn this way and that trying to shake off the weight oppressing
you, which is only made more uncomfortable by the disturbance, just
as cargo while undisturbed puts less strain on a ship, but once it has
spread unevenly just sinks all the faster the part where it has rolled.
Whatever you do, you are acting against your interests and harming
yourself with the movement, since you are jolting a sick man. But   4
when you have eliminated this evil, every change of scene will be
agreeable; you may be driven to the remotest lands and set down in
some random corner of a barbarian region, but that place, whatever it
is like, will be welcoming to you. If you could see this clearly, you   5
would not be surprised that you did not benefit from the variety of
places you constantly visit out of boredom with previous resorts: the
very first of these would have pleased you if you had believed everywhere to be your own country. As it is, you are not travelling but
wandering and being carried onwards, and you change one place for
another, although what you are really looking for, to live well, is provided everywhere. Can anything be as crowded as the forum? Yet you   6
can live calmly there too if you need to. But if I am allowed to choose
my place I will flee far from the sight and proximity of the Forum;
just as unhealthy places assail even the soundest physical health, so
some things are too unhealthy for even a good state of mind if it is not
yet perfected and still recovering.

I disagree with men who wade into deep waters, approving a life   7
full of disturbance, who struggle every day with a mighty spirit
against the difficulties of life. The wise man will endure these but
not choose them, and prefer to be at peace rather than in battle; it is
not much help to have cast out your own faults if you have to quarrel
with those of other men. You may say: 'Thirty tyrants* surrounded   8

Socrates but they could not break his spirit.' What difference does it make how many masters there are? There is only one kind of slavery, and the man who despises it is free, in however great a crowd of oppressors.

9   It is time to stop, but only when I have paid my harbour dues. 'Acknowledgement of the offence is the beginning of recovery.'* Epicurus seems to me to have put this splendidly; for the man who does not know he is blundering does not want to be set right: you

10 must detect yourself before correcting yourself. Some men revel in their faults: do you think they have any thought about a remedy when they treat their offences as virtues? So accuse yourself and scrutinize yourself as much as you can; first act the role of an accuser, then of a judge, and last of all as an intercessor. You must confront yourself sooner or later. Keep well.

Letter 31 (Book IV.2) *This is the first of several letters focused on the recurring theme of defining what is 'the good' (§5) and how it is related to what is honourable. Seneca touches incidentally on the 'vanity of human wishes', a theme which will be central to letter 60. Then he offers various definitions of the good: 'knowledge of life' (§6), 'an even tenor of life and knowledge of things human and divine' (§8), and 'a good and upright spirit' (§11).*

1   I recognize my dear Lucilius; he is beginning to show himself as he had promised. Follow that impulse of the spirit with which you trampled on popular pleasures in pursuit of all that is best; I am not asking you to be greater or better than you were aspiring to be. Your foundations have covered a large area: just do as much as you have aimed to

2   and reconsider the thoughts you have installed in your heart. In short, you will be wise if you shut your ears; it is not enough to block them with wax: you need a stronger obstruction than they say Ulysses used for his companions.* The voice that they feared was beguiling but not official; but the voice we have to fear is resounding not from one rock but from every region of the earth. So sail past not just one spot which you suspect for its treacherous pleasure, but all the cities. Make yourself deaf to those who love you most; with good intentions they are wishing misfortunes upon you. And if you want to be happy, pray to

3   the gods that none of the usual good wishes is your lot. The blessings which those people want to have heaped up are not good; there is only

one good thing, which is the origin and protection of a happy life, to
trust in oneself. But this cannot happen unless you show contempt
for toil and count it among indifferents.* For it is not possible that any
single thing is now good, now bad, now something to be lightly borne,
now to be dreaded. Toil is not good; so what is good? Holding toil 4
in contempt. So I would criticize those who busy themselves on
something pointless, but admire those who strive for honourable
achievement, the more they put effort into it and do not allow themselves to be overcome and bewitched: I will salute them: 'All the
better: rise up and breathe deeply and conquer that slope with one
breath if you can.' Effort nourishes noble spirits. So you have no 5
reason to select from that original wish of your parents the good
things you would like to happen to you, what you are to choose.
Indeed, it is shameful for a man who has already survived great stress
to go on wearying the gods. Why do you need prayers? Make yourself
happy, and you will do so if you realize that those things are good
which contain a share of virtue, and bad which are associated with
vice. Just as nothing glitters without a mixture of light, and nothing
is black unless it contains darkness and has absorbed something shad-
owy, just as nothing is hot without the assistance of fire, and nothing
cold without air, so it is a share in virtue and vice that creates things
honourable and shameful.

So what is good? The knowledge of life. What is bad? Ignorance of 6
life. The shrewd and skilful man will fend off or choose everything
according to circumstance; but he neither fears what he is fending off
nor admires what he chooses, provided his spirit is lofty and unde-
feated. I forbid you to be weakened and oppressed. It is not enough
if you do not jib at effort; demand it. 'What?' you will say; 'Isn't the 7
effort misplaced that is empty and superfluous and brought on by
trivial cases?' No more than the effort spent on noble affairs, since it
is endurance of the spirit which urges it to harsh and tough undertakings and says: 'Why are you hanging back? It is not manly to be afraid 8
of sweat.' Add to this that your virtue should be perfect, an evenness
and consistency in spite of everything, as it cannot be unless there is
knowledge of life and the art of recognizing things human and divine.
This is the supreme good: if you take hold of it you are beginning to
be a partner with the gods and not a suppliant. You say: 'How do I 9
reach that state?' Not over the Apennines or a Greek mountain range
or the wilderness of Candavia; you do not have to go to the Syrtes or

Scylla and Charybdis,* all of which you have passed through, thanks
to your little job as administrator; this journey is safe and agreeable,
one for which Nature equipped you. She gave you the qualities that
will raise you to the level of a god, if you do not let them down.

10   Now money will not make you equal to God, for he has no money.
A magistrate's toga will not do it: God is naked. Renown or self display or the publicity of broadcasting your name among nations will
not do it: no one knows the God and many misjudge him without any
punishment. Nor will the crowd of slaves carrying your litter along
the roads in the city and abroad make you like God. For that most
great and powerful God carries everything himself. Nor can beauty
and strength make you happy; none of these things survives old age.
You must seek something which does not deteriorate day by day, and
11   cannot be obstructed. What is this? The spirit, but when it is right,
good, and great. What else would you call this than God lodging in
a human body? This spirit can as easily fall to a Roman knight as a
freedman or a slave. For what is a knight or a freedman or a slave?
Names won by ambition or injustice. You can leap up to heaven from
a corner, only rise up

> and make yourself worthy
> Of the divine.*

Now you will not shape yourself from gold or silver; no likeness
of God can be modelled from this raw material: remember that when the
gods were well disposed to us they were made of earthenware. Keep well.

Letter 33 (Book IV.4) *Lucilius has reproached Seneca because he has
not quoted any sayings of Epicurus since letter 29. Now he justifies this
at two levels: first by contrasting the nuggets of moral instruction offered
by Epicurus and his followers with the continuous argumentation of Zeno
and his followers; and secondly by criticizing the habit of relying on other
men's sayings instead of working out one's own moral precepts.*

1   You want to have some sayings of our leading thinkers added to
these letters as they were before. Those men were not concerned
with gathering blossoms; their entire argument is manly. You would
recognize that there is some unevenness when memorable sayings
stand out. A single tree does not win admiration when the whole
2   forest soars to the same height. Poems and works of history are full of

these sayings. So I don't want you to think they belong to Epicurus: they are public property, and above all our property, but they are more noticed in his work because they occur seldom, and less expected, because it is a marvel that anything courageous is said by a man who advocated soft ease.

For that is what most people judge, but to me Epicurus is also courageous, although wearing sleeves; courage and energy and a mind ready for war are found as often among the Persians as in men girt for action. So you have no reason to demand snippets and hackneyed 3 sayings: whatever is sampled from other sects is continuously available in our writings. So we don't have those eyecatchers* nor deceive a buyer who will find nothing when he has entered the shop except the objects hung out in the display: we let them take their model wherever they want to pick it up. Now imagine that we want to isolate 4 individual sayings from the crowd; whom shall we credit them to? Zeno or Cleanthus or Chrysippus or Panaetius or Posidonius?* We are not subjects of a king: each man claims his own. But among Epicureans everything that Hermarchus said, or Metrodorus, is credited to one man;* anything someone in that brotherhood uttered was said under the supreme command and auspices of one leader. I tell you, we cannot, even if we try, detach anything from such a host of consistent thoughts.

> It is a poor man's act to count his flock*

Wherever you direct your gaze a thought meets your eye which would be conspicuous if you were not reading it among its peers. So 5 drop that hope of being able to sample in dainty pieces the intellects of great men. You must examine them whole and work through them whole. The composition grows continuously and the creation of the intellect is developed in all its features, so that nothing can be withdrawn without a collapse. Nor am I objecting to you contemplating individual limbs so long as you view them as parts of the man himself. A woman is not beautiful if she is praised for a leg or arm, but if her entire appearance diverts admiration from each separate part. But if you demand full payment I shall not deal with you in such 6 beggarly fashion, but distribute with a full hand: there is a great crowd of sayings scattered here and there which need to be picked up individually, not gathered together. They do not drop but flow, they are unending and interwoven. In fact, I don't doubt that they greatly benefit untrained men listening from outside the school; for

7 short and single items shaped like a verse sink in more easily. That is why we give boys sayings to memorize and what the Greeks call *Chriae*,* because the child's mind can embrace them when it still cannot contain more. But it is shameful for a man who had made some progress to hunt blossoms and prop himself up with a few famous sayings, and rely on his memory: now let him rely on himself. Let him say such things, not hold on to them; for it is shameful for an old man, or one anticipating old age to get his knowledge from other men's notes. 'Zeno said this!' And what have you to say? 'Cleanthes said this.' And what have you to say? How long will you move under another's guidance? Take command and say something worth com-

8 mitting to memory, say something of your own creation. So I believe that all those men who are never originators, but always interpreters hiding in another's shadow, have no spark of nobility, and never dared to do what they spent so long learning. They exercised their memory on other men's thoughts, for remembering is different from knowing. Remembering is keeping safe something entrusted to the memory, whereas knowing is making each thing one's own and not depending

9 on the model and constantly looking back to the teacher. 'This is what Zeno said', 'what Cleanthes said'. Let there be some difference between yourself and the book. How long will you go on learning? Now teach something. Why should I listen to something I can read? The teacher says: 'The living voice contributes a lot.' But not the voice that borrows other men's words and performs like a shorthand

10 writer. Now add the point that men who never come under their own direction first follow their predecessors, in a matter in which no one has failed to rebel from his predecessor, then they follow them in matters still needing investigation. Indeed, the answer will never be discovered if we stay content with what has been discovered. Moreover, the man who follows another does not find anything, indeed he is not even looking.

11   Well then, shan't I tread in my predecessor's steps? For my part I make use of the old path, but if I find another way shorter and less hilly, I will make a path there.* The men who raised these topics before us are not our masters but our guides. The truth is open to all; it has not yet been appropriated, and much of it is left even for those still to come. Keep well.

Letter 34 (Book IV.5) *Lucilius is congratulated on progress, and given renewed encouragement to keep up the good work.*

I grow stronger and more triumphant and rally in energy, casting off 1
my old age, whenever I realize from your actions and writings how
much you have projected yourself beyond yourself—for you long
since left the crowd behind you. If a farmer delights to nourish a tree
until it bears fruit, if a shepherd gets pleasure from the new lambs of
his flock, if no one looks at a nursling except to treat the pupil's youth
as his own, what do you think happens to those who have reared intellects and suddenly see as mature the minds they shaped when still
young and unformed? I claim you for my own; you are my master- 2
piece. When I saw your nature I laid a formal hand on it, I urged you
on and applied goads: I did not let you go slowly but constantly egged
you on; now I am doing the same thing, but now I am encouraging a
man already running at speed and returning my encouragement. 3
'What do you mean?' you say; 'I still want it.' There is a great deal of
importance in this, not just in the way the beginnings of any undertaking are said to anticipate half the task. Our business is based on the
mind, so it is a great part of goodness to want to become good. Do you
know whom I call good? The perfect and completed man whom no
force, no necessity, can compel to do evil. I look forward to you as this 4
man if you persevere and put your weight into it and concentrate on
making all your deeds and words harmonious and matching each
other and stamped with a consistent shape. A man's mind is not in the
right condition if his deeds are dissonant. Keep well.

Letter 35 (Book IV.6) *On the difference between loving and being a true friend. Seneca cites his age and Lucilius' mortality as motives for urgency in developing his love and hastening their reunion.*

When I ask you so earnestly to devote yourself, I am acting in my own 1
interest; I want to have a friend, something that cannot happen to me
unless you persist in developing yourself as you have begun. For as it
is you love me, but are not a friend to me. 'What,' you will say, 'are
these different things?' Yes, quite contrary. The friend loves, but the
man who loves is not automatically a friend; so friendship is always
beneficial, but love sometimes even does harm. If for no other reason, 2

make progress so you can learn how to love. So hurry while you are benefiting me, in case you learn this for another's gain. For my part I already receive the profit, when I imagine that we shall be of one mind and whatever strength fades from my age will return to me from your youth, although there is not a great difference between us; but
3 I also want to rejoice over the reality. Joy comes to us from those we love even when they are distant, but it is light and fleeting; the sight of them, their presence and conversation, had some living pleasure, at least if you not only see whom you want but as you want to see him. So bring yourself to me, an immense gift, and to put on speed, think
4 that you are mortal and I am an old man. Hurry on towards me, but first towards yourself. Make progress, and above all take pains to be consistent with yourself. Whenever you want to test whether something has been achieved, see whether your aim today is the same as yesterday; a change of purpose means that your mind is drifting, and appearing in different places as the wind has carried it. What is fixed with a sure foundation does not wander: that is the success of a perfect wise man, but drifting sometimes happens to a man making progress and launched on the open sea. So what is the difference? The man progressing is disturbed but does not change sides: he wavers, but on the spot; whereas the wise man does not even waver. Keep well.

Letter 36 (Book IV.7) *A friend of Lucilius wants to retire from public service and is meeting criticism. After commending training to face misfortune, Seneca turns to disparaging the fear of death since death is inevitable and brings no suffering.*

1 Urge your friend to despise with a stout spirit those who scold him for seeking the shade and leisure, for abandoning his rank and preferring calmness to everything although he could have advanced further; let him show them each day how profitably he has seen to his own interest. Those men who are envied will not cease to pass on; some will be crushed and some will stumble. Success is an uneasy thing; it harasses itself. It disturbs the brain in more than one way: it provokes different men to different things, some to lack of self-control, others to self-indulgence. It puffs up one group and softens another, slack-
2 ening them completely. 'But some people carry it well.' Yes, as some men can carry their wine. So there is no reason for them to persuade

you that the man who is besieged by many petitioners is happy; men
rush to him as they do to a cistern, which they drain and pollute.
'They call my friend a worthless, lazy fellow.' You know that some
people speak absurdly and mean the opposite. 'They used to call him
successful.' Well then, was he? I don't care that some think him too 3
rough and grim. Ariston* used to say he preferred a young man to be
gloomy rather than cheerful and affable with the crowd, since the
wine that seemed harsh and rough when new became a good vintage:
what was pleasant in the jug did not survive ageing. Let them call him
grim and hostile to their celebrations; that gloom will turn out well in
old age, provided he persists in devoting himself to virtue and absorb-
ing studies worthy of a gentleman—not those of which a smattering
is enough, but studies in which the mind needs to be soaked. This is
the time to learn.

'What? Is there a time when one should not learn?' Not at all, but 4
just as it is honourable to study in all our years, it is not good to be still
training at all times. An old man doing beginner's work is shameful
and absurd; the young man should prepare his knowledge and the old
man should use it. So you will do yourself a great kindness if you
make that friend as excellent as possible; these are the kindnesses they
say one should seek and distribute, without doubt in the highest category, which it is as beneficial to give as to receive. In short, he has no 5
free choice, because he has given a guarantee; but it is less shameful to
default on a creditor than on one's own good prospects. To pay up that
debt the merchant needs a successful voyage, the landowner needs the
natural fertility of the land he farms, and the goodwill of heaven. The
moral debtor can be discharged of his debt simply by his own will.
Fortune has no rights over character. Then let him control it so as to 6
bring the mind to perfection in the most calm condition, a mind
which feels neither what is taken from it nor added to it, but keeps the
same disposition however affairs turn out: if ordinary assets are heaped
upon such a man, he rises above his possessions, but if chance should
dislodge something or everything from them, he is not diminished.

If he had been born in Parthia* he would have stretched the bow in 7
his infancy; if in Germany he would have wielded a slender javelin
from his first boyhood; if he had lived in the time of our forefathers
he would have learned to ride and strike a man at close quarters. This
is what the training of each man's nation urges and demands of him.
So what should he practise? Something that is effective against all 8

weapons and every kind of enemy, to despise death which no one doubts has something terrifying in itself, so that it distresses our minds which nature has shaped to love their own being; otherwise it would not be necessary to be equipped and trained against something which we confront by a kind of voluntary instinct, just as everyone is

9 driven to their own preservation. No one learns how to recline in rose petals if it should be necessary, but he is hardened for this, not to yield his loyalty to torture, so that if it is necessary he will at some time stand when wounded, and keep watch to defend the rampart, and not even lean on his spear because sleep tends to creep up at times on those resting on some prop. Death brings no discomfort, for there would have to be someone whose discomfort it was.

10 If so great a yearning for a longer life possesses you, think that none of the things which pass from our sight and are again buried in the world from which they came and are soon destined to return are destroyed; they cease but are not lost, and death, which we fear and shun, interrupts life but does not snatch it away; the day will come again and restore us to light, which many would shun if it did not bring them back forgetful of their experience.

11 But I will explain more carefully later that everything which seems to be lost is simply changed. A man guaranteed to return should depart in a calm spirit. Watch the cycle of things returning to their own nature: you will see that nothing in this universe is quenched but rises and falls in turn. Summer departs, but another year will bring it back; winter abates, but the right months will bring it back; night buries the sun, but day will immediately drive away night. That deployment of the stars returns to whatever it has passed by; one part

12 of the sky is constantly sinking and another rising. In short, I will bring this to a close if I add this one point, that neither infants nor children nor the mentally handicapped fear death, and it would be disgraceful if reason did not guarantee us the same freedom from anxiety which stupidity allows them. Keep well.

Letter 37 (Book IV.8) *A comparison of the philosopher's oath of service with that of gladiators.*

1 You have promised to be a good man, the greatest bond to ensure a good state of mind, and you have done it on oath. Anyone who tells you the campaign will be soft and easy will be making fun of you.

I don't want you to be deceived. The words of this most honourable
oath and that most shameful one are the same: 'to be burned and
bound and killed by the sword.' But what is enjoined on those who 2
rent out their actions to the arena and pay for their food and drink
with their own blood is that they will suffer such hardships even
against their will: instead, you are enjoined to endure these things
willingly and gladly. They are allowed to lower their weapons and seek
the mercy of the crowd; you will neither lower them nor ask for your
life; you must die upright and unconquered. After all, what is the
benefit of gaining a few days or years? We are born without the chance
of discharge. 'So how shall I acquit myself?' you ask. You can't escape 3
emergencies, but you can defeat them:

Force makes a way*

and philosophy will give you this other way. Take yourself to her if
you want to be safe, carefree, and happy, in short, if you want to be
free, which is the greatest gain: it cannot come to you any other way.
Stupidity is low, contemptible, shabby, slavish, and dominated by 4
many savage emotions. But wisdom, which alone is liberty, sends
away from you these burdensome tyrants who sometimes demand
opposite things and sometimes the same. One way alone leads to this,
and it is straight; you will not wander off: go forward with a sure step.
If you want to subject everything to yourself, subject yourself to
reason: you will rule over many if reason rules over you. From reason
you will learn what to attempt and how; you will not do things by
accident. You will not be able to cite any man to me who knows 5
how he began to want what he wants: he was not brought to this
point by deliberation but driven by an impulse. Fortune does not
come up against us any less often than we come up against her. It is
shameful not to walk but to be carried, and suddenly dazed in the
midst of worldly confusion to ask: 'How did I come to this point?'
Keep well.

Letter 38 (Book IV.9) *Lucilius has asked Seneca to write more
frequently.*

You are right to demand that we increase this exchange of letters. Talk 1
is most beneficial because it slips into the mind bit by bit; set-piece
lectures prepared in advance and poured out in front of a crowd make

more noise but have less intimacy. Philosophy is good advice, but no one gives advice out loud; there are times when one must use, we might say, public harangues, when a man is hesitating and must be driven to action; but when the business is to have him learn, not make him willing to learn, we must adopt these more modest words. They penetrate and stay in the mind more easily, for we don't need many

2 arguments, but effective ones. Words should be scattered like a seed; however small the seed, once it has found the right kind of soil it expands its strength and spreads from the smallest size into an immense growth. Reason is like that. It is not large, if you look at it, but it grows in action. Not much is said, but if the mind receives it well these thoughts gain strength and soar. What I am saying is that moral recommendations behave like seeds. They achieve a lot, and they occupy little space. Just let the right kind of mind, as I said, seize on them and absorb them: then it in turn will produce many ideas from itself and give back more than it received. Keep well.

Letter 39 (Book IV.10) *Seneca answers Lucilius' request for a compendium of recommendations, but sends him to the ethical writers: his noble nature will respond to moral incentives and not be submerged in vice like men ruined by success.*

1 Certainly I will put together fully organized and condensed notes, as you ask: but think whether the regular method may not be more beneficial than what is now called a Compendium, but in the past when we still spoke Latin* was called a Summary. The continuous argument is more necessary for a learner, the other for someone who knows; for the former teaches, whereas the latter simply reminds. But I will supply you with both. There is no reason for you to ask me for one source or another: the man who guarantees their identity is him-

2 self unknown.* So I will write what you ask, but in my own fashion. Meanwhile you have many authorities whose writings I don't doubt are fully systematic. Take up the list of philosophers: just doing this will make you wake up if you see how many have been working for you. You will be eager to become one of them, since this is one of the best qualities of a noble mind, to be spurred on to honourable tasks. No real man of lofty intellect is pleased with humble and sordid matters; it is the sight of great enterprises that summons and rouses him.

3 Just as a flame rises upwards and cannot lie flat and be kept down, any

more than it can rest, so our mind is in motion, all the more nimble
and active as it is more passionate. Happy the man who has directed
this impulse to better purposes: he will set himself beyond the power
and control of fortune; he will moderate success, reduce the force of
failure, and despise what others find admirable. It is the mark of a 4
great spirit to hold great things in contempt and prefer moderate circumstances over excess; for moderation is useful and life-enhancing,
whereas excess harms by its abundance. Just so, excessive growth
weighs down a crop, branches are broken by too heavy a load, and
excessive fertility does not reach ripeness. The same thing happens
to minds burst by excess of good fortune, which they use not only to
harm others but themselves. What enemy was ever so abusive to 5
anyone as some men's pleasures are to them? You can forgive their
lack of control and mad lust only because of one factor; they themselves suffer the consequences of their actions. And it is right that this
frenzy harries them, since lust that has leapt beyond nature inevitably
bursts out beyond measure. For nature's measure has a limit, but
empty desires sprung from lust are beyond bounds. Self-interest 6
measures out what is necessary: but how do you reduce superfluity?
So men wallow in pleasures which they cannot do without, because
these have become a habit, and are most wretched because they have
reached the point where activities that were superfluous have become
necessary. As a result they are enslaved to pleasures and do not enjoy
them, and even cherish their own failings, which is the worst of failings: then their unhappiness is absolute, when shameful activities
not only delight them but are their choice, and there is no longer
a chance of healing when what once were failings have become
character. Keep well.

Letter 40 (Book IV.11) *Seneca believed in the importance of style
because of its power to arouse and convince an audience for philosophical
as well as rhetorical purposes. Here he argues about the appropriate delivery for teaching philosophy. Starting from Lucilius' supposed comment on
the eloquence of the showpiece lecturer Serapion (more sophist than philosopher), Seneca reviews the factors determining the slower pace proper
to philosophers' speech as opposed to speakers in the lawcourts (§8) and
declaimers (§9–10), then contrasts Greek with Roman eloquence and
Cicero with contemporary orators.*

1   Thank you for writing to me often, because you are showing yourself
to me in the only way you can. I never receive a letter from you without immediately feeling we are together. If the portraits of absent
friends please us by refreshing our memory and easing our regret for
them with a superficial and empty comfort, how much more pleasing
are letters, which bring real traces and marks of our absent friend. For
the imprint of a friend's hand on a letter brings recognition, the
sweetest thing about being face to face.

2   You write that you heard a lecture by the philosopher Serapion*
when his ship put in to your harbour: as you say: 'He usually grasps at
words at a great pace, and does not pour them out but urges and drives
them on; in fact, more words come out than one voice can handle.'
I don't approve of this in a philosopher: his delivery should be calm
like his life, but nothing is well ordered that rushes headlong in haste.
So in Homer excited speech following itself without any pause like
snowflakes is assigned to a public speaker, but the mild speech sweeter

3   than honey pours from the old man.* You should take it that the swift
and torrential flow of speech is more appropriate to a storyteller than
to a man arguing a serious and important matter and giving instruction. I am as much against him eking out drips as racing along: he
should neither strain the ears nor overwhelm them. In fact, thin and
scanty speech leaves the listener less attentive, bored with this dragged-
out delivery; yet words that must be waited for sink in more easily than
what flies past. In short, men are said to pass on instructions to their
pupils, but what is fleeting cannot be passed on.

4   There is a further point: since a speech paying attention to truth
should be free of artistry and simple, this popular style of speaking
contains no truth. It aims to stir up the crowd and sweep along unprepared ears with its drive, but it does not offer scope for argument,
being carried away. How can something give direction which is not
directed? Doesn't the speech applied to heal minds need to sink

5   into us? Remedies do not work unless they take their time. Besides,
this copious speech is mostly hollow and meaningless, it makes
more noise than it is worth. The things that terrify me have to be
mitigated, what frets me must be stilled, what deceives me must be
shaken off, self-indulgence must be restrained and greed rebuked:
which of these processes can take place at speed? What doctor cures
the sick in passing? What about the fact that such a din of headlong

6   words without discrimination does not even give pleasure? Just as

it is enough to recognize what cannot be done, so it is more than enough to have listened once to those speakers who simply exercised their language. For what would anyone want to learn or to imitate? What judgement would he make of men whose speech is so disturbed and unleashed that it cannot be brought under control? Just as 7 men running downhill cannot stop when they want to, but are forced to obey the rush of their body-weight, and are carried further than they wanted, so this fast speech is neither under its own control nor fitting for philosophy, which should place its words, not spew them out, and advance step by step. 'Well then, won't it rise in passion 8 from time to time?' Of course, but while preserving the dignified character which that violent and excessive force casts off. Let it have great power, but keep it under control: the stream should flow evenly all year, not in a seasonal spate. I would hardly allow a court speaker such rapidity of speech that it cannot be reined in, proceeding without discipline; for how will the juror follow, who is sometimes raw and inexperienced? Even then, when either the urge to display or some uncontrolled emotion has carried him away, let him only hasten and pour out speech as much as men's ears can endure.

So you will do well not to listen to those who seek to know how 9 much they can say, but not how well, and if necessary you will prefer to listen even to P. Vinicius* speaking. When men asked how P. Vinicius spoke, Asellius said, 'in a long-drawn-out fashion'. For Geminus Varius commented: 'I don't know how you can call him eloquent; he cannot put three words together.' Why shouldn't you prefer to speak like Vinicius? Suppose some stupid fellow interrupted, like 10 the man who asked, when Vinicius was picking out single words as if he were dictating rather than speaking: 'Tell me, are you never going to say anything?' In fact I would want any sane man to keep far away from the racing speed of Q. Haterius, the most celebrated orator of his time: Haterius never hesitated and never stopped, but began only once and ended once.

Indeed I think some things are more or less suited to different 11 peoples. You would put up with this lack of control among the Greeks, whereas we are accustomed to pause and punctuate even when we write. Even our Cicero, from whom Roman eloquence sprang into being, was a measured speaker.* Roman speech is more circumspect and calculates and gives time for calculation. Fabianus,* 12 distinguished in his life and knowledge, and what comes second to

those, in eloquence, used to argue briskly rather than excitedly, so
that you would call this ease rather than speed. I accept this easy flow
in a wise man, but do not demand it: he should utter his speech with-
13 out hindrance, but I prefer it to come out rather than flow out. I am
discouraging you all the more urgently from that affectation because
you cannot achieve that fluency unless you have ceased to feel shame;
you must smooth the blush from your brow and not listen to yourself,
since that unguarded flow will produce many ideas which you would
want to hold back. As I say, this fluency cannot come to you without
risk to your modesty. Besides, it requires daily practice and transfer-
14 ring one's attention from content to mere words. But even if the
words are at hand and can run on without any effort on your part,
they should still be disciplined; just as a fairly moderate pace suits a
wise man, so does speech that is urgent but not rash. So this will be
the chief of these important tenets; I hereby order you to be slow in
speaking. Keep well.

Letter 41 (Book IV.12) *On the divine origin of reason in the human
spirit. Seneca compares the sacred power within a man to our perception
of sacredness when we contemplate mysterious and beautiful elements in
natural landscape. As for divine inspiration or spirit, it is natural and
cannot be simulated by adornment.*

1 You are observing an excellent and beneficial practice if (as you write)
you are aiming persistently at a good state of mind, which it is foolish
to pray for if you can obtain it from yourself. We need not raise our
arms to heaven nor beg the sacristan to admit us to the ear of the
divine image, as if we could then be heard better: God is near you, he
2 is with you, he is within you. That is what I claim, Lucilius, that a
holy inspiration dwells within us as monitor and guardian of our good
and bad behaviour; it treats us as it is treated by us. Indeed, no good
man is without a god; can anyone rise to good fortune without his
help? It is this God who gives us lofty and upright intentions; in each
and every good man,

> <Which God is unknown> but a God dwells in him.*

3 If you bring to mind a grove thick with ancient trees soaring above the
normal height, one that fends off the sight of the sky with the throngs
of branches overlapping each other, that loftiness of the forest and

seclusion of the place and wonder at the shade that is so thick and continuous in the open space will give you the conviction of a deity. If some cavern with its rock deeply eroded holds up a mountain, one not artificial but hollowed out by natural causes into such a gaping void, it will strike your spirit with a kind of religious awe. We worship the sources of great rivers; the sudden emergence of a mighty stream from hiding is given altars; springs of hot waters are worshipped, and either the obscurity or the immense depth of some pools has given them sanctity. If you see a man undeterred by dangers, untouched by 4 desires, happy in misfortunes and calm in the midst of storms, gazing down on men and on gods at their own level, will you not feel reverence for him? You will not say 'that achievement is greater and deeper than is credible in this poor human body'. A divine force comes down 5 and a heavenly power stirs this excellent and modest spirit which passes through everything as if unimportant, laughing at everything we fear and long for. Such a great achievement cannot stand without the prop of divinity, and its greater part remains in heaven where it originated. Just as the sun's rays touch the earth but are up there where they stream from, so a great and sacred mind, sent down for the purpose of helping us to know divinity closer at hand, associates with us but clings to its own origin; it depends on this and gazes and struggles towards it, but is within our world as a superior being.

So what is this spirit? Something that shines only with its own 6 excellence. For what is more stupid than to praise a man for borrowed merits? And what is more crazy than to marvel at things which can at any moment be transferred to another man? Golden reins do not make a better horse. A lion with its mane gilded is given one kind of release into the arena after being reduced to exhaustion, manhandled, and compelled to accept the adornment, while an ungroomed lion of undamaged spirit is treated differently. To be sure, this second lion, fierce in attack as nature wanted him to be, glamorous in his rough appearance, whose beauty we cannot contemplate without fear, is preferred to that tired and gilded creature. No man should be proud 7 except of his own merit. We praise a vine if it loads its branches with fruit, if the sheer weight of what it has borne brings down the props; would anyone prefer the vine from which golden grapes and leaves hang down? The natural virtue of a vine is fertility, and we should praise in a man what is peculiar to him. He may have a handsome staff of slaves and a noble house, he may sow a large estate and put out

large sums at interest, but none of these things is in him, only around
8 him. Praise in him what cannot be taken away or given, what is peculiar to a man. You ask what this is? The spirit, and reason perfected in
the spirit. For as man is a reasoning creature, so his goodness is complete if it has fulfilled the purpose for which he was born. And what is
it that reason demands from him? A very easy thing: to live according
to his nature. But collective folly makes this difficult; we each push
the other into faulty behaviour. How can men be recalled to safety
when nobody pulls them back and the crowd pushes them forward?
Keep well.

Letter 44 (Book V.3) *On the difference between social and moral stand-*
ing. Seneca reproaches Lucilius for feeling socially inferior as a mere knight,
and compares the moral nobility and humble social origin of Socrates and
other great philosophers. References to movement between slavery and free
status point ahead to the direct discussion coming in letter 47.

1 You are belittling yourself to me again and saying that first nature,
then fortune, has been grudging to you, although you can detach
yourself from the crowd and rise to the greatest success among
men. If philosophy has any merit it is this, that it does not look at the
family tree: all men, if we trace them to their first origin, come from
2 the gods. You are a Roman knight,* and it was your enterprise that
raised you to this rank; but by Jove, the fourteen rows shut out many
and the senate does not let in everyone, and even military camps are
selective in choosing whom they welcome into toil and danger: but
good sense is open to all and we are all nobly born for this purpose.
Philosophy does not reject or choose anyone; it shines for everyone.
3 Socrates was not a patrician;* Cleanthes drew water and hired his
services to irrigate a garden; as for Plato, philosophy did not welcome
him as a noble but made him noble; why should you despair of becoming their equal? All of these are your ancestors if you behave worthily
of them; and you will do if you persuade yourself forthwith that you
4 are not surpassed by anyone in nobility. For all of us there are as many
preceding us; there is no one whose origin does not lie beyond
memory. Plato says that no king was not descended from slaves and
no slave was not descended from kings.* A long series of vicissitudes
mixed up all of these ranks and fortune turned them upside down.
5 Who is well born? The man well set up by nature for virtue.

We should look only for this, otherwise if you hark back to the old
days there is no one who does not come from the time before creation.
From the origin of the universe up to this time an alternating sequence
has led us through glorious and humble circumstances. An entrance
hall full of smoky wax masks* does not make us noble; no ancestor
lived in order to give us glory, nor is what occurred before us our
property; it is the spirit that makes one noble, which may rise from
any rank above fortune. So imagine you are not a Roman knight but a 6
freedman: you can achieve this, to be the only free man among the
freeborn.* 'How is that?' you say. If you do not distinguish between
good things and bad on the people's say so. You must fix your gaze not
on the origin of things but their destination. If there is anything that
can create a happy life, then it is good in its own right; for it cannot be
distorted into evil. So where is it that people go wrong, since everyone 7
chooses a happy life? Because they mistake the means of happiness
for the end, and actually flee it while they are seeking it. For although
a firm freedom from care and unshaken confidence is the essence of a
happy life, they gather reasons for anxiety, and not only carry burdens on the treacherous journey of life but drag them along; so they
are always falling further behind from what they are aiming for, and
the more effort they spend, the more they hamper themselves and are
carried backwards. This happens to men hurrying through a maze;
their very speed entangles them. Keep well.

Letter 46 (Book V.5) *Seneca praises the book Lucilius has written
and sent to him (but lets us know nothing about its content).*

I received your book as you had promised me, and opened it, intend- 1
ing to read it at a convenient time; I just wanted to sample it, but then
you beguiled me so that I went on reading. You can see how eloquent
it was, that it seemed light to me, although it was not modestly pro-
portioned like my body or yours but might appear at first sight to be
something by Livy or Epicurus.* However, it held me and drew me
on with such charm that I read it right through without any post-
ponement. The sun was inviting me and hunger nagging me and
the clouds were threatening, but I absorbed it from beginning to end.
I was not just pleased, but I rejoiced. What cleverness it had and 2
what spirit! I would say 'what drive!' if it had spells of calm and
then soared after interludes; but as it is, this was not a drive but

an even pace. The style is manly and chaste, yet at intervals there were passages of sweetness and mildness. Your diction is lofty and upright; this is what I want you to keep to, moving like this. The subject-matter also contributed; so one must choose a fertile topic which

3 beguiles and excites the intellect. I will write more about the book when I have reread it; for now, my judgement is still unsettled, as if I had listened to it but not read it. So let me investigate. There is no need to fear; you will hear the truth. O happy man, to have nothing which would make anyone lie to you at such length! Although even when the motive is removed we lie simply out of habit. Keep well.

Letter 47 (Book V.6) *On the proper treatment of slaves, and how to reform the cruel and insulting behaviour of bad masters at dinner. Seneca's chief arguments are that slavery is the product of chance, which any man can suffer, and that treating slaves with some respect both wins their good-will and brings moral improvement to master and slave.*

1 I was glad to learn from your messengers that you live on friendly terms with your slaves: this fits your good sense and education. 'But they are slaves!' No, they are men. 'They are slaves.' No: companions. 'They are slaves.' No: humble friends. 'They are slaves.' No: your fellow slaves, if you think that fortune has as much power over masters as well

2 as slaves. So I laugh at those who think it shameful to dine with their slave. Why laugh? Except that it is a most arrogant practice that surrounds the master with a crowd of standing slaves as he dines. He eats more than he can hold, and loads with great gluttony his belly bloated and unaccustomed to its function, so that he evacuates with more effort

3 than he swallowed. But the poor slaves may not even move their lips to speak: every murmur is disciplined with the rod and not even accidental sounds, a cough a sneeze a sob, escape blows: silence interrupted by any word is atoned for with a severe beating; for the whole night they

4 keep standing, hungry and silent. This is why those who are not allowed to talk in their master's presence talk about their master. But slaves who not only exchanged talk in front of their masters but with them, whose mouth was not gagged, were ready to offer their necks for their master and avert impending danger onto their own heads; they chattered at dinners but were silent under torture.*

5   Then there is an equally arrogant proverb spread around, that we have as many enemies as slaves; we don't have them as enemies but

make them so. For now I will pass over other cruel and inhuman practices, ways in which we abuse them not even as men but like beasts of burden. When we recline at dinner one of them wipes away our spittle, another is in waiting to gather the products of our drunkenness. Another carves expensive birds:* guiding his skilled hand 6 through their breasts and thighs with sure gestures, he cuts away slices, wretched man, living for this one task, to cut fowl elegantly, except that the fellow who teaches this art for men's pleasure is more wretched than the one who learns it of necessity. Another, as wine- 7 steward, is dressed like a woman and struggling with his own growth to adulthood; he cannot escape boyhood but is dragged back and his appearance, already fit for military service, has been smoothed out, with the bristles pumiced away or completely plucked: he divides the night between his master's drunkenness and lust, as a man in the bedchamber and boy at the dinner party. Another, entrusted with 8 supervising the guests, keeps standing, poor fellow, and waits to see whom flattery and lack of control of appetite or tongue will call back the next day. Add the purchasers who have a detailed knowledge of their master's palate, who know what flavour will excite him, what food delights him by its appearance and what can rouse him by its novelty when he is feeling sated, what he now disdains from surfeit and what he is hungry for that day. He does not put up with dining along with these, and thinks it a derogation of his majesty to come to the same table as his slave—God forbid! How many masters he has among them. I saw Callistus' former master standing at his door,* 9 and the man who had put a label upon him, and presented him among the lots at auction, shut out when others entered the house. The slave paid him back for being thrust into the first batch of sales on which the auctioneer tries out his voice; and he in turn made his excuses and did not think him worthy of his home. His master sold Callistus: but how much Callistus sold to his master!

Just think that the fellow you call your slave was born from the 10 same seeds and enjoyed the same sky, breathed, lived, and died on equal terms! You are just as able to look on him as freeborn as he can look on you as a slave. In the defeat of Varus* Fortune laid low many men of splendid birth aiming at the rank of senator through military service; it made one of them a shepherd, another a janitor. So now go and despise a man whose fortune you may descend to while you are despising him.

11   I don't want to launch into that vast theme and discuss the treatment of slaves against whom we are most arrogant, cruel, and abusive. But this is the gist of my instruction; live with an inferior as you would wish a superior to live with you. Whenever it comes into your head how much you could do to your slave, think that your master

12 could do as much to you. But, you will say, 'I have no master!' You are still young; perhaps you will have one. You don't know at what age Hecuba began to be a slave, or Croesus, or the mother of Darius,

13 or Plato or Diogenes.* Live mercifully with your slave, even affably, and admit him to conversation and discussion and even shared living.

     At this the whole crowd of spoiled darlings will protest: 'Nothing would be more humble or shameful than this!' But I will catch the

14 same men kissing the hand of another man's slaves. Don't you even see how our ancestors removed all ill-will from masters and all insult from slaves? They called the master the Father of the Household,* and the slaves, as is still the practice in mimes, they called Members of the Household. They established a feast-day not as the only day on which slaves ate with their masters, but as one day at least when they permitted the slaves to hold office in the household and hold court,

15 and turned the house into a miniature commonwealth. So what? Shall I bring all my slaves to my table? No more than all free men. But you are mistaken if you think I will thrust away some as performing dirtier tasks, such as, for instance, the muleteer and cowherd. I will not value them by their services but by their character: each man provides his own character, but chance assigns his services. Let some dine with you because they are worthy and others to make them worthy; if there is anything slavish in them from their humble associations, dining

16 with more honoured people will make them shed it. Dear Lucilius, there is no reason to look for a friend only in the forum and senate-house: if you pay careful attention you will find them at home as well. Often good timber is wasted without a craftsman; try it and test it. Just as a man is a fool if he does not look at the beast itself when he is buying a horse, but at its saddle-cloth and bridle, so he is a real fool who assesses a man by his clothing or class, which is wrapped around us like clothing. 'He is a slave.' But perhaps he is free in spirit. 'He is

17 a slave.' Will this do him harm? Show me who is not a slave. One man is slave to lust, another to greed, another to ambition, all of us to hope and fear. I will give you an ex-consul enslaved to an old woman, a rich

man to his maidservant, I will show you the most nobly born young men who have made themselves slaves of pantomime dancers;* no slavery is more shameful than self-imposed slavery. So there is no reason for those disdainful men to discourage you from making yourself agreeable to your slaves and not arrogantly superior; let them be devoted to you rather than fear you.

Someone will say I am now calling slaves to take the cap of liberty, 18 and casting the masters down from their heights, because I said 'let them pay respect to their master rather than fear him'. 'Just like that?' they say: 'You mean they should pay respect like clients, or morning greeters?' The man who says this forgets that what is enough for God is not too little for masters. The man who is paid respect is loved; love cannot be mixed with fear. So I judge that you are acting with abso- 19 lute correctness in not wanting to be feared by your slaves, and using only verbal scolding; only animals are corrected by blows.

We are not harmed by anything that offends us, but self-indulgence drives people to frenzy, so that anything which does not answer their whim calls forth their rage. We have put on the attitudes of kings; for 20 they too, forgetful of their strength and other men's weakness, grow white-hot and rage as if they had been wronged, although their great fortune makes them very safe from any such risk. And they know this perfectly well, but by their complaints are waiting for a chance to do harm; they suffered harm so as to inflict it.

I don't want to delay you any longer, since you don't need encour- 21 agement. This is one of many other advantages of good character; it is content with itself and lasts. Badness is fickle and often changes, not for the better but for its opposite. Keep well.

Letter 48 (Book V.7) *The matter on which Lucilius has requested advice is left unclear: it is merely an opening gambit to enable Seneca to discuss the proper relationship between friends. From §6, however, Seneca is concerned with rejecting syllogistic argument, and his addressee is no longer Lucilius but an imagined philosopher. Unfortunately, several key phrases in §§8–9 are damaged beyond restoration.*

I will write later to answer the letter you sent me on your journey, 1 as long as the journey itself: I need to withdraw myself and consider what course to urge upon you. You too, in asking for advice, spent

some time considering whether you should seek advice. It is more
urgent for me to do this since it takes a greater lapse of time to answer
a problem than to pose it. Especially when a different course is in
2 your interest from what is mine. Am I talking like an Epicurean
again? In fact the same course is in my interest as in yours; or I am
not a friend unless whatever issue arises affecting you is also an
issue for me. Friendship between us makes a total partnership* in
all things, and nothing is favourable or adverse for one of us alone:
we are living for a common purpose. Nor can anyone live happily
if he only observes himself and turns everything towards his own
advantage: you must live for someone else if you want to live for your-
3 self. The careful and scrupulous observation of this partnership,
which associates us as men with men and judges that there is some
right common to humanity, is highly beneficial to developing that
inner partnership in friendship which I was talking about; for the
man who has much in common with mankind will have everything in
common with his friend.
4   This is the kind of advice, Lucilius, best of men, I prefer to receive
from those nice quibblers, what I should guarantee to a friend, to a
man, rather than in how many ways the word 'friend' is used and how
many things 'man' implies. See how wisdom and folly go off in opposite directions. Whom shall I join? Which side do you bid me take?
For one person a man counts as a friend, for another a friend does not
count as a man. The former is making a friend for himself, the latter
is fitting himself to his friend: but you are just twisting the words and
5 distinguishing syllables. I suppose that unless I construct the most
cunning set of questions and fabricate a lie born out of the truth by
a false syllogism, I will not be able to separate the goals we should
pursue from those we should flee. I am ashamed that we as old men
are playing in such a serious business.
6   'A mouse is a syllable, and the mouse eats cheese, therefore a syllable eats cheese.' Just imagine that I cannot solve this nonsense: what
danger is threatening me as a result of that ignorance? Doubtless
I have to fear catching syllables in my mousetrap, or in case a book
may eat the cheese if I am careless. Unless the following syllogism is
more shrewd: 'a mouse is a syllable, but syllables don't eat cheese,
7 therefore a mouse doesn't eat cheese.' Oh what childish stupidities!
Have we furrowed our brows over this sort of thing and let our
beard grow for this? Is this what we teach, looking gloomy and pale?

Do you want to know what philosophy promises the human race? Good judgement. Death calls on one man, poverty sears another, a third is tormented either by another man's wealth or his own; this man shudders at bad fortune, another wants to escape his own success; men treat this man badly, and gods this other fellow.

Why do you set up these puzzles for me? This is not the place to 8 joke: you have been called to support the wretched. You promised to bring aid to the shipwrecked and to captives, to the sick and needy, to men offering their heads to the impending axe; why are you turning away? What are you doing? The man you are playing with is afraid; come to his aid, ease the punishment of those forced to answer these traps. On all sides everyone is stretching out their arms to you, begging some help for their life ruined or doomed to ruin: all their hopes and help depend on you; they are asking you to rescue them from such a great prostration and show the bright light of truth to them, scattered and straggling. Say what nature made necessary, and 9 what superfluous: what easy laws she has established, how pleasant life is and straightforward for those who follow them how bitter and complicated the life of those who trust opinion rather than nature,* if you will first explain what part of them these things are going to relieve. What removes these men's desires? What restrains them? If only desires simply failed to do good! Instead, they do harm. I will make this absolutely clear whenever you want, that your noble nature is being damaged and weakened when it is thrust into such quibbling. I am ashamed to mention the weapons these teachers are offering to 10 men about to fight against Fortune, how they are equipping them. Is this how one marches towards the highest good? Through that philosophical 'whether or unless', and counter-examples shameful and ill-reputed even for jurors seated by the panel? Philosophers,* what else is your intention when you knowingly lead into deception the man you are questioning, if not to make him seem to have failed the prescribed rules? But just as the presiding magistrate reinstates these victims, so philosophy has restored these others to their original condition. Why are you abandoning your mighty promises, and 11 why are you stooping to the basic exercises of grammarians after mighty boasts that you will ensure that the glitter of gold no more dazzles my eyes than the flash of a sword, so that I may trample with great courage on what all men desire and fear? What do you have to say?

'This is the way to the stars?'*

For this is what philosophy promises me, to make me equal to a god; this is why I was invited and what I came for: now keep your promise.

12   So, dear Lucilius, retreat as much as you can from those philosophers' counter-examples and formulae for argumentation; open and simple thoughts are what suit goodness. Even if we had much of our life left, we would need to husband it thriftily to cover necessities. As it is, what folly to learn superfluous tricks when time is in such short supply! Keep well.

Letter 49 (Book V.8) *Seneca is now in Campania, the favourite holiday resort of many elite Romans, and Lucilius' birthplace (he came from Pompeii). Remembered time seems short, but actual time is very short (§4), too short to waste on syllogistic puzzles: instead we must make the most of our life and approaching death by striving to perfect our reason.*

1   Dear Lucilius, it is an idle and careless man who is only brought back to remembering his friend when reminded by a particular place, but familiar places do at times summon back the longing stored in our hearts, and do not so much revive a memory that has been extinguished as rouse it from repose: in the same way that, even if the grief of mourners has been weakened by the lapse of time, either a slave from the deceased man's household or a garment or house renews it. Here we are in Campania, and it is unbelievable how Naples especially and the sight of your hometown Pompeii have made my longing for you fresh again: you are right there before my eyes. I am at the moment of leaving you, I see you swallowing your tears and not resisting strongly enough the emotions which burst forth even under restraint.

2   I seem to have just lost you, for what is not 'just now' when you are remembering? Just now I sat as a boy before Sotion* the philosopher, I began to plead cases just now, I stopped wanting to plead just now, I stopped being able to plead just now. The speed of time is infinite, something more obvious to those looking back. For it slips by those preoccupied with present problems: the passing of its headlong flight is

3   so gentle. You ask the reason for this? Whatever time has passed is in the same condition: it is observed in the same way and buried together: everything falls into the same abyss. And yet there cannot be long lapses

of time in a business that is altogether short. We live for only a point in
time, and so much less than a point, but nature has mocked even this
tiniest thing with the appearance of a longer period: it has made part of
this infancy, part boyhood, part youth, part a kind of sinking from
youth to old age, and a part old age itself. How many stages it has placed
in such a cramped entity! It is just now that I escorted you on your 4
departure, and yet this 'just now' is a good portion of our life, such that
we should reflect that its brevity will one day run out. Time used not to
seem so swift to me: now its pace seems unbelievable, whether this is
because I feel the deadlines being brought closer, or because I have
begun to pay attention and calculate my losses.

So I am all the more indignant that some people waste the greater 5
part of this time, which is barely enough for essentials, even if it is
scrupulously monitored, on superfluous activities. Cicero says that
even if his life was doubled, he would not have time to read the lyric
poets.* I put dialecticians in the same category: they are foolish in
a more dreary way. Lyric poets are openly playful, whereas dialecticians think they are achieving something. Not that I deny that they 6
should be looked over, but only looked over and greeted from the
threshold, for this one purpose, to ensure they do not trick us into
judging that they contain some great and secret good. Why torment
yourself and stew over an investigation which it is more clever to
scorn than to resolve? To explore petty problems is the act of a carefree man, moving on from useful things; when the enemy is at our
backs and the soldier is ordered into action necessity discards whatever idle peace had accumulated. I don't have time to chase ambigu- 7
ous phrases and test my smartness on them.

> See what peoples are gathering, what cities now
> Bar their gates and whet the steel . . . *

I need a heroic spirit to hear that din of war echoing around us.
I would seem crazy to everyone, and rightly so, if, when old men and 8
women were heaping up rocks to fortify the walls, and the young men
under arms were waiting inside the gates for the signal to make a
sortie, or even demanding it, when enemy missiles were whirring in
the gates and the ground itself was trembling with trenches and mines
beneath it, I sat there at ease posing this kind of problem: 'you have
what you have not lost; and you have not lost horns, therefore you
have horns', and other riddles fixed up on the model of this clever

9 aberration. But I may seem to you equally crazy if I waste effort on them: and I am being besieged right now. Then it would have been an external danger that threatened me under siege, and a wall would separate me from the enemy; now these deadly hazards are here with me. I don't have time for those foolish games: I have a huge problem to handle. What am I to do? Death is pursuing me and life fleeing from me. Teach me some remedy for this: bring it about that I am not fleeing death, and life is not fleeing from me. Urge me on against what is difficult and what is inescapable: ease up the constrictions of my time. Teach me that the good of life does not depend on its length, but its employment, and that it is possible, in fact very often so, that a man who has lived a long time has not lived enough. Tell me when I go to sleep: 'You may not wake up,' and when I wake up: 'You may

11 not ever sleep again.' Tell me when I go out: 'You may never return,' and when I come back: 'You may not go out again.' You are mistaken if you think that it is only on voyages that a tiny difference separates life from death: the gap between is as insubstantial in every circumstance. Death does not display itself so close at hand in every place, but it is as close in every place. Shake off these dark mists and you will find it easier to pass on what I am prepared for. Nature made us teachable, and gave us an imperfect reason, but one which could be

12 perfected. Debate with me over justice, over piety, over frugality, over both kinds of chastity, both the kind which abstains from another person's body and the kind which takes care of its own. If you don't want to lead me over trackless paths, I will reach where I am travelling more easily, for as the tragic poet says, 'the speech of truth is simple',* so it should not be complicated: for nothing is less appropriate than that tricky cleverness for minds that are attempting great tasks. Keep well.

Letter 51 (Book V.10) *Seneca's main theme is the avoidance of corrupting resorts, like Baiae, which he claims to have left after less than a day.*

1 Each man does what he can, dear Lucilius. You have Etna there, that noblest mountain in Sicily (though why Messala said it was unique, or Valgius,* for I find the statement in both, I don't understand, since many places erupt fire; not only high places—which is more common, I suppose, because fire rises to the heights—but even low-lying areas).

However, we are making the best we can of Baiae, which I left the day
after I reached it. The place is to be avoided, although it has some
natural merits, because self-indulgence has chosen it to pack with
crowds. So what are we to say? Is it right to declare hatred of any place? 2
Not at all, but just as one kind of clothing suits a wise and decent man
more than another, and yet he does not hate any colour, but thinks
some ill-suited to a man who pursues plain living, so there is a district
which a wise man or one striving for wisdom will shun, as foreign to
good behaviour. So when he thinks of retreat he will never choose 3
Canopus,* although Canopus does not forbid anyone to live plainly,
nor even Baiae, because it has come to be the haunt of vices. There
self-indulgence gives itself the greatest laxity. It is more corrupt, on
the grounds that some licence is allowed to the place. We should choose 4
a place that is healthy not only for the body but for one's morals. Just
as I would not want to live among torturers, so I would not even want
to live among cookshops. To see drunks wandering over the beach and
excursions of men boating and the lakes echoing with the songs of
glee-clubs, and other offences which self-indulgence not only commits as if exempted from the law, but broadcasts to the public—why is
that necessary? We ought to concentrate on escaping as far as possible 5
from the provocations to vice. One's mind must be hardened and
dragged far away from the enticements of pleasure.

One winter in camp there debauched Hannibal,* and the warm
comforts of Campania weakened that man unbroken by snow and the
Alps. He was victorious in battle but vanquished by vices.
We too must campaign, and in a form of campaigning in which rest 6
and leisure are never granted; above all, pleasures must be defeated
which, as you see, have taken possession even of fierce natures. If
anyone imagines how great a task he has tackled, he will realize that
nothing is to be done in a soft or easy way. What use do I have for
those hot pools? What use for sweating-chambers in which dry steam
is enclosed to drain the body? Let all sweat exude through toil. If we 7
did what Hannibal did, and broke off the pace of advance, abandoning
warfare to pay attention to comforting our bodies, no one would be
unjustified in blaming this ill-timed idleness, dangerous even for one
who had conquered, not to mention one in the process of conquest:
we must allow ourselves less than those following the Carthaginian
standards, since there is more danger if we give way and more toil
even if we persevere.

8   Fortune is waging war* with me, but I shall not do what she orders.
I will not accept the yoke, in fact I will shake it off, an action that
demands more valour. I must not let my spirit weaken. If I yield to
pleasure, I shall have to yield to pain, I shall have to yield to toil and
to poverty. Ambition and anger want the same rights over me; I shall
9   be pulled, even torn apart, between so many emotions. Liberty is the
prize. This is the reward of toil. You ask what is liberty? To be enslaved
to no object, no necessity, no chances, to reduce fortune to a level
field? The day I realize I have more power than she, she will have no
more power. Shall I suffer under her when death is in my own hands?
10   A man intent on these thoughts should choose serious and chaste
places. Too many amenities make the spirit effeminate, and without
doubt a location has some power to corrupt one's energy. Pack-
animals whose hooves are hardened on rough ground endure any kind
of route; those stuffed on a soft and marshy pasture are quickly worn
down. A stronger soldier comes from a rocky region; the city fellow or
home-bred slave is slow. Hands transferred from the plough to arms
refuse no hardship, whereas the well-perfumed and glossy fellow fails
11   in the first cloud of dust. The stricter discipline of a simpler place
strengths the mind and makes it fit for great undertakings. Scipio
passed his exile more honourably at Liternum* than at Baiae; his
downfall was not to be placed in such easy circumstances. Even the
men to whom the fortune of the Roman people first transferred the
nation's wealth, Marius and Pompey and Caesar, built their villas in
the region of Baiae, but set them on the highest ridges of the mountains. It seemed more soldierly, with the region stretching far and
wide set deep below this lofty watchtower. See the site they chose, in
what places they raised their buildings and what kind of buildings.
12   You would understand that they were not villas, but camps. Do you
think Cato would ever have lived there, to count the adulteresses
sailing past and so many crafts painted in contrasting colours and
rose petals floating all over the lake, to hear singers exchanging abuse
by night? Wouldn't he have preferred to stay inside the stockade
which he had erected in one night by his own hand? Why wouldn't
any real man prefer his sleep to be broken by the bugle rather than
a chorus?
13   But I have quarrelled with Baiae for long enough, though never
long enough with vices. And this I beg you to do, Lucilius, without
restraint or end. For they too have neither restraint nor end. Cast out

whatever desires are lacerating your heart; if they cannot be pulled out any other way then you must tear out your heart with them. In particular, uproot pleasures and treat them with absolute loathing; like the brigands whom the Egyptians call *Philetae,** they are embracing us in order to strangle us. Keep well.

Letter 53 (Book VI.1) *Seneca starts by reporting his own (rather desperate) reaction to seasickness on a short trip in a private boat from Naples (Parthenope) to Puteoli; after twice making the steersman change his course, Seneca dived out of the boat and swam to land. He is now somewhat amazed (as are we) at his own foolhardiness, but passes quickly (§§5–7) from consideration of physical sickness to ailments of the mind.*

Is there anything I can't be talked into, since I have been talked into 1 sailing? I set out in a calm sea. Admittedly the sky was heavy with discoloured clouds, which usually turn into rain or wind. But I thought the few miles from Parthenope as far as your villa could be stolen even under an uncertain and ominous sky. So to break free more quickly I steered straight across the open sea to Nesis, cutting out all the bays. When I had gone so far that it made no difference to 2 me whether I went forward or returned, the smooth sea which had misled me was first to vanish. There was no storm yet, but already the sea was heaving and suddenly the waves were more frequent. I began to ask the steersman to set me down on some beach, but he said the shores were rough and without harbour over there, and he feared nothing so much in a storm as the land. Now I was too distressed for 3 the danger to come to my aid. For that lingering type of seasickness without an end was tormenting me, stirring up the bile without expelling it. So I pressed hard on the steersman and forced him to seek the shore willy-nilly. As we came close to it I was not waiting for any of Virgil's orders to be followed—'they turn the prows towards the high sea', or 'the anchor is dropped from the prow'*—but recalling my skill as an experienced devotee of cold baths, I launched myself into the sea, wearing my beret as is proper for a cold-water bather. What 4 do you think I suffered as I crawled out over the rough shingle, while I looked for a path and found one? I realized that sailors were justified in fearing the land; it is beyond belief what I endured when I could not endure myself; just understand that it was not because the sea was angered with him that Ulysses was destined to suffer shipwreck

everywhere, but he was prone to seasickness. I too will only reach in
the twentieth year anywhere I am obliged to sail.

5   As soon as I rallied my digestion, which as you know does not
escape seasickness when it escapes the sea, and as I restored my body
with a rubdown, I began to turn over in my mind what amazing forgetfulness of our failings accompanies us, even physical failings which
instantly remind us of their presence, not to mention those which are
6 more hidden for being more serious. A slight upset escapes our notice;
but when it increases and real fever sets in, it forces submission even
on the hardened and enduring sufferer. Our feet hurt, our joints feel
stabs of pain; at this point we still pretend and say we have twisted
our ankle or felt discomfort in some exercise. We lack a name for the
uncertain first stages of the disease, but when it starts to strain the
7 heels and make both feet misshapen we must admit it is gout. It is
quite different with diseases which afflict our minds: the worse a man
is, the less he notices it. There is nothing to surprise you, dearest
Lucilius: for someone who is sleeping lightly perceives visions in his
rest and sometimes while sleeping thinks that he is asleep, but heavy
sleep ends even dreams and buries the mind far deeper, so that it has
8 no consciousness. Why does no one admit his failings? Because he is
still immersed in them: to report a dream requires a man awake, and
admitting one's failings is a mark of health. So let us rouse ourselves
up to convict our blunders. Now only Philosophy will wake us up,
it alone will shake off a heavy sleep; so dedicate yourself wholly to it.
You are worthy of her as she is of you: each of you should seek the
other's embrace. Refuse yourself to all other business, boldly and
9 openly. You do not need to practise philosophy on sufferance. If you
were sick, you would break off your preoccupation with household
affairs and forget your public business and think no one so important
that you should serve as his sponsor in your time of convalescence.
You would concentrate wholeheartedly on freeing yourself as soon as
you could from your sickness. So why don't you do the same thing
now? Dismiss all obstacles and make time for good sense; nobody
attains it while he is preoccupied. Philosophy imposes her dominion;
she grants time, rather than accepting it. She is not a subordinate
matter but the controlling activity, the mistress who is at hand and
10 giving orders. When a city promised Alexander part of its territory
and half of all its possession, he said: 'I came to Asia with the intention not of accepting what you gave me, but of letting you have what

I had left over.'* Philosophy is the same for all men: 'I am not going
to accept the time you have to spare, but you will have only what
I myself find beyond my needs.'

Direct your entire mind this way; sit at her side and pay respect to 11
her; there will be a vast space between you and the rest. You will go
ahead of all mortals in your life, and the gods will not go far ahead of
you. You ask what will lie between you and them? They will exist for
longer, but by Jove, it is the work of a great craftsman to have enclosed
everything in a tiny space. The wise man's time is as wide open to
him as all time is to the gods. And there is one thing in which the wise
man excels a god: a God is not afraid due to nature's gift, but the wise
man is not afraid by his own. This is a great achievement, to have the 12
weakness of a man but the freedom from care of a god. The power of
Philosophy to beat back all the violence of Fortune is beyond belief.
No weapon sticks fast in her body. She is fortified and stands firm;
she parries and exhausts some attacks, evading them in casual dress
like light missiles: others she shakes off and hurls back as far as the
enemy who discharged them. Keep well.

Letter 54 (Book VI.2) *On Seneca's experience of asthmatic seizures,
from which he profits by learning to anticipate death.*

It was my poor health that made my communication slow; it suddenly 1
seized hold of me. You ask: 'What kind of ill health?' You have good
reason to ask, since no kind of sickness is unknown to me. But I am
chronically enslaved by one disease, and I don't know why I should
call it by its Greek name, since it can fittingly be called 'gasping.' Its
onset is short and like a storm; it usually stops within the hour. For
who exhales for long? All the discomforts and dangers of the body 2
have passed through me, but none seems to me more distressing.
How could it be otherwise, since any other condition is sickness, but
this is like breathing one's last. That is why doctors call this 'a rehearsal
for death', for the breath finally does what it has long attempted to do.
You think I am writing this cheerfully because I have survived? I am 3
acting as foolishly, in being delighted with this outcome as if it were
good health, as the man who thinks he has won his lawsuit when he
has postponed the hearing. Yet in the actual moment of suffocation
I did not stop finding repose in happy and confident thoughts. I say 4
to myself: 'What is this? Is death testing me so often? Well, let it then.

But I have had a long experience of this.' 'When was that?' you say. Before I was born. Death is not-being. But I already know what that is like. It will be the same after me as it was before. If this entails any torment, then it must have done so previously, before we came into
5 the light of day. But we felt no trouble at that time. I ask you, wouldn't you say a man was very stupid to think a lantern was worse off when it was put out than before it was lit? We too are put out and set alight: in the time between we have some experiences, but on either side there is deep freedom from care. This is where we are mistaken, dear Lucilius, because we think death is what follows, although it both preceded and will follow us; whatever there was before us is death. What difference does it make whether you have not yet begun or you are coming to an end when the effect of each thing is not to exist?

6 With these and similar encouragements, silent of course, since there was no room for words, I never stopped addressing myself, then gradually that gasping, which had begun to be mere panting, came at greater intervals, and slowed down, and then stayed calm. Even then, although it had stopped, my breath was not flowing naturally; I could feel its hesitation and delay. Let it behave as it chooses, provided I do not gasp in my mind as well.

7 Take this assurance about me: I shall not be trembling at the final moment, I am already prepared, I am not planning a whole day at a time. As for you, praise and imitate the man who is not reluctant to die even when it gives him pleasure to live. For what is the merit in departing when you are evicted? Yet this too is a merit; I am certainly being evicted, but as if I were leaving freely. Indeed, the wise man is never evicted, since being evicted is being driven out from somewhere you leave against your will, but the wise man does nothing against his will. He escapes necessity by willing what it will otherwise compel. Keep well.

Letter 55 (Book VI.3) *Seneca uses his experience in being carried past the luxurious retirement villa of Servilius Vatia to distinguish between a retirement that is death-in-life and proper retirement applied to study and moral self-development.*

1 I have just returned from my ride: I am just as tired as if I had walked as far as I have been sitting. It is an effort to be carried for a long time, and

I rather think the effort is greater because riding is contrary to nature, which gave us feet to do our own walking and eyes to do our own seeing. Our self-indulgence has imposed weakness upon us, and now we have ceased to be capable of doing what we for so long avoided. However, I needed to shake up my body, so that if bile was choking my throat it would be shaken off, or if my breathing was thicker for some reason the jolting, which I felt had done me good, would make it lighter. So I persisted in riding a little longer, enticed by the shore itself, which curves between Cumae and the villa of Servilius Vatia and is enclosed by the sea on one side and the lake on the other, like a narrow causeway. Indeed, it was compacted by the recent weather. For as you know, frequent and fierce breakers flatten it whereas a prolonged calm relaxes it when the juice drains from the sands bound together by the moisture.

However, as is my habit I began to look around to see if I could find anything that would do me good, and I turned my eyes to the villa which once belonged to Vatia. There the rich ex-praetor, known for nothing else but his leisure, grew old and was regarded as a happy man on this account. In fact, whenever the friendship of Asinius Gallus or the hatred, then love, of Sejanus* had ruined a group of men (for it was as dangerous to have offended him as to have held him dear), men used to cry out: 'Vatia, you are the only man who knows how to live!' But he actually knew how to hide, not to live. For there is a great difference between a life of leisure and one of inertia. I never passed this villa during his lifetime without saying: 'here lies Vatia.' However, dear Lucilius, philosophy is so sacred and deserving of worship that even if something resembles it, the deception wins approval. For the common crowd thinks a man at leisure is in retreat and carefree and content with himself, living for himself, although nobody except a man of wisdom can experience any of these conditions. He is not troubled by anything, and knows how to live for himself. For he knows—which is the first requirement—how to live. In fact the man who shuns business and people, who has been exiled by the frustration of his desires, and cannot bear to see other persons more successful, who has gone to ground like a timid and feeble animal, is not living for himself but—a great disgrace—for his greed, his sleep, and his lust; a man does not immediately live for himself because he is living for no one else. However, constancy and persistence in one's intent is such a great achievement that even obstinate idleness has some authority.

6   I cannot write anything specific about the villa itself, because I only know its façade and the parts left open which it displays even to passers-by. There are two open, elaborately constructed grottoes the equal of any large entrance hall, created artificially; one of them does not admit the sunlight, but the other holds it until sunset. A stream flowing through the middle and supplied by both the sea and Lake Acheron divides the plantation of plane trees like a Euripus, abundant enough to rear fish even if it is constantly drained. But when the sea is open to the winds, the channel is protected; when the weather imposes a holiday on the fishermen, one can reach a hand out for ready supplies.

7   But the most convenient feature of the villa is that it has Baiae beyond its wall; it lacks the disadvantages of that place but enjoys its pleasures. I knew personally these assets of the villa, and I think they hold good for the whole year. In fact the villa faces the south wind and takes it in so as to deprive Baiae of the breeze. Vatia seems to have chosen this site quite shrewdly as a refuge for his lazy and elderly

8 leisure. But situation does not contribute much to a man's calm; it is the mind which makes everything commendable to itself. I have known men to be gloomy in a cheerful and pleasant villa, I have known people preoccupied by business while in complete seclusion.

So you have no reason to think yourself unsettled because you are not in Campania. And why are you not settled? Direct your thoughts

9 this far. You are free to converse with absent friends, as often as you like and for as long as you like. We enjoy this greatest of all pleasures all the more while we are apart. For being together makes us fussy, and just because we sometimes chat and walk and sit together, when we have been separated we don't think at all about the men we have

10 just seen. This is why we should accept absence cheerfully, because no one is not often apart even from those who are his companions: count first the nights apart, then the different activities of each man, then their private studies and journeys out of town; you will see that there

11 is not much for travel to steal from us. We must possess a friend in our heart, since it is never away from us: it sees every day whoever it wants. So study with me and dine with me and walk with me; we felt we were living in cramped quarters if there was anything excluded from our meditations. I can see you, Lucilius, and hear you right now. In fact I am so much with you that I wonder whether I should not begin to write notes instead of letters. Keep well.

Letter 56 (Book VI.4) *Seneca has tested his powers of concentration by taking lodging over a public bath-house, and describes its echoing cacophony.*

I'll be damned if silence is as necessary as it seems for a man with- 1
drawn for study! Here a mixed hubbub surrounds me on all sides.
I am living over a public bath. Just imagine all the varieties of cries
that can fill the ears with loathing; when the tougher fellows are
exercising and thrusting arms heavy with lead, when they are either
straining or imitating those under strain, I hear their grunts, and
whenever they let out the breath they have been holding, I hear their
whistles and bitter panting: when I come upon some feeble fellow
content with the common-or-garden massage, I hear the crack of
hands slapping the shoulders, which changes pitch as it hits them flat
or hollowed. But if the umpire of the ballgame joins in and begins to
count the balls, that is the end. Now listen to the brawler and the thief 2
caught in the act, and the man who likes the sound of his own voice in
the bath. Then add those who leap into the pool with a great splash,
as well as those whose voices, if nothing else, are loud and clear.
Imagine the depilator suddenly emitting his thin, shrill cry, calculated to make him more conspicuous, constantly uttering and never
silent except when he is plucking the underarms and forcing the other
man to cry out instead. Now I hear the different cries of the cake-
seller and the sausage-seller and pastrycook and all the hawkers from
the snack-bars selling their wares with a special distinct intonation.

You must be saying: 'You are a man of iron, or stone-deaf, if your 3
mind is firm among such assorted and clashing cries, although constant greeting drives our Chrysippus to death.' But by Jove, I no more
care about that din than about beating waves, or a waterfall, although
I have heard that this was the single reason for a certain tribe moving
their city, that they could not bear the crash of the Nile cataracts.* In 4
fact a human voice seems to distract me more than thudding, since
the former attracts the attention whereas the latter just fills and beats
on the ears. Among the noises which resound all about me without
distracting me I count passing wagons and the tenant carpenter and
the neighbouring ironworker, or the fellow who practises his trumpet
and pipes at the Sweating Fountain,* and does not sing but just shouts
out. But sound is still more of a nuisance when it is intermittent than
when it is continuous. However, I have so hardened myself by now 5

against all these disturbances that I can even hear the coxswain calling out the rhythm to oarsmen in his most disagreeable voice. In fact I am forcing my mind to focus on itself and not be distracted by outside events; let everything be echoing outside, so long as there is no disruption within me, while desire and fear are not quarrelling with each other, while greed and extravagance are not in conflict and neither is bothering the other. For what good is silence in the whole neighbourhood if your emotions are in uproar?

6   Everything was settled in the calm repose of night.*

This is false; there is no calm repose except when reason has settled it; night causes disturbance, rather than removes it, and merely changes our worries. In fact the dreams of sleepers are as troublesome as their days. The real calm is when a good state of mind unfolds.

7   Look at the man who seeks his sleep in the silence of a spacious home, when the whole crowd of slaves have fallen silent and those coming near keep on tiptoe so that no sound can trouble his ears. To be sure, he tosses this way and that trying to catch a light sleep from
8 the midst of his distress: he thinks he has heard even what he does not hear. What do you think is to blame? It is his mind that is disturbing him, that must be appeased, the conflict of his mind that must be quelled. There is no reason to think him calm just because his body is in repose. Sometimes rest itself is restless. This is why we must be roused to action and kept busy by the performance of skilled arts whenever this sloth which cannot bear itself puts us in a bad state.
9 When great generals see their troops are prone to mutiny they control them by some task and keep them busy with exercises: there is never leisure for them to riot when they are kept busy, and nothing is more sure than that the failings of leisure are dispelled by activity. Often we seem to have gone into retreat out of weariness with public affairs and distaste at our unwanted eminence, but in the hiding-place where fear and exhaustion has thrust us ambition sometimes revives. It did not fade because it was forcibly cut out, but out of mere weariness or
10 irritation at hostile circumstances. The same is true of self-indulgence, which sometimes seems to have lapsed, but then harasses men set on pursuing thrift and in their austerity seeks out pleasures which it had not really condemned but simply left behind. It does this all the more violently because it is more surreptitious. All faults are milder when they are open to view; even diseases are on their way to healing,

when they break out of hiding and expose their strength. So you might be sure that avarice and ambition and other sicknesses of the human mind are most destructive when they ebb in a pretence of health.

We seem at leisure, and we are not. For if we are genuinely at 11 leisure, if we have sounded the retreat, if we despise mere show, as I said just now, nothing will distract us, no chorus of men or birds will interrupt our thoughts when they are good and sound and resolved. It is a flighty mind which has not yet withdrawn into itself, that is 12 aroused by speech and external events. It must contain some anxiety and some element of fear to make it alert, and as Virgil puts it:

> Then although no spears alarmed me, or clustering
> Greeks in opposing ranks, each breeze and every sound
> Now terrified me, fearing on tenterhooks,
> Alike for my companion and him I bore.*

The former Aeneas is a wise man whom no whirring spears, no weap- 13 ons jostling among a massed horde, no crash of the city's collapse terrifies. This other is inexperienced, fearing for his possessions, pan- icked at every crackle, a man who hears each sound as threatening and is cast down by it, whom the lightest movements panic; it is his bur- dens that make him scared. Choose any of those lucky men who carry 14 or drag behind them many pieces of baggage, and you will see him 'fearing for his companion and him he bears . . .'. So recognize that you are settled when no shouting will affect you, no voice will shatter you, whether it wheedles or threatens, or raises meaningless din with its hollow sound.

What does this mean? Isn't it sometimes more comfortable to be 15 free of abuse? Yes, I admit it. So I shall move out of this place. I wanted to test it and put myself on trial. What need to suffer any longer, since Ulysses found such an easy cure for his comrades against even the Sirens? Keep well.

Letter 57 (Book VI.5) *Again Seneca describes an extraordinary physical ordeal, perhaps a combination of whirling sandstorm and the kind of claustrophobia engendered by tunnels. He discusses other forms of phobia and distinguishes them from ostensibly reasonable fears, none of which are really justified.*

1 When I was obliged to return from Baiae to Naples I was easily persuaded that there was bad weather to save me from suffering another
sea-voyage, but there was so much mud on the whole route that I may
seem to have made a voyage all the same. I had to endure the whole fate
of athletes* that day: after a coating of mud, a load of sand over-
2 whelmed me in the Neapolitan tunnel. There can be nothing more
prolonged than that prison, nothing darker than the jaws of that
entrance which put us in a state not of seeing through the darkness but
of seeing darkness itself. Anyway, even if the place had some light the
dust would swallow it, dust which is heavy and distressing even in the
open: what do you think it was like there, where it rolls upon itself, and
being confined for lack of breathing-holes, falls back down on those
who stirred it up? We endured two conflicting inconveniences at the
same time: on the same road and same day we toiled through mud and
3 dust. Still, that darkness gave me some food for thought; I felt a kind
of blow to the mind and transformation without fear, caused by the
novelty and vileness of this unfamiliar circumstance. I am not talking
about myself, now, given that I am far from an acceptable, let alone a
perfect, man, but of the man over whom fortune has lost her dominion, for his mind too will be stricken and his colour change.

4   There are some things, dear Lucilius, which no courage can escape;
nature reminds it of mortality, and so the brave man will wince at
grim experiences and shudder at sudden events and be blind with
dizziness if he looks down on an immense depth when standing on its
brink; this is not cowardice but a natural reaction which cannot be
5 overcome by reason. So some brave men, fully ready to shed their
own, cannot look on another man's blood. Some people collapse and
faint at the handling and sight of a fresh wound, others at an old and
suppurating wound. Others find it easier to suffer a sword wound
6 than see it. So as I was saying, I felt not a mental shock but a transformation. At the first sight of the returning light my cheerfulness came
back spontaneously without bidding; then I began to tell myself how
foolishly we feared some things more or less than others, although
they all had the same outcome. For what difference does it make
whether a watchtower or a mountain falls on someone? You will find
no difference. But there will be men who fear the latter more, although
each is equally fatal; but fear is so focused not on effects but on their
7 causes. Now you must think I am talking about the Stoics, who believe
the spirit of someone shattered by a great weight cannot survive but

is immediately dissipated, because it has not had a free path of escape. But that is not what I am doing. Those who claim this seem to me to be badly mistaken. Just as a flame cannot be extinguished because it 8 escapes around the substance which weighs upon it; as air is not harmed or even split by a blow or impact, but pours back around the object to which it gave way; so the mind, composed of the finest particles, cannot be caught or struck within the body, but thanks to its fineness breaks through the substances that press down on it. Just as lightning finds a path of return through a tiny hole when it has struck and blazed far and wide, so the mind, even more insubstantial than fire, has room to escape through every part of the body. So we should investigate whether it can be immortal. Be sure of this at least, that if 9 it survives the body it cannot be crushed by any kind of experience, since no immortality is subject to exception and nothing is harmful to what is everlasting. Keep well.

Letter 59 (Book VI.7) *Like some later letters (63 and 67), this starts from a conventional phrase—'it was a great pleasure to read your letter'— and uses it to discriminate between the popular use of pleasure (*voluptas*) and Stoic values, which regard pleasure as a harmful emotion but value instead joy (*gaudium*) as a genuine response to real moral success. As for Lucilius' letter, Seneca speaks only of its forceful style, giving no idea of its content. (We may compare his treatment of Lucilius' book in letter 46.) This is profoundly frustrating for us as readers if Seneca is referring to actual compositions by Lucilius, but if this is merely a fiction to give the correspondence authenticity, it keeps the focus on the nature of writing itself as a philosophical or ethical exercise.*

The main body of the letter moves from Lucilius' use of didactic analogies to a military analogy used by Sextius, and compares the stupidity of an ill-led force to the folly of the individual who confuses the false pleasure of external and contingent success with the lasting joy that comes only from the achievement of virtue and wisdom.

It was a great pleasure for me to read your letter: allow me to use a 1 social phrase without holding the words to their Stoic interpretation. We believe pleasure is a moral failing: so be it, but we regularly use the word to mark a happy state of mind. I know, as I said, that, if we 2 measure the words against our own code, pleasure is a shameful thing and joy does not come to any one except the wise man, since it is the

exaltation of spirit of a man confident in his own true merits. But this
is how we usually talk, saying we felt great joy at this man's consulate
or marriage or his wife's safe delivery, things which often prove not
joys but the beginnings of sadness to come, for it is inherent in joy
3 that it does not end or turn into its own opposite. So when our beloved
Virgil says, 'And the evil joys of the mind',* he is speaking eloquently
but incorrectly, for no joy can be evil. Virgil applied this name to
pleasures and conveyed what he meant, that men felt delight to their
4 own cost. Still, I did not say I felt great pleasure at your letter without
good reason. For although an uneducated man may have an honourable reason to feel joy, I still call his emotion pleasure, if it is uncontrolled and likely to turn immediately into its opposite, being provoked
by belief in a false good, and so unrestrained and excessive.

   To return to my point, hear what delighted me in your letter: you
keep words under your control, your speech does not carry you away
5 or take you beyond your purpose. Many writers are enticed by the
charm of some appealing phrase into writing something they did not
have in mind, but this has not happened to you; everything is concise
and matched to the topic; you say what you mean and imply more
than you say. This is the mark of a greater merit: it is clear that your
6 mind also has no excess, nothing bloated. However, I find your meta-
phorical language, while not rash, still stretching its limits. I find
extended similes—and if anyone bans us from using them and judges
they are only allowed to poets, it seems to me he has not read any of
the classical authors, whose work is not yet affected by the pursuit of
applause. They spoke plainly so as to make their matter clear, and are
full of comparisons,* which I think necessary, not for the same reason
as in poets, but as props for our weakness, so as to bring both speaker
7 and listener into the immediate context. Right now I am giving special attention to reading Sextius,* a keen and spirited man who practises philosophy in the Greek language but with Roman values. I was
moved by a simile he applied: that an army marches in four-square
formation ready for battle when the enemy could be expected from
any direction; 'this', he says, 'is what the wise man should do. He
should spread out his talents on all sides so that wherever some
hostile action occurs his defences are ready there and can react to the
nod of their commander, without panic.' We see this practised in
armies organized by great commanders, so that all their forces receive
the leader's command at the same time, being so deployed that the

signal given by one man runs at the same time through the infantry
and cavalry, and this, he says, is much more necessary for us individuals. For those armies were often afraid of the enemy without reason, 8
and their safest route was actually the one they had treated with most
suspicion. Stupidity has no capacity for calm: fear is as much above it
as beneath it. It is frightened on both sides, as dangers both come up
behind it and confront it. It is afraid of everything, unready and terrified by its own allies. But the wise man is fortified and alert against
every assault: he will not retreat if poverty or mourning or shame or
distress mounts an attack. He will march against these hazards and 9
amongst them without fear. As for us, many things bind and weaken
us. We have been wallowing for a long time in these vices. It is difficult
to be cleansed, since we are not just stained but soaked in them.

Not to shift from one likeness to another, I shall ask you something
I often turn over in my thoughts: why does stupidity have so firm a
hold over us? First, because we do not fend it off vigorously nor strive
for recovery with our full strength; secondly because we do not trust
the discoveries of wise men enough nor take them in with open hearts,
only take a light stand on such a great matter. How can anyone learn 10
how much effort is needed against vices when he only learns as much
as he is free from them? None of us goes very deep. We have only
sampled the surface, and it was enough for us, busy as we were, to
spend a small amount of time on philosophy.

The chief obstacle is that we are quick to be satisfied with 11
ourselves. If we find someone to call us good men, cautious and principled, we acknowledge him. We are not content with a moderate
eulogy, but accept as our due whatever flattery has shamelessly heaped
upon us. We agree with those who call us best and wisest, although
we know they often utter many falsehoods; we indulge ourselves so
greatly that we want to be praised for a virtue which is the opposite of
our behaviour. A man hears himself called 'most merciful' while he is
inflicting torture, 'most generous' when he is plundering, and 'most
abstinent' in the midst of drunkenness and lust. So it follows that
we don't want to change because we believe we are already excellent.
When Alexander's expedition was going astray in India and laying 12
waste to tribes not even sufficiently known to their neighbours, as he
marched round the walls during the siege of a city looking for the
weak spots in the fortifications he was shot by an arrow, but persisted
in the siege and in completing his plans. Then, when the pain of his

dry wound intensified as the blood was compressed, when his leg had gradually grown numb and was hanging from his horse, he was forced to give up and said: 'They all swear that I am the son of Zeus, but this wound cries out that I am a mortal man.'* Let us behave like this.

13   Flattery makes each man foolish in proportion to its scale. Let us say: 'You call me wise, but I see how many harmful things I desire, how I long for things that will hurt me. I do not even realize what satiety shows animals, what should be the limit of food and drink: I still don't know how much I can handle.'

14   Now I will explain how you can recognize that you are not wise. The wise man is full of joy, cheerful and calm, undisturbed. He lives on equal terms with the gods. Now examine yourself: if you are never sad, if no hope disturbs your mind with anticipation of the future, if by day and night the condition of your spirit is even and unvarying, alert and happy with itself, then you have reached the high point of human good. But if you constantly desire all kinds of pleasures, know that you are as far short of wisdom as of joy. You want to reach this state, but you are misleading yourself in thinking that you will get there surrounded by wealth or honours; that is, you are looking for joy in the midst of anxieties: the very things you seek as if they would give you happiness and pleasure are the causes of your distress.

15   I mean that all men aim for joy in that way, but they don't know the source of stable and lasting success. One man seeks it from parties and self-indulgence, another from ambition and a sprawling crowd of clients, another from his girlfriend, another from the hollow display of culture and from writing that gives him no healing; all those men are deceived by false and short-lived distractions, like drunkenness which pays for the cheerful craziness of a single hour with the discomfort of a long period, or applause and the favour of a supporting crowd, favour won by great anxiety which will have to be atoned for

16   by as much. So think that this is the outcome of wisdom, to achieve evenness in joy. The wise man's mind is like the universe beyond the moon: there it is always fine and calm. So you have another motive to want to be wise, if the wise man is never without joy. Such joy only arises from awareness of one's virtues; no one can rejoice except the brave, just, and temperate man.

17   'What follows? That stupid and wicked men can't feel joy?' No more than lions who have caught their prey. When men have worn themselves out with wine and sexual indulgences, when the night has

run out amongst their vices, when their pleasures, poured into a cramped body beyond its capacity, have begun to rot, then the unhappy creatures cry out that Virgilian line:

> You know how we spent that last night in false joys.*

Self-indulgent men spend every night in false joys as if it were their 18 last, whereas the joy that attaches itself to gods, and to men who use gods as their models, is uninterrupted and does not come to an end. If it had been derived from outside sources, it would come to an end. But because it is not the gift of external circumstances, it is not under external control: what Fortune has not given she cannot snatch away. Keep well.

Letters 60–2 (Book VI.8–10) *The next three letters (60–2) seem to be an experiment in the power of brevity, making up for their shortness by their vivid and compelling language. While letter 60 continues the theme of 59, denounces the external assets desired by ordinary people (and seen as wishes made for the newborn: cf. Persius,* Satire *2 and Juvenal's great Satire 10, 'The Vanity of Human Wishes'), 61 insists on neglecting external concerns so as to be ready for death: its keynote is fitting oneself to circumstance by willingness (key words are* libenter, *'willingly, gladly', and* invitus, *'against one's will'). In letter 62 Seneca returns to an earlier theme, presenting social commitments as a pretence or nuisance which the philosopher will avoid either by directing his attention elsewhere, to philosophical writers, or by spending his time in the company of a man like the Cynic Demetrius, advocate of plain living.*

60 I am complaining, lodging a grievance, I am angry with you. Will 1 you still persist in wishing for what your nurse or attendant or mother wished for you? Don't you yet understand how much evil they were wishing for? How harmful to us are the wishes of our dear ones. And all the more harmful as they meet more success. Now I am not surprised if every kind of misfortune follows us from our earliest childhood, since we have grown up among the curses of our parents. Let the gods finally hear and grant our own free utterance on our own behalf. How long shall we go on demanding things from the gods—as 2 if we cannot yet support ourselves? How long shall we fill territories large enough for great cities with bulk crops? How long will the nations reap for us? How long will many cargo ships, and not even coming from a single sea, import the furnishings of a single table? A bull is satisfied with the pasture of a very few acres; one forest is enough for a number of elephants; but man pastures on land and sea.

3 What are we to say? Did nature give us such an insatiable belly when it gave us such modestly sized bodies, that we should outdo the greed of the most enormous and gluttonous of animals? Not at all. How small a fraction is actually granted to nature! She is satisfied with a little. It is not the hunger of our stomach that costs so much, but our pretentions. So let us count these 'slaves of gluttony',* as Sallust calls them, among animals, not men, and some of them not even among animals but among corpses. A man is living when he is useful to many; a man lives who puts himself to good use. But those who lie around in a sluggish daze live in their home as if it were a burial chamber. You might as well inscribe their name as epitaph on the marble of their doorway, since they have anticipated their own death. Keep well.

1 **61** Let us stop wanting what we used to want. I at least make it my purpose not to wish for the same things as an old man which I wished for as a boy. My days are spent on this one goal, as are my nights: this is my task and my meditation, to put an end to the old evils. I am aiming to make a day the equivalent of my whole life, nor am I snatching it as

2 if it were my last, but I look on it as if it could be my last. This is the spirit in which I am writing you this letter, as if death might summon me in this very moment as I write: I am ready to go, and so I am enjoying my life because I do not pay attention to how long it will last. Before my old age I took care to live well: in old age, to die well, for to die well

3 is to die willingly. Take pains never to do anything against your will; whatever is compulsory for the man who resists is not compulsory for him if he is willing. This is what I mean. The man who willingly obeys commands has escaped the most bitter part of slavery, that is, acting against his will. A person is not wretched for acting on orders, but if he is acting against his will. Then let us order our minds so that we wish for whatever circumstances demand, and especially let us think about

4 our end without sadness. We need to be prepared for death before we are prepared for life. Life is quite well enough equipped, but we are greedy for its trappings; there always seems to us to be something lacking, and will always seem so. It is not years and days that make sure we have lived enough, but our state of mind. I have lived enough, dear Lucilius: I am sated, and wait for death. Keep well.

62 Men are lying when they want it to seem that a mass of business is keeping them from liberal pursuits. They invent commitments and exaggerate them and create their own business. I am at leisure, Lucilius, yes, at leisure, and wherever I am, there I am my own man. I don't surrender myself to business but lend myself, and I don't hunt for excuses to waste time. Wherever I pause, there I review my concerns and mull over something beneficial in my mind. When I have given myself to my friends I do not withdraw from my own concerns or linger with men whom some chance has gathered me to, or some case arising from civic duty, but I spend time with the best men of history. I direct my mind to them in whatever place or whatever age they lived. I carry Demetrius, the best of men,* around with me and abandon those in purple-dyed robes to talk with him in his plain dress and give him my admiration. Why shouldn't I admire him? I have seen that he does not feel the lack of anything. A man can despise all things, but no man can possess all things: the shortest road to riches is through contempt of riches. Now our Demetrius lives, not as if he has come to despise all possessions, but as if he had passed them on for others to possess! Keep well.

Letter 63 (Book VII.1) *Seneca uses the death of an otherwise unknown friend of Lucilius to offer a philosophical version of a consolatory letter. Several of the arguments also appear in his dialogues consoling Marcia for the death of her son and Polybius for his brother's death. We can also compare the famous letter of Servius Sulpicius to Cicero on the death of his daughter Tullia (Cicero,* Letters to His Friends, *4.5).*

I am very sorry that your friend Flaccus has passed away, but I don't want you to grieve more than is appropriate. I hardly dare make a further demand, that you don't grieve at all: and yet I know that is better. But who will enjoy this firmness of mind unless he is already far advanced beyond the reach of Fortune? And this event will pluck at even his heartstrings, but only pluck at them. As for us, we can be forgiven if we sink into tears, provided they have not flowed to excess, if we ourselves have checked them. When we have lost a friend our eyes should not stay dry, nor should they stream with tears: we should weep but not sob. It seems as though I am laying down a harsh law for you, given that the greatest of Greek poets granted the right to weep for a day, when he said that 'even Niobe thought of taking food'.*

Do you want to know the source of lamentation and excessive weeping? We are using tears to show proof of our loss; we are not obeying our grief but displaying it. No one is sad for himself alone. What
3 fruitless stupidity! But there is a kind of striving even for grief. You say: 'So what am I to do? Forget my friend?' It is a short-lived memory you are promising if it is to last only as long as your grief; soon any random thing will turn your frown into laughter. I am not looking ahead to the longer period when all bereavement is soothed, when even the sharpest mourning abates; as soon as you stop watching yourself that semblance of sadness will depart. As it is, you are mounting guard over your grief, but it will slip away even from your guard,
4 and it ends all the faster for being more acute. Let us aim for our memory of lost friends to be pleasant. No one returns gladly to something he will not reflect on without agony, just as it is inevitable that the name of those we loved and lost will come to us with some pain,
5 but even this pain has its peculiar pleasure. For, as our friend Attalus used to say, 'the memory of deceased friends is pleasant in the way some apples are sweet in their sourness, or as even the bitterness of a wine grown too old pleases us, but when some time has lapsed
6 everything that hurt us fades and we receive pure pleasure'. If we believe him, 'to think of friends unharmed is to enjoy honey and cake, but the contemplation of those who have passed away does not please us without some bitterness. For who disputes that these sharp
7 foods containing some astringency stimulate the appetite?' I don't agree: thinking about dead friends is sweet and appealing to me, for I enjoyed them expecting to lose them, and I have lost them as if I still had them.

So, dear Lucilius, act as fits your good judgement and stop putting a bad interpretation on the kindness of Fortune;* she took him away,
8 but it was she who gave him. Let us be eager to enjoy our friends, since it is uncertain how long we can enjoy this good fortune. Let us think how often we will leave them when we set out on a long journey and how often we will not see them even when we are staying in the same place; we will realize that we lost more time during their life.
9 Would you tolerate men who treated their friends most indifferently but mourned them pitifully, and do not love anyone unless they have lost them? In fact they grieve more profusely then because they are afraid of leaving it in doubt whether they loved them: they are looking
10 too late for marks of their emotion. If we have other friends we are

treating them and valuing them poorly, since they are too weak to give solace for the one man's burial. If we don't have others then we have done ourselves a greater wrong than we suffered from Fortune. She took away one friend, but we have not made ourselves any others. Then consider that a man who could not love more than one friend 11 didn't even love that one too much. If someone who has been robbed prefers to lament over one lost tunic rather than looking round to see how to escape the cold and find something to cover his shoulders, don't you think he is very stupid? You buried the man you loved: find another to love. It is better to replace a friend than weep over him. I know that what I am going to add here is hackneyed, but I won't pass 12 it by just because everyone says it; even the man who did not put an end to his mourning by his own decision came to an end with the lapse of time. But weariness with mourning is the most shameful cure for a man of sense: I would rather you abandoned your grief than were abandoned by it, so put an end as soon as possible to doing something which you cannot continue for long even if you want. Our 13 ancestors gave women a year to mourn, not so that they would mourn so long, but so that they would not mourn any longer:* there is no time appointed for men by law because no time is honourable. But out of those poor women barely dragged away from the pyre, scarcely pulled from the corpse, can you name to me a single one whose tears lasted a whole month? Nothing becomes loathsome more quickly than grief; when it is fresh it finds a comforter and attracts some company, but when it persists it is treated as absurd, and rightly so, for it is either an affectation or a stupidity.

So I write this to you, I who wept so excessively for my very dear 14 Annaeus Serenus,* that—a thing I would wish least of all—I count among those whom grief overwhelmed. But now I condemn my own behaviour and realize that my greatest reason for mourning so intensely was that I never realized he could die before me. This one thought came to me that he was younger and much younger, as if the Fates respected order! So let us think constantly as much of our 15 mortality as of all those we love. I should have said then: 'My Serenus is younger; but what difference does that make? He ought to die after me, but he could die before me.' Because I failed to do this Fortune suddenly struck me unprepared. Now I think that all things are mortal and mortal on indefinite terms; anything that can ever happen can happen today. So, dearest Lucilius, let us think that we 16 will soon reach the place where we are now grieving that he came, and perhaps, if only the belief of wise men is true and there is some place to welcome us all, the man who we think is lost to us has merely been sent ahead. Keep well.

Letter 64 (Book VII.2) *Seneca starts from his devotion to his absent friend, whom he has remembered in friendly company. He recalls their dinner-time choice of reading—the wise words of Quintus Sextius (founder of the Roman philosophical school in which Seneca studied as a young man), and the power of this teaching to inspire moral action (§§1–6). This leads him to assert the possibility of both reverencing past teachers and carrying their investigations further; there is work left for even modern devotees of philosophy, and a duty of gratitude to the moral philosophers of old for the teachings he has welcomed into his mind.*

1 You were with us yesterday. You can rightly complain if this was only true yesterday; that is why I added 'with *us*', for you are always with me. Some friends came by to justify a greater steam and smoke of cooking: not the sort of smoke which escapes from smart men's kitchens and often terrifies the watchmen, but the modest smoke which

2 shows that guests have come. We had talked of many different things, as men do at a party, taking no topic to its conclusion but hopping from one thing to another. Then we had a reading from the book of the elder Q. Sextius, a great man, if you believe me, and a Stoic, though

3 he may deny it. What energy he has, great gods, and what spirit! You won't find this in all philosophers; the writings of some with illustrious names are bloodless. They instruct, argue, and quibble, but they don't arouse the spirit because they don't have any. When you have read Sextius you will say: 'He is alive and active, he is free, he is more

4 than a man, he sends me away full of great confidence.' I will admit to you the state of mind I am in when I read him: I want to challenge all chances, I want to cry out: 'Fortune, why are you holding back? Attack me: you will find me ready.' I put on the spirit of a man waiting for an occasion to test himself and display his manliness.

> He longs to glimpse a foaming boar among the passive cattle,
> or for some tawny lion to come down from the hills.*

5 I want to have something to overcome, to train by enduring it. This is another admirable quality of Sextius. He will show you the greatness of a blessed life and yet not create despair of achieving it: you will

know it is elevated but within reach of the man with a will. Virtue 6
itself will supply this to you, to marvel at it and yet still hope for it. At
least for me, the actual contemplation of wisdom usually takes a good
deal of my time: I gaze at it overwhelmed in the same way as I do the
universe itself, which I often see like a new observer. So I revere the 7
discoveries of wisdom and its discoverers, I delight in approaching it
as my inheritance from many men. It is for me that these things have
been sought out, for me they have been worked upon. But let us play
the good householder and increase what we received; let that inheritance pass on from me in increased form to posterity. There is still a
lot of work to do, and there will be, and no man born after a thousand
generations will be denied the opportunity of adding something else.
But even if everything has been discovered by the men of old, what 8
will always be new will be the use and knowledge and application of
what has been discovered by others. Imagine that we were left pre-
scriptions of remedies for healing the eyes; I don't need to look for
new ones, but these still need to be adjusted for diseases and circumstances. Soreness of the eyes is relieved by one ointment, swollen eye-
lids are eased by another, sudden pressure and seeping are avoided by
this other treatment, the sight is made keener by that one; you should
grind these ingredients and choose the right time and apply a proper
dose to each problem. The men of old invented cures for the mind; it
is our task to find out how they should be applied or when. Our pre- 9
decessors have achieved a lot, but they have not completed the investigation. Still they should be revered and worshipped like gods.
Surely I should keep likenesses of great men as stimuli to my spirit
and celebrate their birthdays. Surely I should constantly address and
honour them? The same reverence which I owe to my teachers is due
to those teachers of the human race, the source from which such a
great blessing has flowed. If I see a man with the office of consul or 10
praetor I do everything which regularly makes an office appear an
honour: I shall dismount from my horse, uncover my head, or step
back from his path. Well then, shall I welcome both Catos and Laelius
the Wise and Socrates, with Plato and Zeno and Cleanthes, into my
heart without the highest recognition?* I truly revere them, and
always rise up to salute such great names. Keep well.

Letter 65 (Book VII.3) *A sample of Seneca's more technical letters,
here concerned with epistemology and the evolving teachings of the Greeks
on types of cause. But Seneca's explicit consultation of Lucilius as arbiter*

of the problem is only a pretext; he clearly has formed and now states his
own judgement on the issue, which is to prefer the simple and single causal-
ity of the Stoics (§4) to the ever-multiplying system he attributes to Plato
and Aristotle. And the discussion of 'causes' in terms of the statue and its
craftsman-creator is only a means to the larger discussion of the relation-
ship between God and the world he has created, treated as explanation of
the human spirit cramped in life, but at liberty in death. See B. Inwood,
Seneca's Philosophical Letters (Oxford: Oxford UP, 2007) [henceforth
'Inwood (2007)'], 136–8 and 138–55.

1   I shared the day yesterday with my ill-health; it claimed the morning
for itself but left the afternoon for me. So first I tested my spirit
with reading, then when it accepted this I dared to demand more
from it, or rather entrust more to it. I tried writing something, and
even wrote with more concentration than usual, since I have been
struggling with difficult material and am not willing to be defeated,
until friends came to apply force to me and control me like an undis-
2   ciplined invalid. Talk took the place of writing, and I shall bring to
you the part of it in dispute. I have committed you to be arbiter. You
have more business than you think, for the case is threefold.

   Our fellow Stoics say, as you know, that there are two things in
the universe from which all things are made, its cause and its matter.
Matter lies inert, a substance ready for everything, and will stay in
repose if no one moves it: but the cause, that is, reason, shapes the
matter and turns it wherever it wishes, making a variety of things
from it. So there ought to be a stuff *from* which something is made,
then something *by* which it is made: the latter is the cause, the former
3   the matter. Every art is an imitation of nature, so apply what I just
said about the universe to these activities undertaken by man.*
A statue has both material which experienced a craftsman and a
craftsman to give shape to the material. So in a statue the material
is bronze, and the cause is the craftsman. This is the condition of
all things: they consist of the thing which is made and the maker.

4   The Stoics believe there is a single cause: the maker. Aristotle
thinks the cause can be expressed in three ways: the first cause is the
material, without which nothing can be made; the second is the craftsman; and the third is the form which is imposed on every piece of
work like a statue. For this is what Aristotle calls *eidos*. There is also a
fourth cause added to these, he says, which is the motivation of the

whole work.* I will reveal what this is. Bronze is the first cause of 5
the statue, for it would never have been made if there had not been
the ore from which it is poured and shaped. The second cause is the
craftsman, since the bronze could not have been formed in that shape
if skilled hands had not touched it. The third cause is the shape, for
the statue would not be called *The Spearbearer* or *The Boy Dressing*
if this appearance had not been stamped upon it. The fourth cause is
the purpose of making it, for if this had not existed it would not have
been made. What is the purpose? What provoked the craftsman, what 6
he aimed at in making it. Either money if he made it for sale, or religion if he prepared it as a gift for a temple. So this is the cause on
account of which it is made—or don't you think we should count
among the causes of a piece of work something without which it
would not have been made?

     To these Plato adds a fifth cause—the model, which he calls *idea*:* 7
this is what the craftsman referred to when he made what he intended.
It is not relevant whether he had this model externally to direct his eyes
towards or internally, something which he himself conceived and
imagined. God contains these models of all things in himself and has
encompassed in his mind the quantities and measures of everything to
be accomplished. He is full of these forms which Plato calls *ideas*,
immortal, immutable, inexhaustible. So men do indeed die, but humanity, on which model man is moulded, endures, and while men suffer
and perish, it suffers nothing. Thus there are five causes, as Plato says: 8
the cause *from* which, the cause *by* which, the cause *in* which, the cause
for which, and the cause *on account of* which, and finally the thing which
is made of them all. So in a statue, since we began by talking about this,
the cause *from which* is bronze, the cause *by which* is the craftsman, the
cause *in which* is the form fitted to it, the cause *for which* is the model
which the maker imitates, the cause *on account of which* is the maker's
motive, and the cause which comes from all these is the statue itself.
The universe too has all of these, as Plato says: a maker—this is God; 9
a raw material—this is matter; a form—this is the appearance and
order of the world which we see; a model, according to which God created the immense size of this most beautiful work, and a motive for
which he made it. You ask, what is God's motive? Goodness. So at least 10
Plato says. 'What was the cause for God making the universe? He is
good, and to the good person no good of any man is a source of envy, so
he made it as perfect as he could.'

Now as arbiter cast your vote and declare who seems to you to say the most likely thing, not who says the truest thing—for that is as far
11 above us as truth itself. This host of causes* hypothesized by Aristotle and Plato includes either too many causes or too few. For if men judge something to be the cause of making an object because it cannot be made if that other thing is taken away, they have said nothing worthwhile. Let them include Time among the causes, for nothing can be made without time. Let them include Place; if there was no space for something to come into being it will not even happen. Let them include Motion, for nothing is made or destroyed without it. There is
12 no art, no change, without motion. But just now we are looking for a first and general cause. This should be simple, for matter too is simple. We ask what is a cause? Reason that makes things, that is, God, for all those things you have listed are not many separate causes but depend
13 on one cause, the one that makes. You say form is a cause? It is the craftsman who imposes this on the work: it is part of the cause, not the cause. The model too is not a cause, but a necessary means of the cause. The model is necessary to the craftsman like his chisel and file. His art cannot advance without them, and yet these are not parts or
14 causes of his art. 'The motive of the craftsman,' he says, 'on account of which he embarks on making something, is a cause.' If it is a cause, it is not an efficient cause but a contingent cause. These are countless, but we are looking for the general cause. They have actually said that the whole universe and its perfected form are a cause; but this lacks their usual subtlety, since there is a great difference between the work and its cause.
15   Either cast your vote or, as is easier in this kind of issue, declare the case is not clear and order us to return to the case. You are saying: 'Why does it delight you to waste time in these quibbles, which do not remove any emotion or drive off any desire?' In fact I am pursuing and debating means to calm the mind, and I am examining first myself, then this universe. But I am not even wasting time now, as you
16 think: for all those considerations, if they are not chopped up small and shredded into this useless subtlety, raise and relieve the mind, weighed down as it is with a heavy load and longing to extricate itself and return to its own business. For this body is a burden and punishment of the mind: it is under the body's weight that the mind is bound and oppressed, unless philosophy approaches and orders it to find rest in the contemplation of the world and releases it from earthly

business to that of the gods. This is its freedom, its holiday, at times it escapes from its guard and is refreshed by the open heaven. As 17 craftsmen working on some delicate thing which wearies the eyes with focusing, if their light is inadequate and unpredictable, come out in the open and delight their eyes with the free light in an area dedicated to the people's leisure, so our mind, shut in this sad, dark dwelling, seeks the open as often as it can and rests in the contemplation of the world.

The wise man and the student of wisdom certainly stays in his own 18 body, but is absent in his best part and directs his thoughts to the world on high. Like a man bound by oath,* he thinks this life he lives is his military service, and he is so shaped that he feels neither love nor loathing of life, and he suffers mortal burdens although he knows more lofty things await him. Are you forbidding me to scrutinize 19 the universe, leading me away from the whole and reducing me to study a part of it? Am I not to ask such questions as: 'What are the beginnings of the universe?' 'Who is the creator of things?' 'Who has separated out everything blended into one and wrapped up in inert matter?' Am I not to investigate who is the craftsman of that world? How such a vast entity came under order and control? Who gathered together scattered parts and marked off all those confused into one and allotted an appearance to things lying in one shapeless mass? What is the source of so great a light? Is it a fire or something more brilliant than fire? Am I not to ask those questions? Must I remain 20 ignorant of my origin? Am I to see these things only once or be born many times? Where am I to go from here? What resting-place awaits my soul, freed from the laws of human slavery? Are you forbidding me any share in heaven, that is, ordering me to live with my head lowered? I am greater than that and born for greater things than to 21 be a captive of my body, which I do not see as anything but a chain set around my liberty: so this body is what I oppose in resistance to Fortune, and do not allow any wound to pass through it to me. Whatever part of me can suffer harm is limited to this, that my free spirit lives in this vulnerable dwelling. That flesh will never force me 22 to suffer fear or adopt a pretence unworthy of a good man; I shall never lie for the sake of this body. When it seems right I shall break off association with it; and even now, while we are held together, we will not be partners on equal terms; my mind claims all rights for itself. Contempt for one's body is the surest liberty.

23   To return to my argument, that scrutiny which we were just talking about will also contribute much to this liberty; for universals consist of matter and of God. God controls those elements surrounding us which follow their guide and God. For what he does is more powerful and precious, because he is God, than the matter which undergoes

24   God. The place which God occupies in this universe is the place which mind occupies in man; what matter is within it, the body is in us. So let inferior things obey superior beings; let us be brave against the acts of Fortune; let us not tremble at harm or wounds or imprisonment or poverty. What is death? Either an end or a passing on. I am not afraid of coming to an end (for this is just the same as not beginning) or of passing on, because I shall not be so cramped in any other place. Keep well.

Letter 67 (Book VII.5) *This letter starts from the commonplace of the changing seasons, to present Seneca keeping to his books and enjoying Lucilius' letters as if they were in conversation. He repeats Lucilius' question, 'whether every kind of good is to be desired', and applies it to the good that comes from the wise man's endurance of pain.*

1   To start from commonplaces, spring is beginning to open up, but now it is tending towards summer, when it ought to be hot, it has merely grown warm and cannot be trusted; for it frequently slips back into winter. Do you want to know how untrustworthy it still is? I don't risk using really cold water, but still dilute its severity. You will say: 'That is to endure neither hot water nor cold.' Yes indeed, dear Lucilius; my age is already content with its own chill; it is scarcely thawed in high summer. So the greater part of my time is spent fully clothed.

2   I am grateful to old age for keeping me to my couch; why shouldn't I thank it on this account? Whatever I ought to refuse to do, I cannot do. Most of my conversation is with my books. If ever your letters arrive I feel that I am with you and have the emotions not of writing back to you but talking to you. So we shall examine your question and what it means as if I am talking with you.

3   You ask whether every good thing is to be desired. You say: 'If it is good to be brave under torture and to be noble when suffering surgery and patient when sick, it follows that those experiences are to be desired; and yet I see none of them as worth praying for. At least so far I don't know that any man paid for the granting of a vow because

he was lashed or twisted with gout or stretched out on the Horse.'
But consider them separately, dear Lucilius, and you will realize they 4
contain something to be desired. I would prefer tortures to be far
from me; but if they are to be endured, I shall desire to behave bravely,
honourably, and with spirit in undergoing them. Why wouldn't I
prefer there to be no war? But if it happens, I shall desire to bear
nobly wounds, starvation, and all the hazards brought by the necessity of war. I am not so mad as to want to be sick, but if I have to be
sick I shall make it my desire to do nothing undisciplined or womanish. So it is not the discomforts that are to be desired, but the virtue
with which these discomforts are endured.

Some of our fellow Stoics think that a brave endurance of all those 5
things is not to be desired, but not to be rejected either, since in prayer
we should seek a pure good, serene and set aside from trouble. I don't
agree. Why? First, because it is impossible for a thing to be good but
not to be desired; then if virtue is to be desired, there is no good without virtue and every good is to be desired; then even if <it causes
physical suffering>* the brave endurance of tortures is to be desired.
So now I ask again: is bravery then to be desired? But surely it despises 6
and challenges dangers; the noblest and most wonderful part of it is
not giving way to fires, confronting wounds, at times not even avoiding missiles but welcoming them into one's breast. If bravery is to be
desired then enduring tortures is to be desired; for this is a part of
bravery. But consider the elements apart, as I said, and there will be
nothing to lead you into error. For it is not suffering torture that is to
be desired, but suffering it bravely: I feel desire for that 'braveness'
which is a virtue. But who ever desired this for himself? Some vows 7
are open and explicit when they are made in detail; some remain
obscure, when many things are included in one vow. For example,
I desire an honourable life for myself; and an honourable life is
composed of various actions: it includes Regulus' cage, Cato's wound
torn open by his own hand, Rutilius' exile,* the poisoned cup which
transported Socrates from prison to heaven. So when I desired an
honourable life, I also desired the prerequisites of these honourable
actions.

           Three and four times blessed   8
    Are those whose lot it was to die with fathers watching
    Beneath Troy's lofty walls!*

What is the difference, whether you desire this for someone or
9 admit that it was desirable? Decius dedicated himself for the state,*
and rushed into the heart of the enemy spurring his horse in quest for
death. After him a second Decius, imitating his father's virtue, having
uttered the ritual prayers that were almost peculiar to his family,
charged into the thick of the enemy battle-line, with only one
concern, to win divine approval, and thinking a good death was to be
desired. So do you doubt whether it is best to die worthy of memory
10 and in some act of virtue? When someone suffers torture bravely he
is employing all the virtues. Perhaps one virtue is ready and most
obvious, endurance; but there is bravery, of which endurance and
long-suffering and hardihood are branches; it includes prudence,
without which no enterprise can be undertaken, which urges you to
bear as bravely as you can what you cannot escape; it includes constancy, which cannot be thrust down from its position and does not
abandon its purpose under the torment of any violence. It includes
that inseparable band of virtues. Whatever deed is honourable, virtue
does it alone, but under due advisement,* and whatever is approved
by all the virtues, even if it seems to be executed by one alone, is to
be desired.

11   Well then, do you think that only the things which come with
enjoyment and at leisure are to be desired, the sort of thing marked
with decorated doorways?* Some good things have a grim appearance;
some vows are celebrated not by a congratulatory crowd but by a crowd
12 of men adoring and revering. So do you not think Regulus desired to
return to the Carthaginians? Put on the spirit of a great man and step
aside briefly from the opinions of the common crowd; assume the
appearance of the most noble and magnificent virtue, which we should
13 worship not with incense and garlands but with sweat and blood. Look
at Cato putting his pure hands to his sacred breast and forcing apart
his wounds that had not gone deep enough. Would you say to him: 'I
wish you what you wish yourself' or 'I am so sorry,' or 'may your action
14 turn out well'? At this point I think of our friend Demetrius, who
called a carefree life without any onslaughts of Fortune a Dead Sea.*
To have nothing to rouse you, to stir yourself up, to challenge your
mental firmness with the report of its coming and attack, but simply to
15 lie in undisturbed ease, is not tranquillity: it is softness. Attalus the
Stoic* used to say 'I would rather Fortune kept me campaigning than
in comfort.' I am being tortured, but behaving bravely. That is good.

I am being killed, but behaving bravely; that is good. Listen to Epicurus; he will say that it is sweet as well! I will never put a soft name on such an honourable and serious matter. I am being burnt, but unconquered; how could this not be desirable? Not that fire burns me, but that it does not conquer me. Nothing is more glorious than virtue, nothing more noble; whatever is done at virtue's command is both good and to be desired. Keep well.

Letter 68 (Book VII.6) *Seneca returns to the theme of* otium, *not so much leisure as a deliberate withdrawal from public duties and urban obligations to devote oneself to philosophy. He returns to a warning given in earlier letters (letter 5 and to a lesser extent letter 8), that open and acknowledged retirement will offend people (of his own class); in letter 5 this offence came from resentment at what might seem an affectation of superiority; here offence has become suspicion. For Lucilius, holding an imperial office, actual withdrawal from that service would have been formally recognized; so would, for Seneca and other senators, their absence from sessions of the senate. Thrasea Paetus provoked first suspicion then accusation and condemnation for treason (*maiestas*) when he absented himself from attending Nero's senate. We are reminded of Tacitus' report (see Introduction) that Nero above all resented and suspected any implication that Seneca was withdrawing from his court.*

I agree with your decision, bury yourself in retirement, but you 1 should also bury that retirement itself. Be aware that you will be doing this, if not on instruction from the Stoics, at least from their example, but you will also be acting according to their instructions: you will win your own approval and that of anyone you choose. We Stoics do 2 not send men into every political community, nor always, nor without release: what is more, when we provide the wise man with a political world worthy of him, that is the universe, he is not outside political life even if he goes into retreat; instead, having abandoned one little corner he is passing into a bigger and grander existence, and after taking his position in heaven he realizes how humble a seat he occupied when he was mounting the magistrate's chair or tribunal. Keep this idea stored in your heart, that the wise man is never busier than when things divine and human have come into his view.

   Now I am coming back to the decision I had begun to urge on you, 3 to keep your retirement unknown. You have no need to put the label

of philosophy and quietism on yourself: give another name to your intention, call it ill-health and weakness and idleness. To vaunt one's
4 leisure is a lazy aspiration. Some animals mix up the tracks around their lair so as not to be found: you must do the same, or there will be no shortage of men hunting you down. Many people pass by open doors but explore what is hidden and thrust aside; spaces that are sealed provoke the thief. Whatever is exposed seems cheap; so the housebreaker goes past what is open. These are the ways of the people
5 and all the most ignorant: they long to burst into hiding-places. So it is best not to display one's leisure, and hiding too hard and retreating from the gaze of men is a kind of displaying. That man has withdrawn himself to Tarentum, that other is secluded at Naples, while a third has not crossed the threshold of his house for many years: whoever attaches some explanation to his retirement is calling a crowd to assembly.
6   When you withdraw, you should not aim to make men talk about you, but to talk with yourself. Now what are you discussing? Do what men delight to do about others, offer yourself a bad opinion of yourself: then you will become used to speaking and hearing the truth.
7 And linger most over what you feel to be your weakest point. Each man knows his bodily weaknesses. So one person will ease his stomach with vomiting, another sustain it with frequent meals, another will empty and purge his body by undertaking a fast: men whose feet are attacked by pain either refrain from drinking wine or from bathing; careless of other problems, they confront the disease which often plagues them. So in our minds there are some diseased parts to which we must apply a remedy. What am I doing in my leisure? I am healing
8 my wound. If I showed you a swollen foot, a discoloured hand, or the withered sinews of a damaged calf, you would authorize me to lie in one place and tend to my disease: this is a greater evil, which I can't show you: there is a gathering and abscess in my actual breast. I don't want you to praise me, I don't want you to say: 'Oh what a great man! He has held everything in contempt, and after damning the follies of human life is fleeing from them.' I have condemned nothing but myself. There is no reason for you to want to come to me in order
9 to make moral progress. You are misguided if you hope for any help from this source; it is not a doctor but a patient who lives here. I would rather you say when you leave: 'I used to think him a blessed man and a learned one, I had turned attentive ears to him, but I have

been let down: I have never seen nor heard anything to desire, or to return to.' If you feel this and say this, you have made some progress; I would rather you pardoned my leisure than envied it.

You say: 'Seneca, are you recommending retirement to me? Are 10 you slipping back into Epicurean sayings?' I am recommending retirement in which you may do greater and nobler things than you left behind. Knocking on the doors of the powerful, making an alphabetical directory of childless old men, having the most influence in the market-place is a loathsome and short-lived power, and if you assess it at its true value, a shabby one. 'That man far outdoes me in 11 influence in the courts, another outdoes me in military campaigns, and the status earned by them, another in the crowd of his clients. I can't match them; they have more influence.' It is worth the cost to be outdone by everyone so long as I outdo and conquer Fortune.

If only your heart had resolved long since to follow this purpose. 12 If only we were not considering a blessed life in sight of death. But even now we are not lingering, for we now trust to experience in judging the many things we would have trusted reason to prove superfluous and harmful. Let us behave like travellers who have set out too 13 late and want to catch up time by speeding, and put in the spurs. This advanced age goes well with these studies; it has already calmed down after fermentation, it has already worn out the faults that were not tamed by the first fervour of youth: there is not much left over for it to quench. 'And when', you ask, 'will you benefit from what you have 14 learned as you are leaving life, how will you apply it?' In this, to leave as a better man. But there is no reason to think any age is more suited to good sense than the age which has tamed itself by attempting much and suffering long and frequent remorse, the age which comes to healthy behaviour after calming the emotions. This is the time for this benefit; any old man who has reached wisdom has done so by virtue of the years. Keep well.

Letter 70 (Book VIII.1) *On the approach of death, and the right attitude for the wise man towards death: when and how to end one's life in sickness or under duress. Seneca illustrates his arguments from both a political (coerced) suicide of a minor member of the imperial family under Tiberius, and the suicides of captives denied liberty to escape disgrace. This is the first of several letters on the theme, which was highly relevant to the experience of Seneca and others at Nero's court.*

1 I have seen your beloved Pompeii again after a long lapse of time. I was brought back within sight of my youth; it seemed to me that I could still do whatever I had done there as a young man, and that I had done 2 it just recently. We are sailing through life, Lucilius, and just as at sea, as our dear Virgil says, 'lands and cities withdraw from us'.* So in this voyage of swift time we bury first our boyhood, then our youth, then whatever lies midway between the young man and the old, set on the border of the two, then the best years of old age itself; finally the 3 common end of the human race begins to present itself. We poor fools think death is a reef, but it is harbour to be reached at some time, but never to be rejected; if someone is carried there in his first years, he should no more lament than the sailor who has made his voyage expeditiously. For as you know, slack winds mock and hold back one man, wearying him with the boredom of a sluggish calm, while a persistent 4 breeze carries another swiftly to his destination.

Think that the same thing is happening to us; life has brought some men swiftly to their destination even when they lingered, whereas it has soaked and stewed others. But, as you know, life is not always worth holding on to: since it is not good to live, but to live well. So the 5 wise man will live as long as he ought, not as he can. He will see where he is going to live, with whom, how, and what he will be doing. He always thinks about the quality, not the length, of his life. If many distressing events occur that disturb his calm, he discharges himself, and he does not do this only at the last necessity, but as soon as he begins to suspect Fortune he looks around carefully to see whether he should put an end to it. He does not think it makes any difference to him whether he makes an end or accepts one, whether it occurs later or sooner: he is not afraid as he would be of a great loss; no one can 6 lose much drop by drop. It does not matter whether he dies more quickly or slowly, but it does matter whether he dies well or badly; for dying well is to escape the risk of living badly. So I think that what the Rhodian said* was utterly womanish: when he was thrust into a cage by a tyrant and fed like some kind of wild beast someone urged him to fast to death, and he replied: 'A man should hope for everything as 7 long as he lives.' If this is true, life still should not be bought at any price. Though some things may be great and beyond doubt, I will not come to them out of a shameful admission of weakness; shall I think that Fortune has absolute power over the man who lives, rather than think that Fortune has no power over the man who knows how to die?

But at times, even if death is threatening beyond doubt and a wise   8
man knows he is marked for execution, he will not lend his hand to
his penalty; yet he would lend it to his own needs. It is stupidity to
die from fear of death: if someone is coming to kill you, wait for him.
Why are you anticipating him? Why are you taking on the responsibility for another man's cruelty? Are you begrudging it to your executioner, or sparing him? Socrates could have refrained from food and   9
starved to death rather than die of poison; but he spent thirty days in
prison awaiting death, not in the belief than anything could happen,
as if such a long period allowed for many hopes, but to make himself
obedient to the laws, to give the last days of Socrates for the enjoyment of his friends.* What was more stupid than to despise death
but fear poison? Scribonia, that formidable woman, was the maternal   10
aunt of Drusus Libo,* a young man as stupid as he was noble, hoping
for higher things than anyone in that generation could have hoped
for, or he himself at any time. When he was brought back sick from
the senate with a sparse attendance (for all his acquaintances had dis-
loyally deserted him, thinking him less a defendant than as good as
dead), he began to take advice whether he should take his own life
or wait for death. Then Scribonia said: 'What pleasure do you get in
doing another man's job?' She did not persuade him; he laid hands on
himself, and with good reason. For if a man lives on, knowing he will
die on the third or fourth day at the whim of his enemy, he is doing
another man's business.

So you cannot make a general judgement on this matter, whether   11
death should be anticipated or waited for when an external force has
announced it: there are many arguments that can pull in either direction. If one death will entail torture, and the other is simple and easy,
why should a man not lay hands on himself? As I would choose a ship
to travel in or a house to dwell in, so I shall choose my death as I leave
life. What is more, just as a longer life is not better at all costs, so   12
dying is worse at all costs if it is prolonged. We should follow our own
humour more in dying than in any other business. Let a man take his
leave as his impulse seizes him; whether he is looking for steel or a
noose or some drug to fill his veins, let him proceed and break the
chains of slavery. A man should win others' approval for his life, but
his own approval for death; the best method is the one that appeals.
Men are foolish to think: 'Someone will say I did not act bravely   13
enough, some that I was too rash, some that there was a more spirited

method of dying.' Just think that the decision in your hands is beyond the reach of gossip! Consider this one thing, to rescue yourself as soon as possible from Fortune; otherwise men will be there to make negative judgement on your action.

14   You will even find men claiming to be philosophers who say that one should not do violence to one's life, and think it abominable to be one's own killer: we should wait for the end which nature has decreed. The man who says this does not realize that he is closing off the way to liberty; eternal law has laid down no kinder rule than in giving us

15 one entry into life but many exits. Should I wait for either the cruelty of a disease or a man, when I can escape the crowd of tortures and shake off hostile attack? This is the one reason why we cannot complain about life: it holds no one against their will. Human affairs are well placed because nobody is wretched except through his own fault. Do you like it? Then live. If you don't, then you are free to return

16 whence you came. You often let blood in order to relieve the pressure pains of headache: a vein is tapped to ease the body. You don't need to sever your breast with a gaping wound; the path to that great liberty is opened with a scalpel, and safety is found in a puncture. So what is it that makes us sluggish and inactive? None of us thinks that he must leave this dwelling sooner or later; so the indulgence of the place and sheer familiarity keeps the old tenants even amongst wrongs. Do you

17 want to be free in spite of this body? Then live like someone who is going to move away. Think that you will have to go without this lodging sooner or later, then you will be braver to face the necessity of departing. But how will men's end come into their mind when they

18 are eager for everything without limit? There is nothing whose contemplation is so essential, for other concerns are sometimes mulled over unnecessarily. Our spirit is prepared against poverty; but our riches have survived. We have armed ourselves to despise pain; but the happy lot of our undamaged and healthy body has never demanded the test of this virtue from us. We have instructed ourselves to endure the longing for those we have lost; but Fortune has kept safe all the men

19 we loved. A day will come that demands experience of this too. You need not think that only great men had the strength to break through the barriers of human slavery; you need not think this can only be done by Cato,* who pulled out by hand the life which he had not released by the steel: men of the lowest rank have escaped into safety by a huge effort, and when they could not die conveniently or

take the means of death of their own choosing, they have seized on anything at hand and by their own force made into weapons tools that were not naturally harmful.

Recently in the gladiatorial school one of the Germans who 20 was being got ready for the morning shows* went aside to relieve himself—for he was not granted any other privacy without a guard; there he took the wooden stick with a sponge attached to cleanse one's anus and thrust it right down into his throat, and stifled his breath by blocking his jaws. This was an insult to death. Just so, not very clean or decent, but what is more stupid than to die fussily? What a brave man, worthy to be given a choice of this death! How 21 bravely he would have used a sword, with what spirit he would have hurled himself into the profound depths of the sea or from a jagged cliff! Deprived in all respects, he found out how to create both death and a weapon for himself, to show you that nothing else but willpower delays our dying. Let each man judge this deed of a fierce fighter as he chooses, so long as this is agreed, that the dirtiest of deaths is to be preferred to the cleanest form of slavery.

Since I have begun to use humble examples I will persist, for each 22 man will demand more of himself if he sees that this act could be despised even by the most despised persons. We think the Catos and Scipios about whom we are accustomed to hear with admiration are beyond imitation, but now I will show you that that virtue has as many examples in a gladiatorial school as in the leaders of the civil war. Recently when a fellow sent up to the morning show was riding 23 under guard, he nodded as if sleep was overcoming him and let his head fall so low that he thrust it between the spokes, and kept himself in his seat for the time it took to break his neck with the rotation of the wheel: he escaped by the same vehicle on which he was being carried to his punishment. Nothing prevents a man who is longing to 24 break out and escape: nature keeps us under open guard. If a man's necessity allows, let him choose an easy way out; if he has several means of freeing himself, let him make a choice and consider by what means he prefers to be freed: but if his choice is difficult, let him snatch the nearest thing as the best, whether it is unheard-of or unprecedented. The man who does not lack courage for death will not lack inventiveness. Do you see how even the lowest slaves, when 25 pain has driven them, are roused and cheat the most vigilant of guards? That man is great who has not only imposed death on himself

but found a way to inflict it. I promised you several examples from the
26 same entertainment. In the second instalment of the sea battle one
of the barbarians buried the spear he had been given against his
enemies deep down his throat. 'Why', he asks, 'didn't I escape all this
torture and humiliation long ago? Why did I wait for death when
I have a weapon?' This makes a much more glorious performance, as
27 it is more honourable for men to learn to die than to kill. Well then,
shall men whom long meditation and reason, mistress of all things,
has taught, not have the courage that desperate and criminal men
have? Reason teaches us that Fate has a variety of approaches but the
same outcome, and that it makes no difference where what is coming
28 to us begins. The same reason advises us to die <as you choose> if it
is possible, but <if not> as you can, and seize on whatever comes
before you to do violence to yourself. It is wrong to live by violence,
but most splendid to die by violence. Keep well.

Letter 72 (Book VIII.3) *Seneca postpones answering an unidentified query from Lucilius and turns (§3) to the need not to interrupt one's
pursuit of philosophy. The main, if underlying, theme is of the stages in
the devotee's progress towards wisdom and the three stages on the way to its
achievement (§§7–11: cf. letter 75, §§12–14 for a fuller treatment).*

1 The argument you enquired about was already clear to me (for this is
how I had learned it step by step), but I had not tested my memory
for a long time and so my memory does not obey me easily. I feel that
I have suffered what happens to scrolls which have stuck together
through disuse; I have to unfurl my mind and all the things that have
settled in it must be shaken out so as to be ready when the need arises.
So let us postpone this issue for now, since it requires a lot of effort
and attention. As soon as I can hope for a longer stay in one place I
2 will take it up. For there are some things that you can write even in a
pony-trap, while others need a couch and leisure and seclusion. Still,
let me work on something even in these busy days, and indeed all day
long. For there is never a time when new distractions will not come
up; we sow them, and so several will grow from one seed. Then we
grant ourselves excuses for delay: 'once I have completed this, I will
weigh in with my whole heart', and 'if I settle this tiresome business
3 I will devote myself to studying'. You must not just practise philosophy when you are at leisure but create leisure for philosophy; we must

neglect everything else so as to pay attention to this, since no time is ever enough for it, even if life is prolonged from boyhood to the longest limits of human age. It does not make much difference whether you abandon philosophy or interrupt it, since it does not persist when it is interrupted but, like things which burst when inflated, slips right back to where it started, because it has lost its continuity.

So we must resist distractions, which rather than being solved should be pushed out of the way. In fact, no time is unsuited to a pursuit which brings us health: and yet many people fail to study because they are beset by the troubles which make study necessary. 'Something 4 will happen to prevent it.' Not for the man whose spirit is joyous and eager in every business; gladness is torn apart for those who are still undeveloped, but the joy of the wise man is firmly woven, it is not torn by any issue or fortune; he is always and everywhere calm, since he does not depend on outside circumstances or wait for the favour of fortune or some individual. His happiness is within his control; it would leave his spirit if it had entered in the first place, but it is born there. At times something happens from outside him to remind him of 5 his mortality, but it is trivial and only grazes the skin. I repeat that he will be exposed to some inconvenience, but that greatest of good things is firmly fixed. As I say, some inconveniences come from outside, just as in a strong and healthy body there are some rashes of blisters or sores, but no deep-driven ailment. I tell you, there is the same differ- 6 ence between a man of perfected wisdom and another whose wisdom is in progress, as between the healthy man and one emerging from a serious and prolonged illness; for this man a milder attack is the equivalent of health: if he does not give it attention he will soon be weighed down and sink back into the same condition, but the wise man cannot relapse, nor even fall further into ill-health. For good health in the body is temporary, and the doctor may restore it but not guarantee it—often he is recalled by the same man who had applied to him, whereas one's mind is healed once and for all. I will tell you how 7 you can recognize the healthy man: if he is content with himself, trusts in himself, and knows that all the prayers of mortals and all the favours given and requested have no effect on the blessed life. For if anything can be added to a condition, it is not perfect; if anything can be subtracted, then it is not lasting; let the man whose gladness is to be lasting rejoice in his circumstances. Now all the material things that the common crowd covets ebb and flow: fortune gives nothing as a

real possession. But these gifts of fortune also give pleasure when reason has diluted and blended them; it is this that recommends even
8 external goods, whose use is unappreciated by the greedy. Attalus* used to apply this simile: 'Have you ever seen a dog grabbing with open jaws the pieces of bread or meat thrown by his master? Whatever he catches he instantly eats whole, and is always gaping in hope of what is coming next. This is what happens to us: whatever fortune has thrown to us as we wait for it we instantly swallow without any pleasure, rearing up and obsessed with snatching another piece.' This doesn't happen to the wise man: he is sated; even if something comes his way he accepts it and puts it down without concern; he enjoys the
9 greatest gladness, uninterrupted and in his own power. A man may have good intentions and some progress, but be far from the summit; he is plunged and raised alternately, and at times lifted to heaven, at times lowered to earth. For uneducated and ignorant men there is no end of buffeting; they fall into that Epicurean chaos which is bound-
10 less void. There is also a third kind of men who play at philosophy but have not set hands on it, but they have it in sight and, so to speak, within their reach: they are not shaken or even caught by the ebb; they are not yet on dry land but already in harbour. So, since there are such great differences between the highest and lowest, and an ebb-tide follows even those halfway, and great risk of relapsing into a worse condition, we must not give way to distractions. They must be shut out: if once they get in they will produce others to succeed them. Let us resist them in the beginning; it will be better if they don't start, rather than come to an end. Keep well.

Letter 73 (Book VIII.4) *A new theme: Seneca argues against the claim that students of philosophy are dissidents; on the contrary, they are grateful to rulers who relieve them of civic responsibilities. This is neither a conventional attitude in Athenian political thought nor in traditional Stoic ethics, but it is as near as Seneca comes to asserting his loyalty to the treacherous emperor Nero. In contrast with previous letters (including letter 72) preoccupied with fortune's power to harm men, this letter says nothing of fortune but treats Jupiter and Neptune and other gods as controlling men's lives.*

1 I think critics are mistaken when they believe loyal students of phil-osophy are insulting and rebellious, despising magistrates and kings

or those who administer the state. On the contrary, no people are more appreciative of those rulers, and rightly; since they give no greater benefit to anyone than to those who are free to enjoy a calm ease. So those whose purpose of living well is greatly benefited by public security must revere the source of this good like a father, much more than those anxious men in the midst of public life who owe a great deal to rulers but also charge much to their account, men for whom no generosity can ever satisfy their desires which grow in the process of being filled. For anyone who is thinking of receiving is forgetful of what he has received, and desire has no worse fault than ingratitude. Add to this that no one among those in political life counts the number of men he has outstripped, but only those by whom he is outdone: it is not so sweet to them to see many men behind them as it is distressing to see anyone ahead of them. All ambition has this fault, that it does not look behind. And it is not only ambition that is unstable but every desire, because it always begins again at the end. But the man pure and free of corruption, who has left the senate and forum and all public business in order to withdraw for higher things, loves those who make it possible for him to do this safely, and he alone gives them a spontaneous witness and owes them a great deal although they do not know it. As he reveres and looks up to his teachers whose kindness has taken him from those dead-end activities, so he reveres the rulers under whose protection he can practise honourable disciplines.

'But a king protects others with his power as well.' Who denies it? But just as one of the ship's passsengers who benefit from the same calm weather will judge his debt to Neptune* to be greater because he has transported a greater quantity of more valuable goods on that sea, just as the merchant will pay his vow with more enthusiasm than any ordinary passenger, while among merchants the one who was conveying perfumes and purple and objects worth their weight in gold is more grateful than the man who piled up cheap stuff fit to be future ballast, so the favour of peace which affects everyone comes more profoundly to those who use it well. For there are many elite citizens for whom peace is busier than wartime: do you think the men who spend their peace in drunkenness or lust or other vices which ought to be stopped even by war, owe as much in return for peace? Unless you think the wise man is so unfair that he does not believe he owes anything personally for the advantages of the community. I owe a great deal to the sun and moon, but they don't rise for me alone; I am privately under obligation to the year and the God who controls it, 7 although <none of its phases are formed>* in my honour. The foolish miserliness of men makes a distinction between possession and ownership, and does not believe anything is its own if it is shared with the community; but that wise man holds that nothing is more his own than whatever he shares with the human race. And these things would not be communal if a part of them did not also affect individuals; whatever is shared even in the smallest fractions makes a man a partner.

8   Now add to this that what is really great and good is not divided so that a tiny fraction falls to each individual: good things come entire to each and every man. Men carry away from a public bounty as much as is promised for each individual; a feast and a distribution of meat and whatever can be held in the hand splits into fractions; but those indivisible goods, peace and liberty, are as entire for all men together 9 as for each man alone. So the wise man thinks of the author of his use and enjoyment of these good things, the man who prevents emergency calling him to arms or keeping watch or defending the walls and the many kinds of war tax, and gives thanks to his guide. This is what philosophy in particular teaches, to owe our benefits well and pay well for them; for sometimes even the acknowledgement is a form 10 of payment. So the philosophic man will confess that he owes a great deal to the man through whose administration and foresight he has the good fortune of prosperous ease and the control of his own time and calm undisturbed by official distractions.

> O Meliboeus, it is a God who made this ease for us,
> For he will always be a God to me.*

11 If even those times of ease owe much to their source, whose greatest benefit is

> He let my cattle wander, as you see, and let me play
> What tunes I wanted on the rustic reed . . .

how highly shall we value this ease which is spent among the gods, which makes us gods?

12   This is what I am saying, Lucilius, and summoning you to heaven by a short-cut. For Sextius* used to say that Jupiter had no more power than a good man. Jupiter has more to offer to men, but between

two good men the wealthier is not more good, any more than between two men with equal expertise in steering a ship you would call the one with the more showy vessel superior. How does Jupiter surpass the 13 good man? He is good for longer: but the wise man does not think less of himself because his virtues are limited to a smaller period. Just as between two wise men the one who dies older is not more blessed than the one whose virtue has been limited to fewer years, so God does not outdo the wise man in happiness, even if he outdoes him in age: virtue is not greater for being longer. Jupiter possesses every- 14 thing, but surely he passes it on for others to possess; the only use which is confined to him is that he is the cause of all men's enjoying its use; the wise man sees all other men's possessions and thinks little of them, with the same calm as Jupiter, and even respects himself more because Jupiter cannot use them, whereas the wise man does not want to. So let us believe Sextius when he shows us that most 15 glorious path and cries out, 'this is the "way to the stars" ', this way in keeping with thrift, in keeping with restraint, in keeping with cour- age. The gods are not fussy or jealous: they invite men in and extend a hand to them as they climb towards them. Are you amazed that a 16 man approaches the gods? God comes to men, indeed, which is actu- ally nearer, he comes *into* men; no mind is good without God. Divine seeds are scattered in human bodies, and if a good farmer takes them up they germinate like their origin and grow up like the seeds from which they sprouted; if it is a bad farmer, he chokes them just like barren and marshy ground, and then produces rubbish instead of crops. Keep well.

Letter 75 (Book IX.1) *Lucilius is dissatisfied with the stylistic level of Seneca's letters. Seneca's definition of the proper style for philoso- phy (§§1–7) leads from style to behaviour; to a classification of levels of progress towards wisdom, and what ordinary devotees may hope to achieve.*

You complain that I am not sending you sufficiently polished letters. 1 But who talks with polish unless he wants to talk pretentiously? I want my letters to be unaffected and easy, as our talk would be if we were sitting down or walking together, with nothing far-fetched or artificial. If it could be managed, I would rather show than tell what I 2 think. Even if I were debating, I would not stamp my foot or wave

my arm or raise my voice, but leave that sort of thing to orators, satisfied if I had conveyed my meaning to you, without adorning it or
3 making it colloquial. The one thing I would really like to prove to you is that I believed everything I said, and not only believed it but was committed to it. Men kiss their girlfriend in a different way from their children, but even in this chaste and mild embrace affection is shown quite clearly. I don't want the things I am going to say about serious matters to be dry, by Jove, and meagre (for philosophy doesn't deny itself eloquence), but it is not right to spend much effort on the
4 words. Let this be the chief goal of our purpose: let us say what we think and think what we say; let our talk be in harmony with our lives. A man has fulfilled his promise if he is the same when you see him
5 and when you listen to him. We will see his quality and his greatness; he is a single whole. Let our words give not pleasure but benefit. But if eloquence can be achieved by a man without preoccupation, if it comes readily or costs little effort, let it give support and accompany the noblest subject-matter; it should be such that it presents the subject rather than itself. Other arts belong completely to eloquence, but
6 here we are conducting the business of the mind. The invalid is not looking for an eloquent doctor, but if it works out that the man who can heal him explains neatly what must be done, the sick man will judge him favourably. Yet he will have no reason to congratulate himself that he has hit upon an eloquent doctor; this is as irrelevant as
7 if an expert pilot was also handsome. Why are you purging my ears? Why are you amusing me? Something else is needed. I must be cauterized and cut and made to abstain. You were called in for this, to cure a sickness that is long-standing, serious, and endemic; you have as much business as a doctor in a plague. Are you concerned with language? Be glad if you can cope with events. When will you learn so many things? When will you implant what you have learned in your heart so that it cannot be forgotten? When will you put all these things to the test? For it is not enough, as with other disciplines, to have committed these details to memory; the methods must be tried on the job: the man is not blessed who knows about these things, but who does them.
8   'Well then, are there not levels beneath this? Is it downhill all the way once we leave the wise man?' No, as I believe; for the man making progress is among the stupid, but is separated from these by a large gap. There are also great distinctions among the students making

progress: they are divided into three groups, as some philosophers think.*

The first group are those who do not yet have wisdom but have 9 already come to a stop in its neighbourhood; yet even what is near is still ahead. You ask who these men are? Those who have discarded all emotions and faults, who have learned what should be embraced, but whose confidence is still untested. They don't yet have their good ready for use, but already they cannot fall back into what they have shunned, already they are in a place from which there is no backsliding, but this is not yet obvious to them; as I remember writing in a letter,* 'they don't know that they know'. They already have the good fortune of enjoying their own good, but not being assured of it. Some 10 of them embrace this category I mentioned, of those making such vigorous progress that men say such people have already escaped from the sicknesses of the mind, but not from emotions: instead, they are still standing on a slippery slope, because nobody is beyond the risk of badness unless he has completely shaken it off. And nobody has shaken it off unless he has taken on wisdom instead of badness.

I have often explained before the difference between sicknesses 11 of the mind and emotions. But I will advise you again now. Sicknesses are long-standing and hardened faults, like avarice and ambition: they have entangled the mind too tightly by far and become its everlasting evils. To define it briefly, sickness is a judgement obstinate in its falsity, as if things that are mildly desirable, or not desirable at all, are greatly to be desired, or if you prefer, let us define it like this: to put a high value on something worth little or no value at all. Emotions 12 are reprehensible disturbances of the mind, sudden and excitable, which have created a sickness when they were frequent and overlooked, just as a single onset of catarrh which has not yet become chronic makes a cough, but a persistent and long-standing one creates a consumption. So those who have made the most progress are free from sicknesses, but while nearest to being perfected they still feel emotions.

The second category is of men who have already cast off the great- 13 est evils of the mind and emotions, but in such a way that they aren't yet in possession of their freedom from anxiety; for they can slip back into the same failures.

The third category is free from many great faults, but not from 14 them all. This man has escaped avarice but still feels anger; he is not harassed by lust any longer but is still troubled by ambition; he no longer feels desire but still feels fear, and in his state of fear is firm enough against some evils but gives way to others. He despises death but is fearful of pain.

15   Let us think a bit about this situation: we will have been well treated if we are included in this count. The second rank is obtained by great natural felicity and a great and persistent effort at study; but even the third condition is not to be despised. Think how many evils you see around you: see how there is no wickedness that lacks an example, how far badness advances each day, how greatly men offend both publicly and privately, and you will realize that we are achieving enough if we are not among the worst. You say: 'I at least hope I can become

16 part of a higher rank.' I had longed for this for us rather than promised it; we are preoccupied and striving towards virtue while bound down among faults. I am ashamed to say this, but we cultivate what is honourable only when we are at leisure. But what a glorious reward awaits us if we break away from our preoccupations and our most

17 clinging evils. Desire will not drive us away, nor fear.

Unvexed by terrors and uncorrupted by pleasures we shall dread neither death nor the gods. We shall know that death is not an evil, and the gods do not exist for evil. What harms us is as weak as what is

18 harmed; the best things lack the power to harm. What awaits us, if we ever emerge from those dregs to the sublime and lofty region, is peace of mind and liberty free from the errors which have been driven out. You ask me what that is? Not fearing men or gods; wanting neither what is base nor excessive; having the greatest power over oneself. It is an incalculable good to become one's own master. Keep well.

Letter 76 (Book IX.2) *This is one of several letters (see especially letter 83) in which Seneca describes his routine in retirement. After a brief assertion of the benefits of studying philosophy even at the end of life (§§2–6), he moves to elaborating his previous argument (from letter 74, §§10 ff., not in this selection) that the only 'good' for man is 'the honourable' (honourable behaviour): that is, the only thing worth calling good is what is morally good (*honestum = Greek to kalon). All other good things are external, contingent, and trivial.*

1 You threaten a feud against me if you are left uninformed of any of my daily routine. See how openly I am living with you; I will even trust

---

you with this. I am attending a philosopher's lectures, in fact this is the fifth day that I have gone to his class and listened to him disputing from the eighth hour. 'A fine age for that,' you say. Why wouldn't it be fine? What is more foolish than not to learn just because I have learnt nothing for a long time now? Well then, shall I behave like the cavaliers and young blades? I am doing well if this is the only thing that dishonours my old age. But this school welcomes men of every age-group. 'Are we to grow old for this, to copy young men?' I shall go to the theatre although I am an old man, and be carried off to the chariot-races, and no gladiatorial pair will fight it out without me: and shall I blush to go to a philosopher? 2

You should go on learning as long as you are ignorant, in fact, if we trust the proverb,* as long as you live. And that saying fits nothing so well as this kind of study: you must learn how to live for as long as you live. But I also do some teaching there. You ask what I am teaching? That even an old man needs to learn. It is true that I feel ashamed of the human race every time I have entered the school. As you know, one must pass right in front of the Neapolitan theatre on the way to Metronax's house.* The theatre is packed, and men give judgement on who is a good piper* with enormous enthusiasm; even the Greek trumpeter and the herald has his crowd of fans; but in the place where one is seeking a good man, in which one learns how to be a good man, there are very few in the audience, and they are seen by most people as having no serious business to do; men call them silly and idle. May that mockery fall on me too: we ought to hear the abuse of the uneducated without distress, and the man making his way towards honourable living has to hold contempt itself in contempt. 3 4

Keep at it, Lucilius, and hurry so that you don't suffer my experience of learning as an old man; in fact hurry all the more because you have now tackled a subject which you can scarcely learn completely by the time you are an old man. You say 'how much progress shall I make?' As much as you attempt. What are you waiting for? No man succeeds in being wise by accident. Money will come unbidden, high office will be offered to you, influence and prestige may perhaps be heaped upon you: virtue will not simply descend on you. It is not discovered by trivial work or a small effort; but it is worth the cost for a man to toil when he is trying to take possession of all good things once and for all. For there is only one good thing: what is honourable; you will find nothing genuine or reliable in those things which please 5 6

7 public opinion. I will now explain why the honourable is the only good, since you think I did not achieve this in the earlier letter and you feel this matter was praised rather than proved to you, and then I shall compress my previous arguments into a small space.

8   Everything is to be valued by its own peculiar merit. Fertility and the taste of the wine recommends a vine, speed a stag; in the case of beasts of burden, you assess the strength of their backs, since their only function is to carry a pack; in a hound the sense of smell is most important if it is supposed to track game, its racing speed if it is to chase them, its courage if it is to bite and attack: in every thing that quality should be best for which it was produced and by which it is

9 valued. What is best in a man? Reason. In this faculty he is superior to animals and approaches the gods. So perfect reason is man's peculiar good, and all his other qualities are shared with animals and plants. He is strong: so are lions. He is handsome: so are peacocks. He is swift: so are horses. I am not saying that he is outstripped in all these qualities; I am not asking what he has in the greatest degree, but what is truly his. He has a body: so do trees. He can control his impulse and movements: so can beasts and worms. He has a voice: but the cry of hounds is much louder, the cry of eagles is more piercing, the bellow of bulls much deeper, the song of the nightingale

10 much sweeter and more flexible. What is peculiar to a man? Reason: when this is right and fully developed it fulfils man's happiness. So if everything deserves praise when it has achieved its own good and reached the goal of its nature, and reason is a man's own good, he deserves praise if he has achieved this and reached the limit of his nature. This perfected reason is called virtue, and it is also 'the honourable'.

11   So the only good in a man is the one and only thing that belongs to a man: for now we are not investigating what any good is, but what is the good of a man. If nothing is special to a man but reason, this will be his only good, but it must be weighed against everything else. If someone is bad, he will be reproached, I think; if he is good, he will be approved. So that quality is first and unique in a man by which he

12 is approved or reproached. You don't doubt that this is good; you only doubt whether it is the only good. If a man has everything else, health, wealth, many ancestral portraits, a crowded reception hall,* but he is openly bad, you will disapprove of him; likewise, if someone has none of those things I listed, if he is lacking in money, a crowd of clients,

noble birth, and a sequence of grandfathers and forefathers, but he is openly good, you will approve of him. So this is the only good of a man, and if he has it, even if he is bereft of everything else, he deserves praise; but if he does not have it, despite an abundance of everything else, he is condemned and rejected. What is true of things is also true 13 of man; a ship is called good not for being painted with expensive colours or having a silver or gold beak, or a figurehead carved in ivory, or for being loaded with royal strongboxes and possessions, but for being stable and strong and dense with joints that keep out the water, solid to bear the assault of the sea, responsive to its helm, swift and unaffected by the wind. You would not call a sword good for having a 14 gilded sword-belt or a sheath studded with jewels, but for a sharp blade for cutting and a point that will break through every defensive layer; we don't ask how beautiful a ruler is but how straight; each thing is praised for the quality for which it was designed, what is peculiar to it.

So in man too it is not relevant how much land he has under crops, 15 how much money out at interest, how many clients greet him, how costly a bed he reclines on, how transparent a cup he drinks from, but how good he is. And he is good if his reason is clear and straight and adjusted to his natural will. This is called virtue, and this is honour- 16 able and the only good belonging to man. For since only reason completes a man, only reason makes him completely blessed: the only good is the one and only thing which makes him blessed. We also say that other things are good which derive and are formed from virtue, that is, all its products: but it is itself the only good, because nothing is good without it. If every good is in the mind, whatever strengthens, 17 raises, and enlarges it is good: for virtue makes the mind stronger and more lofty and more capacious. In contrast, other things which provoke our desires weigh down the mind and weaken it, and although they seem to raise it up they bloat it and deceive it with a lot of emptiness. So this alone is good which makes the mind superior.

All the actions of our whole life are governed by consideration of 18 what is honourable and shameful; reason is directed towards doing and not doing these things. I will tell you what this means. The good man will do what he thinks it will be honourable to do, even if it is going to be full of effort, even if it is going to be expensive, even if it is going to be dangerous: again, he will not do what is shameful even if it brings money, if it brings pleasure or even power: nothing

will deter him from the honourable or provoke him to embrace the
19 shameful. So if he follows the honourable at all costs, and avoids the
shameful at all costs, and observes these two values throughout his
life <not thinking anything good except what is honourable> or bad
except what is shameful, if virtue alone is uncorrupted and persists
alone in its course, then virtue is the only good, such that nothing can
happen to prevent it being good. It escapes the risk of change: folly
crawls towards wisdom, but wisdom does not sink back into folly.

20   If you remember, I said that most people trampled on what was
commonly desired and feared with unreflective impulse; but a hero
has been found to spurn wealth, another to put his own hand into
the flames,* another whose smile the torturer could not break down,
one who shed no tear at his children's funeral, another who went to
meet death without trembling; for love, anger, desire have confronted
dangers. What can be achieved by a short-lived perseverance of the
spirit aroused by some stimulus, virtue is far more able to do, since it
does not get its power from impulse or in an instant but constantly,
21 and with lasting strength. It follows that things often despised by
unthinking men and always despised by the wise are neither good nor
bad. So virtue is the only good, and walks proudly between this and
that condition of Fortune,* with a mighty contempt for each kind.

22   If you accept the opinion that there is something else good besides
the honourable, no virtue will escape suffering strain; for none can be
maintained if it looks to anything outside itself. If this is so, it is contrary to reason from which the virtues derive and truth which does
not exist without reason: and whatever opinion is contrary to truth
23 is false. You must admit that a good man practises the greatest piety
towards the gods. So whatever befalls him he will endure with calm
mind; for he will know it arose from the divine law from which all
things originate. If this is true, then the honourable will be the only
good for him: for it depends on this, that he obeys the gods and does
not get enraged at unexpected blows or lament his lot, but patiently
24 welcomes fate and does what is ordained. If the good is anything else
but the honourable, we will be followed by greed for life and greed for
the things that equip life, something intolerable, unlimited, and
unbounded. So only the honourable is good, because it has its limit.

25   We said that the life of man would be happier than that of gods, if
those things are good which the gods do not need, like money and
honours. Now add the argument that if souls survive released from

the bodies, a happier condition awaits them than they have while they move in the body. But if those things are good which we enjoy by means of our bodies, our souls will be worse off when they are released, which is contrary to all belief, that souls enclosed and confined are happier than when freed and given back to the universe. I had also 26
said that that if there are good things which happen as much to man as to irrational animals, then irrational animals will live a blessed life, which is absolutely impossible. We must endure everything for the sake of the honourable, something which we should not do if there was any other good than the honourable.

Although I had developed these arguments more broadly in the earlier letter, I have gathered them together and run through them briefly. For such an opinion will never seem true to you, unless you 27
lift up your mind and ask yourself, if circumstances demand that you die for your country and ransom the safety of all your fellow citizens by your own, whether you will offer your neck not just patiently but also gladly. If you will do so, there is no other good: for you are aban-doning everything in order to have this. See how great is the power of the honourable: you will die for your country, even if you have to do so immediately once you know it must be done. Sometimes a great 28
joy can be felt even for a tiny, brief time, from a very noble act, and although there is no profit from the deed once performed for the man deceased and removed from human life, the sheer contemplation of the future deed gives joy, and the brave and just man when he has considered the rewards of his death, the freedom of his country, the survival of all those for whom he lays down his soul, experiences the highest pleasure and benefits from his own danger. But even the man 29
robbed of this joy provided by the consideration of a last and finest deed will not hesitate but leap to his death, content to be acting rightly and piously. Now confront him with many arguments to deter him, say: 'Your deed will soon be followed by forgetfulness and the ungrate-ful assessment of your fellow citizens.' He will answer you, saying: 'All those things stand outside my achievement, but I am considering the act itself; I know this is honourable, so I am coming wherever it leads and calls me.'

This, then, is the one good, which not only the perfect mind but 30
one nobly born and of good character recognizes: other benefits are trivial and changeable. So they are possessed with anxiety. Even if fortune is favourable and heaps them all on one person, they weigh

down heavily on their masters and always oppress them, sometimes
31 even cheat them. None of those men you see clad in purple is blessed,
no more than those whom plays present with a sceptre and royal cloak
on stage:* when they have entered, spreading themselves and booted
up in front of the people, they take off their footgear and return to
their real size. None of those men whom wealth and office have put
on a lofty summit is great. So why does he seem great? You are meas-
uring him on top of his pedestal. A dwarf is not big even if he stands
on a mountain; a colossus will keep its size even if it is standing in
32 a well. We suffer from this mistake, this is how we are deceived, that
we don't assess anyone by what he is, but we add to him whatever
trappings he is adorned with. But when you want to embark on a true
assessment of the man and know what he is like, look at him naked, let
him renounce his family property, renounce his offices and the other
lies of fortune, let him cast off even his body. Gaze at his mind, to
see its nature and size, and whether it is great with borrowed assets
or its own.

33   If a man sees swords flashing with unflinching gaze and if he knows
it is unimportant whether his life departs through the mouth or the
throat, call him blessed: if, when he is threatened with tortures of the
body, both those which come by chance or by the injustice of a more
powerful man, then he is blessed if he hears calmly the prospect of
chains and exile and the hollow bugbears of human minds and says:

> 'no form of toil,
> Maiden, comes to me new and unexpected,
> I have foreseen and pondered them in my heart.*

You are making these threats today: I have always threatened myself
34 and prepared myself as a man for human suffering.' The blow of an
evil foreseen comes softly. But to fools trusting in fortune every aspect
of things seems new and unexpected; a great part of evil for the
uneducated is its novelty. To confirm this to you, the things men consider harsh they endure the more bravely the more they become
35 accustomed to them. So the wise man is accustomed to future evils,
and what others have made light by long suffering he makes light by
long meditation. We have sometimes heard the comments of the
uneducated, saying: 'I knew this was waiting for me.' The wise man
knows that everything awaits him; whatever has happened, he says: 'I
knew it.' Keep well.

Letter 77 (Book IX.3) *Seneca is back in Campania, at Puteoli, Rome's main port for the Egyptian shipping route, and has been watching the arrival of the grain fleet from Alexandria. His thoughts turn to his new detachment from material preoccupations and spending life in preparation for death. The death of Lucilius' friend Tullius Marcellinus (which pre-echoes some of the circumstances of Seneca's own death) is used to illustrate when it is right to choose death instead of living.*

The Alexandrian ships have suddenly made their appearance, the 1
ones usually sent ahead to announce the approach of the fleet which
follows them; they call them messenger ships. They are a welcome
sight to Campania; the whole crowd of people of Puteoli stands on the
dock and from the actual type of sails recognizes the Alexandrians
even in a great crowd of ships; for they are the only ones allowed to
fly a topsail, which all ships have above the mainsail. In fact nothing 2
so promotes speed as the top part of the sail; a ship is driven forward
best by its resistance. So whenever the wind has grown stronger and
is greater than is advantageous, the topmast is lowered; the gust is less
powerful from low above the waterline. When they have come this
side of Capri and the promontory from which

> Lofty Pallas is sighted with her storm-tossed summit,*

other ships are told to stay content with their mainsail; the topsail is
the mark of the Alexandrians.

In this rush of everyone hustling to the shore I felt a great pleasure 3
from my own laziness, because although I was expecting letters from
my friends, I did not hurry to find out the condition of my affairs and
what news they were bringing: for it is a long time since I have
experienced any material loss or profit. Even if I were not an old man
I should have felt this, but now all the more: however small my wealth,
I would still have more travel money left than travel, especially since
we have embarked on the journey which we don't have to complete.
A journey will be unfinished if you stop in the middle or short of the 4
destination; but life is not unfinished if it is honourable; wherever
you leave off, if you leave off well, it is whole and entire. But often one
must leave off bravely, and not just from the most urgent reasons, for
the causes which keep us in life are not great either.

Tullius Marcellinus, whom you knew very well, a sedate young 5
man who quickly became old, was seized by an illness, not actually

incurable, but long and troublesome and making many demands on him, so he began to deliberate about dying. He called together many friends. Each one either persuaded him of what he had persuaded himself, because the friend was timid, or because he was a flatterer and wanted to please, gave the advice which he suspected would be
6 more welcome to Tullius in his deliberation. But our Stoic friend, a splendid fellow and, to praise him in the words which he deserves, a gallant and energetic man, seems to me to have given him the best advice. This is how he began. 'Dear Marcellinus, do not torment yourself as if you are deliberating about a major issue. It is not a great thing to live; all your slaves are alive, and all the livestock; it is a great thing to die honourably, prudently, and bravely. Think how often now you have kept on doing the same thing; food, sleep, sex—we run through this cycle; so not only a prudent or brave or unfortunate man, but even a fussy man can want to die.'
7   He did not need an advocate but a helper; the slaves were reluctant to obey. So first he removed their fear and showed that the household was only at risk* when it was uncertain whether the master's death had been voluntary; otherwise it would have been as much of a
8 bad example to kill one's master as to prevent it. Then he advised Marcellinus that it was not discourteous, just as the remains of a dinner were distributed to the attendant waiters after the meal was finished, for some reward to be offered (now his life was finished) to those who had been his attendants throughout his life. Marcellinus was of an easy and generous nature even when it concerned his own property; so he distributed tiny sums to his weeping slaves and
9 took the initiative in comforting them. He did not need the sword or bloodshed; he went without food for three days and ordered a tent to be set up in his bedchamber. Then a bathtub was carried in, where he lay for some time, and as hot water was gradually poured in he gradually lost consciousness, not without some pleasure, as he said, as a gentle fainting brings pleasure which we have also experienced when we lost consciousness at times.
10   I have strayed into a story that will not be unwelcome to you; for you will learn that your friend's death was not difficult or unhappy. Although he chose his own death, he still passed away most gently and slipped away from life. But this story will not be harmful either; often necessity requires such examples. Often we ought to die but we
11 don't want to, or we die and we don't want to. No one is so ignorant

that he does not know we have to die at some time; but when death
comes near he backs off, trembles, and wails. Doesn't that man seem
to you most foolish of all who wept because he had not lived a thousand years earlier? But the man is just as foolish who weeps because
he will not be living a thousand years later. These cases are the same;
you will not exist then nor did you before; neither time belongs to
you. You have been tossed into this moment, and if you extend it, how   12
far will you extend it? Why are you weeping? What do you want? You
are wasting your effort.

Cease to hope the gods' own fate can be swayed by prayers.*

Everything is determined and fixed and conducted by a mighty and
everlasting necessity: you will go where everything goes. What is new
in this? You were born for this law; this happened to your father, your
mother, your ancestors, to everyone before you, to everyone after you.
The unconquerable sequence of events, that no power can change,
has entangled and dragged everything with it. What a nation of those   13
destined to die will follow you, and will accompany you! You would
be braver, I suppose, if many thousands were dying with you; and
yet many thousand men and animals are losing their lives in various
ways at this very moment when you are hesitating to die. And didn't
you think that you would some day reach this goal to which you were
always travelling? There is no journey without an end.

Do you think that I am now going to quote to you examples of   14
great men? I will quote one of children. It is reported that a Spartan
boy, still below puberty, cried out when he was taken prisoner: 'I will
not be a slave', in his own Doric language, and validated his words: as
soon as he was ordered to do a slavish and insulting task (he was
ordered to bring a chamber-pot) he smashed his head against the wall
and broke it. Freedom is so near; and does anyone remain a slave?   15
Would you not prefer your son to die like that rather than become
an old man through lack of vigour? So why are you distressed, if even
a child can die bravely? Suppose that you don't want to follow; then
you will be led. Put what is under another's control in your own
power. Won't you put on the spirit of that boy, and say 'I am not a
slave'? Poor fellow, you are a slave to men, a slave to things, a slave to
life; for if you lack the virtue of dying, life is slavery. Do you have any   16
reason to wait? You have used up the very pleasures which delay you
and hold you back: nothing is new to you, nothing is not tedious from

sheer surfeit. You know the flavour of wine and of syrup; it makes no
difference whether a hundred amphoras or a thousand pass through
your bladder; you are just a container. You know very well how
oysters and mullet taste; your self-indulgence has kept back nothing
untouched for future years. And yet these are the things from which
17 you are torn against your will. What else is there that you grieve to
have snatched from you? Your friends? So do you know how to be a
friend? Your country? Do you think so highly of it that you will postpone your dinner? The sun? If you could you would put it out, for
what did you ever do worthy of the daylight? Confess that you will not
be any more reluctant to die from longing for the senate, the forum,
or nature itself; it is the meat market you are reluctant to leave, in
18 which you have in fact left nothing untasted. You are afraid of death;
but how you look down on it in the midst of your mushroom feast!
You want to live. So do you know how to? You are afraid of dying:
what then, isn't that life of yours mere death? When Caius Caesar was
travelling along the Via Latina and one of the file of prisoners under
guard, with a beard trailing onto his breast, asked for death, Caesar
asked: 'So are you living now?' This is what we should answer those
19 for whom death will come to the rescue. You are afraid to die. 'So are
you living now?' But he says: 'I want to live, and I am doing many
things like an honourable man; I am reluctant to leave the duties
of my life, which I am performing conscientiously and vigorously.'
Don't you know that one of life's duties is to die? You are not leaving
20 any duty, for there is no fixed quota which you must fill out. No life is
not short; for if you look back at the world, even the life of Nestor or
Sattia* is short, though she had it inscribed on her monument that
she had lived ninety-nine years. You see someone boasting of a long
old age. How could they have put up with her if she had been able to
complete her hundredth year? Like the play, so is life itself: what matters is not how long it is but how well it has been performed. It does
not matter when you end. End when you want; just put a good closure
on it. Keep well.

Letter 78 (Book IX.4) *Seneca starts from Lucilius' ill-health (*des-
tillationes, *translated by scholars as catarrh but covering a more serious
range of sicknesses): the contemporary medical encyclopedia of Cornelius
Celsus distinguishes (4.5) between ordinary catarrh from the head and*

the catarrh of the throat, which becomes more serious when chronic, and
the catarrh of the lungs which leads to phthisis (tuberculosis). Lucilius'
symptoms and Seneca's recommendations overlap to some extent with those
offered by Celsus. The letter, like 104, shows how Seneca felt his duty to
those who loved him. It also offers a detailed analysis of how to cope with
pain, and triumph over it morally (§§20–4), but leads inevitably to the
problem of when and why to choose death.

Your trouble with constant catarrhal flow and the fevers that follow 1
long attacks that have become chronic is all the more upsetting to me
because I have experienced this kind of ill-health, which I disregarded
at its beginning—my youth could still endure harm and behave defi-
antly towards diseases. Later I gave way and was driven to the point
of suffering this flow, reduced as I was to extreme thinness. I often 2
felt the urge to break off my life; it was the old age of my devoted
father which held me back. For I thought not of the bravery I would
need to die, but of the bravery he would need to do without me.

I will tell you what comforted me then, if I mention first that 3
the actual thoughts which enabled me to be calm had the force of
medicine; honourable comforts turn into a remedy, and whatever has
restored the spirit is also good for the body. Our studies acted as my
salvation: I owe it to philosophy that I rallied and recovered strength;
I owe it my life and nothing less than life. My friends also contributed 4
a lot to my good health, since I was relieved by their encouragement,
vigils, and conversations. Nothing restores and aids a man as much,
Lucilius, best among men, as the affection of friends, nothing does as
much to rescue him from fear in the expectation of death: as long as
I left them to outlive me I did not believe that I was dying. I tell you,
I thought I would live not with them but through them; I felt I was
not pouring out my spirit but passing it on. These things gave me the
will to help myself and endure every torment; otherwise the most
wretched condition is not to have the spirit to live, when you have cast
off the spirit to die. So turn to these remedies. Your doctor will show 5
you how much to walk and to exercise yourself; don't give way to ease,
to which limp ill-health is prone; read quite loudly and exercise your
breath, since its path to the receiving lungs is suffering; sail and shake
up your organs with a gentle tossing around; he will tell you what
food to take and when to call up wine for your strength, when to leave

it out so that it does not irritate and inflame your cough. What I am recommending to you is not just a remedy for this disease but for your whole life: despise death. Nothing is saddening once we have escaped this fear.

6   There are three serious concerns in every illness; the fear of death, pain of the body, and the breaking off of pleasures. I have said enough about death; I will just add this, that this fear does not arise from the disease but from nature. Disease has often postponed the deaths of many, and they survived because they seemed to be dying. You will die, not because you are ill but because you are alive. That fate awaits you even when you are healed: when you recover your strength it will not be death you have escaped, but ill-health.

7   Let us return to the peculiar disadvantage, that disease entails great torments, but the periods of remission make these bearable. For the stress of extreme pain has a limit; no one can feel extreme and prolonged pain. A loving Nature has arranged it so as to make pain either bearable or short. The worst pains occur in the smallest parts of the body; sinews and joints and whatever else is small cause the fiercest pain when they have taken on damage. But these parts quickly become numb and lose the feeling of pain because of the pain itself, either because the life-spirit banned from its normal path and changed for the worse loses the power which gives it the strength to remind us, or because the festering moisture, once it has ceased to have a place to gather, bursts and shatters the sensation in the parts it has overfilled.

9   So gout and arthritis and every pain of the spine and sinews subsides when it has blunted the pains which tormented it; in all those cases the first infection harasses us but the attack is quenched by the lapse of time and the suffering ends in numbness. Toothache, eye-ache, and earache cause the most acute pain because it arises in narrow spaces of the body, no less, by Jove, than an aching head. But if it is too violent it turns into unconsciousness and sleep. So this is the consolation for violent pain, that you must cease to feel it if you feel it too much. But that is what distresses the ignorant about bodily discomfort: they have not conditioned themselves to be content with their mind; they have spent a lot of their life on the body. So a great and cautious man separates his mind from the body and spends much of his time with his better and divine part, but only the least time necessary with this peevish and brittle body. 'But,' he says, 'it is a nuisance to go without the usual pleasures, to go without food, be thirsty and hungry.' These

things are severe in the first phase of abstinence, then the desire subsides when the appetites which make us desire are weary and failing; then the digestion is reluctant, then there is aversion in men who were greedy for food. Our desires too die; for it is not bitter to go without the thing you have ceased to desire. Add to this the fact that 12 no pain is without lulls or at least a remission. Add that we can take precautions on its approach and resist its onset with remedies; for no illness fails to send signals, at least if it is returning in the usual way. The endurance of disease is bearable, if you hold its most extreme threats in contempt.

Don't make your misfortunes worse by your own actions and 13 burden yourself with laments; pain is trivial if opinion adds nothing to it. If instead you begin to encourage yourself, and say 'it is nothing, or at least very little: let us last it out; it will soon end', then you will make it trivial in thinking it so. Everything depends on opinion, it is not only ambition and luxury and avarice that take their cue from it; we are pained according to opinion. A man is as wretched as he 14 believes he is. So I think we should drive away the complaints at past pains and those comments: 'No one ever suffered worse. What torments, what woes I have endured! No one thought I would recover. How often I was given up for dead by my kin, how often abandoned by the doctors! Men fixed on the rack are not torn apart so badly.' Even if those words are true, this is past; what is the point of going over past pains and being wretched because you had been? What, doesn't everyone add much to his woes and lie even to himself? Then, what it was bitter to endure it is pleasant to have endured: it is natural to rejoice in the end of one's illness. So these two conditions must be reduced, the fear of the future and the memory of an old discomfort. The latter no longer affects me, the former not yet. When a man is set 15 amid these difficulties let him say:

Perhaps we will delight to recall this too.*

Let him fight with his whole heart; he will be defeated if he gives way, but he will conquer if he strains against his pain. As it is, most people now bring down on themselves the collapse which they should be resisting. The threat oppressing you, impending, pressing down on you, if you begin to withdraw will follow and weigh down on you more heavily; but if instead you will stand and strive against it, it will be driven off. How many blows fighters receive on their face and their 16 whole body! Yet they bear every torment in the desire for glory, and don't just suffer because they are fighting but so as to fight; their exercise is itself a torment. So let us too win over everything, although our reward is not a garland or a palm or a trumpeter making silence for the declaration of our name,* but virtue, and strength of spirit, and peace won for the future if Fortune is defeated once and for all

17 in a combat. 'I feel severe pain.' So do you not feel it if you bear it like a woman? Just as the enemy is more dangerous to those who flee, so every chance setback presses harder on a man who yields or turns away. 'But it is severe.' Well then, are we brave in order to endure trivial discomforts? Do you want the disease to be prolonged, or violent and short? If it is long it has a lull; it gives room for recovery, it makes a present of plenty of time, and inevitably will both increase and come to an end. A short and sudden disease will do one or the other; it will either come to an end or make an end of him. So what does it matter whether it or I cease to exist? In either case there is an end to pain.

18 It will also help to turn your mind to other thoughts and move away from pain. Think what you have done that is honourable or brave; go over in your mind the good parts; spread your memory over those things you most admired; then let every hero who triumphed over pain come to your mind: the man who persisted in reading a book while he offered his varicose veins to be cut out, the man who did not cease smiling when the torturers, angered by his smile, were trying out all the tools of their cruelty. Will pain not be conquered by

19 reason, when it is defeated by a smile? Name whatever you wish, flows of catarrh and the violence of incessant coughing heaving up parts of one's organs and fever that scorches one's very breast and thirst and limbs twisted so that they are splayed and out of joint; the flame is worse, and the rack and hot-plates, and the pressing on swelling wounds of something to reopen them and press even deeper. But amid all this some hero has not uttered groans. That is not enough; he has not supplicated. Still not enough. He is not answering. Not enough. He has smiled and smiled sincerely. After this do you want to mock pain?

20 'But my disease does not let me do anything, and has taken me from all my duties.' Ill-health possesses your body but not your mind. So it hampers a runner's feet, a tailor's or carpenter's hands; if you are accustomed to employ your mind you will urge and teach, listen

and learn, ask and recall. What more? Do you think you are achieving nothing if you are restrained in your sickness? You will show that disease can be overcome or at least endured. There is room for virtue, 21 believe me, even on a sickbed. It is not only weapons and battle that give proof of a keen spirit untamed by terrors: a brave man shows his courage even in blankets. You have something to do: to struggle well with your disease. If nothing compels you or forces its demands on you, you are presenting a fine model. Oh what great material it would be for glory, if we could be watched when sick! So watch yourself and praise yourself.

Besides, there are two kinds of pleasures. Disease restrains the 22 bodily ones but does not remove them; in fact, if you judge truly, it encourages them. It is a greater pleasure for a thirsty man to drink, food is more appreciated by a hungry man; whatever comes our way after abstinence is taken in more eagerly. As for those pleasures of the mind which are greater and more reliable, no doctor denies them to a sick man. Whoever pursues these and understands them despises all the beguilements of the senses. 'Oh, unhappy invalid!' Why? Because 23 he does not dilute snow with his wine? Because he does not refresh the chill of his drink which he has blended in a lavish cup, by breaking ice into it? Because those famous Lucrine oysters are not opened at his table? Because there is not a riot of cooks around his dining-place, bringing stoves in along with their delicacies? For this is what luxury has dreamed up: so that no food should grow tepid, that nothing should lack heat for the hardened palate, the kitchen now follows the dinner. 'Oh, unhappy invalid!' He will eat as much as he can digest; 24 a wild boar will not lie there in his sight, rejected from the table like cheap flesh, and the breasts of birds (for it is distasteful to see them whole) will not be placed in heaps in the serving-dish. What harm have you suffered? You will eat like a sick man, or rather, at last, like a healthy and sensible man.

But we will endure all of these, gruel, hot water, and whatever else 25 seems unbearable to pampered men wallowing in luxury, more sick in mind than body: just let us stop shuddering before death. And we will stop if we have learned the limits of good and evil, so that finally life will not cause boredom, nor death cause fear. For weariness with one's 26 self cannot take possession of life when it has so many varied, great, and divine matters to report: it is idle ease which tends to bring us into aversion to it. If we survey the world the truth will never turn

27 into distaste; it is false things that will give us surfeit. Again, if death
approaches and calls, however premature it is, even if it cuts off one's
middle years, the fruit of the longest life has already been harvested.
Such a man has come to know nature to a great extent; he knows honourable things do not grow with time; those men must see all of life as
short who measure it by pleasures that are empty and so unlimited.

28   Refresh yourself with these thoughts and make leisure sometimes
for our letters. The time will come one day that brings us together
for common conversation; however little it may be, our knowledge
of how to use it will make it long. For as Posidonius says: 'One day of
learned men extends further than the longest age for the uneducated.'

29 Meanwhile, hold on to this and grasp it; not to yield to hardship, not
to trust prosperity, to keep an eye on all the wantonness of Fortune,
as if she will do whatever she can do. Whatever has been long anticipated comes as a lighter blow. Keep well.

Letter 79 (Book IX.5) *Seneca uses Lucilius' travels in Sicily to
encourage his projected poem on Etna, and moves by analogy from the
ascent of the mountain to the moral ascent (§8) of the aspiring wise man.
But a new theme opens up around §13; contrasting worldly reputation
with the true fame which may elude great thinkers during their lifetime,
but comes all the more gloriously with the appreciation of posterity. Here
Seneca draws on the model of Epicurus' letters to his closest friends.*

1 I am looking forward to your letters in which you will describe to me
what new sights your travels around all Sicily have shown you, and
give a clearer account in all respects of Charybdis* itself. For I am
well aware that Scylla is a reef, and not dreadful for sailors; but I want
a complete report on whether Charybdis lives up to the mythical
tales, and if you have been able to note this (for it is worth your observation), tell us whether it is only churned up into eddies by one wind
or every storm has an equal effect on that part of the sea, or whether
it is true that whatever is swept up by that whirlpool is submerged
and carried many miles, and surfaces near the shore of Taormina.

2 If you write to me all of this then I will dare to instruct you to climb
Mount Etna too in my honour. Some say it is being wasted away
and gradually losing height, arguing from the fact that it used to be
pointed out to sailors from a much greater distance. This may happen
not because the height of the mountain is shrinking, but because the

fire has faded and is carried upwards with less violence and scope, and the smoke by day is also more sluggish for the same reason. Now neither explanation is beyond belief, whether the mountain which is being swallowed shrinks from day to day, or it stays the same, because the fire does not eat away the summit, but is kindled in some underground valley and seethes up and feeds on other things, so that it does not draw its fuel from the mountain itself, but its pathway. In Lycia 3 there is a notorious area (the natives call it Hephaestion) where the ground is pierced in many places, and a harmless fire surrounds it without any risk to what grows there. So the area is fertile and grassy, as the flames do not scorch anything but only glow with a slack and weak force.*

But let us save that topic, and investigate it when you write to me 4 how far from the crater of the mountain the snows lie which are not even melted by summer: they are so safe from the fire nearby. You need not make that task a debt of mine, for you would have given it to satisfy your craving even if no one had instructed you. What can 5 I give you not to describe Etna in your poem, not to touch on this obligatory topic for all poets? The fact that Virgil had already fully treated this did not prevent Ovid from handling it; in fact neither of them deterred Severus.* Besides, this subject has offered itself successfully to everyone, and I don't think those who went first pre-empted what could be said, but opened the way. It makes a great dif- 6 ference whether you are tackling exhausted material or merely well ploughed; it grows day by day and what has been discovered does not get in the way of those seeking to discover. Besides, the late-comer enjoys the best circumstances; he finds the words ready made, and they have a new appearance once he has rearranged them. Nor is he laying hands on them as if they belonged to others, for they are public property. <Legal experts say nothing public can be possessed from mere use.>* Either I don't know you or Etna has whetted your appe- 7 tite; you already want to write something grand and equal to your predecessors. For you won't be allowed to hope for more by your modesty, which is so great that you seem to me to belittle the strength of your intellect, if there is a risk of winning; such is your reverence for your predecessors.

Wisdom has this merit among others, that no man can be outdone 8 by another except when he is climbing upwards. When you have reached the summit everything is level: there is no room for an

increase, and things stand still. Does the sun add anything to its
size? Does the moon travel beyond its regular orbit? The seas do not
9 increase; the universe keeps the same appearance and scale. Things
that have reached their proper size cannot raise themselves further;
whatever wise men are born will be matched and equal to each other.
Each of them will have his own talents; one will be more sociable,
another more businesslike, one will be more prompt in speaking,
another more eloquent; but what really matters, what makes a man
10 blessed, is equal in them all. I don't know whether your Etna can
collapse and fall on itself, whether the constant force of the fires can
diminish this lofty peak, conspicuous across a vast expanse of sea; but
neither flame nor ruin will bring down virtue; this one form of greatness cannot be brought down. Nor can it be advanced or withdrawn,
its size is so determined like that of the heavenly bodies. So let us try
11 to raise ourselves to this. Much of the task has already been achieved;
no, rather, if I want to tell the truth, it is not much. Nor is it goodness
to be better than the worst of men; who would boast of his eyes
who looks up at the daylight? If the sun shines for a man through
the gloom, he may be content for the time being to have escaped the
12 darkness, but he is still not enjoying the good of light. Our spirit will
have something to congratulate itself on when it is released from this
darkness in which it is wallowing and does not see brilliant things
with a frail sight, but admits full daylight and is restored to its heaven,
when it recovers the place which it possessed by the lot of its birth.
Its beginnings call it upwards, and it will be there even before it is
released from this imprisonment, when it shatters its vices and shoots
forth, pure and light, into its divine thoughts.

13   Dearest Lucilius, we are delighted to concern ourselves with this,
to advance towards it with all our vigour, whether few men or even no
one knows it. Glory is the mere shadow of virtue; it will accompany
virtue even against its will. But just as a shadow sometimes precedes
us and sometimes follows and falls behind us, so glory is sometimes
in front of us and offers a chance of seeing itself; sometimes it is
behind us and all the greater because it comes later, when envy has
14 withdrawn. How long it was that Democritus was thought to be
mad! Fame scarcely welcomed Socrates. How long Cato was unknown
by his own community! It rejected him and did not understand
him until it lost him. The virtue and incorruptibility of Rutilius*
would be hidden if he had not suffered injustice; it shone forth while

being abused. Did he not give thanks to his lot and embrace his exile? I am talking about men on whom fortune cast the light while she persecuted them; how many men had their success emerge into renown after them! How many fame did not welcome but rooted out? You see how greatly not only the more learned but this crowd of ignorant men marvels at Epicurus: he was unknown in Athens itself, where he was in hiding. So after living many years beyond his Metrodorus, in a letter in which he sang the praises of his friendship with Metrodorus* with grateful memory, he added this at the end, that nothing had done so much harm to himself and Metrodorus among so many blessings as that the renowned Greek world kept them not just unknown but virtually unheard. So did he fail to be discovered after he had ceased to exist? And did the good opinion of him fail to shine forth? Metrodorus too admits in a letter that he and Epicurus had not become sufficiently well known, but he said that those who wanted to follow the same tracks after himself and Epicurus would have a great name easily won.

No virtue stays unnoticed, and to be unnoticed is no loss; the day will come which broadcasts it, hidden as it is and oppressed by the meanness of its own age. A man is born for a few, who thinks only of the people of his own age. Many thousands of years, many thousands of peoples, will follow on: look towards them. Even if envy imposes silence on everyone who lives along with you, men will come who judge you without prejudice or favour. If virtue has any reward from fame, this too does not perish. The talk of posterity will not affect us at all; but it will worship and pay attention to even those who cannot feel it. There is no one to whom virtue has not given thanks living and dead, if only he has followed her in good faith, if he has not dressed himself up and painted himself, if he has been the same whether he was seen with advance warning, or suddenly and unprepared. Pretence achieves nothing; an external appearance superficially borrowed deceives few, but truth is the same in all its parts. Things that deceive have no solidity. A lie is a thin sort of thing: it is seen through if you scrutinize it carefully. Keep well.

Letter 80 (Book IX.6) *Seneca's meditations on moral issues discussed by his predecessors are disturbed (§2) by sounds of a boxing-match, leading him to contrast physical and moral combat, and see men's public life in terms of mime or tragedy, concealing the moral flaws beneath the stage costume (cf. letter 76, end).*

1   Today I owe my leisure not just to myself, but to the show, which has
    called all the intruders away to the boxing-match. No one will break
    in, no one will hamper my thinking, which is advancing more boldly
    from this very assurance. The door will not suddenly creak, nor the
    curtain be raised: I shall be allowed to go safely, which is all the more
    necessary when one makes ones own way along one's own path. So am
    I not following our predecessors? Yes I am, but I allow myself to dis-
    cover some new thing and to change or abandon others: I am not a
    slave to them but I agree with them.

2   But I have made a great boast: although I promised myself silence
    and seclusion without interruption, now a great shout is being wafted
    from the stadium, and although it does not shake me out of myself,
    it redirects me to contemplating this phenomenon. I think to myself
    how many men exercise their bodies, and how few their intellects;
    what a great gathering there is to see an unreliable show put on in
    play, and what a great isolation around the noble arts; how weak in
3   mind are the fellows whose arms and muscles we admire. And I am
    brooding in particular over the question: if the body can be led on by
    exercise to such endurance that it will bear the fists and kicks of more
    than one opponent, endurance in which a man spends the day suffer-
    ing the most burning sun in scorching dust and soaked in his own
    blood. How much more easily the mind could be strengthened to take
    the blows of Fortune unbeaten, to rise when cast down and trampled
    on. For the body needs many things to be strong, whereas the mind
    grows from itself, feeds itself, and exercises itself. They need great
    quantities of food and drink and great quantities of oil and finally
    prolonged effort. Virtue will come to you without equipment or
    expense. Whatever can make you a good man is there in you.

4   What do you need to be a good man? Willpower. And what better
    wish can you have than to rescue yourself from this enslavement
    which oppresses us all, which even slaves of the lowest class and born
    in this squalor try by every method to cast off? They pay out their
    pocket-money which they have accumulated by cheating their bellies,
    for their personal freedom; and won't you desire to reach freedom at
5   whatever cost, thinking that you were born free? Why are you looking
    at your strongbox? This cannot be bought. So the name of liberty is
    meaningless on the account books, since neither those who bought it
    nor those who sold it possess it. You must give this good thing to
    yourself, you must ask it from yourself. First free yourself from the

fear of death (for this has set the yoke upon us) then from fear of
poverty.

If you want to know how it is void of evil, compare the expressions   6
of poor men and rich: the poor man laughs more often and more
convincingly; there is no anxiety hidden deep down; even if some
concern occurs to him, it passes like a light cloud; the cheerfulness of
those called successful is faked, or a severe and festering sadness, all
the more severe because at times they are not allowed to be openly
wretched, but while they are eating up their heart in woes they are
obliged to play the successful man. I often have to use this example,   7
and no other expresses more powerfully the mime of human life,
since the mime assigns us the parts we play so badly. The man who
strides on the stage spreading himself, and says as he reclines:

> See I am lord of Argos, Pelops left my throne
> Where by fair Helle's strait and Ionian sea
> Is washed the Isthmus,*

is a slave and earns five measures of grain and five denarii a day. The   8
man who speaks, proud and overweening and swollen in confidence
of his powers, saying:

> Unless you fall quiet, Menelaus, this hand will slay you,

gets a daily allowance and sleeps in a patched garment. You can say
the same thing about all those pampered creatures whom a litter sus-
pends above the heads of men and above the crowd; their success is
only a mask. You will despise them if you strip them of their costume.   9
When you are going to buy a horse you have the cloth taken off,
you pull the clothing off slaves for sale to make sure the flaws of their
bodies don't go unnoticed: so do you appraise a man who is swathed
in costume? Slave-dealers hide whatever might offend by some trick
of the trade, and so even their wardrobe is suspect to the purchasers;
and if you saw a bandaged leg or arm, you would have it bared and
the flesh itself displayed. Do you see that man, king of Scythia or   10
Sarmatia,* glorious in his royal headdress? If you want to appraise
him and know what the whole man is worth, undo his diadem: there
is a lot of evil hiding underneath it. Why am I talking about other
men? If you want to weigh yourself up, set aside your money, your
house, your rank, and consider your inner man: for as it is, you are
entrusting to others the gauge of your quality. Keep well.

Letter 82 (Book X.2) *Seneca claims to have noticed Lucilius' new level of moral achievement and encourages him to continue in cultivating a way of life that is calm but not comfortable or self-indulgent. He can protect himself against fortune by seeking nothing that depends on her gift. The letter moves to consideration of death (§8) and how to overcome the fear of death, not through logicians' syllogisms, but through genuine eloquence and emulating heroic examples.*

1 I have stopped being anxious on your behalf. You will say: 'Which of the gods have you taken as guarantor?' Obviously the one who deceives nobody, that is, a soul devoted to the right and good. Your better part is home and dry. Fortune can do you a wrong, but, something more to the point, I am not afraid that you will do yourself any wrong. Go onward as you have begun and settle yourself in that way of life

2 calmly, not indulgently. I would rather things went badly with me than indulgently—take the word 'badly' in the popular sense as meaning harshly, roughly, and strenuously. We often hear someone's life praised with the envious phrase, 'he lives indulgently', by which they mean, 'he indulges himself'. For the mind is gradually made womanly and grows slack like the leisure and slothfulness in which it lies. What then? Is it not better for a man even to grow stiff and cold? <   >* Then pampered men fear the same thing, <the condition of death> which they have made their lives resemble. There is a big

3 difference between leisure and a tomb.* 'So,' you say, 'isn't it better to lie inert like this than to be tossed on those eddies of obligations?' Each condition is abominable, both the pressure and the inertia. I think the man who lies drenched in perfume is as dead as the one dragged away on the hook:* leisure without study is death and the

4 burial of a living person. Then what is the use of withdrawal? As if the reasons for anxiety did not persecute us across the seas. Is there any hiding-place in which the fear of death does not enter? What repose in life is so well fortified and secluded in such a high place that pain cannot intimidate it? Wherever you have hidden yourself, human misfortunes will clash around you. There are many external troubles besieging us, to deceive or oppress us, and many within us which

5 seethe up in the middle of isolation. Philosophy must be set around us like an impregnable wall, which Fortune may assail with many siege-engines but cannot break through.* The mind that has abandoned external desires stands in an unassailable position and protects

itself in its own fortress: every missile falls short of it. Fortune does not have long arms as we think; she does not seize anyone unless they are clinging to her. So let us leap as far away from her as we can—but only the knowledge of oneself and of nature will guarantee this. A man should know where he is going, and where he came from, what is good and what is bad for him, what to seek and what to shun, what is the method for distinguishing between things to avoid and things to seek, and reasoning to mitigate the frenzy of desires and curb the cruelty of fears. Some men believe they have reined in these emotions even without philosophy, but when some chance tests them when they are unsuspecting, acknowledgement comes too late; bold words are forgotten when the torturer demands your hand and when death comes closer. You could say to such a man: 'You found it easy to challenge misfortunes at a distance: here is pain which you said was bearable, here is death, against which you made many spirited boasts; the whips crack and the sword flashes:

Now you need courage, Aeneas, now a strong breast.'*

Persistent meditation will make it strong, if you exercise not your language but your mind, and prepare yourself against death; the man who tries to persuade you by quibbling that death is not an evil will neither persuade you nor rouse you into action. For, dear Lucilius, I love to laugh at the silly arguments of the Greeks, which I have not yet shaken off although I am amazed by them. Our friend Zeno* employs this syllogism: 'No evil is a source of glory, but death is a source of glory, therefore death is no evil.' You have made your point. I am freed from fear; after this I shall not hesitate to offer my neck. You don't want to speak more fiercely or provoke laughter from the man about to die? By Jove, I could not easily tell you whether the man was more silly who believed he could remove the fear of death by this cross-examination,* or the adversary who tried to refute it as if it was relevant. For he set up a counter-examination arising from the fact that we count death among matters morally indifferent, which the Greeks call *adiaphora*. 'Nothing indifferent is a source of glory,' he says, 'but death is a source of glory, therefore death is not indifferent.' You see where this investigation is frustrating itself; death is not a source of glory, but to die bravely is glorious. And when you say 'nothing indifferent is glorious', I agree with you to the extent that I say nothing is glorious except about matters indifferent; for example,

I mean that the following are indifferent (that is, neither good nor
11 bad): sickness, pain, poverty, exile, death. None of these is glorious in
itself, nor is anything glorious without them. For it is not poverty that
is praised, but the man whom poverty does not subdue or weigh
down. It is not exile that is praised, but the man who went into exile
with a braver countenance than if he had been exiling another. It is
not pain that is praised, but the man whom pain could not compel; no
one praises death, but the man whose spirit death took away before
12 it could disturb him. All such things are not intrinsically honourable
or glorious, but whatever virtue has confronted and handled it makes
honourable and glorious. These count as morally neutral things.
What matters is whether badness or virtue has laid hands on them,
for the death which was glorious in Cato's case was immediately disgraceful and shameful in Decimus Brutus.* For this is the Brutus
who withdrew to relieve himself when he was doomed and seeking
ways to postpone death, and when he was called back for death and
told to offer his neck said: 'I will offer it, so may I live!' What folly it
is to flee when you cannot step back. 'I will offer it, so may I live!'—he
almost added 'even under the domination of Antony'. What a man!
He deserved to be surrendered to life.

13   But as I began to say, you see that death itself is neither bad nor
good. Cato handled it most honourably, Brutus most disgracefully.
Once virtue is added everything takes on all the merit which it previously lacked. We call a bedchamber well-lit, but the same place is
14 totally dark at night. The day pours light into it, the night takes
it away; so the things called indifferent and neutral by us, wealth,
strength, beauty, honour, monarchy, and their opposites, death, exile,
ill-health, pain, and other things which we fear to a greater or lesser
degree, are given the name of bad or good either by badness or from
virtue. An ingot is neither hot nor cold by nature: cast into the fur-
nace it gets hot, dropped into water it gets cold. Death is made honourable by whatever is itself honourable, that is, virtue and a spirit
that holds external assets in contempt.

15   But among those things we call indifferent, Lucilius, there is a
major distinction. For death is not indifferent in the same way as your
hair is evenly or unevenly trimmed. Death is among the things which
are not bad but have the appearance of being bad, because self-love
and the innate will to survive and preserve oneself and the rejection
of dissolution <cause fear of death> because it seems to snatch away

from us many good things and lead us away from the abundance to which we are accustomed. This factor too makes death strange to us, that we already know our present conditions whereas we don't know the circumstances into which we will pass away, and we are terrified of the unknown. So even if death is indifferent, it is not something that we can easily overlook: the spirit must be hardened by vigorous training to endure the sight and approach of it. Death should be despised more than we usually despise it, since we have come to believe many things about it, and many intellects have competed to increase its bad reputation: they have described the underworld prison and the realm buried in everlasting night in which

> the vast gatekeeper of Hell?*
> Lying on half-gnawed bones in his gory cave
> Ceaselessly howling terrifies bloodless shades.

Even when you have persuaded men that these are fantasies and nothing is left for the deceased to fear, another fear arises; for just as men are afraid of being in the underworld, so they are afraid of being nowhere. In face of these beliefs infused in us by long-held conviction, surely the brave endurance of death is glorious and among the greatest achievements of the human mind. It will never rise to virtue if it believes that death is an evil, but it will rise up if it thinks that death is indifferent. Nature does not allow anyone to approach something he judges to be bad with a heroic spirit: he will come sluggishly and hesitantly. For no action is glorious if it is done by someone unwilling and backing off; virtue does nothing just because it is necessary. Now add that nothing is done honourably unless the entire spirit weighed into it and lent support, without recoiling in any part of itself. For when we approach a bad thing either from fear of worse, or in hope of good things for which it is worth stomaching such endurance of the single evil, the judgements of the agent are in conflict; on one side he is ordered to complete his purpose, on the other something pulls him back in flight from this suspicious and dangerous thing; so the mind is torn in opposite directions. When this happens, glory is lost, since virtue carries out its resolves with undivided spirit, and does not fear what it is doing.

> As for you, yield not to evils but go more boldly on
> Than this your fortune will allow you.*

19 You will not go forward more boldly if you believe those things are evils. You must uproot this delusion from your breast, otherwise misgivings will cling to you, delaying your initiative; it will suffer being pushed against the evil that needs spontaneous attack.

Our Stoics want Zeno's cross-examination to be true, and the other one opposed to him to be deceptive and false. I am not reducing this to a dialectic law and those tired old knotty tricks: I think the whole technique should be thrown out that makes the man cross-examined think he is being tricked and, when reduced to admission, makes him give one answer but believe another. For the sake of truth we must

20 proceed more straightforwardly, and in face of fear more bravely. As for the riddles which they wrap up, I would rather untangle them and lay them out, to persuade and not to compel. How will the general urge on the army he is leading into battle, an army that is going to die for its wives and children? I present to you the Fabii,* who transferred the whole of the state's warfare onto their single clan. I show you the Spartans arrayed at the very narrows of Thermopylae; they expect neither victory nor a return home. That place is going to

21 be their tomb. How do you urge them on to oppose their bodies and accept the ruin of their whole race and to yield up their life rather than their position? Will you say: 'What is a bad thing is not glorious; death is glorious, so death is not a bad thing'? Oh what an effective speech! After that who will hesitate to impale himself on the hostile blades and die holding his ground?

But how bravely the famous Leonidas spoke to them. 'Fellow soldiers, lunch as if you were going to dine with the dead!' The food did not choke them in their mouths, nor stick in their throats, nor fall from their hands. They eagerly accepted the invitations to both lunch

22 and dinner. What about the Roman leader who spoke like this to the soldiers sent to seize a site by passing through an immense force of enemies: 'Fellow soldiers, it is necessary to go to this place, but it is not necessary to return.'* You see how straightforward and authoritative is virtue: who among men can your verbal snares make more brave or more unyielding? These snares break the spirit, which should least of all be hemmed in, and coerced into petty and thorny places,

23 when it is being rallied for a great action. The fear of death has to be stripped away not from three hundred men but from all mankind. How do you teach them that it is not a bad thing? How do you overcome the beliefs of all the ages, which infuse a man immediately

from his infancy? What aid are you finding for human frailty? What are you saying to make them rush impassioned into the midst of dangers? What eloquence are you using to defeat this unanimity in fear, what powers of intellect, to defeat this conviction of all mankind striving against you? Are you assembling tricky words and stringing together cross-questioning for me? Great monsters are struck with great weapons. Roman soldiers vainly assailed with arrows and slings 24 that savage serpent in Africa,* more terrifying to the legions than the war itself; it was not even vulnerable to the 'Pythian' catapult.* When its enormous size, as tough as its vast bulk, rebuffed iron spears and whatever human hands had hurled, it was finally crushed by rocks the size of millstones. And are you quibblers hurling such petty weapons against death? Are you confronting a lion with a shoemaker's awl? What you say is sharp, and nothing is sharper than an ear of corn, but sheer delicacy makes some things useless and ineffective. Keep well.

Letter 83 (Book X.3) *This letter starts with an account, supposedly requested by Lucilius, of how Seneca spends his days at home (§1–8), then moves on to Zeno's condemnation of drunkenness, first reporting philosophical disputes, then offering Seneca's own contrasting attitudes of tolerance towards drunkenness even in serving magistrates, and condemnation of drunken incapacity for the nausea and disgusting behaviour it causes in individuals. See A. L. Motto,* Essays on Seneca *(Heidelberg: Peter Lang, 1993), 155–62, 'Seneca on Drunkenness.'*

You tell me to describe my daily routines, and describe them in full: 1 you must have a good opinion of me if you think there is nothing in them for me to conceal. Certainly we must live as if we lived open to view, and think as if someone could look into our innermost heart; and so he can. For what is the use of anything being secret from man? Nothing is shut off from God; he shares in our minds and enters into the midst of our thoughts—I say enters, as if there is a time when he leaves. So I'll do your bidding and gladly write to you what I do and 2 in what sequence. I shall start immediately to observe myself, and review my day, a most beneficial procedure. The thing that makes us worst is that nobody looks over his life; we think about what we are going to do, and not often, but we don't think about what we have done. And yet planning for the future comes from the past.

3   Today is uninterrupted, since no one has snatched any part of it
from me. It is divided entirely between resting and reading, with the
least part given to physical exercise, and I give thanks to old age on
that account; it does not cost me much. When I have stirred myself
I get weary, and this is the end of even the most strenuous exercises.

4 You ask about my trainers? One person, Pharius, is enough. He is a
charming boy, as you know, but he will change. I am already looking
for someone younger. He says we are going through the same physical
transition, since both of us are losing our teeth. But already I can
scarcely keep up with him running, and in a few days I shan't manage
it—see what good daily exercise is doing! A great space quickly
increases between two men going in opposite directions: he is rising
at the same time that I am sinking, and you know well how much
faster the second of these processes happens. No, I lied, because my

5 old age is already not sinking but collapsing. Now you ask how today's
race turned out? In a way unusual for runners: we tied. After this
exhaustion rather than exercise I took a cold bath; this is what I call a
bath that is not quite warm enough. I, the mighty cold-water bather
who used to greet the outdoor channel on the first of January, who
used to resolve at the New Year, as one resolves to read, write, and say
something of note, to leap into the Aqua Virgo, first transferred my
campaign to the Tiber,* then to this tub, which, when I am feeling
most brave and everything is scrupulously observed, is warmed by

6 the sun: there isn't much difference from actual baths. Then some
dry bread and a lunch without table service, after which I don't have
to wash my hands. I sleep just a little. You know my habits; I enjoy the
shortest of naps combined with wakefulness; it is enough for me to
have stopped being awake. Sometimes I know I have slept, sometimes
I just suspect it.

7   Now the din of the chariot races* intrudes on me: my ears are
shattered by some sudden and collective shout, but they don't dislodge my thinking or even interrupt it. I put up with the noise most
patiently: many voices blurred into one are like waves or the wind
beating on the forest and other sounds without meaning.

8   So what have I turned my mind to now? I'll tell you. It is a thought
left over from yesterday's meditation, wondering what the shrewdest
of men had in mind when they made the proofs of the most important
matters frivolous and confusing: they may be true, but they seem

9 very like lies. The great man Zeno, founder of this tough and rigorous

school, wants to discourage us from drunkenness. So see now how he argues that the good man will not be a drunkard: 'Nobody trusts secret information to a drunkard, but he entrusts it to a good man, so the good man will not be a drunkard.' Now pay attention to how the contrary is mocked in a similar syllogism (for it is enough to quote one out of many). 'Nobody trusts secret information to a man sleeping, but he entrusts it to a good man, so the good man does not sleep.'

Posidonius defends Zeno's position* as best he can, but as 10 I think, it can't be done even like this. He says 'drunkard' is used in two ways: the first when someone is actually drunk and incapable from wine; the second if he often gets drunk and is vulnerable to this flaw; that Zeno means the man who often gets drunk, not the one actually drunk, since nobody would trust secrets which could be uttered in one's cups to this man. This is false, because the first syl- 11 logism includes the man who is drunk, not the one who will be. You will grant that there is a big difference between the drunken man and the drunkard, since the man who is drunk may be so for the first time and not have this flaw, whereas even the drunkard is often free of being intoxicated. So I understand what is usually meant by this word, especially when it is used by a man who claims to be careful and scrutinize his language. Further, if Zeno understood this meaning and didn't want us to understand it, he was seeking an opportunity for deception through the ambiguity of the word, something that must be avoided in the search for truth. But suppose he realized this; 12 what follows is false, that secret information is not trusted to a man who is often drunk. Think how many times a general and a tribune and a centurion have given orders that had to be kept secret to soldiers who were not always sober. In the assassination of Gaius Caesar, that is, the one who took control of the government after the murder of Pompey, men trusted Tillius Cimber as much as Gaius Cassius.* Cassius drank water all his life, whereas Tillius Cimber overdid the wine and was prone to brawling. He himself joked about this: 'Am I to bear with any man, when I cannot even bear my wine?'

Now let each man name the men he knows who cannot be trusted 13 with wine, but can be safely trusted with information. Still, I can quote one instance that occurs to me in case it is forgotten. For we should equip our lives with distinguished models, and not always resort to the old ones. Lucius Piso,* the warden of the city, was drunk 14 from entry upon his office. He spent the greater part of the night in partying, then he used to sleep until noon: this was his morning routine. Yet he administered his position, on which the protection of the city depended, most scrupulously. Even the deified Augustus gave him secret instructions, when he appointed him governor of Thrace, which he subdued, and so did Tiberius when he set out for Campania, although he was leaving many elements in the city both

15 suspicious and hostile. I think that because Piso's drunkenness turned out well for him, Tiberius later made Cossus the warden of the city, a serious and moderate man, but one sunk in wine and a soak, so much so that on one occasion he passed out completely and was carried out of the senate meeting which he had attended coming straight from a party. Yet Tiberius gave him many instructions in his own writing, which he thought should not be trusted even to his own officials. And no secret, whether private or public, was leaked by Cossus.

16   So let us get rid of those common declamations: 'The mind bound by drunkenness is not under its own control; just as jars are cracked by fermenting wine and the strength of its heat brings up all the dregs from the bottom to the top, so when a man is heated with wine everything hidden below is brought up and comes out in public. As men loaded with undiluted wine cannot hold their food because the wine overflows, so they cannot hold a secret; they pour out equally what is

17 their own and what belongs to others.' Although this often happens, so does its opposite, that we deliberate over urgent matters with men whom we know are prone to drink. So this claim proposed in defence of Zeno's case is false, that a secret is not passed on to a man who often gets drunk.

How much better it is to accuse drunkenness openly and set out its faults, which even a mediocre man avoids, not to mention the perfected wise man. For the wise man it is enough to quench his thirst, and even if being excessively merry for some other reason urges him

18 on, he stops short of drunkenness. Instead we shall consider whether the mind of the wise man is disturbed by too much wine and commits the usual follies of a drunkard. Meanwhile, if you want to infer that the good man should not get drunk, why do you argue in syllogisms? Say how disgraceful it is to swill more than one can hold and not know the capacity of one's stomach; say how many things men do when drunk which make them blush when sober, and that drunkenness is nothing but a willed form of madness. Stretch out this condition of drunkenness for several days; will you doubt that it is madness?

As it is, it is not milder, but shorter. Quote the example of Alexander 19
of Macedon,* who ran his dearest friend Clitus through at a feast and
when he understood his crime wanted to die, as he certainly should
have. Drunkenness both inflames and exposes every fault, removing
the modesty which resists criminal behaviour. For more men refrain
from what is forbidden from shame at offending than from good
intentions.

When too great a quantity of wine has taken hold of the mind 20
whatever evil was hidden comes out. Drunkenness does not create
faults but drags them out; then the lustful man does not even wait for
the bedroom, but allows his lusts everything they demanded without
delay; then the pervert admits and broadcasts his sickness; then the
insolent man does not control his tongue or his hand. Pride swells up
in the arrogant, cruelty in the savage man, and meanness in the envious. Every fault is let loose and breaks out. Add to this that man is 21
unaware of his own behaviour, confused and unclear speech, glassy
eyes and a wandering step, dizziness so that the walls move as if a
whirlwind was driving the whole house around, the sufferings of the
stomach when the pure wine ferments and bloats one's organs. Now
it is just about bearable while maintaining its own force; what about
when it is corrupted by sleep and what was drunkenness becomes
indigestion? Think of the disasters caused by the drunkenness of 22
communities: it has surrendered the fiercest and most warlike nations
to their enemies; it has laid open the fortifications guarded for many
years through persistent warfare; it has driven the most defiant
peoples resisting the yoke under the domination of others; it has subdued with wine men unconquered in battle. Take Alexander, whom I 23
just mentioned. So many marches, so many battles, so many winters
which he passed overcoming the difficulties of seasons and terrain, so
many rivers tumbling from unknown regions, so many seas, all let
him go unharmed: it was his excess in drinking and the deadly goblet
of Hercules* which buried him. What is the glory of being able to 24
hold great quantities? When you have won the prize and men floored
by sleep and throwing up have refused the challenge of your toasts,
when you are the last survivor of the whole party, when you have
defeated them all in your grandiose valour and no one has been as
capable of holding his wine, you are overcome by the cask. What else 25
ruined Mark Antony, a great man of noble mind, and made him desert
to foreign customs and un-Roman faults, except his drunkenness and

his love for Cleopatra, no less than for wine.* This was what made him an enemy of the state, this made him unequal to his enemies; this made him cruel when the heads of the state's leading men were brought to him as he dined, when he reviewed the faces and hands of the proscribed in the middle of the most refined feasting and luxury fit for a king, when loaded with wine he was still thirsty for blood. It was unbearable that he got drunk when was doing such things; how much more unbearable that he did this sort of thing even when he was

26 drunk. Cruelty usually follows on intoxication, since the health of the mind is corrupted and inflamed. As chronic sickness makes men moody and difficult and enraged at the least slight, so constant bouts of drunkenness make the spirit savage. For when they are often out of their mind, the habit of madness is hardened and faults begotten of wine dominate even without it.

27 So tell me why the wise man should not get drunk; show the ugliness and offensiveness of the condition in actions, not words. And what is easiest: prove that those things called pleasures, once they have crossed the limit, are punishments. For if you try this argument, that the wise man is not intoxicated by much wine, and maintains the right behaviour even if he is tipsy, you may as well infer that he will not die after drinking poison, nor sleep when he is overcome by slumber, nor throw up and pass out whatever is sticking in his intestines after drinking hellebore. But if his feet are stumbling and his tongue unsteady, why should you think him partly sober and partly drunk? Keep well.

Letter 84 *(No Book number is preserved.) Seneca moves from reflections on the role of reading in enriching the mind to the nature of literary, specifically stylistic, imitation, and invokes analogies from nature of fusing many ingredients in an emulative style as bees compound honey from many varieties of flower, and or forming an original style in the way a son blends the personality inherited from his father (§8) with his own individual contribution to character, or a choral composition blends the different voices. What is needed for style as for moral virtue is single-minded concentration (§11) and indifference to material things.*

1 I believe those excursions of mine, besides shaking off my sluggishness, help both my physical health and my studies. You can see how they sustain my health; given that the love of literature makes me lazy

and indifferent to my body, I get my exercise from other men's effort. I will show you how they benefit my studying: I have not reduced my reading times. For they are essential, I think, first to prevent me from being content with my own resources, and secondly so that when I have made acquaintance with other men's investigations, I can pass judgement on what has been discovered and deliberate about what still needs discovering. Reading nourishes the intellect and restores it when it is wearied by study, but not without more study. We 2 should not limit ourselves to either writing or reading; the former will depress one's powers and exhaust them, the other will relax and weaken them. One should pass in turn from one to the other and blend one with the other, so that the pen will shape whatever has been gathered from reading into a body. We should imitate the bees, as 3 they say, which wander and harvest from flowers suited to making honey and then organize whatever they have brought back and distribute it over the honeycombs, and as our dear Virgil says:

> pack the flowing honey
> And fill the cells swollen with nectar sweet.*

As to the bees, it is not clear whether they draw the juice from the 4 flowers which immediately becomes honey, or transform what they have gathered by a kind of mixing and peculiar nature of their breath into this flavour. Some authorities believe they do not have any expertise in making honey, only in gathering it. They say that in the land of the Indians honey is found in the leaves of reeds, which is produced either by the dew from that climate or the sweet and rather thick moisture of the reed; they add that the same power is found in our plants, but less obvious and memorable, which the creature designed for this task pursues and compresses. Others believe that what the bees have plucked from the youngest green and flowering things is turned into this substance by its storage and arrangement, not, as they say, without some fermenting agent which makes different elements merge into one.

But not to be diverted into a different subject from our topic, we 5 too should imitate these bees and separate out whatever we have accumulated from the variety of our reading (for they are preserved better if kept apart), then, by applying the care and skill of our intellect, fuse those different tinctures into one flavour so that even if their source is clear, it is equally clear that the product is distinct from

the source. We see that nature does this in our bodies without any
6 effort on our part. The foods we have taken are a burden as long as
they remain of their own nature and swim as solids in the digestion,
but once they have been transformed from what they were, only then
do they pass into our strength and our blood. So let us provide the
same change in the foods that nourish the mind, so that we don't
allow whatever we have swallowed to stay whole, and foreign to us.
7 Let us digest these foods: otherwise they will enter the memory, not
the intellect. Let us accept them conscientiously and make them ours,
so that a single substance is formed from many, just as a single number
is made from individual numbers when one calculation takes in many
smaller and discrepant sums. Let our mind do this; it should hide
everything from which it has received support and only display what
8 it has achieved. Even if there is a resemblance to some model which
your admiration has planted rather deep, I want your words to resemble it as a son does, not like a portrait; a portrait is a dead object. 'Well
then, won't men recognize whose speech you are imitating? Whose
style of argument, whose aphorisms?' I think that at times they will
not recognize even this, if a man of great talent has imposed his own
form on every element that he has derived from some chosen model,
9 so that they merge into a whole. Don't you see how many voices go to
make a choir? Yet one sound is produced from them all. One voice is
high-pitched, another low, another of medium pitch: they add women
to the male voices, and the obligato of pipes: the individual voices are
10 hidden, while the sound of all together is clear. I am talking about the
choir as the philosophers of old knew it; now there are more singers
in our performances than there were once spectators in the theatres.
When the rank of singers has filled all the gangways and the auditor-
ium is ringed with trumpeters and from the stage every kind of pipe
and organ has sounded out, a harmony is made from these divergent
sounds. That is how I want our mind to be; there should be many arts
and many principles and examples taken from many generations, but
all cooperating together.
11   'How can this be achieved?' you ask. By constant concentration;
if we do not do anything unless Reason urges it, and avoid nothing
unless Reason urges against it. If you want to listen to her, she will
tell you: abandon those distractions which men have rushed to
enjoy; abandon riches, which are either a danger or a burden to their
possessors; leave the pleasures of body and mind, which soften and

weaken you; <u>abandon ambition</u>, which is a bloated, hollow, and windy condition, with no limit, as preoccupied with not seeing anyone precede it as not seeing anyone its peer, which suffers from envy, in fact a double envy. For you see how wretched it is when the man envied himself feels envy. Do you see those houses of the powerful, those 12 doorways riotous with the quarrelling of men striving to greet them?* These create a lot of insults for you as you enter and more when you have made your entrance. Go past those stairways of the wealthy and their entrance halls raised on huge platforms; when you stand there it is not only steep but slippery. Instead direct yourself this way, towards wisdom, and aim for its most calm and generous properties.

Whatever skills seem to excel in human life, even if they are small 13 and owe their prominence to comparison with the humblest things, are approached over difficult and steep paths. The way towards the high pediment of rank* is full of pitfalls; but if you choose to climb this peak, to which fortune has bowed her head, you will see everything that is thought to be most lofty beneath you, and yet you will reach the summit over level ground. Keep well.

Letter 86 *(No Book number is preserved.) Seneca has made a journey along the coast to visit the 250-year-old villa of the hero Scipio Africanus at Liternum, where he retired when he met political prosecution after his defeat of King Antiochus in 188 BCE. Seneca uses the contrast between Scipio's bare and simple bath-house and the luxury of modern bath suites to make a predictable contrast between ancient virtue and modern indulgence. In a second phase of the letter (§§14–21) he discusses the methods applied by Aegialus, the current owner of the estate, to transfer and replant olives and vines.*

I am writing this as I rest in the actual villa of Scipio Africanus, having 1 offered reverence to his shades and the altar which I believe is the tomb of the great man. For I am persuaded that his spirit has returned to heaven, from which it came, not because he led mighty armies—for so did Cambyses,* mad and profiting by his madness—but because of his exceptional moderation and piety, virtues more admirable when he left his country than when he defended it. For of necessity either Scipio was to be at Rome, or Rome at liberty.* He said: 'I do not want 2 to diminish her laws and customs in any respect. Let there be equal rights among all citizens. My country, enjoy the blessing I conferred on you without me. I was the cause of your liberty; now I will be its proof. I am departing, if I have grown greater than is in your interest.'

3 How could I fail to admire the nobility of heart with which he withdrew into voluntary exile and relieved the state of its burden? The situation had reached the point where either liberty would harm Scipio or Scipio liberty. Neither course was right, so he made way for the laws and retreated to Liternum, making his country as much a debtor for

4 his exile as for that of Hannibal. I have seen the villa made of squared-off stone, its wall set around a woodland, with towers raised on either side as bulwarks for the villa and a cistern big enough for an army* set below the buildings and nurseries, and a little bath-house cramped and dark in the old fashion; nothing seemed hot to our ancestors

5 unless it was also dark. So a great pleasure came over me as I considered Scipio's ways and our own; in this little corner that 'Dread of Carthage',* to whom it is due that Rome was captured only once, that hero used to wash his body weary with country chores. For he exercised himself with tilling, as was the custom of the men of old, and himself subdued the land. He stood there, beneath this mean and

6 shabby roof. This cheap paving bore his weight, but who is there now who would endure bathing like this? A man seems poor and mean in his own eyes if his walls do not gleam with vast and precious mirrors; unless marble from Alexandria is offset with Numidian overlay; unless the elaborate covering is framed and variegated like a picture; unless the ceiling is hidden by glass; unless Thasian stone, once a rare marvel in a temple, is set around our pools, in which we dip bodies made unhealthy by excessive sweating; unless the water comes from silver taps.

7   And so far I am talking about the plumbing of ordinary men; what will I say when I come to the baths of freedmen? What a quantity of statues and columns that do not support anything but are set as an ornament for the sake of their expense! What a quantity of water cascading like thunder over the steps! We have reached the level of

8 luxury where we are only willing to tread on precious stones. In this bath-chamber of Scipio there are tiny slits rather than windows cut out of the stone wall so as to admit light without risk to the fortified structure, but now they call baths mere moth-traps if they are not fitted out to let in the sun all day long through vast windows, unless men are simultaneously bathed and tanned, unless they see fields and seas from their bathtub. So establishments that won admiring crowds when they were dedicated are rejected as outdated when luxury has

devised something new to outdo herself. But once baths were few 9
and not decorated with any elegance; for why would one decorate
something bought for a penny and invented for utility, not pleasure?
Water was not poured in from below, nor did it always run fresh as
if from a hot spring, nor did they think it mattered how crystal clear
was the water where they shed their dirt. But ye gods, what a joy to 10
enter those dim baths covered with an everyday roof, whose water
you might guess Cato as aedile or Fabius Maximus or one of the
Cornelii had blended with his own hand!* For even the most noble
aediles performed this chore of entering the places which received
the common people and demanding cleanliness and a beneficial and
healthy temperature, not the one recently adopted as hot as a fire, so
much so that a slave convicted of some crime should be sentenced to
be bathed alive. It seems to me that there is no difference whether the
bath is burning or just hot. How some men now condemn Scipio for 11
lack of sophistication because he did not let the day into his hot bath
with wide windowpanes, because he did not stew in broad daylight
and wait to digest in his bath. Poor wretched man! He didn't know
how to live. He did not wash in filtered water but often in cloudy and
even muddy water, when it rained rather heavily. Nor did it matter
much to him whether he washed like that, since he used to come to
wash off sweat, not perfume. What do you think will be men's com- 12
ments? 'I don't envy Scipio: he really did live in exile if he bathed like
that.' In fact, if you only knew, he did not even wash daily, for as men
say who have recorded the early customs of the city, they used to wash
their arms and legs daily, since they had gathered dirt from working,
otherwise they washed all over on market-days. Here someone will
say: 'Obviously they were very dirty.' What do you think they smelled
of? War, work, manhood. Since fancy baths were invented men have
become filthier. When he is going to describe a man of ill-repute, 13
notorious for excessive indulgence, what does Horace say? 'Buccillus
smells of breath-sweetener.'* But if you presented Buccillus now, he
would be like a man smelling of old goat; he would be in the position
of Gargonius, whom Horace actually contrasted with Buccillus. It is
not enough to put on perfume unless it is refreshed two or three times
a day, so it does not fade on the body. And what are we to say when
they glory in this perfume as if it were their own nature?

If these reflections seem too grim to you, blame the villa, in which 14
I learned from Aegialus,* that most careful proprietor (for he is the

current owner of the estate), that any tree, however old, can be transplanted. We old men need to learn this, since none of us is not setting
up an olive grove for another generation,* <and I saw that an example
of three- or four-year-old trees with contemptible fruit could resume
15 producing.> You too will be protected by the tree which

> Grows slowly, bringing shade to late-born grandsons,*

as our Virgil says, who considered not what to say most truthfully but
most elegantly, not wanting to instruct farmers but to delight his
16 readers. For to pass over all the other cases, I will cite here words of
his that I was forced to prove wrong today:

> Spring is for sowing beans; then crumbling furrows
> Welcome the clover and the yearly millet crop.*

Whether they should be set at the same time or either crop has a
spring sowing you can judge from this; I am writing to you in June,
which will soon turn into July; and I saw men on the same day reaping
beans and sowing millet.

17   Let me return to the olive grove, which I saw set out by two methods. Aegialus transplanted the trunks of big trees with their branches
lopped all round and reduced to a single foot with their stock, after
cutting back the roots to leave only the head from which they hung.
He dipped this in manure and buried it in a trench, and then not only
18 heaped up the earth but stamped on it and pressed it down. He says
nothing is more effective than this 'pounding', as he calls it. I suppose
it shuts out cold and wind. Besides, the stock is less disturbed and lets
the new roots emerge and take hold of the ground, which even a light
shaking would uproot while they are flexible and barely clinging. Also
he shaves the stock of the tree before he buries it. For new roots
emerge from every part of the wood that is left bare. In addition, the
trunk should not project above the ground more than three or four
feet. For it will immediately be covered from the base and there will
not be a large part, as in old olive groves, that is dried up and charred.
19 This was his other method of planting: he took sturdy branches
whose bark, like the branches of new young trees, was not hard, and
he planted them in the same way. They grow a lot more slowly, but
although they have sprouted as if from the base they have nothing
20 rough or grim about them. I even saw an ancient vine being transplanted from its bush. Its tendrils should be gathered up as well,

if possible. Then the vine must be pinned down more extensively so that it will even form roots from its body. I saw vines laid out not just in February but at the end of March which are now holding and embracing new elms. In fact he says that all those trees which are 21 big-boled, so to speak, must be helped with water from the cistern, and if it does them good we have control over the rainwater.

I am not planning to give you more instruction, in case I make you into a competitor, as Aegialus made me his. Keep well.

Letter 87 *(No Book number is preserved.) This starts with a lively description of a two-day trip with his friend Maximus by mule cart with only bare supplies and a minimum (!) of slaves, which Seneca proudly contrasts with the false display of wealth by extravagant debtors—an ancient equivalent of the modern society of maxed-out credit cards. At §11 Seneca turns to the disputes of philosophical schools over the nature of the good, and the problem of detaching material goods from their origin in vicious activities. In fact material goods, or wealth, are the underlying issue of the whole letter. As Inwood,* The Stoic Reader *(Indianapolis: Hackett, 2008), 239, says: 'the main theme of the letter is wealth . . . in the conventional sense.' This is why the letter is important to our understanding of Seneca. His own wealth was an embarrassment to him in several ways. Ethically it was an obstacle to moral progress (cf. Mark 10: 23–5, esp. 25, where Jesus tells the rich man seeking to live virtuously that 'it is easier for a camel to go through the eye of a needle than for a rich man to enter into the kingdom of God'). Although Seneca declared in letter 5, §6 that it was a weak soul that could not handle wealth, he knew that his own self-imposed games of poverty were not an answer. Worse, though, was the danger that Seneca's wealth imposed on him. Nero wanted/ needed Seneca's riches, but refused to let Seneca make a present of them (see Introduction, pp. xi–xiv). It was hardly less dangerous to talk about this in personal terms, and the obliquities of this letter discussing whether wealth could be a good or was morally neutral or, worse still, a source of evil, are as near as Seneca approaches to his personal condition. (Letters 20 and 119, not in this selection, are also relevant.)*

The letter is typical of Seneca's hostile and inconsistent engagement with philosophical syllogisms. To make it easier to follow I have used Inwood's numbering of arguments, and set in italics all claims not endorsed by Seneca himself—whether made by Peripatetics, by Posidonius, or by certain other Stoics. For connoisseurs of philosophy there is a full discussion in Inwood, The Stoic Reader, *239–60.*

1 I suffered shipwreck before I even went on board ship; I am not going to add how this happened, in case you think this should be counted among the Stoic paradoxes, which I shall prove are in no case so false or surprising as they seem at first sight, whether you like this or even if you don't Meanwhile this trip showed me how many superfluous things we have and how easily we can deliberately put down things which we don't notice are taken from us when necessity has removed

2 them. I and my friend Maximus* have just finished a very happy two-day journey, with the few slaves one vehicle could hold and without any possessions except what were carried on our bodies. The pillow lies on the ground and I on the pillow; of my two cloaks one became

3 a groundsheet and the other a coverlet. Nothing could be subtracted from lunch; it was ready in less than an hour. We went nowhere without figs and never without notebooks; these serve as a relish if I have bread, and if not, for bread itself. They turn every day into a New Year* which I make 'happy and blessed' with good thoughts and the generosity of my spirit, which is never greater than when it has set aside eternal matters and made its peace by fearing nothing and its

4 wealth by desiring nothing. The vehicle in which I rode is a country cart; the mules prove they are alive by walking; the muleteer is unshod, but not because of summer. I can scarcely persuade myself to want this vehicle to seem my own; my perverse modesty over what is right still persists, and whenever we come into some more elegant company I blush in spite of myself, a proof that those values which I approve and praise do not yet hold a fixed and immovable place. A man who blushes at a shabby vehicle will vaunt himself in a costly one.

5 I haven't made much progress yet; I dare not display my thrift; I still care for the opinions of other travellers. Instead, I should have uttered this protest against the opinions of all the human race: 'You are mad, going astray, gaping at superfluous things and esteeming no one at his own value. When it comes to property you canny calculators establish the accounts of each man to whom you will either trust

6 money or favours (for you count these too as outlay): this fellow has wide possessions, but owes a great deal; the other has a handsome home, but bought with borrowed money; no one will present a more handsome household, but it doesn't match his debts; if he pays his

creditors he will have nothing left. You will have to do the same thing
in assessing the rest, scrutinizing how much each man has.' You think 7
he is rich because golden equipment follows him in the street, because
he has ploughlands in all the provinces, because his account-book is
bulky, because he owns as much land outside the city as a man would
be envied for possessing in the uninhabited parts of Apulia; when you
have said all this, he is poor. Why? Because he has debts. 'How much?'
you say. Everything, unless you judge there is a difference between
borrowing from a man or from Fortune. What difference does it make 8
that his mules are all dressed in one livery? What about those decorated vehicles?

> Winged steeds spread with purple embroidered cloths,
> Gold pendants hang from their breasts, and clad in gold,
> They chew gold bits between their teeth.*

Those things can neither make a master superior nor a mule. M. Cato 9
the censor,* whose birth was as valuable to the state as Scipio's (for one
waged war with our enemies, the other with our morals), used to ride
on a hack with pack-saddles laid upon it to carry his necessities. How I
would love him to encounter one of those cavaliers, displaying their
wealth on the road, driving runners and Numidians and a cloud of dust
before him! This man would certainly seem more refined and better
escorted than M. Cato, this fellow who among all those fancy trappings
is hesitating right now whether to hire himself out to the sword or the
knife.* What a credit to the age that a commander, triumphant general, 10
and censor, indeed something excelling all these things, a Cato, should
be content with one riding-hack, and not even the whole of that: for baggage occupied part of it hanging from either flank. So would you not
prefer that one horse rubbed down by Cato to all those plump ponies
and Spanish thoroughbreds and trotting-horses?

I see there will be no end to this topic unless I impose it on myself. 11
So I will fall silent here as far as concerns those hampers which the
man who first named them doubtless foresaw would turn out hampering.* Now I want to render to you a very few of our men's syllogistic arguments which concern virtue, which we maintain is sufficient
for a blessed life.

'What is good makes men good (for in music what is good makes a 12
musician). But the gifts of Fortune do not make a man good; so they
are not goods.'

(**First argument**) The Peripatetics* answer this challenge by declaring our first proposition false. They say that *'good men are not made at all costs from what is good. In music there is something good like a pipe or string or organ adjusted to the practice of singing: but none of*
13   *these makes a musician.'* We will answer them: 'You don't understand how we have determined what is good in music. For we are not talking of what equips the musician, but what he does. You are dealing with the tools of the art, not the art itself. But if anything is good in the
14   art, that at least will make a musician.' Even now I want to make this clearer. A good thing in the art of music can be meant in two ways, one which helps the effect of the musician, the other which helps the art itself. Instruments, pipes and organs and strings, are relevant to the effect, but not to the art. For a man is an artist even without them; perhaps he cannot use his art. This is not equally ambiguous in a man, for the same thing is the good of a man and of his life.

15   (**Second argument**) *'Anything that can be the lot of the most con-temptible and shameful person is not good: now wealth is the lot of a pimp and a gladiator trainer; so it is not a good thing.'*
         They say: *'What you propose is false; for in grammar and the art of*
16   *healing or piloting we see goods coming to the most humble men.'* But these arts do not claim greatness of the mind, they do not rise to the heights or shun the gifts of fortune; whereas virtue raises a man up and places him above what is dear to mortals; he neither longs for nor fears excessively what are called good or evil. Chelidon, one of Cleopatra's eunuchs, possessed a great property. Recently Natalis,* a man whose tongue was as foul as it was impure, who fellated women, was the heir of many men and made himself many heirs.* Well then, did money make him impure or did he befoul the money? It falls into
17   the hands of some men like a shilling into a sewer. Virtue takes its stand above such things; it is rated in its own coinage; it judges that none of those random incidental things is good. Medicine and pilot-ing do not forbid themselves and their adherents from admiring such things; someone who is not a good man can still be a doctor or a pilot, or a grammarian, as much, by Jove, as a cook. You would say that a man whose lot it is to possess an extraordinary thing is not himself an ordinary man; for a man is what he possesses.

18   An account is worth as much as it contains; indeed, what it con-tains comes into its receipts. Whoever put a price on a full purse except the sum of the amount of money it contained? The same thing

applied to the masters of great properties; they are merely accessories and attachments of the estates. So why is the wise man great? Because he has a great spirit. So it is true that something that can accrue to even the most contemptible fellow is not a good. So I will never call idleness good, since a cicada and a flea enjoy it. I would not even call being calm and free of trouble a good; for what is more at ease than a worm? You ask what makes a wise man? What makes a god. You must give him something divine, heavenly, and glorious; the good does not come to everyone nor suffer any ordinary owner. See

> What each region bears and what it rejects;
> Here crops, there grapes grow up more happily,
> Elsewhere the shoots of trees and grasses sprout
> Unbidden. Don't you see how Tmolus sends saffron,
> India ivory, and soft Sabaeans incense,
> But the bare Chalybes rough iron?*

Those products are separated by regions, so that trade with each other was necessary to mortals, if anyone wanted something from another man. So that highest of goods has its own place, it is not born where ivory or where iron is produced. You ask what is the place of the highest good? The spirit. Unless it is pure and chaste it cannot contain God.

(**Third argument**) '*A good thing is not made out of a bad one: but wealth is made from avarice; so wealth is not a good.*' He says: 'It is not true that a good thing is not born from a bad one; for money is made from sacrilege and theft. So sacrilege and theft are indeed an evil. But this is because it causes more bad things than good; for it gives profit, but along with fear anxiety and torture of mind and body.' Whoever says this must accept that sacrilege, just as it is bad because it causes many evils, is also good in some part, because it causes some good: but what could be more monstrous than this? And yet we have utterly persuaded men that sacrilege, theft, and adultery are thought good. How many men do not blush at theft, how many boast of adultery! For petty sacrilege is punished, but the loot of great ones is carried in triumphal processions.* Now add that sacrilege, if it is at all good in any part, will also be honourable and treated as done rightly: for the action is ours, a claim not accepted by the reflection of any mortal man. So good things cannot arise from bad ones. For if, as you say, sacrilege is bad for this one reason that it brings a lot of evil, if you

cancel the punishments, if you guarantee freedom from risk, it will
be entirely good. And yet the greatest punishment for crimes lies in
25 themselves. I tell you, you are mistaken if you postpone punishment
to the executioner or to prison: these deeds are punished immediately
when they are committed, even while they are being committed. So
good does not arise from evil, no more than a fig-tree from an olive;
shoots match their seed, and good things cannot be inferior to their
origin. Just as what is honourable does not arise from what is shameful, so good does not arise from evil, for the honourable and the good
are the same.

26   Some of our sect answer this as follows: '*Let us think money is good
from wherever it derives; yet the money does not arise from the sacrilege
even if it is taken by the sacrilege. Understand this in this way. There is
gold and a viper in the same vessel; if you take the gold from the vessel
you have not taken it because there is also a viper there, and, I repeat, the
vessel does not give me gold because it contains a viper, but it gives gold
although it also contains a viper. In the same way, profit comes from sacrilege not because sacrilege is shameful and criminal, but because it also
contains profit. Just as the viper in that vessel is a bad thing, not the gold
which lies there with the viper, so in sacrilege the crime is bad but not the
27 profit.*' I disagree: for the circumstances of each situation are totally
different. I can remove the gold from there without the viper, but I
cannot make the profit without the sacrilege; that profit is not attached
to the crime but blended with it.

28   **(Fourth argument)** Anything which makes us fall into many
evils when we want to obtain it is not a good thing: and while we
want to obtain wealth we fall into many evils, so wealth is not a good
thing.

        He says: '*Your proposition has two implications: one, that in wanting
to obtain wealth we fall into many evils. Now we also fall into many evils
when we want to obtain virtue: one man was shipwrecked while he was
29 sailing on a study voyage, another was captured. The other implication is
this; anything which causes us to fall into evils is not a good thing. It will
not be a consequence of this proposition that we fall into evils through
wealth or pleasures; or if we fall into many evils because of wealth, wealth
is not only not a good thing but a bad thing, but you are only saying that
it is not a good thing. Besides,*' he says, '*you admit that wealth has some
benefit; you count it among advantages, but on this same argument they
will not even be advantageous, for through wealth many disadvantages*

come to us.' Some people reply to these arguments: 'You are mistaken ₃₀ in blaming wealth for misfortunes. Wealth does not harm anyone; either each man is harmed by his own stupidity or another's wickedness, just as a sword does not kill anyone: it is the weapon used by the killer. So wealth does not harm you if you are harmed because of wealth.' Posidonius* had a better argument, as I think, in saying ₃₁ wealth was the cause of bad things, not because in itself it had any effect, but because it provoked those who would do harm. For an efficient cause, which inevitably does direct harm, is different from an antecedent cause. Wealth contains this antecedent cause: it puffs up men's spirit and begets arrogance and attracts envy, and carries the mind so far from itself that the repute for money delights us even when it will bring us harm. Now all good things should be free of ₃₂ blame; they are pure and do not corrupt minds or provoke them: they raise them up and expand them but without causing a swelling. Good things create confidence, but wealth creates rashness; things that are good give greatness of the spirit, but wealth gives insolence. Now insolence is nothing but a false appearance of greatness. Posidonius ₃₃ says: 'In that way wealth is even a bad thing, it does not just fall short of being a good thing.' It would be bad if it itself did harm, if, as I said, it contained an efficient cause; but as it is, wealth has an antecedent cause, one that does not incite the mind but attracts it; for it spreads before it a plausible appearance of good believed by most people. Virtue also has an antecedent cause for envy; for many men ₃₄ are envied for wisdom and many for justice. But this case does not come from it nor is it plausible. On the contrary, it is more plausible that virtue presents an appearance to men's minds which invites them to love and admiration.

   (Fifth argument) Posidonius says we should put the question ₃₅ like this: *'Things that do not give greatness or confidence or freedom from anxiety are not good; now wealth and good health and things like these do none of these things, so they are not goods.'* In fact he expresses this problem even more clearly in this way. *'Things that do not give greatness to the mind or confidence or freedom from anxiety, but produce insolence, pride, and arrogance, are bad things; now we are driven into these faults by the gifts of fortune, so they are not good.'*

   In fact, he says, 'on this principle they are not even assets or advan- ₃₆ tages. For the nature of advantages and of good things is different: an advantage is something containing more benefit than trouble; a good thing should be pure and harmless in all respects. A thing is not good which gives more benefit, but which gives nothing but benefit.

37 Besides, an advantage also belongs to animals and imperfect men and fools. So an advantage can be mixed, but it is called an advantage because it is assessed from its greater part; the good only belongs to the wise man; it ought to be free of damage.'

38 **(Sixth argument)** Keep cheerful; only one knot remains but it is the knot of Hercules. *'A good thing does not arise from bad, but wealth comes from many instances of poverty, so wealth is not a good thing.'*

Men of our school don't accept this problem, whereas the Peripatetics both invent it and resolve it. For Posidonius says* that this quibble, tossed around in all the schools of dialectic, is refuted by Antipater

39 in this way: 'Poverty is not named in terms of property, but in terms of loss (or as the men of old used to say, deprivation; the Greeks call this "according to emptiness"); he is not talking about what the poor man has but what he doesn't have.' So nothing can be filled from many empty things; many things add up to riches, but not many deprivations. He says: 'You are not understanding poverty as you should. For poverty is not what possesses few things, but what does not possess many things; so it is not called after what it has, but from what it lacks.'

40 I could express my meaning more easily if there was a Latin word that meant *anhuparxia*—'lack of resources'. Antipater assigns this meaning to poverty; I do not see what else poverty can be than the possession of very little. We will see about that question, if ever we have a lot of leisure, what is the essence of wealth and of poverty; but at that time we shall also consider whether it is better to soothe poverty and remove the arrogance from wealth than to quarrel about words, as if we had already cast our verdict about things.

41 Let us imagine we have been summoned to a public assembly and a law is being passed to abolish wealth. Are we going to support or resist these proposals? By these we shall ensure that the Roman people desires and praises poverty, the foundation and cause of its empire, but fears its own wealth; that the Romans bear in mind that they found wealth in the conquered, and from wealth ambition and bribery and riots invaded this most chaste and restrained of cities, that the spoils taken from nations were displayed too extravagantly, and that what one people snatched from all could more easily be snatched from this one by all of them? It is better to urge this and take their

desires by storm, not just curtail them. If we can, let us speak more boldly; if not, more openly. Keep well.

Letter 88 *(No Book number is preserved.) Seneca makes his topic clear from the beginning; Lucilius has supposedly asked for Seneca's valuation of cultural activities not focused on moral self-improvement. This provokes a disapproving survey of various liberal arts—the recognized ancient disciplines. See also letter 108 below.*

You want to know my opinion of liberal studies? I don't respect any 1 study or count it among good activities if it results in a profit. These are remunerative crafts, useful if they prepare the mind and do not distract it. One should linger in these activities as long as the mind cannot do anything greater; they are our elementary training, not our real work. You see why they are called 'liberal'. Because they are 2 worthy of a free man. But only one study is truly liberal, the one that makes him free: this is the study of wisdom, lofty, courageous, and great in soul: the rest are trivial and childish. Do you think there is any good in those arts whose teachers you see to be the most shameful and scandalous of all men? We ought not to learn these things, but to have learned them.

Some thinkers have judged that we should ask whether liberal arts make a man good; but they don't even promise this and lay claim to this knowledge. Grammar is preoccupied with care for speech, and 3 if it wants to spread further, about histories and, to extend its boundaries to the limit, about poetry. Which of these lays a path towards virtue? The explanation of syllables and conscientious attention to words and memorizing of stories and the law and modifications of verses—which of these removes fear, takes away desire, and reins in lust? Let us pass on to geometry and music: you will find nothing in 4 those arts which forbids one to fear and forbids desire. Whoever is ignorant of this gains nothing from knowing everything else.* < > whether those teachers teach virtue or not; if they don't teach it then they are not passing it on; if they teach it they are philosophers. Do you want to learn how far from teaching virtue they have taken their position? See how different are the studies of all these men among themselves, and yet there would be a resemblance if they taught the same thing. Unless perhaps they persuade you that Homer was a phil- 5 osopher,* but deny it by the very arguments from which they infer it;

for now they make him a Stoic who approved only of virtue and shunned pleasures and did not abandon what was honourable even at the price of immortality; now an Epicurean, praising the condition of a calm society that lives its life between parties and song; now a Peripatetic, who introduces three varieties of goods; now an Academic, who says everything is unknowable.* It is clear that he contains none of these if he contains all, since they are in conflict with each other. Let us concede to them that Homer was a philosopher, for he had become wise before he knew any poetry; so let us learn what made

6 Homer wise. But for me to investigate who was older, Homer or Hesiod, is not more relevant than to know, given that Hecuba was younger than Helen, why she carried her age so badly. What do you

7 think it matters to investigate the age of Patroclus and Achilles? Are you asking the route of Ulysses' wanderings rather than making sure we do not wander for ever? I have no time to hear whether he was tossed around between Italy and Sicily or beyond the world known to us (for such a prolonged wandering could not have occurred in so narrow an area); storms of the mind toss us around daily and bad- ness drives us into all the misfortunes of Ulysses. There is no lack of beauty to trouble our eyes, or enemies; on one side are savage mon- sters gloating over human blood, on the other treacherous charms for the ears, on yet another shipwrecks and so many varieties of evil. Teach me instead how to love my country, my wife, my father, and how I can sail even when shipwrecked towards these honourable

8 destinations. Why are you asking whether Penelope was unchaste, whether she hoodwinked her contemporaries? Whether she suspected Ulysses was the man whom she saw, before she found out?* Teach me what chastity is, and how great a good it contains, whether it is sited in the body or the mind.

9   I pass on to music. You teach me how high-pitched and low notes blend, how there is a harmony of strings that produce different pitches; no, better, make my mind harmonize with itself and my deci- sions will not clash with each other. You show me which are the modes for lament: rather, show me how I shall not utter sounds of lament among misfortunes.

10   The surveyor teaches me to measure my estates rather than teach- ing me how I am to measure what is enough for a man; he teaches me to count and lend my fingers* to avarice rather than teaching me that those calculations are irrelevant to the real issue: that a man

is not better off because his family property exhausts the accountants; rather, he should teach how superfluous are a man's possessions if he will be utterly wretched when he is compelled to count up for himself how much he possesses. What good does it do me to know how to 11 divide an estate into parts, if I don't know how to divide up with my brother? What is the benefit from assembling the feet within the acre and understanding if anything has escaped the notice of the surveyor, if I am saddened by an uncontrolled neighbour who is shaving something off my land? He teaches me how to lose nothing from my boundaries; but I want to know how to lose the whole estate cheerfully. He says: 'I am being driven out of my father's and grandfather's 12 lands', but who held this land before your grandfather? Can you tell me, not to what man but to what community it belonged?

You did not enter on it as a master but as a tenant farmer. Whose tenant are you? If things go well with you, of the heir. The legal experts say that no public property can be made private by possession; but what you are occupying and calling yours is public land, indeed land belonging to all humanity. Oh glorious art! You know 13 how to measure round areas and reduce whatever shape you have taken into square units; you can name the distances between the stars; there is nothing that does not come under your measurement; so if you are a craftsman, measure a man's mind, say how great it is, say how petty it is. You know what a straight line is; what good does that do you if you don't know what is straight in life?

I come now to the man who boasts of his knowledge of the heavens: 14

> Where chilly Saturn's star withdraws himself,
> What orbits heaven's Cyllenian fire explores.*

What good will it do to know this? For me to be anxious when Saturn and Mars stand in opposition or when Mercury will make an evening setting under the gaze of Saturn, rather than for me to learn that wherever they are, they are propitious and cannot change? The unin- 15 terrupted order of the fates and its unavoidable course drives them on; they move to and fro along fixed sequences and either provoke or indicate the outcomes of all events. But whether they cause whatever happens, what advance will the knowledge of an unchangeable phenomenon cause? Or if they only indicate, what use is it to foresee what you cannot escape? Whether you know these things or don't, they will happen.

16   But if you look to the scorching sun and stars
        Following in due order, tomorrow's hour will not deceive,
        Nor will a tranquil night's tricks cheat your trust.

17   I have taken enough and more than enough precautions to remain
safe from treachery. 'So will tomorrow's hour not deceive me? For
anything that happens to a person unawares cheats him.' I don't know
what will happen; I do know what could happen. I will not ask any
remission from this, but expect it all; if anything is remitted I will
be grateful for the favour. The hour deceives me if it spares me, but
it does not even cheat me in those terms. For just as I know that anything can happen, so I know that it will not take place at all costs; so I
expect favourable circumstances but am prepared for bad ones.

18   You must put up with me not following the prescribed order, for I
cannot be persuaded to welcome painters into the number of liberal
arts, any more than statue-makers or marble artists or other servants
of luxury. In the same way, I am thrusting out wrestlers and the whole
science based on mud and oil from these liberal arts; or else I will
also accept perfumers and cooks and the rest of those who lend their
19 minds to provide our pleasures. For, I ask you, what is liberal about
those starving vomiters whose bodies are stuffed with a forced diet
and minds live in starvation and sloth? Do we think this is a liberal
pursuit for our youth, which our ancestors exercised properly, of
hurling spears, twisting stakes, riding horses, and handling arms?
They taught their children nothing that could be learned by men
reclining at ease. But neither these arts nor those teach and nourish
virtue; for what is the gain from riding a horse and controlling his
pace with the reins while being torn apart by the most unreined
desires? What good is it to defeat many in wrestling or boxing, and be
overcome by anger?

20   'So, do liberal studies bring us no advantage?' Much for other
purposes, but nothing for virtue; for even those openly worthless arts
worked by hand contribute a lot to the tools of life, but are irrelevant
to virtue. 'So why do we train our sons in liberal arts?' Not because
these arts can bestow virtue, but because they prepare the mind to
accept virtue. Just as that first lettering, as the men of old called it, by
which the alphabet was passed on to boys does not teach the liberal
arts but prepares a place for taking them in presently, so the liberal
arts do not lead the mind up to virtue but get it ready.

Posidonius says there are four kinds of art:* there are the common   21
and sordid arts, there are arts of entertainment, arts of children,
and liberal arts. The common arts are those workmen's crafts which
depend on the hand and are busy with equipping life, which contain
no pretence of grace or the honourable. The arts of play are those   22
directed to the pleasure of the eyes or ears; you would include in these
the stage-engineers who contrive the platforms rising each on the
other and the storeys soaring silently aloft, and other unexpected
changes, either structures that held together opening to gape apart,
or those which were separate and now suddenly come together, or
those which were raised suddenly sinking down on to themselves.
These fascinate the eyes of the uneducated, who marvel at everything
unexpected because they don't know the causes. Childish arts are the   23
ones the Greeks call *encyclical* and our educators call liberal. But the
only really liberal arts, or to speak truly, free arts, are those preoccupied with virtue, bearing some resemblance to the liberal arts.

Just as one part of philosophy is natural, another is moral, and a   24
third logical, so this crowd of liberal arts is claiming a place for itself
in philosophy. When it comes to natural investigations they depend
on the evidence of geometry, so it is a part of the art which it supports. But many things support us without being a part of us, in fact   25
if they were part they would not support us. Food is support for the
body, but it is not a part of it. Geometry provides us with a service, so
it is necessary to philosophy as a carpenter is, but the carpenter is not
a part of surveying nor is surveying a part of philosophy. Besides,   26
each art has its limits; now the wise man seeks out and knows the
causes of natural phenomena, whose numbers and measures the surveyor explores and calculates. The wise man knows how the heavenly
bodies are maintained, their power and nature; the astronomer
deduces their paths and returning paths and some cycles according to
which they set and rise and sometimes give the appearance of standing still when it is not possible for heavenly bodies to stand. The wise   27
man will know the cause that produces reflections in a mirror; the
surveyor can tell you how far a body should be from the reflection and
what shape of mirror produces what reflections. The philosopher will
prove that the sun is big, and the astronomer how big it is, following
a procedure based on practice and exercise. But for him to proceed
he must first obtain some axioms, for his art is not independent, since
its basis is contingent. Philosophy asks for nothing from any other   28

source, but raises up the whole edifice from the ground; astronomy, so to speak, is superficial and builds on another art: It receives its first premises, and reaches further steps by their favour. If it reached the truth independently, if it could understand the nature of the whole universe, I would say that it contributes a lot to our minds, which grow by the contemplation of the heavenly bodies and draw some knowledge from on high.

29 The mind is perfected by one thing, the unchangeable knowledge of good things and evil; for no other art investigates good and evil things. I would like to go through the individual virtues. Bravery is a despiser of things to be feared; it despises and challenges and breaks down terrible things that would send our liberty under the yoke: so do the liberal studies strengthen this in any way? Faith is the most sacred good of the human heart, and is not compelled to cheat by any necessity, or corrupted by any reward: 'Burn me, flog me, kill me,' it says. 'I will not betray you, but the more the pain seeks out my secrets the more deeply I will hide them.' Can liberal studies make such courage in any way? Temperance controls the pleasures, shunning and driving away some of them, and regulating others, reducing them to a healthy level, and it never approaches them for their own sake; it knows that the best limit on things desired is not how much you want to take but

30 how much you ought to take. Humanity forbids us to be proud towards associates, or bitter; it behaves affably and easily in words, deeds, and emotions to everyone, it thinks no misfortune foreign to itself and loves its own good most of all because it is going to serve as good for some other person. Do liberal studies give any kind of instruction in this behaviour? No more than simplicity, modesty, and moderation, no more than economy and thrift, no more than clemency, which spares another man's lifeblood as if his own, and knows that a man must not be treated wastefully by another man.

31 'So,' someone says, 'when you say that we cannot reach virtue without liberal studies, how can you deny that they contribute anything to virtue?' Because one does not reach virtue without food, but food is not relevant to virtue; timber contributes nothing to a ship, although a ship cannot be made without timbers; there is no reason to think anything is made with the support of the material without which

32 it cannot be made. We can even say that one can reach virtue without liberal studies, for although virtue has to be learned is it not learned through them. So why should I think that a man will not be wise, if he

is uneducated in literature, when wisdom itself does not depend on literature? It passes on facts, not words, and I rather think a memory is more sure when it does not depend on any outside help. Wisdom 33 is a great and extensive thing; it needs space; one must learn about matters, divine and human, about the past and future, about transient and eternal matters, about time. Consider how many questions are asked about time alone: first, does it have an independent existence; then, whether anything is before time and without time; when the universe began or even before the universe, is it true that because something existed, so also did time? There are countless questions 34 just about the mind:* what is its origin, what kind of thing is it, when does it begin, how long does it last, does it pass from one place to another and change its homes, transmitted into different animal forms, or is it only enslaved once, to wander when it is released in the whole universe; is it a body or not; what will it do when it ceases to do anything on our account? How will it use its freedom when it escapes from this cage; does it forget what preceded and begin to know itself from the point where it is led away from the body and retreats into the empyrean? Whatever part of human and divine matters you grasp, 35 you will be wearied by a vast abundance of things to be investigated and learned. In order to give free hospitality to these many and great themes, you must remove superfluous thoughts from your mind. Virtue will not fit itself into these confined quarters; as a great matter wants open space. Let everything else be thrust out and the whole heart lie open to it.

'But the knowledge of many arts gives pleasure.' So let us retain 36 only as much of them as is necessary. Do you think a man should be reproached for procuring things beyond his needs and piling up a parade of costly things, and don't you think the same about the man preoccupied in the superfluous furnishing of culture? To want to know more 37 than is enough is a kind of lack of control. What about the fact that the pursuit of liberal arts makes men troublesome, wordy, tactless, self-satisfied, and so unable to learn the necessary ideas because they have learned superfluous ones? The grammarian Didymus wrote four thousand books; I would feel pity for him if he had read as many superfluous works. In these books the homeland of Homer is investigated, the real mother of Aeneas,* whether Anacreon was more lustful or drunken, whether Sappho was a public whore, and other things which would need to be unlearned if you knew them. Now go and deny that life is long!

38   But when you have reached our philosophers too I will show you
many things to be cut back with an axe. The encomium, 'Oh what a
cultured man!' costs a great waste of time and trouble to other men's
39 ears. Let us be content with this simpler encomium, 'Oh what a good
man!' Is this how things stand? Shall I unroll the records of all nations
and investigate who first composed poetry? Shall I calculate how
much time elapsed between Orpheus and Homer, when I don't have
a chronology? And shall I review the signs with which Aristarchus
edited other men's poems, and spend my life on syllables?* Shall I
stick in the dust of geometry?* Has that beneficial precept escaped
me: 'Be sparing of time'? Shall I know this sort of thing, and what
40 shall I not know? Apion the grammarian, who toured all Greece under
Gaius Caesar and was adopted by all their states in the poet's name,
said that Homer, after completing both epics, the *Odyssey* and *Iliad*,
added a beginning to his work in which he included the whole Trojan
War. Apion adduced as proof that Homer had deliberately put two
41 letters in the first line containing the number of his books. This is
the sort of thing a man should know who simply wants to know a
great deal.

    Don't you want to consider how much time your ill-health is
taking from you, how much time is taken by public duties, how much
by private duties, how much by your daily routine, and your sleep?
42 Measure your life; it cannot contain so many distractions. I am talking about liberal arts; but how much superfluous stuff philosophers
too have, how much remote from usefulness! They themselves have
stooped to the distinction between syllables and the peculiar uses of
conjunctions and prepositions, and have shown envy of grammarians
and geometers; whatever is superfluous in their arts the philosophers
have transferred into their own. So they have brought it about that
43 men know how to speak more scrupulously than to live. Listen to
what harm is done by excess subtlety, and how hostile it is to truth.
Protagoras* says that one can dispute with equal fairness on both
sides about any topic. And about the actual question whether every
thing can be disputed on either side, Nausiphanes says that of what
44 we can see nothing is more existent than non-existent. Parmenides
says that, 'of what we can see, nothing exists in universal terms'. Zeno
of Elea cast out all business from his business: he said nothing existed.
The Pyrrhoneans occupy themselves with the same kind of thing, as
do the Megareans and Eretrians and Academics, who have introduced

a new kind of knowledge, knowing nothing. Throw all of these sub- 45
jects into the superfluous flock of liberal studies; one lot are handing
on a knowledge which will not benefit me, while the others are
removing all hope of knowledge. It is better to know superfluous
things than nothing. But they are not holding out a light to direct our
vision to the truth, while the others are even gouging out my eyes. If
I believe Protagoras, there is nothing that is not doubtful in nature;
if I believe Nausiphanes, this alone is certain, that nothing is certain;
if I believe Parmenides, there is nothing but the one; if Zeno, there
is not even that one. So what are we? What are those things that sur- 46
round and feed and sustain us? The whole world is a shadow, either
empty or deceitful. It would not be easy to say which group angers
me more, those who wanted us to know nothing, or those who did not
even leave us this option, of knowing nothing. Keep well.*

Letter 90 (Book XIV.2) *Seneca starts from the theme of our debt to the
gods and to wisdom itself that we are able to live a good life. In this letter
Seneca presents his view of the wise man's contribution to human civilization, arguing primarily against the first-century* BCE *Posidonius of Apamea
(cf. letters 33, 78, 83, 88 above). Posidonius, a polymath, historian, geog-
rapher, and cosmologist (he wrote on the tides), was the most famous Greek
intellectual of his day (cf. 20), so prominent as a leading citizen of Rhodes
that he was sent as ambassador to represent its interests with Rome. He
worked the wise man into his portrait of social evolution by making him
the 'first discoverer' of key elements in the progress of civilization, not only
moral and social arts, like ethics and rhetoric, but the original technological
inventions: Seneca protests (cf. §7 ff.), partly, no doubt, because he sees
wisdom as strictly a teacher of morality, but partly from social discrimination (going back to Plato's strictures on* banausoi, *and shown also in
Cicero's* On Obligations) *against workers in crafts and trades, who were
often slaves, and seen as incapable of moral or intellectual concerns.*

*Seneca argues that arts such as hunting and carpentry are simply prod-
ucts of cleverness, not wisdom (§11), and are quickly perverted into the
devising of luxuries: basic discoveries such as that of milling grain for bread
and the art of weaving (§§20–3) did not require wisdom, only ingenuity.
He outlines the proper concerns of philosophy (§34) and turns to the innocence of the primitive Golden Age made familiar to Romans by Virgil's*
Georgics, *blessed in its lack of the luxuries which Seneca reviled.*

1   Dear Lucilius, who can doubt that we live by the gifts of the gods, but
    live well by the gifts of Philosophy?* We could be sure that we have
    a greater debt to Philosophy than to the gods, since a good life is
    a greater gift than life itself, if it were not the gods who originally
    bestowed Philosophy upon us: they gave absolute knowledge to no
    man, but the ability to practise Philosophy to us all.

2   If they had made the human good of wisdom common to all and we
    had been born with forethought, wisdom would have lost its finest
    property, of not being among the gifts of fortune. As it is, wisdom has
    this precious and glorious quality, that it does not offer itself, that
    each man owes it to his own efforts, and it is not to be gained from
    others. What would there be for you to revere in Philosophy if it were
3   a gift of favour? It is Philosophy's sole task to discover the truth about
    divine and human affairs; religious scruple, piety, justice, and all the
    other retinue of interrelated and mutually supportive virtues never
    stray from this pursuit. Philosophy taught us to worship things divine
    and love human society, that authority lay with the gods and collab-
    oration with mankind. And this collaboration remained unbroken for
    some time before greed tore apart partnership and brought poverty
    even to those it made most wealthy, since once they craved each his
4   personal property they ceased to possess everything. But the earliest
    mortals and those of their descendants who pursued nature without
    being spoiled shared the same guide and law, being entrusted to the
    decisions of a superior, since it is natural for inferior things to give
    way to more powerful ones. Take herds of dumb animals: either the
    biggest or the strongest creatures have command. It is not the bull
    inferior to his breeding but the one who surpasses the other males in
    size and muscle who goes before the herds; it is the tallest elephant
    who leads the troupe; among men, 'the best' replaces 'the biggest'.
    So the ruler used to be chosen for his intellect, and the greatest
    happiness among nations was enjoyed by those among whom only
    the superior man could be more powerful. A man can safely enjoy as
    much power as he wishes if he believes he only has power to act as
    he should.

5   In the age that men call golden Posidonius* believes that monarchy
    belonged to wise men. They controlled human action and protected
    weaker persons from stronger; they successfully argued for and
    against decisions and showed what was expedient and harmful; their
    foresight ensured that their people lacked nothing; their courage

warded off dangers, their generosity advanced and enriched their
subordinates. To be in command was a service, not a form of domination. No man tested how much power he could wield against those
who had conferred that power upon him, nor did anyone have the
intention or excuse for wronging them, since it was good to obey a
good commander, and a king could make no worse threats to those
who disobeyed than that of resigning from his monarchy.

But as vices gradually developed and monarchies turned into 6
tyrannies, a need arose for laws which themselves were originally
proposed by wise men. Solon, who founded Athens as a democracy,
was one of the seven men known for wisdom:* if Lycurgus had been
born in the same age he would have been counted eighth in the sacred
band. The laws of Zaleucus and Charondas win praise; but these
men did not learn from public life or from the halls of jurisconsults,*
but from the chaste and silent retreat of Pythagoras the laws which
they laid down for Sicily and the Greek society throughout Italy in
their prime.

So far I am in agreement with Posidonius: but I would not grant 7
that the arts of daily life were discovered by philosophy, nor would I
claim for it the glory of manufacture. He says: 'Philosophy taught
men scattered or sheltering in huts or some dug-out cave or the trunk
of a hollow tree to construct buildings.' But I believe that philosophy
no more devised these contrivances of dwellings soaring storey upon
storey and cities weighing down upon cities than it devised fishponds,*
enclosed so that human gluttony would not run the risk of storms, and
luxury would have safe havens however much the seas raged in which
to force-feed its privileged flocks of fish. What do you think? Did phil- 8
osophy teach men to use a lock and key?* What else was this but giving
a signal for greed? Did Philosophy erect these looming structures with
so much risk to their tenants? For it was not enough for men to take
random shelter and find themselves some natural container without
difficulty. Believe me, that age was blessed before the coming of archi- 9
tects and masons. These amenities were invented when luxury was
already coming to birth; to square off logs and split a beam with sure
hand as the saw ran along the marked traces:

For the first folk split the brittle wood with wedges.*

They were not preparing buildings for a banqueting-hall then,
nor was pine or fir conveyed in a long train of vehicles that shook

the streets, just to suspend coffered ceilings made from it and heavy
10 with gold. Forked timbers, supported on both sides, propped up a
hut: they arranged branches packed together and heaped with foliage,
tilting them downwards to serve as a drain for even the most intense
rains. Men lived without anxiety under these shelters; the thatch covered free men, whereas slavery lives under marble and gold.

11   I also disagree with Posidonius in his claim that joiners' tools were
invented by wise men; for on that basis we could say that it was thanks
to wise men that mankind discovered

> How to hunt beasts with traps, cheat birds with lime,
> And to surround great moors with packs of hounds.

For it was the shrewdness of men, not real wisdom, that discovered
12 all these things. I also disagree with the claim that it was wise men
who discovered mines of iron and bronze, when the earth, scorched
by forest fires, poured out molten veins lying near its surface: such
contrivances as these are discovered by the sort of men who exploit
13 them. Nor does it seem to me such a delicate question as it does to
Posidonius, whether the hammer or the tongs were first put to use. In
both cases someone of lively talent, sharp but not great or lofty, discovered them, and whatever else must be found by bending over the
body and turning one's mind towards the ground.* The wise man was
undemanding in his way of life. How could he fail to be? Even in this
14 age he would be eager to live as simply as possible. I ask you, how is it
consistent for you to admire both Diogenes and Daedalus?* Which
of these seems wise to you? The man who devised the saw, or the one
who saw a boy drinking water from the hollow of his hand and immediately took his cup out of his knapsack and broke it, scolding himself
like this: 'Fool that I am! How long I carried superfluous baggage!'
15 The man who tucked himself into a tub and slept in it? Which man
would you now think wiser? The one who discovered how to spray
saffron to a great height from hidden pipes,* who fills channels with
an instant surge of waters or dries them out, and constructs revolving
ceilings for dining-halls so that one shape is formed after another and
the vaults overhead are changed as often as the dinner-courses, or the
man who shows himself and others how nature has made no harsh or
difficult demands on us; that we can be housed without the marble-
cutters and the carpenter, that we can be dressed without the silk
trade, that we can have what is essential for our needs if we are

content with what the earth set out on its surface? And if the human race was willing to listen to him, it would know that a cook is as unnecessary as a soldier.

Those men were wise, or at least like sages, who kept the protection 16 of their body simple. Essentials require simple maintenance; the effort is spent on luxuries. You won't need craftsmen; just follow nature. She did not want us to be hampered; she equipped us for whatever she imposed on us. 'Cold is unbearable for a naked body.' So what? Cannot the skins of wild beast and other animals defend us well enough and lavishly from the cold? Don't most tribes cover their bodies with the bark of trees? Aren't the feathers of birds woven together to form a garment? And don't the majority of the Scythians to this day wear skins of foxes and rodents, which are soft and cannot be penetrated by the winds? What, then? Haven't ordinary men woven wickerwork by hand and smeared it with cheap mud, then covered the gables with straw and other woodland products and passed the winter free of anxiety as the rains ran down the slopes? 'But we 17 need to fend off the heat of the summer sun with a thicker form of shade.' What? Didn't antiquity hide away many places hollowed out into a cave either by the violence of the weather or some other accident? What? Don't the peoples of the Syrtis* lurk in dugouts, and other tribes who find that because of the sun's scorching heat no covering is sufficiently solid to drive off the hot spells except the dry ground? Nature was not so unfair that when she gave all other living 18 things an easy passage through life, man alone could not live without all these crafts; she has not given us any harsh orders or made anything hard to obtain in order that life could continue. We have been born with a ready supply: we have made everything difficult for ourselves by our disdain for easy things. Roofs and coverings and warmth for our bodies and foodstuffs and things that have now become a great trouble were to hand and free of cost, and could be prepared with little effort. In fact our demand for everything was limited to our actual need; we made those things costly and marvellous, we made them things to be acquired by complex and multiple crafts. Nature is enough for her own demands. It is luxury that has rebelled from 19 nature; daily it eggs itself on and has been growing for so many ages and fosters its own faults by its talent. First it began to hanker after superfluous things, then perverse things, and recently it has enslaved the mind to the body and bid it play slave to lust. All those crafts by

which a community is beset and disturbed are working for the body,
for which we once provided all needs as we would for a slave, but now
we prepare them as for a master.* So there are workshops here for
weavers, there for joiners, here again for those cooking up perfumes,
and over there the studios of men who teach effeminate dance-steps
and effeminate and degenerate songs. The natural measure that limited our desires to necessary equipment has given way: now it is a
mark of boorishness and poverty to want what is enough.

20   It is unbelievable, dear Lucilius, how easily the sweetness of eloquence leads even great men away from the truth. Here is Posidonius,
in my opinion one of those who has made the greatest contribution
to philosophy, in the process of trying to describe how some threads
are twisted while others are pulled from the soft loose wool, then how
the loom lets down the warp pulled straight by hanging weights, how
the weft is woven in to soften the hardness of the web pressing down
on both sides and forced by the blade to coalesce and combine. He
claims that the art of weaving too was discovered by wise men: but he
forgets that later a more refined variety was discovered, in which

The warp was bound to the loom, a reed separated the threads,
The weft was interwoven by the sharp-edged shuttles,
Which the teeth set in the comb smooth far and wide.*

What if he had chanced to see the looms of our age, on which a
garment is woven that will conceal nothing, in which I don't say there
21 is no defence for the body, but none for modesty? Then Posidonius
moves on to farmers and describes with equal eloquence the ground
cleaved by the plough and reploughed so that the loosened soil will
open up more easily for the roots, then the sowing of seeds and weeds
picked out by hand so that nothing accidental and wild will grow up
and choke the crop. This too he calls the work of wise men, as if the
cultivators of land are not still today finding many new techniques for
22 increasing fertility. Then he is not content with these crafts, but forces
the wise man into the mill:* for he explains how he began to make
bread by imitating nature. He says: 'When the grain is taken into the
mouth the hardness of the teeth coming together breaks it up and
whatever falls out is returned to the teeth by the tongue; then it is
mixed with moisture so as to pass more easily down the slippery
throat; when it reaches the stomach, it is digested by the constant
23 heat, and then finally is added to the body. Someone followed this

model and put a rough stone on top of another like the teeth, and the fixed part waits for the action of the other; then the grains are smashed by the rubbing of the two stones and are returned frequently until by constant grinding they are reduced to minute size; then water was sprinkled on the flour and by constant handling used to soften it and form bread, which was first cooked through by hot ash and a scalding tile, then gradually ovens were discovered and other types of container whose heat would satisfy demand.' He almost went to the length of saying cobbling was discovered by wise men.

All of these things reasoning discovered, but not right reasoning. 24 For these are the inventions of man, not a wise man, as much as the boats in which we cross rivers and seas, with their sails fitted to catch the motion of the winds and tillers attached in the rear to twist the ship's course this way and that. The model is derived from fish, which steer themselves by their tail and with a light thrust on either side turn their speeding course. He says: 'Yes, the wise man invented all of 25 these things, but he gave tasks too petty for him to handle to more humble servants.' In fact these things were discovered by the same people who take care of them even today. We know that some inventions only emerged within our memory, like the use of windows passing the light through a transparent pane; like the fittings of baths and the tubes pressed into the walls through which the heat was spread around so that it warmed the lowest and highest levels equally.* Need I mention the marbles which make temples and house gleam? What about the massive stones shaped to be round and smooth, on which we support porticoes and buildings big enough to hold nations? What about the signs for words which catch even the swiftest speech, letting the hand keep up with the speed of the tongue? These are contrivances of the lowest kind of slaves: wisdom has a more lofty seat, and does not teach the hand: it is the teacher of minds. Do you want 26 to know what it has unearthed and achieved? Not graceful movements of the body nor different tunes for the trumpet and pipe, which catch the breath and form a sound either in its passing or its emission. Wisdom does not devise arms or walls or weapons of war, it supports peace and summons the human race to harmony. It is not, I insist, the 27 craftsman and inventor of tools for essential use. Why do you assign such petty things to it? You are looking at the craftsman of life itself. It has other arts under its mastery, for if life itself is subservient to anything then so are the ornaments of living; but otherwise

philosophy is aiming towards a blessed condition, it leads there and
28 opens up the way to it. It shows what is bad and what seems so; it casts
the emptiness out of minds and gives them real, solid greatness,
trimming back what is swollen and showy but hollow, and it does not
let the difference between great and bloated things go unnoticed;
it passes on knowledge of the whole of nature and of itself. It makes
clear the gods and their nature, the nature of the gods of the underworld, of the household and personal spirits, and of the souls that
have suffered their full life to become a secondary form of divinity,*
where they dwell, and what are their activities, powers, and will.
These are wisdom's initiations, which open up not some local shrine
but the vast temple of all the gods, the universe itself, whose true likenesses and appearances it has brought forth for minds to perceive;
29 for human eyesight is too blunt for such great visions. Next wisdom
returned to the beginnings of things and the eternal reason which
infuses it all and the force of all the elemental seeds which individually delineates each kind. Then it began to investigate the mind, its
origin, place, duration, and divisions. Next it transferred itself from
bodies to things without body and explored the truth and its proofs;
after that how ambiguities of life and speech were distinguished; for
in both false things are mixed in with true.

30   The wise man has not withdrawn himself from those arts (as it
seems to Posidonius), but never came near them. For he would have
found nothing worth discovering unless he judged it to deserve continuous use; he would not have taken up things to be put down again.
31 Posidonius says: 'Anacharsis invented the potter's wheel, which shapes
vases by its rotation', then because a potter's wheel is found in Homer
he preferred the verses to be thought false rather than this myth.

    I argue that Anacharsis was not the inventor of this technique, and
if he was, then its inventor was certainly a wise man but he did not
invent it *qua* wise man, just as wise men do many things as men, and
not as wise men. Imagine that the wise man is very swift; he will over-
take everyone in a race by being swift, not by being wise. I wish I could
show Posidonius a glass-blower, who can form glass with his breath
into various figures such as could hardly be shaped by a careful hand.
    These skills were discovered after we had stopped seeking wisdom.
32 He says: 'Democritus* is said to have invented the arch, so that the
curve of the stones gradually sloping would be held together by the
central keystone.' I shall say this is false; for there were inevitably
bridges and doorways, before Democritus, whose upper surfaces

are curved. Further, you have forgotten that the same Democritus is 33
supposed to have discovered how to soften ivory, how pebbles could
be heated and turned into emeralds, a process by which stones suited
for this are coloured today. Suppose the wise man invented these
processes, he did not do it *qua* wise man; for he does many things
which we see are performed either with more skill or more practice
by the least wise of men.

You ask me what the wise man has explored, what he has brought 34
into the daylight? First the truth and nature, which he did not follow
with his eyes like other living creatures, since eyes are sluggish for
seeing divine things; then a code of law of life, which he has shaped to
match the universe, and he not only taught men to know the gods but
to follow them and to receive things that occurred by accident in the
same way as what was commanded. He forbade men to obey false
opinions and he weighed up by a true reckoning what each thing was
worth; he condemned pleasures that entailed remorse and praised
goods that would always please us, and he made it obvious that the
man is most blessed who does not need blessedness, and most powerful who has himself in his own power. I am not talking about that 35
philosophical sect which has placed the citizen outside his own country and the gods outside our world, which has made a present of virtue
to pleasure,* but about that philosophy which thinks nothing good
unless it is honourable, which cannot be beguiled by the gifts of man
or fortune, whose price is that it cannot be taken in by any price.

I do not believe that this philosophy existed in that raw age when
crafts were still lacking and useful skills were learnt from experience
itself. <Next came> blessed times, when the generous gifts of nature 36
lay there in public for general use, before avarice and luxury forced
mankind apart and taught them to separate from their partnership
and fan out for raiding: these were not yet wise men, even if they did
what the wise must do. One could feel more admiration for any other 37
condition of the human race, nor would God, if he allowed someone
to give shape to earthly things and customs to their tribes, have given
more approval to any other condition than the society which is
reported to have existed among men:

> No farmers tilled the fields
> Nor was it right to mark the plain with bounds,
> Men sought from a common source and earth itself
> Produced most lavishly without any man's demand.*

38 What was more blessed than that race of men? They enjoyed the
world in common; earth, like a mother, was sufficient for the protection of all men; this protection was the carefree possession of public
resources. Surely I could call that race of men most wealthy, since you
could find no poor man among them! Avarice broke into these fine
conditions, and in wanting to divert something and turn it to its own
use, it put everything beyond its control and reduced itself from
unlimited abundance to a narrow compass. Avarice imported poverty,
39 and by lusting after many things lost them all. So though it may try to
replace what it lost, while it adds estates to estates, driving out a
neighbour either by bribery or injustice; while it extends its lands
to the scale of provinces and calls a long journey abroad through his
own lands possession; no extension of our boundaries will restore
things to the point from which we departed. When we have gone to all
40 lengths we will have much; but we once had it all. The earth itself was
more fertile when it was not tilled, and it was generous for the benefit
of people who did not plunder it. Whatever nature had produced, it
was no less a pleasure to have discovered it than to show what was
discovered to another; for there could not be either a surplus or a
shortage for anyone since the produce was shared out among men in
harmony. The stronger man had not yet set his hand upon the weaker,
the miser had not yet shut out another from even essentials by hiding
away what was stored for his own use; there was equal concern for
another and for oneself.
41   Weapons of war were idle and hands unstained by human blood
turned all ill-will towards wild beasts. Men whom a thicket had protected from the sun, who lived safe from the savagery of winter or
rainstorms, in a cheap hideaway under the foliage, passed calm nights
without sighing. Anxiety makes us toss in our purple and rouses us
with the sharpest goads; but how soft a sleep the hard earth gave to
42 them! They were not overhung by engraved ceilings, but the stars
glided overhead as men lay in the open and the universe swept onward
as a glorious show for the nights, performing this great task in silence.
The panoramas of this most beautiful home lay open as much by day
as by night; it was their pleasure to gaze on the constellations sinking
from the midpoint of the sky, and others again rising from their hidden
43 sources. How could men fail to rejoice in wandering among such
widely spread marvels? But you panic at every sound from your roof,
and if anything creaks among your paintings you flee thunderstruck.

Fall of man when left nature

They did not have dwellings on the scale of whole cities; they had breezes and free flow of air among the open spaces and the light shade of a rock or tree and crystal-clear springs and streams not distorted by digging or any pipe or forced conduit but running freely, and meadows lovely without artifice, among these a country home cleaned by a country hand—this was a home according to nature, in which it was a delight to live, neither fearing the structure nor on its behalf; for now our residences are a great part of our fear.

But although their life was exceptional and free from deceit, there 44 were no wise men, since this name is now given to the greatest achievement. Yet I wouldn't deny that there were men of lofty spirit, men sprung, so to speak, freshly from the gods; nor is there any doubt that the universe yielded superior things when it was not yet worn out. Just as the character of all men was braver and more ready for toil, so there were not yet intellects perfected in all things. For nature does not give us virtue; it requires an art to become good. Indeed, they did 45 not hunt for gold or silver or transparent stones in the deep dregs of the earth, and they still spared unreasoning animals; so far were they from the state when a man kills another not in anger or fear but just to watch the show. They did not yet have embroidered clothing, gold was not yet woven into fabric, nor was it even mined from earth at that time. So what is the issue? They were innocent out of ignorance 46 of worldly matters, and it makes a great difference whether someone does not want to offend or does not know how to. They did not have justice, or forethought, or temperance and courage. This primitive life had things similar to all these virtues, but virtue does not come to a mind unless it is trained and taught and brought to its highest condition by constant exercise. We are certainly born for this goal, but without it, and even in the best men before you educate them, there is the raw material of virtue, but not virtue itself. Keep well.

Letter 91 (Book XIV.3) *The great fire of Lyons. This event of August 64 CE provides the main key to the dating of the correspondence. Founded by Munatius Plancus in 43 BCE (as Seneca tells us), the city became the administrative centre for the three Gauls, and seat of the imperial cult. Given its position at the confluence of two great rivers, the Saône and Rhone, it is amazing that no part of the city seems to have escaped destruction, and it has been suggested that the alleged immensity*

*of the fire, and indeed the whole narrative, may be a substitution for the
very recent fire of Rome (compare §15 below, and see Tacitus, Annals,
XV.38–43) which Seneca would avoid mentioning because of the popular
rumours blaming Nero. Seneca uses the disaster as an illustration of the
mortality of both men and their creations, and a warning that we cannot
know how soon cities and men may perish. From §16 Seneca is concerned
with the personal lesson of such disasters, adding in §19 as a subsidiary
theme the misrepresentation of death by shallow human gossip.*

1 Our friend Liberalis* is upset at the announcement of the fire which
burnt down the colony of Lyons; this disaster could have distressed
anyone, all the more a man devoted to his native city. This accident has
made it a struggle for him to recover his strength of mind, which I
suppose he had exercised over fears he thought could be expected. But
I am not surprised if this unforeseen and almost unheard-of calamity
was not feared, since it was also without precedent; for fire has damaged many communities but never annihilated any of them. Even when
fire has been unleashed against houses by enemy action it fails in many
places, and although kindling instantly, it seldom consumes everything so absolutely as to leave nothing for demolition. Even among
earthquakes there has not been any so dreadful and ruinous that it
overthrew whole towns. In short, no fire ever sprang up anywhere so
2 deadly that nothing was left for a second fire. So many noble structures, each fit to give glory to individual cities, were laid low by one
night, and in this time of such peace a disaster occurred so extreme
that men would not have feared it even in war. Who would believe it?
When warfare was lulled everywhere, when secure peace was spread
throughout the world, Lyons, once the pride of Gaul, is nowhere to
be seen. Fortune allows everyone whom it strikes down on this public
scale a chance to fear what they were going to suffer; no great entity
does not require some span of time for its ruin, but in this case one
night came between a mighty city and nothing. In fact I am taking
longer to tell you of its destruction than that destruction took.

3 All these events are depressing the mood of our friend Liberalis,
although he is strong and upright in the face of his own misfortunes.
Nor was he shaken without cause, for unexpected disasters weigh
more heavily; novelty adds weight to calamities, and there is no mortal
man who has not felt more grief at something that left him in amaze-
4 ment. So we should make sure nothing is unforeseen; we must send

our mind ahead to face everything and think not of whatever usually happens but whatever can happen. For is there anything that fortune does not drag down from even the most flourishing success when she chooses to? Is there anything she does not assail, and shatter all the worse because of its brilliance and glitter? What is hard or difficult for her? She does not always attack by a single approach, not even 5 the common one; sometimes she invites our own action against us, sometime she is content with her own power and devises dangers without a human agent. No occasion has been missed: the causes of grief arise in the midst of our pleasures. War breaks out in the midst of peace and the troops maintaining our security turn into a source of fear; a friend becomes a foe, an ally becomes an enemy. The calm of summer is driven into sudden storms worse than winter weather. We suffer enemy attack without enemies, and if there are no other causes for disaster, excessive good fortune finds them for itself. Disease attacks the most abstinent of men, consumption the strongest, punishment the most innocent, rebellion the most withdrawn; chance finds some new device to heap up its violence on men who seem to have forgotten her. Whatever a long sequence of time has built up 6 with huge effort and through great indulgence from the gods, a single day strews and scatters in ruins. The man who talks about 'a day' has set a long delay for misfortunes that rush on to us; an hour or minute of time is enough to overthrow empires. It would be some consolation for our weakness and our enterprises if everything was as slow to perish as to come into being; but now progress advances slowly and there is haste only to suffer loss. Nothing is stable in private or 7 public life; the fates of men are turned around as quickly as those of cities. Terror arises in the calmest circumstances, and without any external provocation disasters spring from the least expected sources. Kingdoms that stood through internal and external wars collapse without anyone assailing them; how rare is the community that has enjoyed continuous happiness! So we must consider every possibility and reinforce our spirit against whatever could happen.

Imagine exile, tortures, wars, and shipwrecks. Chance can take 8 you from your country, or take away your country itself, it can drive you into the desert, and even this situation in which one is stifled by crowding can become a desert. Let us set the whole condition of human destiny before our eyes, and anticipate in our mind not what great misfortune often occurs but the greatest that can occur, if we don't want to be overwhelmed and dazed by these unaccustomed blows as if they were new; we must consider fortune in its full form.

9 How often the cities of Asia and Achaea have fallen with one earth-tremor! How many cities in Syria and in Macedonia have been engulfed! How often this disaster has laid waste Cyprus! How often has Paphos* collapsed on itself! The ruin of whole cities has often been announced to us, and yet we who so often receive these announcements are just a small part of mankind. So let us rise up against the acts of Fortune and know that whatever happens is not as dreadful as

10 rumour claims. A wealthy city has been burned down, and an ornament of the provinces to which it had been both added and incorporated, and yet it was built on one hill, and that not particularly broad; time will wipe away the traces of all those communities which you now hear spoken of as magnificent and noble. Don't you see how in Achaea even the foundations of glorious cities have been swallowed up and nothing stands to show that they actually existed?

11 Not only human handiwork falls apart; time does not overthrow only the products of human artifice: mountain ridges collapse, whole regions have subsided, areas have been covered by the waves which once stood far from the sight of the sea; the wild power of fires has eaten away the hills on which they glowed and has brought down to sea-level what were once the loftiest peaks, reassurance and beacons to those sailing past. The works of nature herself are harried, and so

12 we should bear calmly the destruction of cities. They stand, but are destined to fall; this end awaits all of them, whether it is the internal force of winds and gusts made violent by enclosure that have shaken off the mass that weighs upon them; or the force of torrential streams, all the wilder for being concealed, has broken down everything in its path; or the violence of flames has shattered the solid ground; or sheer age, from which nothing is safe, has bit by bit taken these places by storm; or the harmful climate has expelled peoples and neglect has rotted the deserted areas. It would be a long task to list all the paths of the fates. I know this one thing: all works of mortal men are doomed to mortality, and we live among things destined to perish.

13 So I am applying these and similar consolations to our friend Liberalis, who burns with an incredible patriotism, although his country was perhaps destroyed in order to be raised up in a better form. For often injustice has made space for a greater fortune; many things have fallen in order to rise to a greater height. Timagenes,* the enemy of our

city's success, said the fires of Rome were only a cause of grief to him because he knew that the parts consumed would rise up in superior form. In this city too it is likely that everyone will compete to restore its 14 buildings on a greater and more lofty scale than those they lost. If only they may be long-lasting and founded under better auspices for a longer age! For this is the hundredth year of this colony since its foundation, an age not extraordinary even for a man. It was founded by Plancus and grew to this large population because of its excellent location; but how many severe misfortunes it has endured within the space of human old age! So let our mind be shaped to understand and endure 15 its own fate and know that there is nothing Fortune will not dare, and that she has the same rights against empires as against their rulers, and the same power against cities as against men.

There is no reason to be indignant about this; we have come into a world where life is lived by these laws. If you like it, obey; if not, then leave by whatever way you choose. You are indignant if anything unfair is decided against you personally; but if this necessity binds both high and low, be reconciled with fate, by which all things are brought to their conclusion. There is no reason to measure us by 16 tombs and those monuments which fringe the road so unevenly; since ash reduces everything to the same level. We are born unequal, but die equal. I am saying the same thing about cities as about their inhabitants; Ardea was captured, just like Rome.* That founder of human law has distinguished us not by our birth or the glory of our names, except while we live; but when we come to the end of mortal things he says: 'Depart, ambition; let the selfsame law hold force for all that weigh down the earth.' We are equal in suffering all things; no one is more brittle than another, no one more sure of himself for the coming day.

Alexander, king of Macedon, began to learn land-measurement, 17 poor fool, wanting to know how small the earth was, of which he had occupied only the least part. So I say 'poor fool', for this reason: he should have understood that he was wearing a false title; for who can be Great in a puny existence? The knowledge passed on to him was subtle and required learning with careful attention, not the sort of thing a madman would grasp who sent his thoughts ranging over the Ocean itself.* He said: 'Teach me easy things!' and his teacher said: 'This knowledge is the same, and equally difficult for everyone.' Think 18 that Nature is saying: 'Those things you complain about are the same

for everyone; I cannot give easier material to anyone, but whoever wants will make it easier for himself.' How? By calmness of mind. You must feel pain and thirst and hunger and age (if you enjoy a longer stay among men), you must be sick and lose something and be lost in
19 death. But there is no reason to trust the rumours that create disturbance all round you; none of these is bad, nothing is intolerable or hard. Fear of them comes from human agreement. You fear death like gossip, for what is more foolish than a man who fears words? Our Demetrius* often says cleverly that he regards the words of the ignorant as just like their farting bellies. 'What difference does it make to
20 me whether they sound off above or below?' What madness it is to fear being defamed by the infamous! Just as you feared gossip without reason, so you were afraid of things you would never fear if gossip had not ordered it. Would a good man suffer any loss for being spattered
21 with unfair scandal? This talk amongst us should not even discredit death, and it has a bad reputation. None of those who accuse death have experienced it; until then it is rash to condemn what you don't know. But you do know this, how many people it has been useful to, how many it frees from torture, poverty, laments, punishment, weariness. We are not in any man's power, when death is in our power. Keep well.

Letter 95 (Book XV.3)   *In letters 94 (not selected) and 95 Seneca tackles at dialogue length the issue of teaching by particular instructions (*praecepta, 94*) or by deduction from fundamental first principles (*decreta, Greek* dogmata*). As one might expect, he recommends teaching through general principles, from which particulars can be derived as needed, but naturally sees the benefits of combining both methods. Letter 95 is more interesting in its arguments and illustrations and incorporates his main points from 94 into the opening section. Thus Seneca twice uses analogies from the traditional Greek arts of medicine and piloting, and twice leaves his main theme for invective against luxury, especially in dining (§§20–8, 40–2); he also introduces two brief, important passages giving his beliefs about how we should treat the gods (§§47–50) and our fellow men (§§51–3), an exhortation to altruism relatively rare in Seneca.*

1 You have asked me to anticipate the discussion I said should be postponed until its proper time, and to tell you in writing whether the part

of philosophy which the Greeks call *paraenetice* and we call prescriptive is sufficient to bring philosophy to perfection. I know you will take it well if I refuse. That is all the more a reason for promising and not allowing the common saying to go to waste: 'After this don't ask for a favour you will wish had not been granted.'

For at times we ask urgently for something we would refuse if 2 anyone offered it. Whether this is fickleness or childish behaviour, it should be punished by making easy promises. There are many things we wish to seem to want, but we do not actually want them. A recitalist brings with him a huge history written in tiny writing and closely rolled up, and when a great part of it has been read, he says: 'I'll stop now, if you like.' The reply, 'No, go on reading, go on!' comes from men who long for him to fall silent at that point. Often we want one thing but choose another and don't even tell the truth to the gods, but the gods either do not listen to our prayers or take pity on us. I will abandon pity and avenge myself by thrusting a huge letter upon 3 you, and if you read it reluctantly, tell yourself, 'I brought this on my own head!' and count yourself among those whom a wife, wooed with great urgency, torments; amongst those whose riches, acquired with immense sweat, give them trouble; amongst those whose offices, sought with every conceivable trickery and effort, torture them; and other men once they have obtained the evils they pursued.

But to drop the introduction and tackle the real topic, men say: 4 'The blessed life consists of right actions; rules and instructions lead to right actions; so instructions are sufficient for the blessed life.' Yet instructions do not always lead up to a blessed life, but only when the mind is obedient; sometimes they are applied without success if corrupted opinions beset the mind. Then even if men act rightly they do 5 not know they are acting rightly. For no one who is not formed from the beginning and ordered by the full use of reason can go through all the routine to know when he should do something or how long, or with whom and how and why. He cannot strive for honourable behaviour with his whole heart, not even consistently or gladly, but will look back for help and be caught fast.

'But if honourable action comes from instructions,' the opponent 6 says, 'instructions are enough for a blessed life; however, the first premiss hold good, therefore so does the other.' We will answer that honourable actions can be achieved even from instructions, but not only from them.

7   'If other arts are content with instructions, then so will wisdom be
content, for this too is an art of living. But the man who gives this
kind of instruction: "Move the helm like this, lower the sails like this,
make use of a favouring wind like this, and resist an adverse wind like
this, and take control of a wind that is uncertain and wavering in this
way," is training a pilot. And instructions shape other craftsmen, so
8   they will have the same power over this craftsman of living.' All those
other crafts are preoccupied with the tools of living, not with life as a
whole, hence many external factors hem them around and hamper
them: hope, desire, fear. But this craft, which claims to be the art of
life, cannot be prevented by anything from exercising itself; for it
shakes off hindrances and tosses away obstacles. Do you want to know
the difference between the circumstances of other arts and this one?
In them it is more excusable to commit an error deliberately than by
accident, but in this art the greatest fault is to go wrong on purpose.
9   This is what I mean. A grammarian will not blush at a solecism if he
has committed it on purpose, but will blush if he made it inadvert-
ently: a doctor, if he does not realize that the patient is failing, commits a greater blunder against his art than if he conceals his
understanding; but in this art of living the guilt of deliberate offenders is more shameful. Now add to this that most arts—indeed, the
most cultured among them all—have their own axioms, not just
instructions, as does medicine; so the school of Hippocrates is different from that of Asclepiades and the school of Themison is different
10   again.* Besides, no theoretical art goes without its principles, which
the Greeks call *dogmata*, and we can call either decrees or laws or
principles; you will find these in both geometry and astronomy. Now
philosophy is both theoretical and active: it both examines and acts.
You are mistaken if you think it only promises earthly enterprises; it
aims higher. It says: 'I examine the whole universe and do not hold
myself within mortal apprenticeship, contented just to persuade or
dissuade you; great things summon me that lie above you:

11   For I shall begin to debate the supreme nature of heaven
          And the gods, opening up the first seeds of our world,
          From which nature creates, increases, and sustains
          All things, returning them to dissolution,*

as Lucretius says.' So it follows that since philosophy is contempla-
12   tive, it has its own first principles. And what about the problem that

no one will handle what is to be done correctly unless he has been
given a method of going through all the routines of proper behaviour? The man who has received instruction for one situation and not
for all will fail to observe these routines. Instructions are inherently
weak and, so to speak, rootless, if they are given for particulars. It is
principles which fortify us, which protect our freedom from care
and our tranquillity, which contain within them all of life and all the
universe. The difference between the principles of philosophy and
instructions is like that between first principles and particulars; these
depend on the elementary principles, while the principles are the
causes of both these particulars and of everything else. The opponent 13
claims that 'ancient wisdom did nothing except give instructions in
what to do and to avoid, and men were far superior then: once learned
men appeared there has been a shortage of good men; for that simple
and open virtue turned into an obscure and tricky science and we
teach how to argue, not how to live.' As you say, that ancient wisdom 14
was rough and ready, especially as it came to birth, just like other arts
whose subtlety has grown during their progress. But there was not
yet a need for careful remedies. Wickedness had not risen to such
heights or spread itself so far abroad: simple remedies could resist
simple failings. Now inevitably our defences have to be so much more
laborious because the forces attacking us are so much more violent.

Medicine was once the knowledge of a few plants to staunch flow- 15
ing blood and knit wounds together: after that it gradually reached
this manifold variety. It is not surprising that it had less business
when human bodies were sturdy and solid, with a simple diet not corrupted by artifice and pleasure; after men began to seek out food not
to remove hunger but to provoke it, and a thousand seasonings were
discovered to stimulate greed, foods that were nourishment for those
who craved them became a burden once they were sated. Hence those 16
sallow faces and the trembling of sinews steeped in wine and thinness
more pitiable when it comes from indigestion than from hunger;
hence unsteady feet and a constant stumbling as if due to drunkenness; hence moisture building up under the whole skin and
a swollen belly ill-adjusted to holding more than it could contain;
hence a flow of lurid bile and a discoloured complexion and the rot of
internal decay,* and gnarled fingers with twisted joints and the numbness of sinews inert without sensation or quivering as they tremble
without cease.

17   Need I mention dizziness in the head? Or the tortures of eyes and
ears and the pricking of a seething brain, and all the parts which serve
to excrete afflicted with internal ulcers? Besides there are countless
varieties of fever, some raging in their attacks, others insinuating with
a subtle sickness, and others that come with shuddering and extended
18   shaking of the limbs. Need I mention countless other diseases, the
punishments of luxury? Men who had not yet weakened themselves
with pampering were immune to these woes, men who controlled
themselves and tended their own needs. They hardened their bodies
with toil and real effort, worn out either with racing or hunting or
tilling the earth; food sustained them which could only please really
hungry men. So there was no need for such a mighty pharmacopoeia,
or so many instruments and jars. Their health was simple, and from
19   a simple source; it was many dishes that made many sicknesses. See
the extent to which luxury, that plunderer who lays waste land and
sea, has mixed up food destined to pass down a single throat. Inevitably
such different ingredients clash and, once swallowed, are badly
digested as each conflicts with the other. It is not surprising that the
sickness from this inharmonious food is intermittent and variable,
and when those ingredients from opposed parts of nature are forced
into the same stomach they overflow. This is why we are sick in as new
a fashion as our life is newfangled.
20   The greatest of doctors and founder of this science said women
did not lose their hair or suffer from gout; but now they go bald and
are sick in the feet. The nature of women has not changed, but has
been overwhelmed; for in matching the licence of men they have also
21   matched the afflictions of male bodies. They stay up all night no less
than men, they drink no less, they challenge the men in both oil and
wine; they throw up food heaped on to their unwilling organs and
return all their wine in vomiting; they nibble snow as much as men,
as comfort for a feverish stomach. They don't even give way to men
in lust; born to be penetrated* (may the gods and goddesses curse
them!), they have dreamed up such a perverted kind of indecency
that they penetrate men. So why should we be surprised that the
greatest of doctors, most expert in nature, was caught making a false
statement when there are so many bald and gouty women? They have
destroyed the advantage of their sex by their vices, and because they
have cast off their womanhood they have been condemned to the
ailments of men.

Doctors in the old days did not know how to give food repeatedly 22
or prop up sagging veins with wine, they did not know how to let
blood and ease persistent sickness with bathing and sweating, they
did not know how to revive the dormant strength of legs and arms
by binding them and summon circulation from the centre to the
extremities. There was no need to look round for many kinds of help
when there were few kinds of danger. But now how far the evils of 23
ill-health have advanced! This is the price we pay for the pleasures we
crave beyond limit and decency. You will not be surprised by the diseases beyond counting; just count the cooks. Every serious study is
idle, and men who teach liberal disciplines sit in empty corners without any audience; there is a void in the schools of rhetors and philosophers; but how crowded are the kitchens, what a great throng of
young men presses around the hearths of spendthrifts!

I pass over the unhappy boy slaves,* who can expect other insults 24
in the bedchamber after the dinner is completed; I pass over the columns of fancy men grouped by tribes and colour so that they all share
the same smoothness, the same phase of their first down, the same
type of hair so that no straight-haired man is mixed in with curly-
haired men; I pass over the crowd of bakers, the crowd of waiters who
run here and there to bring in dinner when the signal is given. Ye 25
gods, what a number of men one belly keeps busy! What, do you think
those mushrooms, that luxurious poison, do not work any secret spell
even if they have no instant effect? Do you think that summer snow
does not harden their livers? Do you think those oysters, that most
idle flesh, force-fed on mud, contribute none of their slimy weight?
What about that Company's relish,* the costly decay exuded from
bad fish, do you think it fails to burn the intestines with its salty rot-
tenness? Do you think those festering foods, all but transferred from
the fire to the mouth, can be quenched in the internal organs without
harm? How loathsome and unhealthy are their belches, what disgust
men cause even themselves as they breathe out their stale hangovers.
You could tell that what they have eaten is rotting, not being digested.
I remember there was once mention in conversation of a notorious 26
dish in which the tavern, eager to ruin itself, had heaped up whatever
usually passes the time among the connoisseurs: there were shellfish
and mussels, and oysters were marked out, sliced around just to the
point where they were eaten, and sea-urchins . . . and mullets filleted
without any bones were spread over them. Men are not satisfied to eat 27

things one at a time; the flavours are forced into one dish. So what
ought to happen in the stomach happens at the dinner; I expect that
food will soon be served ready chewed. But how much less trouble
it is to pick out the shells and bones, and have the cook perform the
work of our teeth? 'It is heavy duty to indulge in luxury in single
items; let everything be served at once and turned into the same flavour. Why should I reach out my hand for one thing at a time? Let all
the foods come together, let the centrepieces of many dishes merge
28 together and be fused together. Men who used to say that gourmets
were seeking something to boast of and glory from these dishes should
know that these things are not being shown off, but confined to the
diner's own personal pride. Let foods which are usually set out separately be treated alike, soaked in a single juice, let there be no difference: let oysters, sea-urchins, mussels, and mullets be shaken up and
cooked before being served.' Food consumed by men throwing up
29 would not be more badly messed up. As those delicacies are jumbled
together, so from them diseases do not happen in single form, but are
impossible to interpret, contrary and manifold, so that medicine too
has now begun to arm itself against them with many methods of treatment and forms of observation.

I can tell you the same story about philosophy. It was once more
simple among men whose offences were smaller and curable with
even slight attention; but now every remedy has to be tried against
so great an inversion of our behaviour. If only this great plague could
30 be overcome in this way! But we are mad not only as private persons
but publicly. We chastise murders and individual slaughter, but what
about war and the vaunted crime of massacring whole tribes? Avarice
and cruelty know no limit. In fact, as long as they are done surrepti-
tiously by individuals such acts are less harmful and unnatural; but
now savage actions are imposed by senatorial decrees and decrees of
the plebeian assembly, and things forbidden privately are officially
31 ordered by the state. Things that men would pay for with their lives,
if they had done them privately, we now praise because men in general's cloaks have perpetrated them. Man, that gentlest of creatures,
feels no shame to rejoice in reciprocal bloodshed and waging wars and
passing them on to their children to wage, although even domestic
32 and wild animals enjoy peace among their own kind. Philosophy
has become more elaborate to counter such powerful and widespread
frenzy, and has taken on as much strength as the evils had accumulated

which it was meant to fight. It was a quick job to scold men drinking
undiluted wine and seeking a fancier kind of food; the mind did not
need great force to restore it to the thrift from which it had fallen a
little short:

> Now we need swift hands, now your masterful art.* 33

Men seek pleasure from everything; no vice stays within its limits;
luxury rushes headlong into avarice. Forgetfulness of what is honourable has taken over; nothing is shameful if the price is right. Man,
who should be sacred to man, is now killed in sport and play, and the
young man whom it was abomination to train in inflicting and suffering wounds is now brought on naked* and unarmed, and men find
enough entertainment in a fellow man's death. So amid this pervers- 34
ity of behaviour something more violent is missing that would shake
off these chronic evils; we must use first principles to pull down the
false persuasions that have been so deeply absorbed. If we add to
these principles instructions, consolations, exhortations, they will be
able to prevail; alone they are ineffectual. If we want to keep men 35
under restraint and tear them away from the evils which now beset
them, let them learn what is evil and what is good, let them know
that all things except virtue change their name and are now bad, now
good. As the first bond in military service is reverence and love of
the standards and treating desertion as an abomination, and from
then on orders and instructions will be easily exacted from those
bound by oath, so you must lay the first foundations in those whom
you want to lead to the blessed life and instil virtue into their hearts.
Let them be held by a kind of religious devotion to it, let them love it;
let them want to live with virtue, and refuse to live without it.

'Well then? Haven't some men grown up virtuous and achieved 36
great progress without any subtle training, while simply obeying bare
instructions?' Yes, I admit it, but their nature was fertile and absorbed
beneficial lessons in passing. For just as the immortal gods did not
learn virtue, since they were generated possessing it whole, and it is
part of their nature to be good, so some men who have inherited an
exceptional nature reach the usual level or instruction without a long
apprenticeship, and have embraced honourable values as soon as they
heard them: this is the source that made their intellects so absorbent
of virtue, or even spontaneously productive. But other men, either
dull-witted and blunt or hampered by bad habits, must have the rust

37 rubbed away from their minds for a long time. For the rest, as the teacher who passes on to them the chosen principles of philosophy is more quick to lead men with a natural instinct for good to their highest potential, he will also help the weaker men and rescue them from bad beliefs; and you can see how necessary these principles are. There are elements lurking in us which make us sluggish for some tasks and rash in attempting others; that boldness cannot be restrained nor that slothfulness aroused unless we remove their causes, false respect and false fear. As long as these vices hold us in thrall you can say: 'This is what you should do for your father, this for your children, this for your friends, this for your guests.' But as a man tries to do it avarice will hold him back. He knows he ought to fight for his country, but cowardice holds him back; he knows he must sweat to the last drop for his friends, but his pampered life forbids him; he knows that a mistress is the worst kind of offence against a wife, but his lust drives him

38 in the opposite direction. So it will be useless to provide instructions unless you have first cleared away the obstacles to those instructions, just as it will be useless to set out arms in full sight or bring them closer, unless the hands are made ready to use them. For the mind to

39 embark on the instructions we give, it must be released. Let us imagine someone is doing what he ought; he will not do it constantly, nor consistently, since he will not understand what he is doing. Some things will turn out right either by chance or practice, but he will not have the ruler on hand to check them, to trust that what he did is straight. A man who is good by accident gives no guarantee that he will always be good.

40   Then instructions will perhaps enable you to do what you ought, but will not guarantee that you do it in the way you should; and if they don't guarantee this they do not lead all the way to virtue. A man will do what he ought when reminded, I admit; but that is not

41 enough, since glory lies not in the deed but in its motivation. What is more scandalous than an extravagant dinner that consumes a knight's whole property? What so worthy of a censor's condemnation, if, as those gluttons say, someone offers this treat 'to himself and his good spirit'? And yet inaugural dinners* have cost otherwise thrifty men a million sesterces. If the same expenditure is made out of gluttony, it is shameful; if to honour the office, it escapes reproof; for it is not the

42 luxury but the outlay that is customary. A mullet of enormous size— why don't I add its weight and provoke the gluttony of some fellows?

They say it weighed four-and-a-half pounds—was sent to Tiberius Caesar, who had it carried to the market and put up for sale. 'My friends,' he said 'unless I am utterly mistaken either Apicius or P. Octavius will buy that mullet.' His guess succeeded beyond expectation; they bid against each other, and Octavius won and achieved immense glory among his boon companions, for buying for five <thousand> sesterces the fish that Caesar had sold and not even Apicius had bought. To pay out the price was disgraceful only for Octavius, not to the man who had bought it in order to send it to Tiberius, though I would reproach him too: he marvelled at a thing he thought worthy of the emperor. A friend keeps watch beside a sick 43 man; we approve. But he is doing it to obtain a legacy; he is a vulture, waiting for the corpse. The same actions can be either disgraceful or honourable; it matters why or how they are performed. Now every action will be honourable if we have committed ourselves to the honourable and judged it and what comes from it to be the only good in human affairs; the rest are only good for the time being. So conviction 44 should be implanted that will affect one's whole life; this is what I call a first principle. Our actions and deliberations will match this conviction; and our life will match as these actions. It is not enough to persuade in some details a man who is organizing the whole. In 45 his treatise *On Obligations*, Marcus Brutus* gives many instructions for parents and children and brothers, but no man will perform them as he should unless he has a standard against which to measure them. We ought to set up the mark of the highest good so as to strive towards it, so that our every deed and word will look to it, just as sailors must direct their course by some constellation.

Life wavers without a purpose: if one must be set up at all costs, 46 then principles begin to be essential. You will grant, I think, that nothing is more disgraceful than a man hesitant and uncertain and backing off in timidity. This will happen to all our affairs unless we eliminate the faults that check and hold back our spirits, forbidding them to go forward and attempt things wholeheartedly.

It is customary to give instruction on how to worship the gods. Let 47 us forbid a man to light lamps on the Sabbath,* since the gods do not need light and not even men take pleasure in soot. Let us forbid men to perform morning greetings and crowd around the doorways of temples; human ambition may be charmed by such homage, but a man worships a God if he knows him. Let us forbid men to carry towels and strigils to Jupiter and hold a mirror up to Juno; a God does not look for servants.* Why would he? He himself gives service to the whole human race and stands by everywhere and for everyone.

48 Although a man may learn what limits one should keep in sacrificing, how far we should recoil from troublesome superstitions, yet he will never have made enough progress unless he conceives in his mind what a God should be like, one who possesses everything and

49 shares out everything, freely conferring kindnesses. What is the gods' reason for giving kindnesses? It is nature. If someone thinks they do not want to do harm, he is mistaken; they simply cannot. They can neither suffer wrong nor inflict it: for being harmed and harming are bound together. Those whom nature, that highest and most beautiful of beings, has made exempt from danger she cannot make dangerous

50 to others. The first form of worship of the gods is to believe in them, then to credit them with their own grandeur, to credit them with the loving-kindness without which there is no grandeur; to know that it is they who govern the world, who moderate the universe by their power, who exercise guardianship over the human race, while at times being inattentive to individuals. They neither cause evil nor possess it: but they punish some offenders and discipline them and demand penalties and at times punish under the appearance of doing good. Do you want to make the gods propitious? Be good. Whoever has emulated them has given them enough worship.

51   Here is another investigation: how should we treat men? What do we do? What instructions do we give? To spare human blood? How little it is not to harm the one you ought to benefit! A great glory, to be sure, if a man is gentle with another man. Shall we instruct him to stretch out his hand to the shipwrecked, show the way to a lost traveller, divide his bread with the hungry? Why should I mention everything that should be done or avoided? Instead I can briefly pass on

52 to him this definition of human duty: everything you see, in which things divine and human are comprehended, is a unity; we are members of a great body. Nature gave birth to us as kin when she begot us from the same sources and for the same ends; she gave us mutual love and made us inclined to collaborate. She shaped what is fair and just; it is by her ordinance that it is more wretched to harm than to be harmed; it is by nature's command that hands are ready for helping.

53 Keep that line in your breast and on your lips:

         I am a man and think no man's lot foreign to me.*

Let us have possessions for common use; it is for common use that we were born. Our society is like a vault, which is held up by the fact that its stones would fall if they did not each thrust against the other.

After considering gods and men, let us examine how we should 54 treat objects. We will be tossing around instructions superfluously if we have not previously handled such topics as the opinions we ought to have about each issue, about poverty, about wealth, about glory, about disgrace, about one's country, about exile. Let us assess each one, putting aside popular belief, and ask what they are, not what they are called.

Let us pass on to virtues. Someone will instruct us to put a high 55 value on foresight, to embrace courage, and apply justice, if possible, even more closely than the other virtues; but this will achieve nothing if we do not know what virtue is, whether it is single or multiple, separate or intertwined, or whether the man who possesses one virtue possesses the others, and how they differ amongst themselves. A builder does not need to ask what is the beginning of construction, 56 what its purpose, any more than a pantomime artist needs to investigate the art of dancing; all those arts know themselves, nothing is missing, for they do not affect the whole of life. But virtue is the knowledge of both other things and itself; you must learn about it so that it may be learned. An action will not be upright unless the inten- 57 tion behind it is upright, for the action depends on it. Again, the intention will not be upright unless the condition of the mind was upright, for that is the source of intention. But the condition of the mind will not be in the best state unless it has understood the laws of life in its entirety and gone through what judgement it must form of each thing, unless it has reduced matters to the truth. Tranquillity will only come to those who have acquired an unchanging and fixed judgement; others will fall away instantly and subside and fluctuate alternately between what they have let go and what they are seeking. What is the cause of their buffeting? That nothing is clear to those 58 relying on that most unreliable steersman, public opinion. If you want always to have the same desire, you must desire true things. We do not reach the truth without principles: they hold life together. Good things and bad, honourable things and shameful, just and unjust, pious and impious, the virtues and their uses, the possession of advantages, our reputation and prestige, health, strength, beauty, the sharpness of our senses—all of these need an assessor. Let us be

free to know what value to report for each item in our account of
59 property. For you are mistaken and think some things worth more
than they are, you are so mistaken that the things thought most
valuable among us—wealth, influence, power—should be rated at a
mere sesterce. You will not know this unless you examine the system
by which they are assessed among themselves. Just as leaves cannot
turn green unaided, but need the branch to which they cling and
from which they draw the sap, so those instructions wither if they are
left alone; they need to be grafted onto a system.

60   Moreover, men who eliminate principles do not realize that their
instructions are strengthened by the very thing used to eliminate
them. For what are they saying? That life is sufficiently explained by
instructions, that the principles of wisdom <that is, the dogmas> are
superfluous. And yet the very thing they claim is as much a principle,
by Jove, as if I now claimed we should retreat from instructions as
superfluous, and employ principles and devote our attention to them
alone: in the very act of denying that we should concern ourselves
61 with instructions, I would be instructing. Some topics in philosophy
require advice, others a proof, and a substantial one to boot, because
they are involved and scarcely can be opened even with the greatest
care and subtlety. If proofs <are necessary> then so are principles
which infer the truth from proofs. Some things are open to view,
others veiled; the open ones are understood by the senses and by the
memory; the veiled ones lie beyond these methods. For reason is not
satisfied with the obvious; its greater and finer part is in hidden elements. Hidden things require a proof, and proof cannot occur without
62 principles; so principles are necessary. What makes sense common
also makes it perfect, that is a sure conviction of things; if everything
floats in the mind without this, then principles are necessary to give
63 minds an unbending judgement. In short, when we advise someone
to count his friend as dear as himself, to think that an enemy can be
turned into a friend, to rouse love in the former and temper hatred in
the latter, we add: 'This is just and honourable.' Now it is reason that
maintains the just and honourable elements of our principles: so
64 reason is necessary, since they will not exist without it. But let us
combine the two; for branches are useless without roots and the roots
themselves are helped by the parts they gave birth to. Nobody can be
unaware of the immense usefulness of men's hands, since they give us
open assistance; but the heart through which the hands have life,

from which they take their motion, by which they are moved, remains
hidden. I can say the same thing about instructions: they are open,
whereas the principles of wisdom are in hiding. Just as only the initi-
ated know the more sacred elements of ritual, so in philosophy those
secrets are shown to those admitted and received into the rites; but
instructions and other such details are known to outsiders as well.

Posidonius judges that not just instructional method (for nothing 65
prevents us using that word), but also persuasion and consolation and
exhortation are necessary: he adds to these the investigation of causes
(and I don't see why we dare not call this *aetiology*, since grammarians, those custodians of the Latin language, call it that as of right).
He says that the description of each virtue will also be useful; this is
what Posidonius calls *ethologia*, but some call *characterismos*,* which
presents the signs and marks of each virtue and vice, by which similar
conditions can be told apart. This process has the same effect as 66
instructing; for the instructor says, 'do those things if you want to be
abstinent', while the man who describes says, 'an abstinent man is
one who does such things, who abstains from them'. Are you asking
what is the difference? One gives instructions for virtue, the other
a model. I admit that such descriptions, and—to use the word of
tax-collectors—identification marks are customary: let us present
things as praiseworthy and an imitator will be found. You think it 67
useful to be given features by which to recognize a thoroughbred so
that you will not be deceived when you buy it, or waste your effort on
an inferior one? How much more useful it is to know the marks of an
excellent spirit, which we can transfer to it from that other field.

> At once the pure-bred colt treads on the land,   68
> Prancing and setting hocks down daintily;
> It is first to lead the way and breast fierce streams
> With daring, trusting itself to the unknown bridge,
> Not dreading empty din. Its lofty neck
> And nimble head, short belly and fat back,
> Its breast with spirit flaunts its sinews . . .
>   . . . Then if warfare sounds afar
> It cannot rest, but pricks its ears with limbs agog,
> Gathering beneath its nostrils whorls of fire.*

Without intending to, our friend Virgil has described a gallant hero; 69
I at least would not give any other image for a great man. If I need to

describe Marcus Cato unafraid amid the crashes of civil wars and
first to assail armies brought down from the Alps,* going to confront
the civil war, I would not attribute to him any other expression or
70 demeanour. Certainly no one could have been more high-stepping
than the man who simultaneously reared up against Caesar and
Pompey and, when some groups supported the power of Caesar and
others those of Pompey, challenged them both and demonstrated that
there was also a party of the free republic. For it is not enough to say,
in Cato's case, 'not dreading empty din'. How could it be? When he
does not shudder at a real din close at hand, when in the face of ten
legions and the Gallic squadrons and barbarian weapons mixed with
citizen arms, he raises a free battle-cry and exhorts the state not to fail
on liberty's behalf, but to attempt everything, since it will be more
71 honourable to fall into slavery than to go towards it. What vigour and
spirit was in him, what confidence amid public panic! He knows he is
the one whose condition is not at issue, since the issue was not whether
Cato should be free, but should be among free men—hence his contempt for dangers and swords. We may well say, in admiration for the
man's unconquered courage as he did not weaken among the public
collapse, 'his breast with spirit flaunts its sinews'.

72   It will be helpful not just to describe the nature of good men and
outline their form and features, but to narrate and set out how they
behaved: Cato's last and bravest wound which let liberty release his
spirit, the wisdom of Laelius and his harmony with his friend Scipio,
the splendid deeds of the other Cato at home and abroad, the wooden
couches of Tubero,* when he was setting out a public feast, with goat-
skins instead of tapestries and earthenware jugs for the guests arrayed
before the shrine of Jupiter himself. Wasn't this like dedicating poverty on the Capitol? If I have no other deed of his to include him
among the Catos, do we think this is not enough? That was a censor-
73 ship, not a dinner. How men eager for glory are ignorant of what it is,
or how it should be sought! On that day the Roman people saw the
furnishings of many statesmen, but only marvelled at this one man.
All their gold and silver has been broken and melted a thousand times,
but Tubero's earthenware will survive for all ages. Keep well.

Letter 97 (Book XVI.2) *After a brief contrasting letter criticiz-*
ing Lucilius' mood of complaint, ending with the war-cry: 'To live is

to campaign!' Seneca moves in letter 97 to invective against bribery and
corruption, paraphrasing and quoting an early letter of Cicero to Atticus.
Although Nepos (Life of Atticus, 16.3) reports that Atticus supervised
the publication of the letters he received from Cicero (and Seneca himself
refers to this correspondence in De Brevitate, *5.2), this seems to be the*
first actual quotation from the correspondence. As in letter 95, Seneca's
interest in the generation of the civil wars leads again to Cato, whose
integrity is highlighted by the contrast with his peers. (Historically this
is less than accurate, but it is part of Cato's received image.) But his real
purpose in reporting this anecdote only surfaces after §10, with the dis-
tinction between immediate detection and material punishment, and the
enduring punishment of a guilty conscience.

You are mistaken, dear Lucilius, if you think our generation has 1
a monopoly of vices like luxury and indifference to good behaviour
and the other faults which every man reproaches in his own age: these
are the faults of mankind, not of a given time. No age has been free
of guilt, and if you begin to calculate the licence of each age, I am
ashamed to say it, but offences were never more blatant than in Cato's
presence. Can anyone believe that money changed hands in the trial 2
in which Publius Clodius was accused on grounds of the adultery
which he had secretly committed with Caesar's wife—after he had
violated the religious scruples of that rite which is supposedly 'for
the people', when all men are so comprehensively removed from the
enclosed space that even the paintings of male animals are covered
up? Yet cash was paid out to the jurors, and—a thing even more disgraceful than this bargain—fornication with married women and
noble young men was imposed to seal the bargain. There was less 3
offence in the charge itself than in his acquittal; the man accused of
adultery dished out adulteries, and was not sure of his escape until
he had made the jurors corrupt like himself. These things happened
in that trial where, if nothing else, Cato had borne witness. I will
set down Cicero's actual words,* because the story beggars belief.
'He summoned them to him, made promises, intervened, gave bribes. 4
Now—(ye gods, what a desperate case!)—even nights with specific
ladies and introductions to noble youths served as a bonus to the pay
of certain jurors.' I don't have time to complain about the price, there 5
was more offence in the bonuses offered. 'Do you want the wife of
that grim fellow? I will give her. Or of that rich man? I'll guarantee

you bedding with her. If you don't commit adultery you can condemn him. That beauty you lust after will come to you. I am promising you a night with her and not postponing it: the guarantee of my promise will be given before the adjournment.' It is more effective to spread around adulteries than commit them; but this is really a war declared

6 against wives and mothers. These Clodian jurors asked the senate for a bodyguard, which should not have been needed unless they were going to condemn,* and they got their request; so Catulus made a witty comment to them when the defendant was acquitted: 'Why did you ask us for a bodyguard? Was it to prevent your bribes being stolen?' But among those jokes Clodius got away with his adultery before the trial and acted as pimp during it, escaping condemnation

7 more disgracefully than he had earned it. Do you think anything ever was more corrupt than the public behaviour which left lust undeterred by sacred rites or trials, trials in which worse sins were committed than the offence investigated in this special inquiry held by decree of the senate? The investigation was whether a man could be safe after an adultery; it was manifest that no one could be safe without it.

8 This crime was committed between Pompey and Caesar, between Cicero and Cato, the same Cato whose presence in the audience led to the people's refusal to demand the usual sport of stripping the courtesans at the Games of Flora*—in case you believe that men acted at the shows with more severity than at trials. That kind of behaviour will happen and did happen. And the licence of cities may shrink at some time from discipline and fear, but never of its own

9 accord. So you have no reason to believe that we have made the most concessions to lust but the least to the laws: for contemporary youth is much more thrifty than at that time, when the defendant denied committing adultery to the jurors, but the jurors admitted it to the defendant, when fornication was carried on to serve the verdict, when Clodius, popular for the same vices of which he was guilty, practised procuring as he pleaded the case. Would anyone believe this? The man exposed to condemnation for one adultery was acquitted by many of them.

10 Every age will produce Clodii, not every age a Cato. We are prone to worse behaviour, since neither a leader nor a companion is wanting, and the affair itself goes on without a leader or a companion. Mankind is not just inclined to vice but enthusiastic, and—something that

makes most of them incorrigible—blunders in every other art cause shame to the craftsmen and offend the man who has gone astray, but offences in life give men pleasure. The helmsman feels no joy when ₁₁ the vessel capsizes, the doctor does not rejoice when the patient is buried, the pleader does not rejoice if the defendant loses the case through his fault, but each man's moral offence gives him pleasure; he delights in an adultery where he was actually incited by its difficulty: he delights in its precautions and stealth, and feels no distress at his guilt until its outcome distresses him. This comes from the depravity of our practices. However, to show you that there is some sense of ₁₂ goodness even in minds seduced to the worst behaviour, and that disgrace is not unknown but disregarded, everyone covers up their offences and although they have come off successfully, they exploit the benefit but suppress the actual offences. But a good conscience wants to come out and be seen; wickedness fears even the dark.

So I think Epicurus spoke with discrimination when he said: ₁₃ 'a guilty man may be lucky enough to go unnoticed, but he cannot be confident of staying unnoticed',* or if you think this meaning can be better explained like this, 'offenders do not gain by passing unnoticed because even if they have the luck to pass unnoticed, they have no certainty of it'. That is, crimes can be safe but not free of anxiety. I don't think this offends against our school if it is explained like ₁₄ this. Why? Because the first and worst penalty of offenders is having offended, and no bad deed goes unpunished, even if Fortune enriches it with her gifts, even if she protects it and claims its safety, since the punishment for a bad deed lies in the deed itself. Even so, those second penalties press hard and pursue him, to be always afraid and panicking and with no trust in escaping trouble. Why free wickedness of this penalty? Why not leave it always in suspense? Let us disagree ₁₅ with Epicurus when he says nothing is just by nature and crimes should be avoided because fears cannot be avoided; let us agree with him when he says that bad deeds are lashed by guilty conscience and the greatest mass of tortures attack crime because perpetual anxiety oppresses and beats upon it, because it cannot believe the guarantors of its own freedom from trouble. For this is itself proof, Epicurus, that we are naturally repelled by crime, because no man is without fear even in safe circumstances. Fortune frees many people from their ₁₆ penalty, but no one from fear. Why is this, if not because we have an inherent loathing of what nature has condemned? So confidence of

escaping never arises even for those who do escape notice, because
their bad conscience convicts them, and shows them to themselves.
And fear and trembling are inherent properties of the guilty. And
since many crimes escape the law and an avenger and prescribed
punishments, we would have suffered badly if men did not pay to
their own immediate cost for those natural and serious offences and
fear did not take the place of endurance. Keep well.

Letter 99 (Book XVI.4) *An apparent anomaly, this letter consists
of an opening paragraph to Lucilius forwarding an extensive letter of
consolation to Marullus, who has lost a young son. Romans generally
show little interest in the development of young children, and the boy's
(or child's) age is difficult to determine from the letter. Marullus himself
is otherwise unknown. It is noteworthy that Seneca regards the loss of a
friend (cf. letter 9, §§8–18) as more substantial than that of a child, but
then young children died far too frequently for parents to have too firm a
hope of their survival*

*Another exceptional feature of this letter is the quotation in Greek from
the Epicurean Metrodorus' letter to his sister (§25): Seneca had already
paraphrased Metrodorus' consolation in letter 98, §9 'I think Metrodorus
made an excellent comment in the letter in which he consoles his sister
for her loss of a son of fine character: "every good thing for mortals is
itself mortal."' There, as in letter 99, Seneca distinguishes the good things
dependent on fortune from the true good of virtue beyond fortune's reach.
The theme of letter 98 is the harm of anticipating misfortune, apparently
unprompted by any bereavement of Lucilius. Perhaps composing 98 triggered Seneca's attachment of the undated letter to Marullus as the substance of letter 99. His quotation of the collection before citing the Greek
in letter 99 suggests that he only knew Metrodorus' letter to his sister from
its inclusion in a wider collection of his letters which Seneca himself possessed. This may be the collection he refers to in letter 79, §16 above.*

1 I have sent to you the letter I wrote for Marullus when he had lost his
little son and was said to be bearing up rather self-indulgently. I did
not follow the usual practice in this, nor did I think I should handle
him gently, since he deserved reproach rather than consolation. For
we need to give way for a little while to someone stricken and suffering a great wound rather badly: he will wear himself out or at least
2 shake off the first blow; but men who have chosen to mourn should be

scolded immediately and learn that there is foolish behaviour even in weeping.

Are you expecting consolation? Listen to a scolding. Are you suffering your son's death so indulgently? What would you do if you had lost a friend? Your son died with uncertain prospects and very young: only a little space of time has been lost. We look for pretexts 3 for grief and want to complain about Fortune even unfairly, as if she will not provide fair causes for complaining; but I swear, you seemed to me to have enough courage in face of solid misfortunes, not to mention those shadows of woe at which men groan because it is customary. Take the greatest of losses, if you had lost a friend, you should have tried to rejoice that you had enjoyed him rather than grieve because you had lost him. But most men do not calculate how much 4 they have received, and how much enjoyment they have had. That kind of grief includes this failing among others, that it is not only superfluous but ungrateful. So your effort is wasted because you once had such a friend? Has nothing been achieved by so many years, so close a sharing of life, such intimate association in studies? Are you burying your friendship along with the friend? And why are you distressed at having lost him if there was no profit from having him? Believe me, a great share in those we have loved, even if chance has taken them from us, stays with us: the time past is ours, and nothing is in a safer position than what has happened. We shall be ungrateful 5 towards past benefits, out of hope for the future, as if future events, should they happen, will not soon turn into the past. The man who is only happy at present circumstances restricts the enjoyment of things too narrowly; both future and past events delight us, the former in anticipation, the latter in remembrance; but the first is suspended and may not happen, the second cannot cease to have existed. So what madness is it to be disappointed in what is most guaranteed? Let us be content with what we have already absorbed, if we were not drinking with a leaky soul that passed on whatever it had received.

There are countless examples of men who buried their sons as 6 young men without tears, who returned from the bier to the senate or some public duty and instantly attended to another task. And rightly: for first of all, it is superfluous to grieve if you do no good by grieving; then, it is unfair to lament about what has happened to one person but awaits everyone: then, the lament over missing someone is foolish when there is so little time apart between the lost and his mourner.

So we should be more calm because we are following those we have
7 lost. Consider the swiftness of rushing time, think of the shortness
of this course along which we race at a gallop, and watch this company
of the human race straining towards the same goal, separated by the
slightest of intervals, even when they seem largest: the man you
think lost has been sent on ahead. Now what is more crazy than to
weep over the man who has preceded us, when you have to complete
the same journey? Does anyone weep for the event he was well aware
8 would take place? Or, if he did not think of death in this man's case,
he was deceiving himself. Does anyone weep over an event which he
kept saying was bound to happen? Whoever laments that someone is
dead is lamenting that he was a man. The same preconditions have
9 bound us all: death awaits whoever has been born. We are separated
by intervals but assimilated in our departure. The time between the
first and last day is uneven and uncertain: if you count the inconveniences, it is long even for a child; if you count its speed, it is too short
even for an old man. Nothing is not slippery and deceptive and more
restless than any squall: everything is buffeted and turned into its
opposite at the bidding of fortune, and in such a whirlwind of human
circumstances nothing is certain for any man except death, and yet all
men complain about the one thing in which no one is deceived.

10 'But he died as a child.' I won't yet tell you that the one who ends
life quickly is better off; but let us pass over to the man who has grown
old; how short is the time by which he outstrips the infant! Imagine
the immensity and depth of time and encompass it all, then compare
what we call a human life with this measureless amount; you will see
11 how tiny is the quantity we long for, which we stretch out. How much
of this is occupied by tears and anxieties? How much by death, longed
for before it comes to us, how much by ill-health and by fear? How
much is delayed by unripe or useless years? And half of that is slept
through. Add to this the hardships and bereavements and dangers,
and you will realize that even in a long life the portion that is actually
12 lived is very small. But who admits to you that a man is not better
off if he can return from life quickly, whose journey is completed
before weariness sets in? Life is neither good nor bad; it is the space
for both good and bad. So he has lost nothing except a toss of the
die more likely to bring a loss. He might have grown up modest and
prudent, he might have been moulded for better things under your
care, but, as is more rightly to be feared, he could have become like

the majority. Look at those young men from the most noble families 13
cast by their own prodigality into the arena, look at those who indulge
their own and others' lust in alternating indecencies, who let no day
pass without drunkenness and some conspicuous scandal; it will be
obvious that there was more to fear than hope. So you ought not to
rally reasons for grief and pile up trivial disadvantages in indignation.
I am not urging you to strive and arouse yourself: I don't have such a 14
poor opinion of you that I believe you need to summon all your valour
against this blow. That is not grief but a pang; you are making it into
grief. Undoubtedly philosophy has been of good service, if you are
missing with a stout spirit a boy still better known to his nurse than
his father.

So am I urging you now to become hardened, and do I want your 15
features to grow stiff at the burial, and am I not even allowing your
spirit to shrink? Not at all. That is inhumanity, not valour, to see the
burial of one's dear ones with the same eyes that see them alive, and
not be distressed by the first severance of family members. Now suppose I forbid it; some actions are under their own control: tears fall
even from those holding them back, and relieve the heart by being
shed. What then? Let us permit them to fall, not order it; let it flow 16
as much as the emotion has thrust it out, not as much as imitation
demands. But let us not add to our mourning, nor inflate it to match
another's example. The display of grief demands more than grief
itself: how rarely is a man sad for himself alone! They groan more
loudly when they are overheard, and being calm and silent when they
are in seclusion, when they see someone they are roused to new bursts
of tears: then they lay violent hands upon their head (which they
could have done more freely with no one to stop them), then they
invoke death for themselves, then they toss about on their couch;
grief is idle without a spectator. As in other matters, so in this too, we 17
commit the fault of adjusting ourselves to the examples of the majority, and look not to what is proper but to what is customary. We abandon nature and give ourselves to the common people, no good source
for any action, and most volatile in this as in all these other matters.
The crowd sees some man enduring in his grief and calls him impious and savage; it sees someone collapsing and clinging to the body,
and calls him womanish and gutless. So everything must be reduced 18
to the measure of reason. Truly, there is nothing more foolish than to
chase a reputation of melancholy and give approval to tears which I

judge are sometimes allowed to fall by a wise man, and at other times produced by their own force. I will explain the difference. When the first news of the bitter death has struck us, when we hold the body that is about to pass from our embrace into the pyre, a natural necessity forces out tears and the spirit, stricken by the blow of grief, shakes the eyes, whose nearby moisture it squeezes and forces out, just as

19 it shakes the whole body. These tears fall from the impact against our will: the tears which we allow to escape when we go over the remembrance of those we have lost are different, and there is something sweet in the sadness when their pleasant talk, their cheerful speech, and their attentive devotion come to our mind; then the eyes are

20 released as if in joy. We indulge in them, whereas we are overcome by the others. So there is no reason to contain or express your tears because of someone standing or sitting nearby; they never stop or flow as shamefully as when they are faked; let them follow their own bent. But they can come from calm and peaceable men: often they have flowed without challenging the authority of the wise man, with

21 such moderation that they lack neither feeling nor dignity. I am saying that you can obey nature while preserving your severity. I have seen men to be respected at the funeral of their dear ones, on whose face love shone forth without any playacting of mourning: there was nothing except what was granted to true emotions. There is a proper measure even in grieving: the wise man must observe this, and just as in other matters so in tears, there is a sufficient amount: in foolish men griefs have overflowed just like joys.

22 Accept what is necessary with a calm spirit. What happens that is new or beyond belief? Right now a funeral is being contracted for so many men, their burial clothes are being bought, how many are mourning after your mourning. Whenever you think that he was a boy, think also that he was a man for whom there is no certain promise, whom fortune is not leading automatically to old age; she

23 discharges him whenever it suits her. But talk often about him and celebrate his memory as much as you can; it will come back to you more often if it comes without bitterness; for no one gladly associates with a sad person, still less with sadness itself. If you had heard any of his chatter or his childish jokes with pleasure, return to them more often and boldly declare that he could have fulfilled your hopes which

24 you had formed with a father's heart. Indeed, to forget dear ones and carry out their memory along with their bodies and to weep lavishly

but remember sparingly is the act of an inhuman soul. That is how birds and beasts love their nurslings, their love is excited and almost frantic, but is completely quenched once they are lost. This is not right for a sensible man; let him persist in remembering but cease to mourn.

I don't in the least approve of what Metrodorus says, that there is 25 a pleasure kindred to sadness which must be aimed for at that sort of time. I have written the actual words of Metrodorus.* *From the letters of Metrodorus to his sister. There is a kind of pleasure akin to grief, which we must hunt at this time.* I have no doubt what you will think about 26 this; for what is more disgraceful than to seek pleasure in grief itself, indeed, through grief, and to seek out what will gratify even among tears? These are the philosophers who object to our excessive rigour and slander the hardness of our recommendations, because we say grief should either not be admitted to the mind or quickly driven from it. But what is either more unbelievable or more inhuman, not to feel grief at the loss of a friend or to lay snares for pleasure in the midst of grief? What we recommend is honourable, when emotion 27 has shed some tears and, so to speak, boiled over: that the soul must not be surrendered to grief. What, are you saying that pleasure should be mixed with grief? This is how we comfort children with a rusk, or soothe their weeping by pouring out milk. You do not allow pleasure to be idle even at the time when your son is burning or your friend is breathing his last, but you want to add spice to your mourning? Is it more honourable to remove grief from your mind, or to invite pleasure to join grief as well? Do I say 'invite'? It is hunted down, even by the mourner. He says: 'There is a kind of pleasure akin to 28 sadness.' We Stoics are free to say that, but you Epicureans are not. You only know one good, pleasure, and one evil, pain; what kinship can there be between good and bad? But imagine there is; is this the best time to root it out? Shall we examine grief itself, to see whether it has in it something pleasant and pleasurable? Some medications 29 which are beneficial to certain parts of the body cannot be applied to others because they are disgusting and unseemly, and what would be helpful elsewhere without any loss of modesty is dishonourable in the wounded part; aren't you ashamed to heal mourning with pleasure? That blow must be healed more severely. Rather, urge the mourner that no feeling of woe reaches the deceased, for if it reaches him he has not died. I repeat, nothing hurts the man who does not exist: if he 30 is hurting he is living. Do you think he is badly off because he does not exist or because he is still someone? But he cannot feel suffering, either because he does not exist (for what feeling does nothing have?) or because he exists, for he has escaped the worst hardship of death, not existing. Let us also tell the man weeping and longing for the child snatched away in first youth: in terms of the shortness of life, if you compare everyone on a universal scale, young men and old, all are on equal terms. For a smaller part has come to us from the whole age than what anyone might call the least part, since there is a least part; the period we live is next to nothing; and yet, alas for our folly, it is spread far and wide.

32   I have written this to you not because you were waiting for such a delayed remedy from me (for it is clear to me that you have been telling yourself whatever you are going to read), but to chastise that little lapse in which you have fallen away from yourself, and to exhort you for the future to raise your eyes against Fortune and keep a lookout for all her weapons, not as if they could reach you but as if they were bound to reach you in any case. Keep well.

Letter 101 *(No Book number is preserved.) This letter returns to the theme of death, starting from the sudden death of a respected but worldly man, Cornelius Senecio (§§1–4). Its suddenness points to the need for men to live each day as if it were their last. But one should not hang on to life regardless of its quality, like Maecenas (see letter 114) or Virgil's Turnus fearing death in combat with Aeneas: death can be a favour from nature.*

1 Every day and every hour shows us how worthless we are, and reminds us with some fresh proof of our vulnerability when we forget it: then it forces us, planning for eternity, to look back towards death. You want to know the meaning of this opening? You knew Cornelius Senecio, a splendid and active man of equestrian rank; he had advanced from a humble beginning and his progress to other elements of success was already a gentle downhill path, since prestige

2 grows more easily than it begins. Money too suffers the most hindrance at the level of poverty; it sticks fast while a man is crawling out of penury. Senecio was already about to grasp wealth, indeed, two most efficient talents were bringing him that way, expertise in earning and in conserving possessions, either of which could have made him

3 rich. This man of the greatest thrift, no less careful of his property

than his health, came to see me in the morning, as was his custom,*
then kept vigil until nightfall by a friend lying seriously ill without
hope of recovery. Then, after dining cheerfully, he was seized by a
sudden attack of ill-health, a constriction which narrowed his throat
and choked his breath so that he barely prolonged life until the dawn.
So he died within a few hours, after performing all the duties of a hale
and hearty man. This man, who was keeping his money busy on land 4
and sea, who had also embarked on public business leaving no form
of profit untried, was snatched away in the full transaction of his successful affairs and the full momentum of moneymaking.

Now graft your pear-trees, Meliboeus, set out your vines.*

How foolish it is to organize one's life when one is not even master
of the morrow! How great is the delusion of men embarking on long-
term hopes! I shall buy this, build that, lend this sum, recall that, hold
these honours and then withdraw my weary and fulfilled old age in
leisure. Believe me, everything is uncertain even for the fortunate; 5
no one should promise himself anything in the future; even what he
already possesses slips through his hands, and chance cuts off even
the hour which we are about to seize. Time rolls on by a law that is
fixed, but beyond our ken; indeed, what difference does it make to
me whether something is known to nature which is unknown to me?
We plan long voyages and a delayed return to our native land after wan- 6
dering over foreign shores, warfare and the slow rewards of our hardships on campaign, administrative positions and advancement in office
through other offices, and all the time death is at our side, and since it
is never thought of except as something affecting others, we constantly
have examples of mortality heaped upon us, which will not stay in our
minds beyond the duration of our surprise. And yet what is more fool- 7
ish than to be surprised that something has happened on any day which
can happen on them all? For our boundary stone is fixed where the
inexorable necessity of the fates has planted it, but none of us knows
how near he is to that boundary. So let us shape our minds as if we
have reached the end. Let us not postpone anything, let us engage in 8
combats with life each day. The greatest fault in life is that it is always
unfinished, that something is being postponed. The man who has put
the finishing touch on his life each day is not short of time; and it is
from this shortness that fear is born and a greed for the future that eats
up the soul. Nothing is more wretched than hesitation about things to

come and how they will turn out; the mind, anxious about the length
9 and quality of its remaining time, is harassed by unending fear. How
shall we escape this tossing and turning? There is only one way: if our
life does not extend itself but gathers itself in; for the man whose
present is incomplete is kept in suspense for the future. But when whatever I have owed to myself is paid back, when the mind is firm and
knows there is no difference between a day and an age, it sees as if from
on high whatever days and events are to come thereafter and thinks
about the ordering of circumstance with an unstinting smile. For how
will the variety and volatility of chance disturb you, if you are sure in
10 the face of the unsure? So make haste to live, my dear Lucilius and
think of each single day as a single life. The man who has equipped
himself like this, who has had a whole life each day, is free of care: for
those who live in hope each coming instant slips away and greed
advances on him with the fear of death, itself most wretched and
making all things wretched. Hence that disgraceful prayer of Maecenas
in which he does not jib at feebleness and ugliness and finally the sharpened stake,* so long as his life is prolonged among these evils:

11   Make me feeble in hand, feeble with limping foot,
     Impose a hunchbacked swelling, loosen my slippery teeth;
     While there is life I am fine; keep it going for me
     Even if I sit impaled on a sharpened stake.

12 He is wishing for what would be most wretched if it came upon him,
and asking for a prolongation of his torment as if it were life. I would
think him beneath contempt if he wanted to live on up to the moment
of the stake. He says: 'You can make me weak, so long as my breath
persist in a broken and useless body; you can corrupt me, so long as
some time is added to my repellent and distorted life; you may crucify
me and put a sharpened stake beneath for me to sit on.' Is it worth so
much to drive in one's own wound and hang stretched from a cross, so
long as it postpones the best part of all misfortunes, the end of one's
torment? Is my living breath worth so much that I am ready to give it
13 up? What would you wish for this fellow if not obliging gods? What is
the meaning of this disgraceful and unmanly poem? What is the object
bargained by this crazy fear? What the aim of such vile begging for
life? Do you think Virgil ever uttered to this man his words:

     Is dying wretched to so great a degree?*

He is wishing for the worst of misfortunes and longs for what it is most grievous to suffer to be prolonged and extended; in return for what? Simply the price of a longer life. But what kind of living is it to 14 die at length? We have found someone who wants to rot in executioner's tortures and perish limb by limb and lose his life-breath so many times drop by drop, rather than breathe it out once and for all? We have found someone who wants to be impaled on that ill-omened plank, already weak, already distorted and crushed into that loathsome protrusion of shoulders and chest, a man who had many motives for dying even before the stake, yet wants to draw out a life that will draw on so many tortures? Now try to deny that it is a great kindness of nature that we must die. But many people are ready to bargain for 15 worse things yet: even to betray a friend so that they may live longer, and hand over their children for violation so that they may see the light which has witnessed so many crimes. We must cast off the lust for life and learn that it makes no difference when you suffer what must be suffered at some time or other; what matters is how well you live, not how long; indeed, living well often depends on not living long. Keep well.

Letter 103 *(No Book number is preserved.) This is one of Seneca's shortest letters (cf. letters 60–2 above). The motive for its brevity may simply be a quest for variety, after the relative copiousness (and technical arguments) of letter 102. Its message is a variant on letter 101, since it warns against preoccupation with the future, but it is in a sense the opposite of 101, since it focuses not on too confidently anticipating one's own future plans, but on too timorous a fear of accidents and misfortunes. However, this theme is subordinate to a second warning, not against accidents, but against the deliberate malevolence of other men (§2). The proverb* homo homini lupus *('man is a wolf to man') was known before Seneca, but is not cited by him; indeed, this is the only letter explicitly condemning men for their treachery.*

Why do you keep looking round at the troubles which may possibly 1 happen to you, but may also not happen? I mean fire, collapse, and other things that befall us but are not sent as a trap for us; instead, look at and avoid the schemes which watch and entrap us. Disasters, even serious ones, are rare, such as shipwreck or overturning a coach, whereas the danger from man to man is an everyday hazard. Prepare

yourself against this, gaze on this with eyes alert; no misfortune is
2 more common, none more persistent, none more beguiling. A storm
threatens before it swells up, buildings creak before they collapse,
smoke is a herald of fire, but ruin from man is instant, and is concealed all the more carefully as it comes nearer. You are mistaken if
you trust the expressions on the faces of those you meet; they have
the features of men but the spirits of wild beasts, except that beasts
are deadly at the first encounter but do not seek out those they have
passed. For only necessity incites them to do harm; they are compelled into battle either by hunger or fear, whereas a man delights in
3 ruining another man. So consider what kind of risk comes from man
by considering what is a man's function; watch another man to avoid
being harmed, and do not yourself harm another. Rejoice in everyone's blessings and be distressed by their misfortunes, and remember
4 what you ought to offer and what you should avoid. What will you
gain by living like that? Not that they cannot harm you, but they
cannot deceive you. So withdraw into philosophy as far as you may;
she will protect you in her bosom, and in her shrine you will either be
safe or at least safer. Men do not butt into each other unless they are
5 walking on the same path. As for philosophy itself, you should not
vaunt it: it has been a source of danger to many by being arrogantly
and insultingly displayed; let it strip you of your faults, not reproach
others with theirs. It should not be alien to the behaviour of society,
nor aim at seeming to condemn whatever it does not practise. It is
possible to be wise without display and without provoking ill-will.
Keep well.

Letter 104 *(No Book number is preserved.) This wide-ranging letter
focuses chiefly on Seneca's health and the relationship between travel and
both physical and mental troubles, but it opens with a unique portrait of his
relationship with his wife Paulina. He barely mentions her elsewhere and
we depend on Tacitus' account of Seneca's suicide* (Annals, XV.61–5 f.)
*for what we know about Paulina, who wished to share his death but was
prevented at the last minute from following his example. Surprisingly,
Seneca does not quote Horace's famous verdict: 'men who rush across the
sea change the climate but not their own mood'* (Epistles, I.11.27).

1 I have taken refuge in my estate at Nomentum from—what do you
think?—the city? No: the fever that is creeping up on me; it has

already laid hands on me to claim me. The doctor said that it was
setting in when my veins were upset and erratic, and disturbed from
their usual rhythm. So I immediately ordered them to get a cart ready,
and although Paulina held me back I insisted on leaving. I had on my
lips that comment of milord Gallio:* when he began to feel fever in
Achaea he immediately embarked on shipboard, protesting that this
sickness came not from his body but the place itself. This is what I 2
told my dear Paulina, who makes me concerned for my health. For
knowing her life depends on mine, I begin to consider my own needs
in order to consider hers. Although old age has made me more resolute in face of many challenges, I have lost this gift of my age, since I
am reminded that in the case of this old man there is also a young
woman to be spared. So since I cannot persuade her to love me more
resolutely, she persuades me to love myself more carefully. For we 3
ought to indulge in honourable emotions, and at times, even if reasons to die press hard upon us, our life must be recalled to honour our
dear ones, even when in agony, and kept when it is hovering on our
lips to depart, since a good man should live not as long as it gives him
pleasure but as long as he is obliged to; the man who doesn't think his
wife or friend worth staying alive longer for, who will persist in dying,
is a pampered fellow.

Let a man's mind demand this too from itself, when the advantages
of his family and friends require it, not just if he wants to die, but if
the process is beginning; let him suspend it and keep himself available
to his dear ones. It is a mark of great courage to return to life for the 4
sake of another person, something great men have often done; but I
also think it a mark of the highest humanity to pay more attention to
one's old age, whose best application is to look after oneself with less
anxiety and use one's life with more spirit, if you know that this is
sweet and helpful and desirable to one of those you love. And this 5
brings no ordinary joy and reward; for what is more pleasant than to
be so dear to your wife that you become dearer to yourself on this
account? So my dear Paulina can hold me in her debt not only for her
fear but for my own.

So you want to know how my plan of going away turned out? 6
As soon as I left the polluted atmosphere of the city and that smell
of smoky kitchens which pour out all the sickening steam they have
inhaled, mixed with dust, I immediately felt my physical condition
changed. And how much do you think I gained strength once I

reached my vineyards? Released into pasture,* I fell upon my nourishment. So I recovered myself, and that languor of an uncertain and
discomforted body did not persist. I am beginning to study with my
7 whole heart. Place does not contribute much to this unless the mind
makes itself ready—it will have seclusion even in the midst of distractions, if it wants; but the man who picks and chooses his locality
and hunts for leisure will find something to distract him everywhere.
They say that when a fellow complained to Socrates that his travels
had done him no good, Socrates replied: 'It serves you right, for you
8 are travelling in your own company.' How well things would go for
some people if they strayed away from themselves! As it is, they
trouble themselves, harass and spoil and intimidate themselves.

What is the point of crossing the sea and changing cities? If you
want to escape the burdens that oppress you, you should not be
somewhere else, but someone else. Imagine you have come to Athens,
imagine Rhodes, choose any city at your whim: what difference does
9 it make what way of life the city has? You are importing your own. You
will think riches are a good thing; false poverty will torment you,
which is the most wretched fate. For, however great your possessions,
still because another man has more you will seem to fall short by
as much as you are overtaken by him. If you think public office is a
good thing it will distress you that so and so has been elected consul,
or another re-elected; you will feel envy whenever you read someone
mentioned more often in the records. The frenzy of ambition will be
so great that no one will seem to be behind you as long as anyone is in
10 front of you. You will judge death to be the greatest of evils, although
there is no harm in it except being feared, which precedes it. Not only
dangers but suspicions will keep you terrified, you will always be harried by empty fears. For what good will it do

to have fled countless Greek cities
And made your escape through the thick of the enemy?*

Even peace will supply fears; you will not even have faith in safe
circumstances once your mind is panicked, but having developed the
habit of unforeseeing fear, the mind cannot ensure its own survival.
It does not avoid trouble but runs away from it, and we are more
11 exposed to dangers when our back is turned. You will judge it the
worst of evils to lose someone you love, although this is as foolish as
weeping because the leaves are falling from the pleasant trees that

adorn your home. Whatever delights you, look on like green leaves, make use of them while they are flourishing. Chance will shake off different men on each day, but just as the loss of foliage is easy because it will be born again, consider as easy the loss of those you love and think the pleasures of your life, since they will be replaced even if they are not resurrected. 'But they won't be the same.' Neither will 12 you be the same: every day and every hour changes you, but in other matters what is stolen is more obvious, this theft is hidden because it does not take place in the open. Other men are taken from us, but we are withdrawn from ourselves by stealth. Will you not think about any of these considerations nor apply remedies to your wounds, but sow causes for anxieties for yourself by hoping for some things and despairing of others? If you have any sense, blend one with the other; do not hope without despair nor despair without hoping.

What can travelling in itself do to benefit any man? It has not 13 restrained his pleasures, nor reined in desires, nor checked anger, nor broken the untameable passions of love; in short, it has not removed any evils from the soul. It has not given him judgement, nor shaken off delusion, but held him back for a little while with some novelty of circumstance like a child who marvels at the unknown. What is more, 14 it provokes mental instability, which is a great sickness, and sheer disturbance makes it more fickle and unstable. So men leave the very places they had sought with intense eagerness yet more eagerly, and migrate like birds, going away faster than they came. Travelling will 15 give you a knowledge of foreign peoples and show you the contours of new mountains and the expanse of plains not seen before and valleys watered by year-round streams; it will place the unique nature of some river under your observation, whether it swells like the Nile with its summer flooding or is snatched from sight like the Tigris, then after completing its buried course is restored to its old size, or like the Meander, the exercise and sport of all poets,* is entangled in constant bends and often brought close to its own course, bending away before it flows into itself; but this will not make the man better or more healthy.

We must busy ourselves with our studies and the sources of wisdom 16 so as to learn what we seek, and investigate what has not yet been discovered: this is how we should rescue our mind from a most wretched enslavement and restore it to liberty. As long as you do not know what to shun and what to seek, what is necessary and what

is superfluous, what is just and what unjust, what is honourable and
17 what dishonourable, this will not be travelling but going astray. That
rushing around will bring you no assistance, since you are travelling
with your own emotions and your misfortunes are following you. If
only they just followed! Then they would be further away, but as it is
you are carrying them, not leading them. So they weigh down on you
18 everywhere and sear you with equal discomfort. A sick man needs
medicine, not a resort. If a man has broken his leg or twisted a joint, he
does not get into a vehicle or boat but summons the doctor to get the
broken limb healed, so that the dislocated joint is restored to its place.

So do you think a mind broken and distorted in so many places can
be healed by changing places? That is too great a sickness to be cured
19 by being carried around. Travel does not make a doctor or an orator;
no skill is learned from a place: well then, do we gather wisdom, that
greatest of all arts, along the way? Believe me, there is no journey
which will set you down free of desires, of anger, of fears, or if there
were such, the human race would make its way there. Those sicknesses will weigh down upon you and make you stew as you wander
over earth and sea as long as you are carrying the sources of your sick-
20 nesses. Are you surprised that flight is not doing you any good? The
things you are fleeing from are with you. So correct yourself, take off
your burdens and shrink your desires within a healthy limit: scrape all
the wickedness out of your soul. If you want to have pleasant journeys, heal your companion. Greed will cling to you as long as you live
with a greedy and miserly person; arrogance will cling to you as long
as you associate with a proud man; you will never cast away cruelty in
company with a torturer; gatherings of adulterers will inflame your
21 lusts. If you want to shed your vices you must move far away from
models of vice. A miser, a briber, a cruel and treacherous man, men
who would do you much harm if they had been near you, are actually
within you. Desert to the better cause; live with the Catos, with
Laelius, with Tubero.* And if you also enjoy associating with Greeks,
keep company with Socrates and Zeno; the former will teach you to
22 die if it is necessary, the other to die before it is necessary. Live with
Chrysippus, with Posidonius: they will pass on to you the knowledge
of things human and divine, they will bid you put things in practice
and not just speak smartly and throw out phrases to delight your
audience, but stiffen your soul and rear it up against threats. For there
is only one harbour for this wave-tossed and troubled life, to despise

what may happen, to stand confidently and ready, opposing your breast to receive the blows of fortune, neither hiding nor wavering. Nature has brought us forth great of soul, and as she has given 23 savagery to some animals, trickery to another group, and timidity to others, so she has given us a lofty spirit loving glory and seeking how it may live most honourably, not most safely. Just like the universe which it follows and emulates as far as is permitted to mortal steps: the spirit presents itself and believes itself praised and admired. It is 24 master of all and above all, so it does not humble itself to anything, nothing seems too heavy for it, nothing such as to bow a man down.

> Shapes dreadful to behold, both Death and Toil.*

Not dreadful at all, in fact, if a man can gaze on them with open eyes and break through the darkness; many things that are thought terrible by night the day turns into absurdity.

> Shapes dreadful to behold, both Death and Toil.

Our friend Virgil put it splendidly when he said these were not dread– 25 ful in reality but to behold, that is, a matter of seeming not being. For what aspect of them is as fearful as rumour has reported? What reason is there, I ask you Lucilius, for a man to fear toil, and a mortal to fear death? I so often meet men who think nothing is possible which they cannot do themselves, and who say we are speaking of things greater than human nature can bear. But how much more highly I think of 26 them. These men too can do this, but they are unwilling. Finally, what man have these hardships ever left helpless when he made the attempt? Who has not found them easier in the performance? We do not fail to dare because they are difficult, but they are difficult because we do not dare.

But if you want an example, take Socrates, that long-suffering old 27 man, tossed around in every kind of harsh circumstance, but unde-feated by poverty which his household burdens made more serious, and by the military hardships which he also endured. What hardships exercised him at home, whether his wife,* with her savage behaviour and wanton tongue, or his undisciplined children, more like their mother than their father; whether he was harried either in war or under tyranny or in that liberty which proved more savage than wars and tyrants. The war was fought for twenty-seven years;* after 28 the end of conflict the state was surrendered for its offence to the

Thirty Tyrants, most of whom were his enemies. Last of all came his condemnation, filled with the most grievous charges; he was accused of violating religion and corrupting the youth which he was said to be launching against the gods and their fathers and their state. After this came prison and poison. These blows had so little power to move Socrates that they did not even change his expression. Oh what a marvellous and unique achievement! Right up to the end no one saw Socrates either too cheerful or too gloomy; he kept an even temper in such great unevenness of fortune.

29   Do you want another example? Take the younger Cato, whom Fortune treated both more hostilely and more persistently. When he resisted her everywhere, last of all in death, he showed that a brave man could live against the will of Fortune and die against her will. All this age was spent either in civil warfare or in <civilian life> when it was already giving birth to civil war, and you may say that he <lived among slaves> no less than Socrates, unless you happen to think

30   Pompey and Caesar and Crassus were allies of liberty. No one saw Cato change when the state was changed so often; he showed himself to be the same in all conditions, in his praetorship, at his electoral defeat, in his accusation, in his province,* at the meeting of the public assembly, in the army, in death. Finally, in that nationwide panic, when Caesar was on one side relying on ten good legions, fighting-fit, supported by all foreign peoples, and on the other side Pompey, Cato was one man sufficient against them all. When some men were leaning towards Caesar and others towards Pompey, only Cato formed a

31   party of the free state. If you want to imagine in your heart an image of that time, you will see the common people and all the crowd eager for revolution on the one side, and on the other the elite and equestrian order, whatever chaste and refined elements there were in the state, with two beings left in the middle, the free state and Cato. You will marvel, I tell you, when you notice

Atrides and Priam and Achilles raging at both,*

32   for Cato is angry with both and disarms them both. This is his judgement on each: he says that if Caesar wins he will die, and if Pompey wins he will go into exile. What did he have to fear, since he had decided as his fate, whether defeated or victorious, whatever the most enraged enemies would have decided? So he died by his own deci-

33   sion. You see how men can endure hardship: he led his army on foot

through the midst of Africa's deserts. You see how he could endure thirst: dragging the remains of the conquered army over dry hills without any equipment, he bore the lack of water weighed down by his breastplate, and whenever there was a chance of water he was the last to drink. You see that he could despise honour and discredit: on the day of his electoral defeat he played ball in the place of assembly. You see he was able to feel no fear of the power of stronger men: he challenged at one time both Pompey and Caesar, although no one dared to offend the one unless he was doing service to the other. You see that death could be as well despised as exile: he imposed exile on himself and death, and war in between them. So we can have as much courage as his against such things, if we only choose to withdraw our neck from the yoke. But first of all we must reject pleasures; they weaken and make womanly and make great demands; but we must also make great demands upon fortune. Then we must despise wealth: it is the indenture of slavery. Abandon gold and silver and whatever else is a burden to family happiness: liberty cannot be won for nothing. If you value it greatly, then everything else must be valued little. Keep well.

Letter 107 *(No Book number is preserved.) Seneca's pretext is a complaint from Lucilius that some of his slave household has run away. The opening text is damaged, so that it is not clear how Seneca makes his contrast between the seriousness of being deceived by friends and by mere slaves; the argument suggests that another group of men had been resentful of Lucilius' quest and obstructed his efforts.*

Where is that good sense of yours? Where is your shrewdness in esti-   1
mating problems? Where your greatness of soul? Does such a puny matter disturb you? Your slaves thought your preoccupation was an opportunity to run away. If your friends were deceiving you <let them have that name, if you please, which our mistake has imposed on them, and be called friends so that they will not behave more shamefully>* . . . but in all your business you are free of those who were wearing out your effort and believed you were being troublesome to others. None of this is unfamiliar, none of it unexpected; it is   2
as absurd to be offended by such matters as to complain because you are splashed <in the baths or jostled> in the public street or stained by mud. Life is like public baths, a crowd, a journey; some things will

be aimed at you, others will just happen. Living is not a dainty activity. You have just embarked on a long journey; so you must slip and get buffeted and fall and be weary and cry out 'Oh death!'—that is, you must tell lies. You will abandon a fellow traveller in one place, bury your companion in another, fear your companion in another; this rough and bumpy track must be travelled to the end through that
3 kind of discomfort. Does a man want to die? Then let his spirit be prepared against all eventualities; let him know he has come where the thunderbolts rumble; let him know he has come where

> Mourning and avenging cares have laid their beds
> Where pallid sickness dwells and grim old age.*

This is the company in which we must pass our life. You cannot escape these things but you can despise them; and you will despise them if you often meditate and consider the future ahead of time.
4 Everyone approaches with more courage a hazard for which he has long squared himself, and resists even harsh circumstances by contemplating them in advance. But the man without preparations panics at even the lightest troubles. We must see to it that nothing comes to us unexpectedly, and since novelty makes all things more burdensome, constant meditation will guarantee that you are not a raw recruit for any misfortune.
5 'My slaves have left me.' They robbed another man, they accused another, they killed another, they betrayed another, they beat up another, they plotted against another with poison and yet another with accusations: whatever you mention has happened to many . . . in short, many different weapons are aimed at us. Some have pierced us, some quiver in flight and are approaching this very moment, some
6 graze us on their way to strike other men. We should not be surprised at any of these nuisances for which we were born, which no man should complain about since they are the same for everyone. That's what I say: they are the same; for a man could have suffered even what he escaped. The law is fair, not as everyone experienced it but as it was legislated for us all. Let us command a sense of fairness from our
7 spirit, and pay the tax of mortality without lament. The winter has brought cold: we must shiver. The summer brings back heatwaves: we must sweat. The bad weather tries our health: we must be sick. And a wild beast will confront us somewhere, and man, worse than all wild beasts. Water will snatch something from us, and fire some

other thing. We cannot change this state of affairs. What we can do is
put on a mighty spirit worthy of a good man so as to suffer the blows
of Fortune bravely and acquiesce in Nature. Now Nature controls 8
this realm that you see with its seasonal changes: sunny days follow on
cloudy ones; the seas are disturbed after being calm; the winds blow
in their turn; day follows night; part of the sky rises and part sinks
(into Ocean); the eternity of the world is composed of oppositions.
Our spirit must fit itself to this law: let it follow and obey it; let it 9
think that whatever happens should have happened, and not choose
to scold Nature. It is best to suffer what you cannot set right and
accompany without a protest God, who has made all things advance:
it is a bad soldier who follows his commander grumbling and groan-
ing. So let us receive our orders tirelessly and eagerly, and not aban- 10
don the progress of this most noble creation into which whatever
we suffer is woven; and let us address Jupiter, the pilot of this vessel,
as our Cleanthes* addresses him in most eloquent verses, and as our
most eloquent Cicero's example allows me to adapt in our own language. If you like them, you will take it well, but if they don't please
you, you will know that in this I followed Cicero's lead:

> Lead me, father and lord of heaven's lofty pole   11
> Where'er you choose; I'll not delay obedience;
> Here I am, active. If I'm reluctant, I will follow groaning,
> A bad man suffering what the good man chooses.
> The Fates lead on the willing but drag behind the laggard.*

Let us live and speak like this; let fate find us ready and unflagging. It 12
is a great spirit which has submitted to Jupiter, but on the other hand,
a man is petty and worthless who struggles against him and disap-
proves the ordering of the world and prefers to set the gods right
rather than himself. Keep well.

Letter 108 *(No Book number is preserved.) This extended letter shares
a common theme, the integration of moral knowledge into one's behaviour through life, across two sections, one focused on worldly men's failure to apply philosophical teaching, with a digression on Seneca's own
youthful pursuit of asceticism, framed by allusions to Attalus (§§3, 13),
Pythagoras, Sotion, and Attalus again (§23: cf. letter 110, §§13–20).
Starting at §24, the second part of the letter goes through forms of liberal*

*art which do not focus on the moral imperatives implicit in two of Rome's
key texts. The letter offers important evidence that Cicero's treatise* On
the Republic *(now partly lost) was as central to education as the* Aeneid.
*It also offers (partially conflicting) evidence for how literature was taught
by critics, some with a focus on language, others on historical and mythical
content and antiquarian interest in the early poetry of Ennius. See also
letter 88 and Appendix.*

1 What you ask about is one of those things which it is only relevant
to know for its own sake. All the same, since it is relevant, you are
impatient and will not wait for the books that I am assembling just
now, which contain the whole division of moral philosophy.* I will
send it off immediately, but I will write first how you can control the
eagerness to learn which I see burning in you, so that it does not trip
over itself.

2 Ideas are not to be picked at random or greedily assaulted *en masse*;
one reaches the whole through its parts. The burden should be fitted
to our strength and not taken hold of beyond what we are able to support. You must drink in not as much as you want but as much as you
can contain. Only be of good cheer; you will take in as much as you
want. The more your spirit receives, the more it expands itself.

3 I remember Attalus* giving us this instruction, when we were
besieging his school and entered first and left it last, even calling him
out as he walked to some disputations, though he was not only ready
for his pupils but reaching out to them. He said: 'The teacher and
pupil should have the same purpose, so that the teacher wants to do
4 him good and the other to do well.' The man who comes to a philosopher ought to take something good home with him daily; let him
return home, if not more healthy, then more susceptible of health.
For he will return. Such is the force of philosophy that it helps not
only those studying but those associating with it. The man who comes
into the sunlight, even if this was not his intent, will become tanned;
men who have sat in perfume shops and lingered a bit too long take
the smell of the place with them; and those who have been with a
philosopher must take with them something that would benefit even
indifferent people. Mark what I am saying, indifferent, not hostile
people.

5 'What then? Don't we know folk who have sat on for many years
with a philosopher and not even taken on a tincture of thought?'

Of course I know them. They are persistent and constant, men I call
not pupils of the philosophers but tenants. Some come to listen but 6
not to learn, just as we are led into the theatre for pleasure, to enter-
tain our ears with speech or song or stories. You will see that a great
part of these listeners finds the philosopher's school a clubhouse for
their leisure. They are not concerned with discarding any failings
there, or receiving a law of life by which to curb their behaviour, but
to enjoy an entertainment for the ears. Some even come with notebooks, not to record ideas but words, which they repeat with as little
benefit to others as they hear them without benefit to themselves.
Some are roused by grandiose utterances and enter into the speaker's 7
passionate emotions, eager in expression and mind, excited just like
eunuchs raving on command at the sound of the Phrygian piper.*
The beauty of the matter sweeps them along and stimulates them,
not the sound of empty words. If there is any fierce saying against
death, or any defiant saying against fortune, then it is a delight to do
immediately what you hear. They are moved by these sayings and
behave as they are ordered, if only that form would persist in their
minds, if the people, always arguing against what is honourable did
not immediately resist their glorious impulse; very few have been able
to take home the purpose they had conceived. It is easy to rouse a 8
listener to desire what is right; for nature has given all men foundations and a seed of virtues. We were all born for all of these merits;
when a challenger approaches, then these goods of the spirit are
roused as if from sleep. Haven't you seen how the theatres resound
whenever something is said which we acknowledge in public and bear
witness to their truth in common agreement.

Poverty lacks much but avarice everything: 9

A miser is good for no one, worst for himself.*

Even the most miserly of men applauds this verse and rejoices that
his own vices are being abused; how much more do you think this will
happen when these things are said by a philosopher, when the verses
are included among healing instructions, so as to sink them more
effectively in the mind of the ignorant? For as Cleanthes said: 'As our 10
breath produces a louder sound when a trumpet pours it out through
the narrow neck of a long channel with an opening that widens at the
end, so the narrow constriction of verse makes our meanings louder.'
The same words are heard more carelessly and have less striking

effect as long as they are uttered in prose; when rhythms are added and fixed feet have framed a smart saying, the same statement is, as
11 it were, hurled by a more vigorous arm. There are many sayings about the contempt of money, and this sort of instruction is given in the longest speeches: that men should think wealth is in the mind, not in ancestral property; that the man is wealthy who has adjusted to his poverty and made himself rich with a little possession; but the minds are more affected when songs of this kind are uttered:

> Least needy is the man who least desires.
> He has his wish who only wants enough.

12 After hearing these and similar sayings we are brought to an admission of the truth; but those for whom nothing is enough are amazed and applaud, declaring open hatred of money. When you see them in this condition, urge them, press this point and load it on them, abandoning ambiguities and syllogisms and quibbles and other games of futile wit. Denounce avarice, denounce luxury; and when you seem to have succeeded and affected the minds of your audience, press more passionately: it is unbelievable how much this kind of speech will succeed, bent as it is on healing and entirely directed to the good of the listeners. For malleable natures are very easily won over to love of what is honourable and good, and truth lays hands on men still teachable and only slightly corrupted, if it obtains a proper advocate.

13   Certainly, when I heard Attalus reach his climax against vices, errors, and the evils of life, I often pitied the human race and believed him to be lofty and higher than the summit of human achievement. He himself called himself king, but he seemed to me to go beyond ruling, since he was able to conduct a censorship of the ruling class.*

14 But when he began to recommend poverty and show that whatever went beyond need was a superfluous weight and a burden to whoever carried it, I often felt delight to leave school as a pauper. When he began to belittle our pleasures and praise a chaste body and sober table and a mind pure not only of unlawful pleasures but even of unnecessary ones, I delighted to restrict the greed of my throat

15 and stomach. From that inspiration some resolves have persevered, Lucilius, since I came to everything with a great urgency, then once I returned to the life of the community* I kept a few of the good practices I had begun. From that stimulus I renounced oysters and mushrooms for my whole life, for they are not foods, but delicacies forcing

well-filled men to eat (most welcome to the greedy, stuffing themselves beyond their capacity), stuff that easily goes down and is as
easily brought up. From that motivation I abstained from perfume all 16
my life, since the best smell for a body is no smell. From that my
stomach is now free from wine. From that I shunned the baths for
all my life; I believed it useless and pampered to distil the body and
void it by sweating. The other practices I cast away have returned,
but on these terms, that I keep a moderate measure of the things
I dropped from abstinence, something close to abstinence in fact,
though I rather think more difficult, since some things are cut off by
the mind more easily than they are restricted.

Since I began to explain to you how my eagerness to approach phil- 17
osophy was so much greater when I was young than in persevering as
an old man, I will not be ashamed to admit the love which Pythagoras
generated in me. Sotion* used to tell us why he abstained from animal
flesh and why Sextius abstained after him. The two men had different
motives, but glorious ones in each case. Sextius believed man had 18
enough nourishment without shedding blood, and that the practice
of cruelty began when dismembering had developed into a pleasure.
He added that the material of luxury ought to be reduced; he inferred
that mixed foodstuffs foreign to our bodies were detrimental to good
health. But Pythagoras said there was kinship with each other among 19
all creatures, and an exchange of souls passing successively into
different forms. If you believe him, no soul perishes, in fact it is not
even interrupted except for a very short time, while it is being poured
into another body. We shall see how it passes through shifts of time
and when, after wandering through several dwellings, it returns into
human form; meanwhile this belief created a dread of crime and kin-
murder in men for fear they should unwittingly assail their parent's
soul and violate it with arms or jaws, if a kindred spirit was housed in
any body.

When Sotion had set this out and rounded it out with his proofs. 20
He asked: 'Don't you believe that souls are assigned to different
bodies, and what we call death is merely a change of abode? Don't you
believe that that soul once belonging to a person lingers in these
domestic or wild animals or those living underwater? Don't you
believe that nothing is lost in this world, but just changes its setting?
That it is not only the heavenly bodies that revolve on fixed orbits,
but that living things also go through sequences and souls are driven

21 through the world? Great men have believed this. So suspend your judgement, but keep all options open for yourself. If those statements are true, it is a matter of innocence to abstain from living things; if they are false, it is an economy. What loss is incurred by your willingness to believe? I am rescuing you from the diet of lions and 22 vultures.' Inspired by this argument I began to abstain from living creatures, and after a year the habit was not only easy for me but welcome. I believed that my spirit was more lively, and I would not declare today that it was not so. You wonder how I stopped? The time of my youth coincided with the beginning of Tiberius Caesar's principate: foreign rites were stirring and abstinence from some living creatures was counted as evidence of superstition.* So at my father's request, not because he feared false accusations but he loathed philosophy, I returned to my earlier habit, and he had no difficulty in 23 persuading me to enjoy better dinners. Attalus used to praise a pillow that offered resistance to the body: I still use one of these as an old man, such that it shows no imprint.

I have told you these details in order to prove to you how passionate were the beginner's urges towards every good choice, if anyone urged them on, if anyone incited them. But there is some blundering through the failure of instructors; they teach us to argue, not to live; and some error among pupils, who bring to their instructors not the purpose of developing their soul but their intelligence. So what used to be philosophy, the love of wisdom, has become philology, the love of argument.

24 Now the purpose with which you approach each activity is very relevant. The intending teacher of literature examining Virgil, does not read that famous statement,

Time flees beyond recall,*

as: 'We must be alert; unless we hurry we will be left behind; the swift passage of time drives us and is driven; we are swept on unwittingly; we postpone everything to the future and are slow in circumstances that rush ahead.' Instead, he reads it to note how often Virgil uses the word 'it flees' of the swiftness of times:

The best day of life for unhappy mortals
Is first to flee; disease comes and grim age,
And toiling and harsh death unmerciful.*

The student thinking in terms of philosophy applies the same words   25
where he should. He says: 'Virgil never says the day passes, but it
flees, which is the most urgent form of running, and that the best days
are first to be swept away; then why are we slow to urge ourselves on,
so as to match the speed of the swiftest object? The better times fly
past us and the worse take their place.' Just as the purest liquor is first   26
to flow out of the jar, while what is most heavy and clouded sinks, so
in our age what is best is at the beginning. Shall we allow it to be emp-
tied for others while we keep the dregs for ourselves? Let this lesson
stick in our mind and please us as if it were sent by an oracle:

> The best day of life for unhappy mortals
> Is first to flee.*

Why the best? Because what is left is uncertain. Why the best? Because   27
as young men we can learn, we can turn our mind still flexible to
better things; because this time is suited to toils, suited to keep our
intellects busy with study and exercise our bodies in hard work; what
is left is more listless and languid and nearer to the end. So let us
concentrate with our whole hearts and, leaving aside our distractions,
toil for one purpose, not to delay understanding the swiftness of this
most nimble-footed time, which we cannot hold back, until we have
been left behind. Let each day please us like the best and be brought
into our control. We must seize what is fleeting. The man who reads   28
the poem with the eyes of a literary interpreter does not think that the
first day is best because sickness follows and old age oppresses us and
is looming overhead while we still think in terms of youth, but he tells
us that Virgil always combines sickness and old age—and he is not
mistaken, for old age is itself a sickness. 'Besides,' he says, 'he applied   29
this epithet to old age, he calls it "grim":

> . . . replaced by sickness and grim old age;

and he says in another passage:

> Pale sicknesses dwell there and grim old age.'*

You need not be surprised that each man gathers what is suited to
his own pursuits; in the same meadow the ox seeks grass, the hound a
hare, and the stork a lizard.* When some student of language, or some   30
literary critic or a devotee of philosophy takes up Cicero's book *On the
Republic*, each one focuses his attention in a different direction.

The philosopher is amazed that it was possible to say so much against justice.* When the literary interpreter approaches the same passage, he makes this note: that there were two Roman kings of whom one had no father and the other no mother. For there is uncertainty about Servius' mother; Ancus had no father, but was called the grandson of

31 Numa.* Besides this, he notes that the officer we call a dictator, and who is named as such in the histories, was called 'master of the people' by the men of old. This survives in the augural books to this day, and it is evidence that the man named by him is called 'master of the cavalry'. He also notes that Romulus died during a solar eclipse; that there was Appeal to the People even under the kings, and this is given in the priestly records as some other writers think and Fenestella.*

32 When a scholar of language opens up the same books, he first enters into his notebook that Cicero used the form *reapse*, that is, *reipsa* [in reality] and no less *sepse*, that is, *se ipse* [he himself]. Then he passes on to what the usage of the age has changed, as for example that Cicero says 'since we have been recalled from the very heelmark of addressing him'. For what is now called the chalk in the

33 chariot racetrack the men of old called 'the heel'. Then the scholar assembles lines of Ennius, especially those written about Scipio Africanus:

> whom no citizen nor stranger
> Could pay the price of service for his deeds.*

And he claims to understand from this that *ops* meant not only help but service, to the men of old. For Ennius says that no citizen or

34 stranger could pay him the price of his work. Then he thinks himself clever to have found the source for Virgil's words: 'above him the mighty gate of heaven thunders.'* He reports that Ennius stole this from Homer, and Virgil from Ennius; for there is this epigram by Ennius in the same work, *On the Republic* of Cicero:

> If it be right for anyone to rise to heaven's realms
> Then me alone the mighty gate of heaven takes in.

35 But to avoid slipping into the role of student of text or literary critic, I want to remind you that listening to philosophers and reading their work is for the purpose of attaining a blessed life, not so as to hunt archaic or artificial language and extravagant images and figures of speech, but to learn beneficial instructions and glorious and spirited

sayings which will presently be turned into action. May we learn such
things so thoroughly that what were words become deeds. For I think 36
nobody deserved worse of all mortal men than those who learned
philosophy as if it were a saleable skill, who live in a fashion different
from how they declare that one should live. They are parading themselves around as examples of a useless training, open to every failing
that they denounce. Such a teacher cannot benefit me any more than 37
a seasick pilot in a hurricane. One must hold on to the helm as the
breakers snatch it and struggle with the seas itself, one must rescue
the sails from the wind; what help can a ship's steersman give me who
is stupefied and throwing up? Yet how much worse a storm buffets life
than tosses any boat? We must not talk but steer. Everything these 38
men say, everything they throw out as the crowd listens to them, is
borrowed property: Plato said that, or Zeno said it, or Chrysippus
and Posidonius* and an immense squadron of so many names of this
kind. I will tell you how the speakers can prove that these sayings are
their own: let them practise what they preached.

Since I have now said what I wanted to convey to you, I will soon 39
satisfy your desire, transferring what you demanded complete into
another letter, so that you are not weary when you come to read this
thorny matter, which should be heard with keen and inquisitive ears.
Keep well.

Letter 110 (Book XI.1) *The opening, with its place of dispatch
and formal good wishes, is a gesture towards epistolary conventions, but
Seneca quickly gets down to the main theme: for happiness, we must be at
peace with ourselves, and guard ourselves against material desires. Seneca
illustrates this from two kinds of material things or two aspects of luxury:
food and drink not just for gluttony, but much more for display, like costly
equipment. Men should be contemplating the universe, not grubbing for
precious metals, which will harm their souls. The last third of the letter
is given over to an (undated) harangue of Attalus denouncing a parade
which is clearly a Roman triumph; the passing parade is an analogy for
the passing distractions of life, but a common man's desire even for basic
food and drink enslaves him and denies him freedom.*

I send you greetings from my place at Nomentum, and bid you enjoy 1
a sound mind, that is, the favour of all the gods, whom each man finds
appeased and favouring if he has first propitiated himself. For the time

being set aside the tales that some thinkers like, that a divine escort is given to each of us, not an official one but one of lower rank such as Ovid calls 'gods from the common crowd'.* I want you to set this aside while keeping in mind that our ancestors who believed this were Stoics:

2 indeed, they gave a Genius and a Juno to each individual.* Next we will consider whether the gods have so much leisure that they can look after the affairs of private citizens; meantime, be sure of this, that whether we are allocated to their care or neglected and left to fortune, you can wish no worse curse on any man than if you curse him with suffering his own hostility. But there is no reason to wish that anyone whom you think deserves punishment should have the gods against him. He has, I tell you, even if he seems to be escorted by their favour.

3 Apply your usual care and examine what our life is and not what it seems, and you will know that more evils come to us as consequences than accidents. How often something that was at first called a blow has proved the origin and beginning of good fortune! How often an affair welcomed with great congratulation has built steps up to a precipice and raised further to this point someone already distinguished, as if he was still standing where a fall can be safe.

4 But this 'falling' contains no misfortune if you look to its outcome in death, beyond which nature thrusts no one down. The end of all things is near, it is near, I tell you, that position from which the fortunate man is cast down and the unfortunate one is released: but we stretch out these conditions and make them longer by our hope and fear. But if you are wise, measure everything by the human condition: compress both what gives you joy and what gives you fear. For it is worth the cost of not rejoicing long over anything to escape fearing long over anything.

5 But why am I touching on this misfortune? You have no reason to fear anything; the troubles which disturb us and petrify us are hollow. None of us has discovered what was true, but simply handed on his fear from one to another; no one has dared to come close to what disturbed him and find out the nature and good aspect of his fear. So a false and empty notion is still believed because it has not been

6 refuted. Let us think it worth while to direct our gaze: it will soon be obvious how short and indeterminate and harmless are the things we fear. The confusion of our spirits is just as it seemed to Lucretius:*

> Just as boys tremble, fearing everything
> In blinding darkness, so we fear in light.

Well then! Aren't we more stupid than any child, to fear in the light? But this is false, Lucretius: we don't fear in the light, because we have 7 made everything dark for ourselves. We see nothing, neither what harms us nor helps us; throughout life we stumble over things and we don't pause or step any more carefully for that reason. For you can see what a crazy thing it is to rush around in the dark. But by Jove, we are determined to be called back from a greater distance, and while we don't know where we are being swept to, we press on swiftly to our goal. But the dawn can come, if we only want. There is only one way 8 it can happen: if a man takes in this knowledge of things human and divine, and does not just sprinkle it over himself but steeps himself in it; if he goes over the same things repeatedly, although he knows them and refers them to himself; if he seeks to know what things are good and what bad, the things to which this name is falsely assigned; if he inquires into things honourable and shameful; if he inquires into providence. Nor does human shrewdness stop within these bounds. 9 He is eager to look out beyond the universe, to see where it is being moving onward and where it originated, to what outcome such universal speed is hastening. We have dragged our spirits away from this divine contemplation towards shabby and low matters, to be a slave to avarice, to abandon the universe and its limits and its masters who control all things, to scan the ground and explore what evils it can dig out, not content with what has been offered. Whatever will be 10 good for us our God and father placed near at hand; he did not wait for our explorations, and gave things of his own accord. He buried harmful things as deeply as possible. We cannot complain of anything but ourselves; against the will of nature who has hidden them, we have fetched out what will destroy us. We have enslaved our spirit to pleasure, whose indulgence is the beginning of all evils; we have surrendered it to ambition and repute and other things equally hollow and empty.

So what am I urging you to do now? Nothing new—for we are not 11 looking for remedies for new evils—but first of all to distinguish in your mind what is necessary and what superfluous. The things you need will be found everywhere; but superfluous things have to be constantly and obsessively sought out. Now you have no reason to 12 praise yourself excessively for despising golden couches and jewelled equipment: for what is the virtue in despising superfluities? Admire yourself when you despise necessities. You are not scoring any great achievement if you can live without a king's equipment, if you don't hanker after wild boars weighing a thousand pounds or the tongues of flamingoes and other monstrosities of a luxury that now disdains complete animals and singles out specific parts from each variety; but I will admire you when you despise even cheap bread, if you persuade yourself that grass, when it is necessary, grew not just for cattle but for humankind, if you know that the tips of trees can serve to fill the belly into which we have heaped up such costly products. It should be filled without fussiness: for what does it matter what the belly takes

13 in, since it is going to lose whatever it took in? You take delight in an array of dishes hunted by land and sea, some of them all the more welcome if they are delivered to the table still fresh, others if they have been force-fed and fattened to overflowing and scarcely able to hold in their stuffing. The artificial glamour of these foodstuffs appeals to your fancy. But by Jove, those dishes anxiously examined and spiced in different ways, once they enter the belly, will be taken over by the same single disgusting mess. Do you want to despise the pleasure of food? Then think of its outcome.

14 I remember Attalus making this speech to everyone's admiration: 'Riches deceived me for a long time. I used to gape when some of these trappings glittered in one place or another: I thought what was hidden was like what was displayed. But in some parade I saw all the wealth of a city,* engraved both on gold and silver and materials that outdid the cost of gold and silver, rare and refined colours and clothing imported not just from beyond our boundaries but beyond those of our enemies; here we see flocks of slave-boys conspicuous in grooming and beauty, there flocks of women, and other things which the fortune of the greatest empire brought forth to review its posses-

15 sions. I said: "What else is this but provoking the desires of men, already sufficiently excited? What is the point of this parade of money? Have we assembled in order to learn avarice?" But by Jove, I brought away with me less greed than I had taken there. I despised riches not because they were superfluous but because they were too petty.

16 Have you seen how that procession, slow and carefully organized as it was, passed within a few hours? Will this sort of thing occupy our entire life, when it could not even occupy a whole day? And this other thought came to me, that these things were as superfluous to their

17 possessors as they had been to the spectators. So I say to myself, whenever something like this has dazzled my eyes, whenever a glittering house meets my eyes, a refined troupe of slaves, a litter on the

shoulders of handsome attendants: "What are you amazed at? Why are you gaping? This is just a parade. These things are being displayed, not possessed, and are passing on even as they please you." Instead turn towards real wealth: learn to be content with a little, and 18 with lofty spirit cry out that popular saying: "We have water, we have porridge, let us challenge Jupiter himself in good fortune." Let us do that, I beg you, even if we run out of these necessities; it is shameful to base a blessed life on gold and silver, but just as shameful to base it on water and porridge. "So what should I do if they are lacking?" You 19 are asking for a cure for poverty? Hunger ends hunger; otherwise what is the difference whether the things that force you into slavery are great or tiny? What does it matter how little Fortune can deny to you? Even water and porridge fall under another man's control, but a 20 man is free not if Fortune is given little power over him, but if she has no control. That's how it is: you should desire nothing if you want to challenge Jupiter, who desires nothing.'

This is what Attalus said to us, and nature has said to us all; and if you are willing to think this over often, you will be aiming to be happy, not appear so, and to appear happy to yourself, not to others. Keep well.

Letter 112 (Book XIX.3) *This very short letter echoes the pattern of ordinary private correspondence recommending or concerning mutual friends. We are to imagine that Lucilius has recommended a loser, but the purpose of the letter is to portray a particular stage when a man is not ready to attempt self-discipline.*

Be assured, I really want your friend to be shaped and educated as you 1 request, but he has proved to be a tough case—or rather, which is worse, a very soft case, broken down by long practice of bad habits. I 2 want to give you a sample from our own craft. A vine does not accept any random graft:* if it is old and eaten away and weak and slender it will either not accept the slip or not nourish it and attach it to itself, nor will the slip take over the stock's quality and nature. So we usually cut it away above ground level, so that if it has not responded we can attempt a second chance, and the slip is replaced and inserted below the soil. This man you write about with your instructions has no 3 strength; he has been indulging his faults. So he has become flabby and hardened at the same time; he cannot accept reason, he cannot nourish it. 'But he himself is eager!' Don't believe him. I am not saying that he is lying to you: he thinks he is eager. His luxurious habits have made him queasy, but he will soon be reconciled to them.

4 'But he says he is offended by the way he lives.' I would not deny that, for who is not offended? Men love and hate their faults at the same time. So we will pass our verdict on him when he has convinced us that he really loathes luxurious living: for now they are just on bad terms with each other. Keep well.

Letter 114 (Book XIX.5) *This letter is chiefly famous for its stylistic message, blaming corrupt style (*corrupti generis oratio*) on the corruption of character (*animus*), which links decadent writing and behaviour through the intellectual aspect of the mind (*ingenium, *a word also used by literary critics for style, and even for the authors and poets whose style is at issue). Seneca has already used the work of Maecenas, his great predecessor as an imperial adviser, twice in his letters, quoting with approval in letter 92, §35 (not in this selection) Maecenas' poetic statement of indifference to burial: 'Nor do I care for a tomb; Nature buries the abandoned corpses.' (Maecenas' poetry can be found in E. Courtney, *Fragmentary Latin Poets *(Oxford: Oxford UP, 1993), but prose passages are not included; a reference in our manuscripts to 'Maecenas de cultu suo' looks like the title of a lost prose treatise.) He returns to Maecenas in letter 101, §11 to illustrate the shameful content of Maecenas' poem clinging to life at any price.*

*Here, however, Seneca's preoccupation is not with the content of Maecenas' writing but with his style (*oratio, ingenium*). Seneca uses the brief samples from Maecenas to illustrate loose, ambiguous, and disordered writing. Are they verse (it is hard to recognize any metre, even lyric cola), or more likely prose? At §13 Seneca turns to historical writing and changes of fashion. Thus he illustrates the mannerisms of historians from the lost *Punic Wars *of Arruntius (§§17 f.), with its excessive and clumsy imitation of Sallustian mannerisms. But it is not imitation of others that marks moral corruption (§20), but rather deliberate affectation of corrupt writing: like a mind unbalanced by drink or fashionable indulgence, it becomes a disease. Seneca blames both corrupt style and corrupt lifestyles on men's failure to realize their limitations and mortality: the goal should be restraint (§§26–7).*

*Although Seneca himself would be singled out by Quintilian (*Institutions of Oratory, *10.2. 125–31) as a bad stylistic influence, he himself employs* *a very classical framework of analysis. Thus Seneca's criticism of language (*dictio/lexis*) follows the Aristotelian tradition, proceeding through the choice and combination of single words (rejecting basic terms for archaisms, neologisms, poetic vocabulary, and bold metaphor), to criticism of arrangement (*compositio*) that damages clarity, euphony, and rhythm, and of loose syntax*

On Seneca's judgement of Maecenas see the annotated translation of the first half of the letter by Winterbottom in Ancient Literary Criticism, *ed. D. A. Russell and M. Winterbottom (Oxford: Oxford UP, 1978).*

While the formal topic of this letter is corruption of style, Seneca himself clearly intended his critical discussion to be subordinate to the denunciation of moral laxity. The theme is continued in letter 115.

You ask me why a corrupted fashion of speech has appeared at certain 1
times, and how the tendency of personal styles towards certain failings originated, so that at times a grandiose expository style was popular and at others a fractured style drawn out like an incantation; why sometimes daring sentiments going beyond credibility have been in fashion and at other times brusque and suggestive aphorisms, in which one had to understand more than one hears: you ask why there was a period which exercised the right to metaphor without any sense of shame. The answer is what you commonly heard said, and has become a proverb with the Greeks: men's style is like their lifestyle. Now as each and every man's delivery <can be similar, so the prevail- 2
ing> style itself sometimes imitates public behaviour, if the moral standards of a community have come under pressure and given way to indulgence. Wantonness of style is evidence of public luxury, if it is not just a feature of one or two persons, but has been generally approved and welcomed. A man's style and his spirit* cannot have 3
different complexions. If the spirit is healthy and sedate, serious, restrained, then the style too is sober and sound; when the spirit is corrupted then the style too is affected. Don't you see how, if a man's spirit has lost vigour, his limbs drag and their feet move sluggishly? If it is womanish, how the softness is manifest in the man's walk? If it is keen and fierce, how the pace is excited? If it is frenzied, or—and this is close to frenzy—angry, then the body's movement is deranged and does not walk but is carried away. Don't you think this happens much more to the intellect, which is completely fused with the spirit: is shaped by it, obeys it, and seeks its code from it?

4   How Maecenas lived is too well known for any need to report now the
       way he walked, how indulgent he was, how he wished to be conspicuous,
       how he did not want his failings to go unnoticed. Well then, wasn't his
       speech as slack as he was loose in his clothing? Aren't his words as con-
       spicuous as his grooming, his escort, his house, his wife? He would have
       been a man of great talent if he had conducted himself in a more correct
       fashion, if he had not avoided being understood, if he had not sprawled
       even in his speech. So you will observe the contorted eloquence of a
5   tipsy fellow, straggling and full of licence.* What is more shameful than:
       'with stream and forest sprouting on the bank'? See how 'they plough
       the channel with skiffs and churning up the shallows, reflect the gar-
       dens'. What do we say, if someone 'curls at a woman's wink and coos
       with his lips and begins sighing, as the tyrants of the glade wilt on lan-
       guid necks'? 'An incurable gang grazes at the banquet and challenges
       the homes with the pitcher and demands death in their hope.' 'A spirit
       barely witness to its feast day', 'threads of fine wax', and 'crackling
       milled salt'. 'His mother or wife dress up the hearth.'
6   Won't it come to mind immediately reading his words that this is the
       man who always walked through the city in loosened tunics (for even
       when he was performing the role of Caesar in his absence he issued the
       watchword in undress)? This is the man who appeared on the magis-
       trate's dais, on the speakers' platform, in every public gathering, cover-
       ing his head with his cloak, with his ears protruding on either side, just
       like the runaway slaves of a wealthy man in the mime;* this was the
       man who, especially in the din of civil wars when the city was troubled
       and under arms, had two eunuchs as his escort in public who were
       more men than he was; this is the man who married a thousand times,
7   although he had only one wife.* These phrases so badly assembled, so
       carelessly dropped, arranged so contrary to everybody's custom, show
       that his way of life was just as strange and perverted and exceptional.
       He is most praised for being merciful: he was sparing with the sword
       and refrained from bloodshed, and only showed his power by his
       licence. But he spoiled this source of credit by those indulgences in
8   monstrous diction: it is clear he was soft, not mild. Those contortions
       of arrangement, those words askew, those amazing statements, often
       grand in intent but weakened in utterance, will make this obvious to any
       man: his head had been turned by too much good fortune. This is
9   sometimes the fault of a man, sometimes of a generation. When good
       fortune has spread luxury far and wide, first men's grooming begins to

be too particular, then there is a preoccupation with furnishings, then care is lavished on the houses themselves, to make sure they expand into the open country, that the walls gleam with marbles imported across the seas, that the roofs are set off with gold, that the gleam of the floor matches the ceilings; then the display is transferred to dinners and courted with novelty and variation of the usual order, so that courses which usually end the dinner are served first, and the dishes customarily offered to those arriving are given to those departing. When the mind has become accustomed to disdaining what is custom- 10 ary and normal things are treated as contemptible, it seeks novelty even in speech, and now recalls archaisms and outdated words and utters them, now invents <unknown words>* and turns them aside, or else, as has recently become increasingly common, bold and frequent meta- phor is treated as elegance.

There are writers who cut short their sentences and hope for 11 appreciation if the utterance is left hanging and creates a suspicion of its meaning in the hearer; there are others who extend and prolong their statements; others again do not just carry this to a fault (as is inevitable for anyone trying something grandiose) but actually love the fault itself.

So wherever you see that corrupt speech has won favour, there will be no doubt that behaviour too has abandoned correct usage. As the luxury of dinner parties and of dress are marks of a sick society, so licence of speech, if it is common, shows that the minds from which the words proceed have collapsed. Don't be surprised that corrupt 12 mannerisms are welcomed not just by the humbler spectators but even by this more cultivated crowd; for they differ in their togas, not their judgement. There is more reason for surprise that not only faulty speech but the actual faults win praise. For this has always hap- pened; no intellect has won approval without indulgence. Give me any man you like of great reputation; I will tell you what his gener- ation pardoned in him, what it knowingly overlooked in him. I will cite many examples of men whose faults did not harm them, and some whom they benefited. In fact, I will cite men enjoying the greatest reputation and counted among marvels, but if anyone corrects their speech, he destroys it: their faults are so thoroughly fused with merits that they drag the virtues down with them. Add to this that speech 13 does not keep a fixed rule: the habits of the community, which has never stood still in one place for long, keep it changing. Many people

seek their diction from another age and talk like the Twelve Tables. For them Gracchus and Crassus and Curio are too polished and recent; they go back as far as Appius and Coruncanius.* Some, on the other hand, want only what is hackneyed and in common use, and
14 fall into shabby diction. Each choice is corrupt in a different way, as corrupt, for heaven's sake, as refusing to use anything except glorious, resonant, and poetic vocabulary, while shunning basic and traditional language. I would call this man as much at fault as the other: one grooms himself more than is proper, the other neglects himself more than is proper. The former depilates even his legs, the latter not even his armpits.

15 Let us pass on to arrangement. How many ways shall I suggest of going wrong in this aspect of style? Some approve a jerky and rough arrangement: they deliberately disrupt anything that has flowed too calmly; they don't want a combination without a jolt; they think that what strikes the ear with its unevenness is manly and strong. Some men do not go in for arrangement, but a kind of incantation: it
16 caresses so much and glides so softly. What am I to say about those sentences in which words are postponed and, after being long awaited, scarcely turn around at the clausula?* What about that style which slows down for the ending, like that of Cicero,* sloping downhill and gently holding back, never differing in its habitual rhythm from his customary way.

Not only <being finicky> in the style of one's sayings is a fault, but if they are either trivial and childish or aggressive, daring more than is possible without damage to one's modesty, if they are flowery and too sweet, if they end in futility and do nothing more than resound without impact.

17 Faults like these are introduced by a single man, whose influence dominates the eloquence of the time, then others imitate him and pass it on one to another. So when Sallust was in fashion, truncated sayings and phrases ending prematurely and ambiguous brevity passed for elegance.* L. Arruntius, a man of exceptional economy, who wrote histories of the Punic War, was a Sallustian who strove for that kind of style. In Sallust you find, 'he made an army with his silver', that is, procured it with money. Arruntius began to fancy this and set it down on every page. He says somewhere, 'they made a rout for our men'; elsewhere, 'Hiero, king of the Syracusans, made a war'; and in another place, 'this news made the Panormitans surrender

themselves to the Romans'. I just wanted to give you a sample; his 18
entire book is woven together like this. Things that were rare in Sallust
are frequent and almost uninterrupted in this man, and not without
reason; for Sallust came upon these turns of phrase, while Arruntius
was seeking them out. You see the consequence when a fault becomes
a model for someone else. Sallust said, 'when the waters were wintry', 19
so Arruntius in Book I of his *Punic War* says, 'suddenly the storm
became wintry', and in another place, when he wanted to say that the
year had been cold, he says, 'the whole year was wintry', and in another
passage, 'then he sent out sixty cargo ships, lightly loaded except for
the soldiers and sailors' kinsmen, when the north wind was wintry'. He
never stopped inserting this word in all these passages. In one passage
Sallust says: 'while he sought good reports of fairness and justice amid
the civil conflict.' Arruntius couldn't stop himself from putting, immediately in his first book, that there were 'great reports' about Regulus.

So faults like these, imposed on a writer by imitation, are not 20
marks of luxury or a corrupted mind, since it is by the man's own
self-made faults that you should assess his condition. The speech of
an irritable man is irritable, that of a disturbed man too excited, that
of an indulgent man dainty and fluid. And you see men follow this 21
pattern when they either pluck their beard or partly pluck it; men
who shave their lips too closely and graze them, while preserving and
letting grow the other part; men who choose cloaks of an improper
colour, or a transparent toga, who don't want to do anything which
can slip past men's eyes: they provoke them and turn them towards
themselves, they even want to be reproached, so long as they are
noticed. Such is the style of Maecenas and all the others who do not
make mistakes by accident, but knowingly and willingly. This comes 22
from a serious mental affliction: just as in drinking the tongue does
not stumble until the mind has sagged under its load and is either
overturned or collapsed, so those faults of speech are just tipsiness,
a nuisance to no man unless the mind gives way. So take care of your
spirit; our meaning and our language come from it, our deportment,
expression, and gait come from it. When it is healthy and strong our
speech too is sturdy, strong, and manly; if it sinks down the rest will
follow its collapse.

> When the king is safe they are unanimous;   23
> Without him they break faith.*

The spirit is our king: when it is safe the rest stay at their task, they obey and take heed; when it has wavered a little, that is when they hesitate. But when it has given way to pleasure its skills and actions grow flaccid, and every enterprise is affected by languor and looseness.

24   Since I have made use of this analogy, I will continue. Our spirit is sometimes a king and sometimes a tyrant, a king when it aims at honourable goals, and cares for the well-being of the body entrusted to him, giving it no shameful or shabby commands; but when it is beyond control, covetous and indulgent, it assumes the dread and accursed title and becomes a tyrant. Then uncontrollable emotions seize on the tyrannical mind and oppress it; at the beginning it exults like a crowd glutted with a bounty* that will do it harm and clutching

25 what it cannot swallow. But when sickness increasingly consumes the mind's strength, and self-indulgence has sunk into its marrow and sinews, it will still delight to see those things which provoked the greed that made it useless, but instead of its own pleasures the mind will delight in the spectacle of other men's indulgences,* becoming a purveyor and witness of the lusts which it lost the ability to enjoy by heaping them on itself. In fact it does not give the tyrannical mind as much pleasure to be copiously supplied with pleasant things as bitterness, that it is not passing all these delicacies through its throat and belly, that it is not wallowing with the whole crowd of fancy boys and women: it actually grieves that a great part of its happiness is inactive, prevented by the limitations of its body.

26   Isn't it madness, dear Lucilius, that none of us thinks that he is mortal, none us thinks himself feeble? Indeed, none of us thinks that he is just one person? Look at our kitchens and our cooks rushing around between so many fires; does it seem to you that all this confusion of food is being prepared for just one belly? Look at our storage rooms and cellars full of the vintages of many ages; do you imagine that the wines of so many years and regions are being stored for a single belly? See in how many places the earth is being churned up; how many tenant farmers plough and dig; do you imagine that estates

27 are sown in Sicily and Africa for a single belly? We will be healthy and moderate our desires only if each of us counts himself and measures his body and knows he cannot take in anything in quantity or for long. However, nothing will be so helpful to you in practising general restraint as if you constantly recall how life is short, and uncertain at that: whatever you do, keep death in mind. Keep well.

Letter 115 (Book XIX.6)   *This letter begins and ends with the theme of good style (*compositio*) already touched in letter 114, but its main body is occupied by a paean to the man of real all-round virtue, presented as a kind of divine epiphany and so assimilated (a little oddly) to the disguised Venus met by her son in* Aeneid, I. *From §7 on Seneca inveighs against wealth and the desires it provokes in unphilosophical men. He blames early childhood upbringing for these false values reflected in the misjudgement of theatre audiences, for prevailing envy of wealth that will only provoke bad behaviour to obtain it and anxiety when it is won.*

I don't want you to be too troubled about words and their arrange-   1
ment, dear Lucilius: I have more serious matters for you to see to.
Ask for something to write about, not how to write, and do it not for
the sake of writing but of forming judgements, so as to apply your
judgements better to yourself and mark them. If you notice any man's   2
utterance being fussy and refined, be sure that his mind too is obsessed
with equally trivial things. The great man's speech is more relaxed
and carefree: whatever he says reflects more confidence than concern.
You know those over-groomed young fellows, gleaming in hair and
beard, straight from the bandbox; you would not expect anything vigorous or sturdy from them. Speech is the mind's grooming; if it is
trimmed all around and dyed and set by hand it shows that the speaker
too is not healthy but affected by some feebleness. Patterning* is
not an ornament for men. If we were allowed to examine the soul of   3
a good man, what a noble countenance we would see, how pure and
gleaming with grandeur and calmness, with justice balanced by courage, all glowing with temperance and prudence! Besides these virtues
thrift and self-control and tolerance and generosity, affability and
humanity, a rare good quality in men (who would believe it) would
shed their light upon him. Then what beauty—ye gods!—what
weight and severity his foresight and elegance would add to this,
with great-heartedness, the most conspicuous of these virtues! Surely
his authority and charm would be immense! Everyone would call it
worthy of both love and respect. If anyone sees this man's counten-   4
ance, more exalted and radiant than it is usual to see in human affairs,
wouldn't he stop, dumbstruck, as if encountering a god, and silently
pray that it might be lawful to have seen him, then wouldn't he be led
on by the sheer kindliness of the divine features to worship and sup-
plicate? Then after long contemplation of its exceptional eminence,

raised beyond the scale of what we are accustomed to look upon, as its
eyes blazed with a mild but no less vivid flame, wouldn't we utter the
saying of our Virgil in reverence and astonishment

5   What shall I name you, maiden, for your features
          Are not mortal, your voice no human sound . . .
          Be blessed and ease our hardship, whoever you be.*

This divine being will be at hand and ease us if we want to worship.
But it is not worshipped with the fat bodies of slaughtered oxen nor
the hanging of gold and silver votives nor cash contributions poured
6 into her treasury, but by a pious and upright intent. I tell you no one
would fail to burn with love of this being if we chanced to see it; but
for now many things intrude and either dazzle our sight with excess
glitter or hold it back in darkness. But just as eyesight can be sharpened and cleansed by some medications, if we are willing to free our
mind's vision from obstacles we shall be able to see virtue even when
it is buried in the body, even with poverty set in front of it, even
when lowness and shame beset it; I tell you, we shall see that beauty
even covered over with disfigurement.

7   On the other hand, we shall observe the badness and the sloth of
a troubled spirit, although the great brilliance of riches shining all
round hampers us and the false light of offices and mighty powers
8 beats down on us as we gaze. Then we will be able to understand how
contemptible are the things we marvel at, like children for whom
every toy is precious; they prefer cheaply bought trinkets to their parents and even their brothers. So what is the difference between us and
them, as Ariston says, except that we are crazy about paintings and
statues, a more expensive foolishness? Little pebbles found on the
seashore with some difference of shape or colour delight children; the
splotches of vast columns, whether they are imported from the sands
of Egypt or the desert of Africa, delight us, as they carry the weight
9 of some portico or dining-hall big enough for a community We marvel
at walls covered in a thin marble veneer, although we know the nature
of what they are hiding. We deceive our own eyes, and when we have
drenched the ceilings in gold, what are we rejoicing in except a lie?
For we know that ugly timbers are skulking beneath that gold. And it
is not just walls and ceilings which this thin adornment is screening.
The happiness of all those men whom you see proudly parading
is just so much gold leaf. Look if you wish to know what evil lurks

beneath that thin layer of dignity. Since money, the very thing that   10
obsesses so many magistrates and judges, that creates magistrates and
judges, has come to be held in honour, the true honour of things has
sunk, and we are turned into traders and merchandise for sale, asking
not what is the quality of any object but what its price. We are devout
for pay and impious for pay and follow honourable purposes as long
as there is some hope of profit, deserting and changing sides if criminal acts promise more gain. Our parents have instilled admiration   11
of gold and silver in us, and the covetousness which steeped us as
little children has settled more deeply and grown within us. Then the
entire community, clashing over other matters, is agreed on this: they
respect this and wish it for their dear ones, and dedicate this wealth
to the gods when they want to seem grateful, as if it is the greatest
of human possessions. Finally our way of life has been brought down
to this, that poverty is a curse and shame, despised by the rich and
loathed by the poor. Add to this the verses of poets, setting a torch   12
to our emotions, as they praise riches as the only glory and ornament
of life. The gods seem to them to be able to give or to have nothing
better.

> The sun king's palace soared with lofty columns,   13
> Agleam with brilliant gold.

Then look at the king's chariot:

> Its axle was of gold, its yoke-pole gold,
> Golden the wheel's rim and silver its spokes.*

Then they call the age which they want to seem best 'golden'. Nor is   14
there any shortage of characters in the Greek tragic poets to exchange
innocence, safety, and good repute for profit.

> Let me be called wicked, if they call me rich.

> We all ask if he is rich, not if he's good.

> They ask how much you have, not why or whence.

> In every place a man was worth what he possessed.

> You ask what it is shameful to possess? Nothing.

> I choose either to live wealthy or die poor.

> Whoever dies at a profit has a good death.

Money, that great blessing of the human race,
Cannot be matched by any mother's joy
Or children or a father rightly revered.
If any such sweetness shines in Venus' face
She rightly stirs the loves of gods and men.*

15 When this last set of lines was uttered in a Euripidean tragedy the whole audience rose in a single surge to throw out the actor and the poem, until Euripides himself leapt into their midst, asking them to wait until they saw what became of the speaker of these words. Bellerophon paid the penalty in that play which each man pays in 16 his own drama. For no covetousness goes unpunished, even if it is itself quite enough punishment. What tears and toils it demands! How wretched in both what is longed for and what is won. Add the daily anxieties which torture each person in proportion to his possessions. The torture of owning money is worse than that of earning it. How hugely men groan over their losses, which fall in large quantity but seem even greater. Finally, even if Fortune does not take anything away from them, whatever we do not gain seems one more loss.

17 'But men call this fellow happy and wealthy, and long to win as much as he possesses.' I admit it. What of it? Do you think anyone is in a worse position than men who suffer both poverty and envy? If only men took counsel with the wealthy before they began to hanker for wealth! If only they took counsel with ambitious men who had won the highest rank of dignity before seeking office! Surely they would change their prayers, since their advisers take on new ambitions when they have condemned their earlier ones. For no one is satisfied by his own success, even if it comes at speed. Men complain about their plans and their advancement and always prefer what 18 they have left behind. So this is what philosophy will guarantee you, something which I hold nothing surpasses: you will never be dissatisfied with yourself. Those neatly interwoven words, that gently flowing speech, will never carry you to this solid happiness which no storm can overthrow; let the words go as they will, provided the arrangement of your mind holds steady. Such a mind is great and indifferent to opinions and content with itself for the very things which offend others; such a mind assesses its advancement by its life, and judges that it only has knowledge in remaining immune to desire or fear. Keep well.

Letter 116 (Book XIX.7) *Seneca does not directly tell his readers that Lucilius has written in mourning for the death of a dear friend, but reveals it obliquely in §2. It leads to a brief discussion of the main dispute between the Peripatetic followers of Aristotle and the Stoics, for whom any emotion was a weakness to be resisted. Seneca solves this issue by distinguishing desires from a more disciplined kind of wishing (§1), but warning against fostering one's own desires. The letter deserves to be better known because it is exceptional in discussing the problem of romantic love (§§5–6) before reverting to the theme of moderating desire.*

Philosophers have often investigated whether it is better to have moderate emotions or none. Men of our school reject them, the Peripatetics moderate them. For my part I don't see how any middling level of sickness can be healthy or useful. Don't be afraid. I am not snatching from you any of the emotions that you don't wish denied to you. I will show myself easy and indulgent to the causes you aim at and think either necessary for life or useful or pleasant: I shall take away the fault in them. For when I forbid you to desire things, I shall permit you to wish for them, so that you can act in the same way without fearing and with a more reliable intention, so that you can even be more aware of those pleasures: surely they will reach you more effectively if you command over them than if you are their slave? 1

But, you will say: 'It is natural for me to suffer from the loss of my friend: grant a just right to my tears that fall so justly. It is natural to be moved by the opinions of men and saddened by their adverse judgements; why don't you allow me this honourable fear of bad opinion?' There is no fault without a patron's encouragement; no fault is not modest and curable at the start, but it spreads more widely from this first stage. You won't succeed in ending it if once you let it begin. Every emotion is weak at first, then it rouses itself and gathers strength as it advances; it is more easily kept out than driven out. Who denies that all emotions originate in a natural beginning? Nature has entrusted us with care for ourselves, but when you indulge in it too much, it is a fault. Nature has mixed pleasure in with necessary things, not so that we would seek it, but so that this additional gain would make the things we cannot live without more pleasing. If you let it come in its own right, then it is luxury. So we must resist pleasures as they enter because, as I said, it is easier to admit them than to get them to leave. 'Well, allow me to grieve up to a certain point, 2 3 4

to fear up to that point.' But your 'up to a certain point' extends a long way and does not come to an end when you want. A wise man can safely keep watch over himself without anxiety, and he will staunch his tears and pleasures when he wants: in our case, since it is not easy
5 to step back, it is best not to step forward at all. It seems to me that Panaetius* gave an elegant reply to a young man who asked whether the wise man would fall in love. 'We will find out about the wise man,' he said, 'but for you and me, still far away from the wise man, we can't risk falling into a condition that is troubled, uncontrolled, enslaved to another and cheap in our own eyes. For if the beloved looks kindly on us we are provoked by that person's kindness, but if the beloved despises us we are inflamed by pride. Ease in love is as harmful as difficulty; we are beguiled by ease but struggle with difficulty. So let us keep aloof, staying aware of our weakness: let us not trust our weak spirit to wine nor beauty nor flattery nor anything that attracts
6 with charm.' What Panaetius said to the man who asked about love I am saying about all emotions: let us withdraw from the slippery slope as far as we can; even on dry ground we are not standing firmly enough.

7   At this point you will counter with that popular criticism against the Stoics: 'You promise too much, and your instructions are too severe. We are poor ordinary fellows and cannot deny ourselves everything. We will mourn, but not excessively; we will feel desire but
8 moderately; we will be angry but we will be appeased.' Do you know why we cannot do that? Because we don't believe we can. No, I swear it, another factor is involved: we defend our faults because we love them and prefer to excuse them rather than shake them off. Nature has given man enough strength if we use it, if we gather our powers and rouse them all up on our behalf, or at least not against our interests. The real issue is that we won't, it is only a pretence that we can't. Keep well.

Letter 118 (Book XX.1) *This letter is a main source for our understanding of how Seneca imagined the correspondence. It may have been written to bolster the reality of a two-way exchange of letters; it is perhaps more tendentious in rejecting the political gossip of the moment which fills many of Cicero's letters to Atticus. From §5, however, it is preoccupied by working out a definition of 'the good' which will distinguish it from mere* '*goods*' *or material assets. The distinction drives the repetitious chain of syllogistic statements which assume that* '*the honourable*' *(honestum) does not need definition, and the good can best be defined in terms of honourable behaviour. This is best understood by recognizing that* '*the honourable*' *is externally defined, as behaviour which other men rightly honour, whereas* '*good*' *covers anything material as well as moral, which is seen as a benefit or asset*

Seneca's last argument (at §§14 ff.), that something can change character purely by reaching a critical size, is unconvincing, but almost certainly borrowed from a philosophical predecessor.

You are demanding more frequent letters from me, so let us compare 1
our accounts: you will find you cannot pay off your debt. In fact we
had agreed that your letters would come first: you would write and I
would write back. But I am not going to be difficult; I know that it is
safe to be your creditor. So I will give you a letter in advance and not
do what that eloquent man Cicero ordered Atticus to do, so that even
'if he has nothing to say, he should write whatever comes into his
mouth'.* I can never lack something to write, even though I pass over 2
all the sort of things that fill Cicero's letters: which candidate is falling behind; who is competing with borrowed resources, who with
his own; who is seeking the consulate on Caesar's credit and who
on Pompey's, and who on his strongbox; what a harsh moneylender
Caecilius is, from whom his own kinsmen cannot budge a penny at
less than 1 per cent interest.* It is better to deal with one's own misfortunes than other men's, to examine oneself and see how many
things one is seeking like a candidate, and not canvass for votes.

This is excellent, dear Lucilius, this is safe and free, to seek for 3
nothing and pass over all the elections run by Fortune. How pleasant
do you think it must be, when the tribes have been called to vote,
when the candidates are in suspense in their temples and one is
naming his bribe, another acting through an agent, another wearing
out with kisses the hands of men from whom he will withhold his own
hand once he is elected, when all are eagerly awaiting the herald's
voice, to stand at ease and watch that marketplace without buying or
selling anything? How much greater happiness* is enjoyed by a man 4
free of care, because he is observing not the praetorian or consular
elections but those great contests in which some men seek commem-
orative honours or perpetual powers, while some seek successful

outcomes of wars and triumphs, others riches, others marriages and children, others their own survival and that of their dear ones! What spirit it demands to be the only man not seeking anything, nor appealing to any man, but who can say: 'I have nothing to do with you, Fortune, I am not giving you any access to me. I know that in your books men like Cato are rejected, and men of this world like Vatinius are elected. I am not asking for anything.' This is to strip Fortune of her powers.

5   So we are free to write this kind of thing instead and pour out this ever-fresh material as we look around at so many restless thousands of men, who in order to obtain something noxious and destructive strive for evil ends by evil means, seeking things that they will presently need to shun or even despise. Who ever found the prize good

6   enough once he had won it, which seemed excessive when he longed for it? Happiness is not, as men think, greedy but petty, so it satisfies no one. You think those goals lofty because you lie far beneath them, but they are low for the man who reaches them. I am deceived if he is

7   not still trying to climb; what you think the summit is just a step. It is ignorance of truth that misleads everyone. They are swept on towards apparent goods, deceived by gossip, then after obtaining them with many troubles they see that these are evils or hollow or less than they hoped. But the majority marvels at things deceiving them at a distance, and generally good things are equated with big ones.

8   So that this doesn't happen to us too, let us ask what the good is. Its interpretation has been very different and each man expresses it in a different way. Some people define it like this: 'The good is what attracts minds and calls them to it.' To this there is the immediate counter-claim; supposing this does indeed attract minds, but to their ruin? You know how many bad things are appealing. There is a difference between the true and the plausible. So what is good is associated with truth, for it is not good unless it is true. But what attracts to itself and entices is only plausible; it creeps up and pesters and draws men

9   to it. Some people have defined it like this: 'The good is what provokes desire for itself or what provokes an impulse of the spirit straining towards it.' But the same objection can be opposed to this, since many things provoke an impulse of the spirit that are sought at the cost of the seekers. Those who have defined it like this do better: 'The good is what stirs up the urge of the mind towards itself in keeping with nature and must only be sought when it becomes desirable.'

For now it is also honourable, and this must absolutely be sought. This point in the argument reminds me that I ought to say what the difference is between the good and the honourable. They share something mixed and inseparable, for nothing can be good unless there is something honourable in it, and the honourable is in any case good. So what is the difference between the two? The honourable is the perfect good, by which the blessed life is realized, and other things also are made good by contact with it. What I mean is this: there are some things neither bad nor good, like military service, an embassy, or administering justice. When these are honourably conducted they begin to become goods and pass from ambiguity into being good. The good is created by association with the honourable, but the honourable is intrinsically good. The good flows from the honourable, but the honourable is such of itself. What is good might have been bad, but what is honourable could not have been anything but good.

This is the definition some have produced: 'The good is what is in keeping with Nature.' Pay attention to what I am saying; what is good is in keeping with Nature; this does not mean that whatever is in keeping with Nature is automatically good. In fact many things are in harmony with Nature but they are so petty that the name of good is not proper for them, since they are trivial and to be held in contempt. No small and contemptible thing is good, for as long as it is tiny it is not good: once it begins to be good it is not tiny. So how do we recognize the good? If it is completely in keeping with Nature. 'You are admitting', you say, 'that what is good is in keeping with Nature: this is its peculiar quality. But you admit that other things are in keeping with Nature which are not good. How is that good when these are not? How does it achieve a different quality when that feature is common to both, of being in keeping with Nature?' By its size, I suppose, and it is nothing new, for some things change by growing. There was a baby; it became a youth; his quality becomes different, for the one is irrational, but the youth is rational. Some things by growing not only become greater but different in nature. Our objector says: 'What becomes greater does not become different; it makes no difference whether you fill a jug or a cask with wine; both have the quality of wine. And a small quantity of honey and a big do not differ in flavour.' You are proposing examples of a different kind, for the same quality remains present in them: although they are increased, it stays the same. Some things when magnified remain of their kind

and quality, others, after many instalments of growth, are changed by the final increment which imposes on them a condition different from their previous one. One stone makes an arch,* the one which has wedged the sloping sides and bonded them by coming in between them. Why does the last increment, even when very small, achieve so much? Because it does not just increase, but brings the whole to com-
17 pletion. Some things in progress cast off their old shape and change into a new one. When the spirit has let something extend for a long time and wearies of following its greatness, the thing begins to be called infinite, because it has become very different from what it was when it seemed large but finite. In the same way we have sometimes thought that a thing was difficult to divide; but in the last stage as the difficulty increased, it was found to be indivisible. That is how we move on from a thing that is barely moved, and with difficulty, to something immovable. On the same principle, an object may have begun by being in keeping with Nature; then its great size transformed it into another quality, and made it good. Keep well.

Letter 121 (Book XX.4) *The novelty in this letter comes in its second part. First comes argument that good behaviour is according to man's nature and best for his condition as a man; then (from §5) to demonstrate what it means for something to be according to or in keeping with man's nature, Seneca turns to a comparison between man and irrational animals and infants. He shows great powers of observation as he explains and illustrates the principle of adaptation to one's nature in animals and in human infants—close to the modern notion of instinctive self-preservation. (This is related to Stoic* oikeiosis, the principle by which men treat themselves and their kin and country as their proper (oikeios) concern, and so take care of them.) The discussion in this letter of a feature men have in common with animals (and infants), though at different levels, can be compared with the exposition in letter 124 on reason, the distinguishing feature of mankind which animals and children lack: it is reason which men have in common with the gods.*

1 I can see that you will quarrel with me when I set out for you today's little investigation, which has preoccupied me for some time. For you are going to cry out again: 'What has this got to do with moral behaviour?' But go ahead and cry out, while I first provide you with other adversaries to quarrel with, Posidonius and Archidemus* (they will

take on the lawsuit), and then tell you this: it is not true that whatever
is a matter of custom and practice produces good behaviour. One 2
thing serves to feed a man, another to exercise him, another to dress
him, another to teach him, and another to amuse him, but all these
things serve man's needs, even if they do not all make him a better
person. Different things concern different aspects of behaviour: some
correct character and set it straight, some investigate its nature and
origin. When I ask why Nature produced mankind, why she preferred 3
him to other animals, is it your verdict that I have left morals far
behind? That is false. For how will you know what behaviour should
be cultivated unless you have discovered what is best for a human
being, unless you have scrutinized his nature? You will only understand what you must do and what you must avoid when you have
learned what you owe to your nature. You will say: 'I want to learn how 4
I can feel less desire and less fear. Shake the superstition out of me;
teach me that this thing called happiness is trivial and hollow, something which adding the syllable *un-* can easily transform.'* I will satisfy your desire by urging on the virtues and giving a good beating
to the vices. Though somebody may judge me to be excessive and
unrestrained in this matter, I will not give up harassing badness and
restraining the most unbridled emotions and stifling pleasures that
will turn to pain and heckling your prayers. Why shouldn't I, when
we have been wishing for the worst of evils and whatever cause we
have for consolation has arisen from subjects of congratulation.

Meanwhile allow me to open up matters that seem a little more 5
distant. We were asking whether all living things had a perception of
their own condition. That they do is most obvious from the way they
move their limbs neatly and nimbly just as if they were trained for this;
no creature lacks flexibility in its own limbs. A craftsman handles his
own tools easily, a pilot turns the helm of the ship smartly, a painter
quickly marks out the many different colours he has set in front of
him to portray a likeness, and alternates between the pigments and
the board with easy gaze and hand;* just so, a creature is flexible for all
its needs. We often are amazed at expert dancers because their hand is 6
ready to express all events and emotions and gesture keeps up with the
speed of words; it is art that supplies them with this, but nature supplies animals. No one wields his own limbs with difficulty, no one hesi-
tates in handling himself. This is what creatures do as soon as they are
born; they emerge with this knowledge and are born trained.

7   You say: 'Creatures move their parts neatly because if they moved
differently they would feel pain. So, according to what you say, they
are compelled and it is fear, not will, that moves them in the right
fashion.' But this is false. Actions driven by necessity are sluggish,
but agility comes from voluntary motion. Far from the fear of pain
driving them to this, they actually strive to achieve their natural
movement even when pain prevents them.

8   This is how the infant trying to stand and getting used to moving
himself, as soon as he begins to test his strength falls over and gets
up again and again weeping until he has trained himself by means of
pain for what nature demands. Some creatures with hard shells, once
they are overturned, twist themselves and thrust out their feet and
bend them sideways until they are put back in place. The capsized
tortoise feels no torment, but it is unsettled when deprived of its
natural condition and does not stop struggling and shaking itself
9 until it is standing on its feet again. So everything has a sense of its
own composition, hence its quick mastery of its limbs, and we have
no greater proof that they came into life with this familiarity than that
no animal is untrained in handling itself.

10   The counter-argument says: 'One's composition is as you say,
the commanding element in the mind, guiding itself somehow in
relation to the body. How does an infant understand this complicated
and subtle relationship which is somehow beyond even your explanation? All creatures have to be born capable of argument in order to
understand this definition which is impenetrable to most citizens
11 in their togas.'* But there would have been an objection you can make,
if I had said that animals could understand the definition of their
composition, instead of their composition itself. Nature is more easily
understood than described. So that infant does not know what his
composition is, but he knows his composition and an animal doesn't
know what it is, but feels it is an animal.

12   Besides, he only understands his composition crudely and superficially and vaguely. We too know we have a mind, but we do not know
what the mind is, where it is, what is its nature and from what source.
Just as we are aware of our own mind, although we do not know its
nature and place, so all animals are aware of their own composition.
For they must necessarily feel the organ by which they feel all other
things; they must necessarily have a feeling they obey and by which
13 they are governed. No man among us fails to understand that there is

something that stirs his impulses; but he doesn't know what it is. And he knows he has an impulse, but he does not know what it is or its origin. So infants too and animals have a perception of their governing part, but it is not yet sufficiently clear or articulate.

The counter-argument objects: 'You are saying that every animal is 14 first adjusted to its own composition, but that the composition of a human is rational and so a person is adjusted to himself as a rational being and not like an animal; for a person is dear to himself in that part which makes him human. So how can an infant be adjusted to his rational composition when he is not yet rational?' Every age 15 has its own composition, one phase for an infant, another for a child, another for a youth, another for an old man; all of them are adjusted to the stage of composition which they occupy. The infant has no teeth, and he is adapted to this feature of his composition. His teeth come into being; he is adapted to this new composition. For the plant that is going to become seed and grain has a different composition when it is young and barely emerging from the furrow, and another when it has grown strong and rests on a stalk that is soft but able to support its weight, another when it turns golden and aims for the threshing-floor and its ear has grown firm; whatever composition it reaches it protects it and forms itself into it. The successive ages of an 16 infant, a child, a youth, and an old man are distinct, but I am the same man who was an infant and a boy and a youth. So although the composition of each being is different, the adaptation of its composition is the same. For nature is not commending me to myself as a boy or youth or old man, but as myself. So the infant is adjusted to what at that time is an infant's composition, not what is going to be a young man's composition, and if there is any greater condition for him to take on it is still true that whatever he was born with was in keeping with nature. First the animal is adjusted to itself: for there has to be 17 a point of reference to which other things are related. I want pleasure. For whom? For me. So I am exercising concern for myself. I shun pain. For whom? For me. So I am exercising concern for myself. If I am doing everything out of concern for myself, then my concern for myself is paramount. This is inherent in all animals, and is not grafted on but born within them. Nature produces her fruits, and does not 18 reject them: and because the most reliable protection is from the next of kin, each being is entrusted to itself. So as I said in earlier letters, even raw young animals, freshly dropped from their mother's womb or egg, immediately know what is hostile and avoid deadly creatures. Animals vulnerable to birds of prey even feel terror at the shadow of birds flying overhead. No animal comes into life without fear of death.

19   'How', says the objector, 'can a newborn animal have recognition of a beneficial or deadly thing?' The first question is whether it understands, not how it understands. For their possession of understanding is obvious from the fact that if they have understood, they will do nothing further. Why does a chicken not run from a peacock or goose, but from the hawk, which is so much smaller and an unknown quantity? Why do chickens fear a cat but not a dog? Obviously they have knowledge of what will do them harm, but not based on experience,

20   for they take precautions before they can test it out. Then, so that you don't assume this happens by chance, they are not afraid of anything except what they should fear, nor do they ever forget this self-protection and carefulness; their flight from anything destructive is consistent. What is more, they do not become more timid as they live longer, so it is obvious that they don't reach this state by experience but from an innate love of their own safety. What experience teaches is both slow and inconsistent, whereas whatever nature

21   passes on is instant and consistent for everyone. But if you insist, I will explain how every animal is compelled to understand what is destructive. It knows it is made of flesh, so it realizes what instruments can cut flesh, or burn it and crush it, which animals are armed to hurt it: it takes the sight of them as harmful and hostile. Those two conditions are associated; for at the same time each being is adjusted to its own survival and seeks what will help while shunning what will harm. Urges towards beneficial things come from nature, so are rejections of their opposite: whatever nature has taught is without any thinking process to spell this out, and happens without deliberation.

22   Don't you see the immense cleverness of bees in shaping their homes, and their intense cooperation on all sides in sharing out their tasks? Don't you see how the weaving of the spider is beyond imitation by any mortal man? What a task it is to spin the threads, dropping some straight down as reinforcements while others run round in a circle spaced out from thick to more fine, so that the smaller creatures for whose ruin these threads stretch out are held fast as if entangled

23   by nets? That art is born, not learnt. So no animal is more learned than another: you will see the cobwebs of spiders are the same, and

the hole of every corner in honeycombs is the same. Whatever art passes on is uncertain and disproportionate; what nature has spread around is even-handed. Nature has passed on nothing more than self-protection and expertise in it, and this is why creatures begin to live and learn at the same time.

Nor is it surprising that animals are born with this instinct, since 24 they would be born to no purpose without it. Nature contributed this as the first tool of all for survival, adaptation to one's self and fondness for it. They could not have been safe if they had not wanted to be, and this would not in itself have done good to them, but without it nothing else would have done them good. But you will not find a low valuation of itself in any creature, nor even indifference. Even silent and stupid creatures, sluggish for all other activities, have shrewdness in staying alive. You will see that creatures useless to others do not fail themselves. Keep well.

Letter 122 (Book XX.5) *Seneca uses the shortening days of autumn as a trigger for discussing the best use of daylight, and attacking the fashionable practice of keeping (very) late hours: this is one of several customs which he condemns as contrary to nature, and he illustrates such fashionable debauchery with two amusing anecdotes.*

The daylight is now suffering some loss;* it has receded quite a bit, 1 but enough for there to be generous free time if anybody, as one might say, rises with the day itself. A man is more helpful to others and better if he anticipates the day and catches the first light: whereas it is a disgrace if someone lies half-asleep when the sun is high and begins his period of wakefulness at midday; and this is still before dawn for many! There are men who have reversed the functions of 2 day and night, and don't open their eyes, heavy with last night's hangover, before night has begun to come on. This is supposed to be the state of those whom nature, as Virgil says, has placed under our feet and opposite to us:

> And when the rising sun first breathes on us with panting steeds
> The ruddy evening star kindles its tardy lights for them.*

Yet with these fellows I mentioned it is not their location but their life which is completely opposed to us. Some men are our opposites 3 in the same city, men who, as Cato said, see neither the rising nor the setting sun. Do you think these men know how one ought to live, given that they don't know when to live? And do these men fear death, although they have buried themselves in it while still alive? They are as ill-omened as the birds of night.* They may consume their darkness in wine and perfume, they may stretch out the entire time of their unnatural wake in feasts, and those of many courses, but they are not partying but enacting their own funeral rites. At least the rites for the dead are paid by day. But I swear no day is long for an active man. Let us stretch out our life, but its purpose and content is action.

4 Let night be cut back and a part of it transferred to day. Birds purchased for serving at dinner-parties are kept in the dark so that they will fatten easily from not moving. So a bloated sluggishness takes hold of them as they lie without any exercise and <in the arrogant shade>* the proportion of limp stuffing increases. But the bodies of men who have committed themselves to darkness look unhealthy because their complexion is more dubious than in men pale with sickness: they are white, languid, and fading, and the flesh on these live creatures is moribund. I would say this is the least of their woes! There is so much more darkness in their minds. One man feels dazed, the other blacks out and envies actual blind men. Who ever had eyes for the sake of the darkness?

5 You enquire how this distortion of the mind happens, shunning the day and transferring all one's life into the night? All vices fight against nature; they all desert the proper order: this is the aim of luxury, to delight in reversals and not just stray from the right but go as far away

6 from it as possible, and finally to stand on the opposite side. Don't men seem to you to live contrary to nature when they drink without having eaten, when they take wine into empty veins and pass on to food when they are tipsy? And yet this is a common practice among young men who are building their bodily strength, to drink at the very entrance to the baths among those who have stripped; in fact they drink in order to shake off the sweat they have roused by constant rounds of hot drinks. It is vulgar to drink after lunch or dinner; that is what country householders do who are ignorant of real pleasure: the pure wine gives pleasure because it is not kept afloat on food and freely infiltrates the sinews; that tipsiness gives pleasure which comes on an empty stomach.

7 Don't men seem to you to live contrary to nature who exchange their clothes with women? Don't men live contrary to nature when

they aim for the glow of boyhood at an unsuitable age? What practice
could be more cruel or wretched? Shall he never become a man in
order to be able to suffer the violence of men for a longer period? And
shall not even age rescue him when it should have rescued him from
sexual insult? Aren't men living contrary to nature who covet the 8
rose in winter and force the lily in midwinter by bathing it in warm
water and cleverly changing its location? Aren't men living contrary
to nature who plant apple orchards on high towers? Whose coppices
tremble on the roofs and gables of houses, with their roots starting up
where it would have been out of place for them to thrust their treetops? Aren't men living contrary to nature who extend the foundations of their bathing-pools into the sea and don't think themselves
to be swimming in style unless their hot pools are beaten by waves
and storm? When they have made it their routine to want everything 9
against the custom of nature, they end by utterly rebelling from her.
'It's light; time for sleep!' 'It is rest-time; let us exercise now, let us
take a ride, let us lunch. Now the daylight is approaching; it is time
for dinner. It is not right to do what ordinary folk do; it is drab to live
in a hackneyed and common way. Let us abandon the public part
of the day, and let morning be our private and personal time.' To me 10
these men are like the dead; they are so close to their funeral, and a
bitter one, living by torches and tapers.

We remember that a lot of people used to live this life at the same
time, among them the praetor Acilius Butas, whom Tiberius rebuked
when he had consumed his vast family property and was admitting
poverty: 'You woke up too late,' he said. Iulius Montanus, a moderately 11
good poet, known for his friendship with Tiberius and his frigid verse,
was reading a poem. He loved to insert descriptions of dawns and sun-
sets, so when someone was complaining that he went on reciting all day
long and declared no one should go to hear his recitations, Pinarius
Natta said: 'I can't treat him more generously than this, I am ready to
listen to him from dawn to dusk.' When he recited these lines: 12

> Phoebus begins to extend his burning flames,
> Ruddy day to spread; now the sad swallow
> Returning starts to feed her nestlings shrill
> And doles out shares with gentle throat,

the Roman knight Varus, a companion of M. Vinicius and an enthusi-
ast for good dinners which he earned by the wickedness of his tongue,

13 cried out: 'Butas is beginning to sleep.' Then when Montanus contin-
    ued to recite:

> Now shepherds settled flocks within their pens
> Now slothful night gives silence to tired lands . . .

the same Varus said: 'What are you saying? Is it night already? I will
go and give Butas the day's greetings.'*

Nothing was more notorious than his life turned around to its
reverse; something which as I said many men practised in that period.
14 For some the motive to live like this is not because they believe night
has anything more pleasant about it, but because nothing normal
pleases them, and light is burdensome to a bad conscience, and when
a man lusts after or despises everything according to its costly or
cheap price, free daylight provokes their distaste. Besides, luxury-
loving men want their life to be gossiped about while they live, for if
there is silence they think they are wasting their efforts. So on many
occasions they do something to provoke gossip. Many devour their
property, many have girlfriends; to make a name among them you
will have to do something not just luxurious but scandalous, since
15 ordinary badness does not find report in such a busy city. We heard
Albinovanus Pedo's* tale (and he was a smart storyteller) of his
experience living above the house of Sextus. Papinius. Papinius was
one of that crowd of light shunners. Pedo said: 'About the third hour
of night I hear the sound of lashes. I ask what he is doing and I am
told he is reviewing his accounts. About the sixth hour of night I hear
a furious shouting. I ask what that is, and am told he is exercising his
voice. At about the eighth hour of night I ask what is the meaning
16 of the sound of wheels, and they say he is going for a ride. About
daybreak men start running around, slaves are summoned, and the
cellarers and cooks are kicking up a din. They say he has called for
his aperitif and *hors d'oeuvre* and has left the bath. The dinner', Pedo
said, 'barely extended into the daylight, in fact he lived quite eco-
nomically; the only thing he used up was the night.' So when others
said he was miserly and mean, Pedo said: 'No, you would really call
him one who lives by the lantern.'
17   You must not be surprised if you find such great aberrations in
vices; they are widely different and have countless appearances, and
their varieties are beyond imagining. Maintaining what is right is
simple; what is wrong takes many forms, and allows as much as you

like for new deviations. The same thing is true of behaviour. The behaviour of those who follow nature is easy, relaxed, and with tiny differences; but warped men differ from each other and in every respect. But I think the special cause of this affliction is contempt for 18 ordinary life. As men distinguish themselves from others in their grooming, in the fastidiousness of their dinners and refinements of their vehicles, so they want to set themselves apart even in their organization of time. They don't want to commit routine offences, since they see notoriety as the reward of their sins. This is what all 19 those men want who live backwards, so to speak. So, Lucilius, we must keep to the path which nature prescribed for us and not diverge from it: if we follow it, everything will be easy and ready, but if we struggle against it, life is just like men rowing against the current. Keep well.

Letter 123 (Book XX.6) *Seneca's starting-point is a late arrival in one of his country villas, where nothing has been prepared for him. This turns into a meditation on the need for patience and simple expectations.*

After completing a journey more uncomfortable than long I have 1 reached my place at Alba late at night; I find nothing is ready except myself. So I rest my weariness on a little couch and make the best of the delay of my baker and cook. For I am telling myself that nothing is serious if you take it lightly, how nothing deserves indignation <provided you add nothing> by your own state of indignation. My 2 baker has no bread, but the bailiff has some, and the doorman, and the tenant. 'Bad bread!' you will say. Wait, and it will become good; hunger will make even this soft and refined, so you should not eat before hunger orders it. So I shall wait and not eat until I either begin to have good bread or stop turning up my nose at bad bread. One must get used to a little; many difficulties of place and time arise 3 even for men well off and well equipped to <prevent and obstruct the man wanting something.> No one can have whatever he wants, but he can make a point of not wanting what he does not have and cheerfully making use of what is to hand. A well-behaved stomach tolerant of abuse is a great part of liberty. You cannot imagine how much 4 pleasure I derive from the fact that my own weariness makes its own repose; I don't need massage or a bath or any other remedy than time. For rest removes the discomfort which effort has brought on. Such as

5 it is, it is sweeter than any inaugural dinner. So I made an immediate test of my spirit; this is more simple and fair. For when patience has prepared itself and imposed an order, it is not so obvious how much real resolve it has: the most reliable evidence is what patience offers on the spot, if a man considers nuisances not just calmly but with good humour; if he has not turned white with anger or made a fuss; if he makes up for what should have been provided by not feeling desire, and thinks that something may be missing from his regular routine but he himself lacks nothing.

6   We did not realize how many things were superfluous until they began to run out: we made use of them not because we were obliged to but because we had them. What a lot of goods we accumulate because others have accumulated them, because they are in most people's possession. Among the causes of our misfortunes is that we live by the models we copy and are not ordered by reason but misled by habit. But if only a few men acted like this we would not want to imitate them; but as more have begun to do so we follow them, as if it were more honourable because it is more common, and error takes the place of what is right with us, once it has become a public pattern.

7   Nowadays everybody travels abroad with a squad of Numidian horsemen* going ahead of them and a column of runners in front of them; it is shameful not to have anyone to thrust men coming their way out of the road, and to show with a great a cloud of dust that a respectable man is approaching. They all have mules to carry crystal goblets and cups of myrrhine engraved by the hands of great artists; it is shameful to be seen with nothing but luggage that can be shaken up without damage. Everybody's slave troupes ride with oil smeared on their faces so that the sun and the cold will not harm their fresh young complexion; it is shameful for there to be no boy in your retinue whose healthy face is without medication.*

8   You must avoid chatting with all these men; these are the ones who pass on failings and transfer them from one place to another. It used to seem that the worst kind of men were those who paraded stories, but some men now parade their failings instead. Their conversation does a lot of harm; for even if it does not have immediate effect, it leaves seeds in the mind and follows us even when we have left them,

9 an evil that will revive later. Just as people who have listened to a choir carry the melody and the sweetness of the singing with them in their

ears, hampering their thoughts and not allowing them to direct
their attention to serious matters, so the conversation of flatterers and
those who praise corrupt practices clings longer than the time it takes
to hear it. It is not easy to dislodge a sweet sound from the mind; it
accompanies us and persists and sometimes comes back again after
a lapse of time. So we must block our ears to evil comments and from
the beginning; for when they have made a beginning and are let in,
they are more daring. Hence we come to this kind of comment: 10
'Virtue and philosophy and justice are a tinkle of empty words; the
only happiness is to do well in life, to eat, drink, enjoy one's family
property, this is living, this is remembering that one is mortal. The
days flow by and life runs down beyond recovery. Are we hesitating?

What is the point of being wise and imposing thrift on an age that
will not always be able to enjoy pleasures, while it is still able and
demanding them? In this way anticipate death and whatever it is
going to take with it. You don't have a girlfriend or a slave boy to provoke your girlfriend's envy;* you go out soberly each day; you dine as
if you were aiming for your father's approval of your account-book;
this isn't living but being part of someone else's life. What folly it is 11
to look after your property for the benefit of your heir and deny yourself everything so that a great inheritance will turn your friend into
an enemy? For the man who receives more from your death
will rejoice at it all the more. Don't give a damn for those grim and
haughty censors of other men's lives, enemies of their own and moni-
tors of the people, or hesitate to prefer a good life to a good reputation.' You should shun these remarks just like the Sirens 12
whom Ulysses refused to sail past unless he was bound.* They have
the same power. They seduce you from your country, your parents,
your friends and the virtues and in hope mock life as being wretched
unless it is shameful.* How much better to follow the right path and
lead yourself to that point where only what is honourable is pleasant
to you! And we will be able to reach this goal if we know that there 13
are two kinds of things which either entice us or drive us away. Wealth,
pleasures, beauty, ambition, and other beguiling and smiling things
entice us; toil, death, pain, shame, and a more severe diet drive us
away. So we should exercise ourselves not to fear these things, and
not to desire those others. Let us fight against them and withdraw
from what entices us, while rousing ourselves against things which
seek us. Don't you see how different is the deportment of those going 14

downhill and those climbing up? Men who go downhill tilt their
bodies backwards, but those going uphill incline them forward. For
to place one's weight forward if you are going down, and pull it back
if you are going up, is to collaborate with vice, Lucilius. The way to
pleasures is downhill, whereas one must bend to approach what is
rough and harsh; we thrust our bodies in this direction, but rein them
in from the other.

15   Do you think my point in this argument is that only men who
praise pleasure and inculcate the fears of pain, themselves quite fearful enough, are ruinous to our ears? I think those other men also harm
us who urge us to faults in the guise of the Stoic sect.

    For they make this boast that only the wise and learned is a lover.
'He is the only man fitted to this art, and the wise man is also most
expert in drinking and partying. So let us investigate up to what age

16 young men are to be objects of love.' Let this sort of thing be a concession to Greek practice, but let us rather turn our ears towards this
warning: 'No one is good by accident; virtue has to be learned. Pleasure
is a low and trivial thing to be held worthless, something we have in
common with dumb animals, to which the smallest and most contemptible creatures flock. Glory is something hollow and fleeting, and
more volatile than air itself. Poverty is not an evil for anyone unless he
jibs against it. Death is not an evil; you ask what it is? The only impar-
tial law binding the human race. Superstition* is a crazy delusion; it

17 fears the gods we should love and violates those it worships. For what
is the difference whether you deny the gods or slander them?' These
are things we must learn, in fact learn by heart; philosophy should not
pile up excuses for faults. The sick man has no hope of recovery if his
doctor is urging him to self-indulgence. Keep well.

Letter 124 (Book XX.7) *Seneca refutes the notion that we can perceive the good, or what is good, by the use of our senses, which only mis-
lead us into a love of pleasure. Instead he affirms that reason should be in
control, and contrasts what can be expected of an infant as opposed to an
adult. Starting at §15 he introduces a further argument, demonstrating
the limits of animal reason from their inability to comprehend any time
and any events except the immediate present.*

1   I can offer you many teachings of the ancients
           If you do not recoil, impatient to know small cares.*

Now you are not recoiling, and no subtlety is driving you away: it is not a feature of your fastidiousness to pursue only great issues, just as I approve of your behaviour in reducing everything to some source of moral advancement, and only jibbing when nothing is achieved by the greatest subtlety. And I will toil to prevent that happening now.

The question is whether the good is understood by the perceptions 2 or the intellect, and a related issue is that it does not exist in dumb animals and infants. Everybody who sets pleasure as the chief object judges the good to be perceptible, but we instead see it as intelligible, and assign it to the mind. If the senses passed judgement on the good we would not reject any pleasure, for there is none that does not invite and appeal to us; and on the contrary, we would not willingly undergo any pain, for there is no pain that does not jar the senses. Besides 3 those who choose excessive pleasure and whose greatest fear is of pain would not deserve reproach in that case. But surely we do condemn those given to gluttony and lust and we despise those who will not attempt any manly deed from fear of pain. Now what is their offence if they obey the senses, that is, as judges of good and evil? For you have surrendered to them the decision whether to seek or to shun. But clearly reason has been put in charge of this matter: it has 4 made decisions on good and evil as it has on the blessed life, on virtue, and on the honourable. For among that school the verdict is given to the lowest part of the mind over the superior one, letting the perceptions pronounce on the good although they are a dull and blunt thing, more sluggish in men than in other animals. Supposing some- 5 one wanted to distinguish tiny things not with his eyes but with his touch. No perception is more subtle than the eyes, and would be more focused, enabling man to distinguish good and evil. You see the vast ignorance of truth that besets blindness, and how the man whose touch makes judgement of good and evil has cast away matters lofty and divine.

The objector says:* 'As every science and every art should have 6 something apparent and grasped by the perceptions from which to form and grow, so the blessed life takes its basis and beginning from things apparent, and whatever is object of perception. In fact you yourself say that the blessed life takes its beginning from apparent things.' We say that what is in keeping with nature is blessed, 7 and it is openly and immediately apparent what is in keeping with nature, just like what is undamaged. What is in keeping with nature, which happens as soon as one is born, I do not call the good but the beginning of the good. You grant infancy the greatest good, pleasure, so that the baby at birth can begin from the point which the perfect man reaches: you are putting the treetops where the root should be.

8 If anyone said that when it was sheltered in its mother's womb, with its sex still unknown, raw and unfinished and shapeless, it was enjoying some good, he would be obviously misled. And yet how little difference there is between the baby at the moment when it receives life and the creature that is a hidden burden to its mother's flesh. As far as the understanding of good and evil is concerned each is equally ripe, and the infant is no more capable of good than a tree or some dumb animal. Why is there no good in a tree or an animal? Because they have no reason. That is why there is no good in an infant, for it too lacks reason. It will come to reach the good when it has reached reason.

9 There is an unreasoning animal and another that is not yet reasoning; there is also a reasoning but unfinished animal; but there is good in none of these, because it is reason that brings the good with it.

So what is the difference between those groups I have cited? The good will never exist in what is unreasoning; in what is not yet reasoning the good cannot exist then; <in what is reasoning but unfinished>

10 the good will soon be able to exist but it does not yet. This is what I am saying, Lucilius: the good is not found in any random body or any age, and it is as remote from infancy as the last from the first, as the perfected man from the beginner, so it is not in the raw little body still

11 forming itself. Why would it be? No more than in a seed. Put it like this: we know some good quality for a tree or a plant; it is not in the first foliage at the moment when it first breaks through the ground. There is a good for wheat; this is not yet present in the sappy grass nor when the soft ear emerges from the leaf, but when the summer and proper ripeness has cooked the grain. As every nature does not produce its good until it is perfected, so the good of man is not in man

12 except when his reason is perfected. So what is this good? I will tell you; the free spirit, upright, subordinating other things to itself but subordinated to nothing. Infancy is so far from not permitting this good that boyhood does not hope for it and youth hopes for it unreasonably; old age does well if it reaches this after long and intense devotion. If this is good, then it is intelligible.

13 The objector says: 'You have said that there was some good in a tree and in grass, so there can be in an infant.' True good does not occur

in trees or dumb animals; the sort of good there is in them is called good on sufferance. 'What is it then?' you ask. Whatever is in keeping with each thing's nature. Now the good can in no way occur in a dumb animal; it belongs to a more blessed and fertile nature. Unless there is room for reason there is no good. There are these four natures, of 14 a tree, an animal, a man, and a god; the last two, because they are reasoning, have the same nature, but they are different in that the one is immortal and the other mortal. So the good of one of these Nature herself achieves, that is of the god, but the other—of man—is achieved by care. The other things are merely perfect in their own nature, not truly perfect, since they lack reasoning. For in short only that thing is perfect which is perfect in keeping with universal nature, and universal nature is reasoning; the rest can only be perfect in their own kind. And the blessed life cannot exist in that kind nor the 15 efficient cause of blessed life: further, the blessed life is achieved by good things. The blessed life does not exist in a dumb animal, <nor its efficient cause>; there is no good in a dumb animal.

The dumb animal understands the present circumstances by per- 16 ception; it recalls the past when it comes upon something which reminds the perceptions, as a horse recalls the road when it is brought to the starting-point. But in its stable it has no memory of the road, however often it has been trodden. As for the third time, the future, it has no bearing on dumb creatures. For how can their nature seem 17 complete when they do not have the full use of complete time? For time consists of three tenses, past, present, and to come. Only the shortest of these is given to animals, and that in passing, the present. Their memory of the past is sparse and is never recalled except in encounter with present circumstances. So the good of a perfect nature 18 cannot exist in an imperfect nature, or if nature does have it, so do crops. I don't deny that dumb animals have powerful and excitable urges towards what seem in keeping with their nature, but these are disordered and confused, and the good is never disordered or con- fused. 'Well then,' you say, 'do dumb animals move in confusion and 19 disarray?' I would say they moved in confusion and disarray if their nature was capable of order, but as it is they move in keeping with their nature. For something is disordered when it can also at times not be disordered; something is worried if it can also be free of anxiety. No one has a fault unless they can also have a corresponding virtue; to dumb animals that movement comes from their nature. But not to 20 hold you back for long, there will be some good in a dumb animal, there will be some kind of virtue and something perfect, but it is neither good nor virtue nor perfection in an absolute sense. These things are only available to reasoning beings, who have the power to know why, how far, and in what way. So good is not present in anything unless it has reason.

21 You are asking where this disputation is leading and what benefit it will give your mind? I am telling you; it exercises it and sharpens it and at least holds it back with an honourable activity when it is about to take a decision. For even a cause for delay benefits those hastening towards bad deeds. But I am adding this point, that I cannot benefit you more in any other way than by showing you what is your good, by separating you from dumb animals, by putting you alongside God.

22 I ask you, why do you nourish and exercise your body? Nature granted greater strength to cattle and wild beasts. Why do you groom your looks? When you have tried everything you will still be outdone by dumb animals. Why comb your hair with immense care? When you let it flow like Parthians or bind it up like Germans or, as the Scythians do, spread it out, you'll see a thicker mane tossed by any horse, and it will bristle more handsomely on the necks of lions. When you train

23 yourself for speed, you will still not match the hare. Won't you abandon things in which you are bound to be defeated while you are striving for other creatures' excellence, and return to your own good? What is that? Obviously it is a corrected and pure mind, aspiring to match God, raising itself above human achievements, and putting no part of itself outside itself. You are a reasoning animal. So what is the good in you? Perfect reason. So call it back on duty to pursue its goal,

24 and let it grow abundantly, as much as it is able. Then judge that you are blessed, when all your joy comes to you from yourself, when after seeing what men snatch, long for, and keep under guard you find nothing—I won't say that you would prefer—but nothing you would even want. I will give you a short rule of thumb by which to measure yourself, by which you will perceive that you are now perfect; you will have your own good when you understand that the successful are the most unsuccessful. Keep well.

APPENDIX

EXCERPTS FROM THE LOST BOOK XXII
PRESERVED BY AULUS GELLIUS,
ATTIC NIGHTS, XII.2

We will set down Seneca's criticisms of Cicero and Ennius and Virgil, in 2
order to assess their quality. For in the twenty-second book of the *Letters on* 3
Morality he composed for Lucilius he says that Ennius wrote ridiculous
verses about that ancient man Cethegus:

> He was once called by his own citizens,
> Men who lived then and passed their years,
> Choice flower of his people, marrow of persuasion.*

And then he wrote about those verses as follows: 'I am amazed that men of 4
the greatest eloquence devoted to Ennius praised ridiculous verses as if
they were excellent. At any rate Cicero includes even these among Ennius'
good verses.' Indeed, he even says about Cicero: 'I am not surprised that a 5
man existed to write these verses when there was one to praise them; unless
perhaps Cicero, that great orator, was pleading his own case and wanted his
verses to seem good.' After that he even added this, most foolishly: 'and 6
you will find in Cicero himself some phrases in prose from which you will
guess he did not read Ennius to no effect.' Then he sets out what he con- 7
demns in Cicero as Ennian; that Cicero wrote the following words in the
Republic: 'as there was a certain sweet-speaking pleasantness in the Spartan
Menelaus', and that he says in another place, 'let him cultivate short-
speaking in his oratory'. And then this trifler asks pardon for Cicero's er- 8
rors, and says, 'this was not the fault of Cicero but of his generation; one
was bound to speak like this when one read words like that'. Then he adds 9
that Cicero inserted these actual words to escape the discredit of speech
that was too flighty and polished.

He also set down these words in the same passage about Virgil: 'And our 10
dear Virgil wrote certain harsh and shapeless verses, dragging on beyond
their measure, for no other reason than so that the people of Ennius would
recognize a touch of antiquity in the new poem.'

I am already tired of Seneca's words, but I shall not pass over these say- 11
ings of the foolish and tasteless fellow: 'some of Ennius' sentiments are so
great that although they were written among men smelling of goat they can
give pleasure among men smelling of perfume.' And after criticizing the

verses about Cethegus which I wrote down above, he says: 'those who love this kind of line clearly would also love the couches made by Sotericus.'

12   How worthy Seneca seems of reading and study by young men, when he compares the distinction and colour of ancient speech to the couches of Sotericus, as if—to be sure—they were of little charm, discarded in contempt! Yet you could hear recalled and quoted a few phrases that this same Seneca had expressed effectively, such as his criticism of the avaricious and greedy man thirsty for money: 'what difference does it make how much you possess? What you don't have is far greater.'

EXPLANATORY NOTES

1.1　*dear Lucilius*: this is not a formal greeting (none of the letters has a formal opening phrase). In this case Seneca avoids any formalities by shaping his first letter as a reply to Lucilius' resolve not to lose any time for moral self-improvement (repeated in letter 2). This has the effect of subordinating his own role as moral trainer to Lucilius' initiative. Seneca's letters are styled as responses, each one discreetly incorporating encouragement to new techniques of self-discipline.

　　　greatest part: I have not translated the Oxford text (*magna . . . maxima*) but the reading of the manuscripts which moves from *maxima* to *magna*.

1.5　*bottom of the barrel*: this aphorism from Hesiod, *Works and Days*, 369, begins the pattern of closing each letter with a quotation.

2.3　*strength to the body*: Seneca relies on many physical analogies to support his teaching; a favourite is digestion as conversion of food to energy (cf. letter 84).

2.5　*honourable condition*: this is the first of many sayings from Epicurus (founder of the rival philosophical school to the Stoics) cited in the first thirty letters. See also note to 4.10, 7.8, and letter 33.1–4.

3.2　*recommendations of Theophrastus*: Theophrastus, Aristotle's successor as director of the Peripatetic school, wrote many works, including three books on friendship (Diogenes Laertius, *Lives of the Philosophers*, V.45), known to the Romans but now lost.

3.6　*Pomponius*: unidentified. Perhaps Seneca's contemporary, the tragic poet Pomponius Secundus. If so, this prose saying must come from one of his prefaces, or a treatise.

4.2　*escorted to the forum*: upper class Roman boys wore a child's bordered toga until they reached puberty, when their father (or a stand-in) presented them with the toga of a free man, before introducing them to public business in the forum.

4.4　*when a fugitive*: since the previous examples include both free and slave, this third instance could be either a slave fleeing from his master or a free man in flight or exile during civil war.

4.5　*thinking this over*: a regular Stoic precaution to avoid distress was anticipating misfortune (*praemeditatio malorum*).

4.7　*lost his life to Chaerea*: as illustrations of great men overthrown, Seneca begins with Pompey, assassinated after his defeat in 48 BCE by the eunuch minister of the Egyptian boy-king Ptolemy, then his fellow triumvir Crassus, defeated (and beheaded) by the Parthian commander at Carrhae. Gaius Caesar is not here Gaius Julius Caesar but the cruel emperor Gaius (Caligula) who had Aemilius Lepidus (his brother-in-law) murdered and was himself assassinated by the military officer Cassius Chaerea.

4.10 *other men's gardens*: a pun on the 'garden of Epicurus'. The following quotation is Epicurus' fr. 477 in the standard edition by Usener, quoted again in letter 27.

4.11 *wear out our toga*: the toga was required formal dress, so worn for negotiating business contracts, for lawsuits and court cases, and senate meetings.

5.7 *in our Hecato*: when Seneca calls a philosopher 'our', this marks him as a Stoic. Hecato (1st century BCE) was a pupil of Panaetius: his work on morally appropriate actions was used by Cicero, *On Obligations*.

6.6 *his own code*: Seneca illustrates his maxim of sharing moral truth first from Zeno, founder of Stoicism, and his successor Cleanthes, then from the pupils of Socrates, Plato (founder of the Academy), and Aristotle (founder of the Peripatetics), then from Epicurus and three of his senior pupils. Seneca himself read and quotes Metrodorus in later letters.

7.1 *avoid the crowd*: compare the quotation from Democritus and Epicurus, fr. 208 (Usener), referred to at 7.10–11 below.

7.6 *Socrates or Cato or Laelius*: Socrates and Cato the Younger recur in these letters as examples of self-denial and martyrdom for their political integrity. Laelius, nicknamed 'the wise', is a less spectacular figure: consul in 140 BCE and friend of Scipio Aemilianus, he gained his exemplarity from Cicero who featured him in *On the Republic* and made him the mouthpiece of his dialogue *Laelius: On Friendship*.

7.10 *Democritus*: the fifth-century atomist and sage whose teachings were revived and developed by Epicurus.

8.3 *gifts of Fortune*: Seneca personifies the ancient goddess Fortuna (Greek *Tychē*) to an extraordinary degree. She is held responsible for all external misfortunes (thus exonerating God/Providence/Nature from making bad things happen to good men). Above all she is the virtuous and wise man's supreme adversary. Already in the second chapter (2.9) of the dialogue *On Providence*, addressed to the same Lucilius, Seneca presents (bad) *Fortuna* and the gallant man as engaged in a gladiatorial contest, worthy combatants for God to watch (*par deo dignum*). I shall capitalize this personification wherever it occurs, e.g. 14.6 below, 36.5, 38.5.

8.4 *off the track*: the image is drawn from chariot racing, Rome's favourite sport.

8.7 *true liberty*: Epicurus, fr. 199 (Usener).

toga dramas: serious plays set in Rome or Italy, as opposed to the *Palliata* comedies set in Greece.

Publilius: the ex-slave Publilius Syrus was a successful composer of mimes in the time of Julius Caesar; his plays would be performed in the slippers of comic actors, not tragic dress. He was soon credited as author of many moral sayings used in children's education, and will reappear in these letters at 115.15; he may also be author of several anonymous moral verses cited by Seneca.

9.1   *Stilbo*: the encounter of Stilpon (Stilbo) of Megara with Demetrius the Besieger (*c*.300 BCE) is reported by Plutarch in his *Life of Demetrius*, and by Diogenes Laertius (II.115).

9.2   *unfeelingness*: this is Seneca's equivalent of Greek *apatheia*, rising above emotion, which he aims to distinguish from mere cold-heartedness.

9.3   *contented with himself*: again a technical concept, not of smug self-satisfaction but to describe being self-contained or independent (Greek *autarkēs*).

9.4   *to have lost them*: the Stoics classified material assets like health, strength, beauty, wealth, and status as 'indifferents', because they were not morally necessary, but saw no merit in rejecting assets which made it easier to practise virtue.

9.5   *Pheidias*: the great Athenian fifth-century sculptor is often used by Greek and Roman theorists to illustrate the autonomy of the artist.

9.7   *The philosopher Attalus*: an older contemporary of Seneca who practised (and preached) Cynic austerity. He is next quoted in 63.5 and 67.16.

9.13   *Chrysippus:* the second director of the Stoic school, and a copious author of (lost) treatises on ethics and politics.

9.16   *universe has dissolved*: orthodox Stoics before Panaetius thought the universe was liable to cyclic destruction through fire (*ekpyrosis*), but this would not affect Jupiter who was above and beyond the universe.

10.1   *disciple of the same Stilbo*: Crates of Thebes is treated by Diogenes Laertius (Book VI) as a Cynic and pupil of Diogenes, but here as a pupil of Stilbo; see note to 9.1 above.

10.5   *Athenodorus*: Athenodorus of Tarsus, a contemporary of Cicero and court philosopher of Augustus; his views on peace of mind are discussed extensively in *On the Tranquillity of the Mind* (*Dialogues*, IX.3.1–8), but mentioned only here in the letters.

11.4   *Fabianus*: Seneca's examples of blushers contrast the ruthless dictator Sulla with the more vulnerable Pompey and the morally impeccable Papirius Fabianus, a Stoic declaimer whom the young Seneca had heard and admired in both capacities (cf. 40.12; 52.11; 58.6; 100).

11.9   *guardian and attendant*: cf. 12.2. Romans believed that a guardian spirit (*genius*) watched over them from birth (like the *daimōn* of Socrates which warned him against taking foolish actions). Citizens made private offerings to their own *genius* and public offerings for their group or block (*vicus*) to the *genius* of the emperor. In 12.2 Seneca's slave typically swears by the *genius* of his master.

12.2   *by my guardian spirit*: see note on 11.9.

12.3   *your old pet*: adult Romans often treated slave children as clowns or jesters.

12.7   *Heraclitus*: the pre-Socratic Heraclitus of Ephesus was known as 'The Obscure' for the mystic ambiguity of his sayings.

12.7   *a day . . . the daylight*: the text is not recoverable; I have italicized my
        paraphrase.

12.8   *il a vécu*: this Roman governor isolated in a corner of empire has his
        slaves perform a kind of Greek mime anticipating his death, as does
        Trimalchio in Petronius' *Satyricon*.

12.9   *that Fortune gave*: Seneca appropriates Dido's self-epitaph at *Aeneid*,
        IV.653. This is the first of many quotations from Virgil, either from the
        Aeneid (mostly identifying the earnest Stoic aspirant with Aeneas) or
        the *Georgics*. The next quotations are at 18.12; 21.5, but they become
        much more frequent once Seneca has dropped the regular quotations
        of Epicurus in his first thirty letters.

12.10   *It is bad . . . in necessity*: Epicurus, fr. 487 (Usener).

14.8   *Charybdis churns up the waters*: Seneca is reporting Lucilius' crossing
        of the Straits of Messina to take up his administrative position, but it
        is surely a convenient fiction that the pilot aimed his course near the
        whirlpool Charybdis. He takes the opportunity to make a sophisticated
        adaptation of the Homeric sea-hazard so often used allegorically in
        rhetoric (cf. 31.9; 79.1).

14.12   *both at the same time*: a century after the republican civil war between
        Caesar and Pompey, Seneca could dissociate the conflict from any con-
        temporary allusion. Cato notoriously deplored the political actions of
        both commanders in the years from 59 BCE to Caesar's final victory in
        46. But when Caesar crossed the Rubicon in 49 Cato urged Pompey to
        declare a state of armed emergency against Caesar, and served him as gar-
        rison commander in Sicily, Greece, and Africa, but not as a combatant.

15.1   *. . . I am well*: for this greeting, compare Cicero, *Letters to His Friends*,
        V.2, written to Metellus Celer in 62 BCE; it was often reduced to the
        initials SVBE, as in Pompey's military message included at Cicero,
        Letters to Atticus, VIII.11.C, and Balbus at *ibid*. IX.7.B.

15.3   *oil and wine*: the oil was for external application. There was a Roman
        saying, 'Oil for outside, wine for inside!'

15.4   *of the Salii . . . of a fuller*: the Salii, or 'leaping priests' of Mars, danced
        around the bounds of the ancient city at the beginning and end of each
        campaigning season. Fullers cleaned heavy woollen togas by trampling
        and leaping on them in vats of urine.

        and easy exercise: here and in 15.8 below the text is not recoverable: I
        have italicized my paraphrase.

15.6   *Riding in a litter*: the elder Pliny also recommends being carried as a
        form of exercise; for Seneca's habit of *gestatio* cf. letter 55.1.

15.7   *pitches and fixed rhythms*: Cicero reports that it was customary for ora-
        tors to strengthen their voices by exercise, but distinguishes exercising
        for public speaking (often in the open forum) from the more exotic
        vocal exercises of theatrical *phonaskoi*. With no real political life to

preoccupy them the Roman elite seem to have reached our own pampered routines of gymnasia and personal trainers.

15.8   ... *sink moderately*: the text cannot be recovered; I offer an approximate paraphrase.

16.7   *you will never be rich*: Epicurus, fr. 201 (Usener).

18.1   *December now*: for Romans of the first century CE December meant the Saturnalia (feast of Saturn), originally one day, 17 December, then expanding to fill most of the month; it was marked by parties and presents and a free-for-all in which masters served their own slaves.

18.2   *changed our dress*: the most common use of 'changing dress' at Rome was to put on ritual mourning, changing into a dark toga and smearing ash on the forehead. This practice was not restricted to actual bereavement but was adopted when, for example, a friend was prosecuted, or, as in Cato's case, when he felt the republic was endangered.

18.3   *felt-capped crowd*: another use of dress to indicate status. Slaves put on felt caps when they were manumitted and became freedmen, but during the Saturnalia it seems that all Romans put on this slavish headgear. But this sentence assumes another aspect of changing dress. To relax at parties Romans wore not the toga but the Greek pallium or a special dinner outfit called *synthesis*.

18.7   *dinners of Timon*: this is the notoriously inhospitable misanthrope in Athenian lore. Compare Epicurus, 'Letter to Menoeceus' (in Diogenes Laertius, X.131).

     full on a dupundius: with the '*as*' (9), these are the lowest small change used at Rome. I have left them untranslated because any modern equivalent would quickly become obsolete.

18.9   *when Charinus was in office*: Seneca quotes the Athenian date (by the *archōn* who gave his name to each year) given by Epicurus in the text of his letters. He must have been in possession of an autograph manuscript of Epicurean correspondence since he similarly quotes the actual Greek of Metrodorus' letter to his sister at 99.25.

18.10   *barley groats ... barley bread*: barley was cheaper than wheat, but the poor had no ovens, so they had to make do with *polenta* (porridge or groats) instead of bread.

18.12   *Dare ... worthy of the divine*: spoken to Aeneas by his host Evander at *Aeneid*, VIII.364–5, quoted again by Seneca in letter 31. But does Seneca want his readers to think of the original where Aeneas was invited to model himself on Hercules (who became a god), or to understand 'worthy of becoming divine'?

18.14   *Excessive anger leads to insanity*: Epicurus, fr. 484 (Usener).

18.15   *This passion*: anger, a particularly harmful emotion in a society where the powers of masters over slaves (and emperors over citizens) were absolute and unchallenged. Seneca wrote three books *On Anger*, perhaps twenty years before this correspondence, giving special attention not to palliating others' anger, but to keeping one's own rage in check.

19.6   *... of desires*: the Latin text has been corrupted.

19.9   *Maecenas*: this is the first of five references to Augustus' civilian adviser Maecenas (see also 92.35, 101.11–13, 114.4–8 and 22; 120.20 is trivial). Seneca saw in Maecenas, a man of great wealth and culture, and an intimate adviser of Augustus, who held no formal office, a precedent for his own role towards his youthful (and much less rational) emperor. It is strange that Seneca's allusions all cite examples of Maecenas's poetry or prose, although his criticism shows that he saw such self-indulgent writing as a deplorable illustration of a debauched character. See especially114.22, which condemns Maecenas not for accidental blundering, but deliberate (*sciens volensque*) perversion.

19.10   *harsh and upright terms*: I have translated here what I believe to be the sense of Reynolds' text <*nisi*> *in aspero et probo*, intended as a criticism of the words of Maecenas quoted above.

21.1   *those fellows you wrote about*: another cue to Lucilius' imagined letters. The fellows could be connected with the threatening court case which opens letter 24.

21.3   *make you cherished*: Epicurus, fr. 132 (Usener). This is a strong indication that Seneca modelled his own moral exchanges on those of Epicurus.

21.4   *Atticus' name to be forgotten*: Pomponius Atticus was Cicero's oldest and closest friend, a man who kept his distance from politics and so remained on good terms with both Antony and Octavius. His daughter Attica married Octavian's best friend and colleague Agrippa, and their daughter, Vipsania, was the first and best-loved wife of the future emperor Tiberius, and mother of the short-lived Drusus Caesar, Tiberius' heir.

21.5   *Rome's great father rules*: Seneca quotes Virgil's address at *Aeneid*, IX.446–9 to the tragic pair of lovers Nisus and Euryalus, in which the poet promises to immortalize them.

21.9   *common property*: after citing Epicurus (fr. 135, Usener) Seneca adopts the language of a civil arbitrator who assigns private property to one party or another, but declares this item common to all. Compare the fuller statement of this at 33.1–4.

21.10   *the highest good*: the 'garden' of Epicurus at Athens welcomed all friends and students to share in the simplest diet of the poor (see 18.10 above).

21.11   *natural, but not necessary*: Epicureans divided pleasures into three categories, in order of merit: natural and necessary; natural but not necessary (and so permissible if they otherwise did no harm); and neither natural nor necessary—what Seneca calls 'superfluous'. Stoics made a similar distinction between virtuous desires that should be satisfied and morally neutral or 'indifferent' objects of desire.

24.4   *Rutilius . . . Metellus*: these are Ciceronian examples of honourable conservatives unjustly exiled. Rutilius Rufus (consul 105 BCE) was condemned in the late 90s on a false charge of exploiting the provincials of Asia: when pardoned by Sulla ten years later he refused to return; Metellus Numidicus (consul 109 BCE) was exiled for refusing to swear to support a radical bill, but recalled. Their hardships were nothing worse than exile. The other exemplary figures, like Socrates, who respected his (unjust) death sentence and refused the chance Crito offered him to escape, suffered more harshly.

24.5   *Mucius*: Mucius earned his name Scaevola ('Lefty') by thrusting his right hand into the fire to prove to Porsena, king of Clusium, that he was resolved to fight for Rome's new republican freedom at all costs. He is, then, the example *par excellence* of pain willingly undergone.

24.6   *telling me about Cato*: this is Seneca's cue for a detailed account of Cato's self-imposed death. Caesar himself is mentioned only once, although Cato died to avoid falling into his hands. It is Fortune (as in *On Providence*) who takes the rap for Cato's undeserved defeat. With letter 14 (12–14) on Cato's other heroic moment, when he provoked the conservatives' decision to enter the Civil War, Seneca has now set out his reasons for treating Cato as a Stoic hero.

24.9   *Pompey's father-in-law*: this is Metellus Scipio (consul 52 BCE), commander of the republican force which fought on in Libya after Pompey's death and was defeated by Caesar at Thapsus. The 'fated glory of the Scipios in Africa' refers to the victories of Scipio Africanus and his grandson Aemilianus over Carthage in the Second and Third Punic War, and the prophecy current during the campaign against Caesar that a Scipio would lead the victorious force.

24.14 *executioners all around you?*: Seneca's scenario is somewhat rhetorical. Roman citizens of high status were exempt from the death penalty and especially from torture, but under the tyrannical principates of Gaius (Caligula) or Nero men politically suspect were executed and could be tortured.

24.18 *Ixion . . . Sisyphus . . . Cerberus . . . bare bones*: Ixion and Sisyphus were classic sinners against the gods with peculiar punishments in the underworld: next Seneca alludes toTityos, whose liver was reborn and eaten by a vulture each day. Cerberus was the three-headed watchdog of Hades. These myths of the underworld were also repudiated by the Epicurean Lucretius.

24.20 *the water-clock*: a mechanism like an egg-timer, used for timing proceedings in trials.

24.21 *death's last phase*: this hexameter presumably comes from an actual poem by Lucilius.

24.23   *fear of death?*: the three quotations in this letter are Epicurus, frr. 496, 498, and 497 (Usener).

26.8   *Practise death in advance*: once again Seneca has introduced his saying of Epicurus (fr. 205, Usener) with the language of private borrowing, including a notional fee for conveying the letter.

27.5   *Trojans and Achaeans*: the *Iliad* was the stock reading-matter of elite Roman boys, but Calvisius, like the uneducated Trimalchio in Petronius' *Satyricon*, cannot even get his Homeric heroes straight. (Personal assistants served politicians by supplying the names of whomever they met in the forum.) Hesiod was much favoured for his moral maxims, but the nine lyric poets are far less likely to have been part of a Roman's repertoire, and the purchase of nine slaves, one for each poet, was surely added by Seneca to enliven the story.

27.7   *to go along with it*: Seneca's account of this professional parasite includes two untranslatable puns on his greed and mockery. 'To pick up the crumbs' paraphrases a Greek term (*analectas*) for waiter; in elegant households slaves were (supposed to be) Greek-speaking and specialists had Greek designations. But grammarians too were often Greeks.

27.9   *Poverty . . . is wealth*: Epicurus, fr. 477 (Usener).

28.1   *not your surroundings*: Seneca knew and was clearly influenced by Horace's first book of *Epistles*, but adapts without acknowledgement the closing line of *Ep*. I.11.27 (*caelum non animum*). In contrast, for the next two quotations he proudly names Virgil as his source for Aeneas' experiences in *Aeneid*, III.72 ('cities grow distant') and VI.78–9 ('the prophetess grows frantic').

28.8   *Thirty tyrants*: when Athens was defeated at the end of the Peloponnesian War (402 BCE) the Spartans imposed a rule of thirty oligarchs (some of whom had studied with Socrates), but when the thirty voted to condemn citizens to death Socrates resisted the vote and withdrew from any political role. But it was not the oligarchs but the restored democracy which in turn condemned Socrates to death in 399.

28.9   *beginning of recovery*: Epicurus, fr. 522 (Usener).

31.2   *for his companions*: When Ulysses had to pass the Sirens, who lured sailors to their deaths by promising them universal knowledge, he made his sailors block their ears with wax but tie him up so that he could listen without breaking loose.

31.3   *among indifferents*: that is, among objects neither intrinsically good nor bad, which may be chosen if they do not entail harm.

31.9   *Scylla and Charybdis*: Seneca extends the metaphor of ascent to include traversing mountain ranges, then the mountainous region of Candavia near the Roman Via Egnatia in Macedonia, then (returning to maritime hazards) the Libyan Syrtes (treacherous sandbanks) and the two hazards of the Sicilian straits confronted by Ulysses: Scylla off the Calabrian coast and Sicilian Charybdis (see letter 14.8).

31.11   *worthy* | *Of the divine*: this is the second time Seneca has quoted *Aeneid*, VIII.364–5; cf. letter 18.12.

33.3   *eyecatchers*: Seneca introduces a unique Latin form *ocliferia*, 'drawing the eyes'.

33.4   *Zeno . . . Posidonius*: the Stoics are cited in order of succession: first the three heads of the sect, Zeno, Cleanthes, and Chrysippus, then the Stoics who brought knowledge of the sect to Rome, Panaetius, contemporary of Scipio Aemilianus (*c.*150–120 BCE), and Posidonius of Rhodes, contemporary of Pompey and Cicero. Although Seneca ranks Posidonius with the masters, he will not show close interest in Posidonius' ethics or anthropology until letter 83, when he clearly has started to read him as a stimulus to argument.

     credited to one man: that is, Epicurus, who appropriated his followers' wise words.

     to count his flock: this is the boast of Polyphemus at Ovid, *Metamorphoses*, XIII.824, and perhaps extends to implicit mockery of Epicurus.

33.7   *the Greeks call Chriae*: one form of grammatical education consisted in making the pupils take a chosen wise saying and rephrase it in different syntactical patterns.

33.11   *make a path there*: Seneca is not comparing himself to a walker, but to a road-builder (the verb is *munire*, to construct a road), who will therefore make paths for others to use after him.

36.3   *Ariston*: the Stoic Ariston of Chios, a pupil of Zeno, is mentioned in several later letters. Cicero used his treatise *Tithonus: On Old Age* as one of his sources for *Cato Maior: On Old Age*.

36.7   *born in Parthia*: this argument from the training of future warriors in different societies goes back to the ethnography of Herodotus, and recurs in Caesar and Tacitus' accounts of Gallic and German societies.

37.3   *Force makes a way*: Seneca turns around Aeneas' account of the Greek violence in capturing Troy to fit a context in which the good man must make his way by force (*Aeneid*, II.494).

39.1   *when we still spoke Latin*: Seneca is not contrasting a word borrowed from Greek (which are common in his own letters) with a Latin formation, but objecting to a new name, *breviarium* (first attested in this letter), which would have a long future.

     the man . . . is himself unknown: Seneca is punning on the technical business terms *notor*, 'knower' or identifier, and the adjective *ignotus*, 'unknown'.

40.2   *Serapion*: this otherwise unknown lecturer was presumably touring Sicily giving epideictic displays at the time.

     honey . . . from the old man: the two types of oratory described are based on Homer's descriptions in *Iliad*, Book III of Ulysses (whose speech fell like snowflakes), and Nestor the wise old counsellor; they became standard models for teachers and are used by Cicero in *Brutus*, his history of rhetoric.

40.9 *P. Vinicius*: the declaimers Vinicius, Varius Geminus, and Q. Haterius would all be known to Seneca from his father's memoirs (*Contr.* I. 7.5, 11–12). Both Tacitus (*Annals*, IV.61) and Seneca the Elder discuss the unstoppable fluency of Haterius (cf. *Contr.* 4.6–11). Only Asellius seems to be unknown; could this perhaps be a scribal error for Arellius (Fuscus), one of Seneca's teachers?

40.11 *a measured speaker*: first-century critics like Aper in Tacitus' *Dialogue on the Orators* found Cicero and most of his contemporaries too slow in pace. 'Measured' here translates the epithet for a sedate walking horse.

40.12 *Fabianus*: this is Seneca's admired teacher Papirius Fabianus, previously mentioned in letter 11 (see note).

41.2 *a god dwells in him*: Seneca is adapting Evander's account of the future Capitoline Hill in *Aeneid*, VIII.352 to describe not a place, but a man: his argument will be that a virtuous man is the embodiment of God. The editor has inserted a half-line into Seneca's text to complete Virgil's statement.

44.2 *You are a Roman knight*: the second order at Rome, inferior only to the senatorial order, was called equestrian, because originally men of this property class served as cavalry officers (knights). They were privileged to sit in the front fourteen rows at the theatre. The Roman pyramidal hierarchy was of senatorial families, then equestrians or knights, then freeborn citizens: beneath them were the freedmen or former slaves, and below them only actual slaves; even among slaves, the home-bred *vernae* were deemed superior to slaves purchased in the market, and Greek-speaking slaves to 'barbarians'.

44.3 *Socrates . . . not a patrician*: Socrates was a craftsman (stonemason), but the word patrician, denoting a restricted birth-caste at Rome, is doing duty for the Greek concept of being *eupatrid*, 'of good father'. The Stoic Cleanthes apparently worked with his hands, but Plato was an aristocrat, so Seneca makes a different point; the word 'noble' originally meant 'well known', and only later denoted a man whose family had held high office.

44.4 *not descended from slaves . . . kings*: defeat in war turned queens like Hecuba, queen of Troy, and royal daughters into slaves who gave birth as concubines to children of Greek kings.

44.5 *smoky wax masks*: families descended from Roman magistrates kept waxen death-masks of their ancestors in the formal atrium, and paraded them in aristocratic funerals.

46.1 *Livy or Epicurus*: Livy's *History of Rome from its Foundation* filled 143 books: Epicurus' writings were equally voluminous. Only a small proportion of the letter survived the onset of Christianity.

47.4   *under torture*: under Roman law (as also in Athenian law) slaves' evidence was only acceptable if they had spoken under torture, and they could only be saved from this if their master manumitted them. Another law declared that if a master was killed at home all slaves of the household were to be executed as complicit in the crime.

47.6   *carves expensive birds*: this specialization and many of the other details in this letter occur in the undisciplined household of the ex-slave Trimalchio in Petronius' *Satyricon*: once he is drunk he even invites the cook and other kitchen slaves to share his dinner couch, throwing aside all decorum.

47.9   *at Callistus' door*: Callistus became a freedman of the emperor Claudius, and used his power to humiliate the private citizen who had been his earlier master. The Stoic philosopher Epictetus, a former slave of Nero's freedman Epaphroditus, tells similar tales of reversals of fortune.

47.10   *defeat of Varus*: the destruction of a Roman army under Publius Quinctilius Varus in 9 CE by German tribes led by Arminius.

47.12   *mother of Darius, or Plato or Diogenes*: like Hecuba (see note to 44.4 above), Sisygambis, mother of Darius, was technically the slave of Alexander, but he famously treated her with respect. Plato was captured by pirates and sold into slavery at Aegina, but ransomed by a former pupil. Diogenes of Sinope (cf. Diogenes Laertius, Book VI) was first exiled then enslaved; he advertised himself as expert in teaching his masters how to behave.

47.14   *Father of the Household*: the Latin *paterfamilias* denoted the father figure as lord over both his freeborn descendent family and his slave *familia*.

47.17   *pantomime dancers*: these were the pop-singers of the Roman world, idolized by Maecenas, for example, whose lover was Bathyllus a pantomime, and taken as lovers, like Mnester and Paris, by empresses.

48.8–9   *come to his aid . . . rather than nature*: the text is damaged but seems to be drawing a comparison between giving aid to the socially distressed and giving intellectual aid to those trapped by syllogistic reasoning. Certainly in 48.10 Seneca compares the syllogisms of such 'philosophers' to court-room tricks.

48.10   *Philosophers*: Seneca suddenly switches to a plural addressee.

48.11   *way to the stars*: this half-line is spoken by Apollo to encourage young Ascanius in *Aeneid*, IX.641. Seneca quotes it again in letter 73.15.

49.2   *Sotion*: a pupil of the Stoic Sextius, Sotion was young Seneca's first teacher. He is mentioned again in 108.17.

49.5   *the lyric poets*: this has been identified as fr. 12 of Cicero's now lost *Hortensius*, a protreptic to philosophy. But the 'Nine' Greek lyric poets may have become much more fashionable in Seneca's own day: see letter 27 above, and compare the syllabus of Statius' schoolmaster father listed in his *Silvae*, V.3.

49.7   *Bar their gates and whet the steel* . . . : this is quoted from *Aeneid*, VIII.385–6.

49.12   *speech of truth is simple*: Seneca is adapting Euripides, *Phoenissae*, 469.

51.1   *Etna . . . Messala . . . Valgius*: Etna, hymned by Pindar and Virgil, was the most famous volcano active before the eruption of Vesuvius in 79 CE. Letter 79 talks of it as a subject for poets, and Messala and the elegist Valgius presumably both called it unique. Baiae was a volcanic region of unstable terrain, and remains subject to seismic disturbance to the present day.

51.3   *Canopus*: this Egyptian town on the Nile delta must have been popular as a resort; certainly it gave its name to the luxurious canals and water-features of Roman villas.

51.5   *debauched Hannibal*: Livy (XXIII.18) reports that Hannibal and his army were weakened by their comfortable winters in Capua, chief city of Campania.

51.8   *Fortune is waging war*: this resumes the imagery of the virtuous man's combat against Fortune which is particularly well developed of Cato in 24.7 above; see note to 8.3.

51.11   *Liternum*: see letter 86, written from (and about) Scipio's villa at Liternum.

51.13   *Egyptians call Philetae*: the culture of Roman Egypt (where Seneca had spent some years when his uncle was governor) was predominantly Greek, and *philetae*, 'the lovers, embracers', is an ironic Greek nickname.

53.3   *dropped from the prow*: this and the previous half-line come from Virgil's description of landings at *Aeneid*, VI.3 and III.227.

53.10   *I came to Asia . . . left over*: for this story see e.g. Plutarch, *Life of Alexander*.

55.3   *Asinius Gallus . . . Sejanus*: Asinius Gallus, son of Pollio, offended Tiberius (Tacitus, *Annals*, I.12.6); Sejanus, on the other hand, was Tiberius' favourite and praetorian prefect: he even aspired to become Tiberius' heir, until the reclusive emperor was disillusioned by his sister-in-law Antonia and ordered the fall of Sejanus in 31 CE. Seneca's brother Gallio seems to have suffered for his earlier friendship with Sejanus.

56.3   *crash of the Nile cataracts*: Seneca mentions this story of the Nile cataracts in his account of the course of the river in *Natural Questions*, IVb.2.5.T.

56.4   *Sweating Fountain*: this seems to be the only record of a *Meta Sudans* at Baiae: it will have been a conical fountain trickling from multiple spouts; perhaps, as in public baths, its flow offered acoustic enhancement to the players.

56.6   *calm repose of night*: Seneca's father (*Contr.* VII.1.27) cites this line as coming from Varro of Atax, and echoed with variations by both Virgil and Ovid.

56.12   *him I bore*: in *Aeneid*, II.726–9 Aeneas describes his panicked flight from Troy, pulling his son by the hand (my companion) and carrying his crippled father Anchises.

57.1   *fate of athletes*: ancient wrestlers used to coat their bodies in mud and grit to improve their grasp of the adversary.

59.3   *the evil joys of the mind*: Virgil, *Aeneid*, VI.278–9, includes malicious glee among the monsters and diseases besetting the gates of Hades.

59.6   *similes . . . comparisons*: Seneca himself, like other ancient moralists and teachers, uses many didactic analogies to drive home his message. Seneca is particularly fond of military analogies, as well as analogies of gladiatorial combat.

59.7   *Sextius*: presumably C. Sextius, a Roman who taught philosophy in Greek in Seneca's youth; see Seneca's more detailed comment in letter 64.2–4.

59.12   *When Alexander's expedition . . . a mortal man*: the story of Alexander's wound and his denial of immortality appears in the elder Seneca's *Suasoriae*, 1.5, and in Plutarch, *Life of Alexander*, 28 and *Fortune of Alexander* (*Moralia*, 341c), and in Diogenes Laertius (IX.60).

59.17   *false joys*: these lines are spoken by Deiphobus to Aeneas in *Aeneid*, VI.513–14, describing how the Trojans rejoiced on the night of Troy's fall, misled by stories that the Greeks had withdrawn, leaving the Trojan Horse which would bring the city luck.

60.3   *slaves of gluttony*: so Sallust describes degenerate Romans in *Catiline*, 1.1.

62.3   *Demetrius, the best of men*: on the Cynic Demetrius compare letter 20.9 (where he is also described as 'naked', meaning that he wore only a tunic, not the formal toga, still less the expensive Tyrian ('shell-dyed') purple of magistrate's togas).

63.2   *even Niobe . . . food*: Seneca quotes Achilles' words of comfort to the bereaved Priam in *Iliad*, XXIV.602. Priam had lost his best son Hector, but all of Niobe's fourteen sons and daughters were struck dead by Apollo and Artemis. A more common version of her myth, which would be known to Seneca from Ovid, *Metamorphoses*, Book VI, had her turn into the rock Sipylus, streaming with the flow of her tears.

63.7   *Fortune*: it was traditional to invoke personified Fortune to explain unforeseen deaths and natural (or military) disasters. While this provided an escape for Stoics wishing to explain how events could go against divine providence (see 8.3 above), it is not philosophically justifiable.

63.13 *longer*: women were allowed to mourn for a year, men for a shorter time.

63.14 *Annaeus Serenus*: prefect of the guard, and addressee of Seneca's dialogues *On the Tranquillity of the Mind* and *On Leisure*, Serenus was among a number of guests who died of mushroom poisoning at a court banquet (Pliny, *Natural History*, XII.96).

64.4   *come down from the hills*: Virgil, *Aeneid*, IV.158–9, describes the eagerness of the teenage Ascanius for the hunt, a foreshadowing of his enthusiasm for battle. Philosophical investigation is often expressed in the imagery of hunting.

64.10 *both Catos . . . recognition*: Seneca has introduced morally virtuous Roman statesmen Cato the Censor and his great-grandson Cato of Utica (see note to letter 24), and Laelius, nicknamed 'The Wise' (see letters 7.6; 11.10; 25.6), to balance the Greeks, from Socrates and Plato to the Stoic founder Zeno and Cleanthes, his successor as director of the Stoa.

65.3   *activities undertaken by man*: see Inwood (2007), 10–14, 133–55. Using the craft of sculpture as a model by analogy with the Greek tradition of a craftsman-god found in e.g. Plato, *Timaeus*, Seneca explores the development of philosophical ideas about causes, starting from the simple Stoic notion that there was only one cause (the maker) and the raw material to constitute any object. Going back to the three causes named by Aristotle, the material, the craftsman, and the immanent form (exemplified in both the statue, an artefact, and the universe created by God), he adds a fourth Aristotelian cause, the craftsman's purpose. When Seneca claims (§7) that Plato added a fifth cause, the *Idea* or model, he is going against the chronology of the two philosophers, in order to preserve his own explanatory pattern of increasing complexity.

65.4   *fourth cause . . . whole work*: on Aristotle's innovation of the fourth cause see Inwood (2007), 140.

65.11 *host of causes*: as Inwood shows (see previous note), this phrase reflects a traditional Greek rejection of excessive multiplying of entities and explanations. On these multiple causes he superimposes Reason (§12), as a general cause, which seems to put an end to the supposed debate. It is by no means clear what, if anything, Seneca expects Lucilius to contribute to this structure; instead he moves on to the relationship between soul and body (§§16–18) and the urgent obligation (as binding as the military oath, *sacramentum*, §18) to complete his assigned tour of duty (*stipendium*) by pursuing natural philosophy, returning in §23 to the world constituted of its raw material by its creator god (the sole cause in Stoic thinking).

65.18 *bound by oath*: Roman soldiers swore allegiance when they were enlisted.

67.5   *it causes physical suffering*: the text is damaged and a clause roughly to this effect must have been lost. Torture is desirable only inasmuch as it provides an opportunity to show endurance.

67.7   *Regulus' cage . . . exile*: Regulus led an unsuccessful expedition against Carthage in the First Punic War, and was sent back to Rome to negotiate a ransom for himself and fellow captives. But he urged the Romans not to pay the ransom, then kept his promise to return to Carthage, where he was put to death. The story was made famous by Cicero's version in *On Duties*, and Horace, *Odes*, III.5. On Cato and Rutilius see notes to letter 24.4–6.

67.8   *. . . Troy's lofty walls*: this is the wish of Aeneas, the survivor, in the storm of *Aeneid*, I.94–6.

67.9   *Decius dedicated . . . state*: two Decii, father and son, Roman commanders a generation apart, ritually vowed to give their lives to the gods of the underworld by charging into the thick of the enemy in exchange for a Roman victory, first against the Samnites at Sentinum and later against Pyrrhus of Epirus at Asculum.

67.10   *under due advisement*: a legal term declaring a decision valid.

67.11   *decorated doorways*: generals honoured by a triumph had the right to fix captured trophies over their doorways.

67.14   *our friend Demetrius . . . a Dead Sea*: on the Cynic Demetrius see note to 63.2

67.15   *Attalus the Stoic*: see letter 9.7 for his views on friendship, and 63.5 on the emotions of recalling deceased friends. Letter 72.8 offers a longer example of his thought, based perhaps on Aesop's fable about the dog and the cheese.

70.2   *withdraw from us*: *Aeneid*, III.72, already quoted in letter 28.

70.6   *what the Rhodian said*: this man, Telesphorus of Rhodes, is quoted as an extreme example of cruel punishment in *On Anger*, III.17.3–4, but is used here to illustrate the cravenness of any victim who does not prefer death to a dishonoured life.

70.9   *Socrates could have refrained . . . his friends*: a counter-example, because Socrates stayed alive from obedience to the laws (cf. Plato's *Crito*) and to give his company to his friends.

70.10   *of Drusus Libo*: Libo, a remote kinsman of the imperial family, was accused of planning a conspiracy against Tiberius and formally condemned to death. His aunt Scribonia, the penultimate wife of Augustus and mother of his only child Julia, took the line that committing suicide (as was expected in these circumstances) would be sparing his executioner the responsibility of killing him. Compare Tacitus, *Annals*, II.27.2.

70.19   *Cato*: Cato notoriously first stabbed himself, then when his surgeon tried to replace his entrails, disembowelled himself with his bare hands.

70.20   *one of the Germans . . . for the morning shows*: he was scheduled for public execution (see letter 7), like the man who deliberately entangled his
neck in the axle of his cart (§23), not in a combat on equal terms in
which he could have shown courage. The barbarian equipped with a
spear for the mock naval battle (§26) makes a new point; he realized that
now he had a weapon and could use it against himself.

72.8   *Attalus*: on Attalus see note to 67.15 above.

73.5   *his debt to Neptune*: talk of Neptune and Jupiter (§12), as well as quotation of Virgil's worshipful words about Augustus in *Eclogues* 1, suggest
that Seneca has abandoned his Stoic cosmology in this letter in order
to accommodate the right level of loyalty to the ruler.

73.6   *none of its phases are formed*: Reynolds does not believe the text can be
recovered, but Seneca's point is that he benefits from the ordering of
the seasons even though they have not been ordered for his sake.

73.10   *he will always be a god to me*: at the beginning of Virgil's first *Eclogue*
(1.6–7) the shepherd Tityrus claims he will always see the divine young
man (Octavian) as a god, because he 'let my cattle wander, as you see'
(1.9–10). The key point is that the good ruler (and, it seems, the bad one
too) enables the subject to enjoy *otium*, leisure for his intellectual needs.

73.12   *Sextius*: see note to 64.2; he compares Jupiter (or the neutral *theos* of
the Stoics?) to the good man, and invokes Apollo's praise for the young
Ascanius' first success in warfare at *Aeneid*, IX.641 (previously quoted
at letter 48.11).

75.8   *three groups, as some philosophers think*: compare letter 72.8–10 above.

75.9   *writing in a letter*: this refers back to letter 71.4 (not in this selection).

76.3   *trust the proverb*: perhaps the closest model is Solon's famous saying
that he grew old by learning something new each day, cf. Cicero, *On
Old Age*, 26; Valerius Maximus, VIII.7.14 (3).

76.4   *Metronax's house*: Seneca learns of Metronax's death from Lucilius less
than a year later; cf. letter 93.

   a good piper: Seneca uses the Greek *pythaules*, which refers to a piper as
accompanist.

76.12   *portraits . . . reception hall*: so too 'noble birth and clients' in the next
sentence refer to political assets of birth and influence.

76.20   *hand into the flames*: Mucius Scaevola again. See note to letter 24.4.

76.21   *condition of Fortune*: Roman moral tradition thought in terms of both
Fortunes, good (success) and bad (failure). Seneca is credited with a
work on the remedies of each kind of Fortune.

76.31   *royal cloak on stage*: Seneca invokes the common analogy between roles
in life and role in drama; cf. the same argument in the same context at
letter 80.7–8.

76.33   *no form of toil . . . heart*: Aeneas to the Sibyl, *Aeneid*, VI.103–5.

77.2   *storm-tossed summit*: the quotation is unknown, but probably applied to a different temple of Pallas.

77.7   *household was only at risk*: both the younger Pliny (the death of Larcius Macedo, *Letters*, III.14) and Tacitus (*Annals*, XIV.42–5) report scandals when a hated master was killed at home by a slave. The law was that all slaves under his roof must be executed, and in the very recent scandal of Pedanius Secundus (in the 60s CE) 400 slaves were publicly executed, despite the people of Rome's protests.

77.12   *swayed by prayers*: Seneca quotes the Sibyl's rebuke to Aeneas at *Aeneid*, VI.376.

77.20   *life of Nestor or Sattia*: Nestor's age was proverbial; he outlived three generations of men. Seneca counters this with the humble slave epitaph of Sattia. Pliny the Elder collects examples of longevity (no doubt from earlier sources available to Seneca) in the seventh book of his *Natural History*.

78.15   *delight to recall this too*: one of the most famous tags from the *Aeneid*, uttered by Aeneas after shipwreck: *Aeneid*, I.203.

78.16   *name*: as victor of athletic contests.

79.1   *Charybdis*: the Straits of Messina were narrow (3 miles), and flanked by two monstrous hazards, Scylla near Reggio and the whirlpool Charybdis on the north-east coast of Sicily. Both Odysseus and Aeneas were warned against them, and Aeneas successfully navigated past Charybdis.

79.3   *slack and weak force*: this looks like one of the natural wonders gathered by Seneca for his *Natural Questions*, but does not occur in the only reference to Lycia there (III.25.11).

79.5   *deterred Severus*: Virgil was the first Latin poet to describe Etna in any detail; Ovid was more brief in his Cyclops episode in *Metamorphoses*, Book XIV. Cornelius Severus wrote a *Sicilian War* some time after Augustus' victory over Sextus Pompeius, but it has not survived. Seneca clearly thought Severus was writing after Ovid.

79.6   *possessed by mere use*: editors have rejected this as interpolation, probably by a reader recalling Horace's strictures in his *Ars Poetica* on distinguishing between plagiarizing private intellectual property and reworking what is common usage

79.14   *incorruptibility of Rutilius*: Seneca starts with the natural philosopher Democritus, an older contemporary of Plato, then moves through a canon of wise and good men victimized in life but winning fame in death: Socrates and the Stoic saints, Cato the Younger and Rutilius Rufus (see letter 24.4).

79.15   *Epicurus . . . Metrodorus*: Epicurus' correspondence with several friends was known to Seneca, but is now largely lost; the letter mentioned here without addressee presupposes the death of Metrodorus. See B. Inwood, 'The Importance of Form in Seneca's Philosophical Letters', in R. Morello and A. D. Morrison (eds.), *Ancient Letters: Classical and Late Antique Epistolography* (Oxford: Oxford UP, 2007), on Seneca's use of Epicurus' letters as a model.

80.7   *See . . . the Isthmus*: this unidentified quotation must be spoken by Agamemnon, and may come from Ennius' lost *Iphigenia at Aulis*. Certainly the second quotation ('Unless you fall quiet . . .') would fit excellently Agamemnon's protests in his quarrel with Menelaus over the sacrifice of his daughter.

80.10   *Scythia or Sarmatia*: there were kings of Scythia (like Thoas) on the Greek and Roman tragic stage, but Sarmatia (roughly southern Poland) is a name not used before the first century, perhaps in some lost Roman tragedy.

82.2   *<lacuna>*: an element of the argument has been lost.

        leisure and a tomb: compare Seneca's treatment of Vatia in letter 55.

82.3   *dragged away on the hook*: under the Principate the bodies of those condemned for treason, like the disgraced Sejanus, were dragged down to the river and set adrift.

82.5   *but cannot break through*: the image of a city fortified against misfortune echoes letter 74.19.

82.7   *now a strong breast*: addressed by the Sibyl to Aeneas at *Aeneid*, VI.261.

82.9   *Our friend Zeno*: Zeno of Citium, founder of the Stoa, will return in letter 83.

        cross-examination: Seneca uses *interrogatio* (courtroom questioning of witnesses, which involved torture when slaves were interrogated) to translate the Socratic *elenchus*, which forces the interlocutor by successive questions to deny what he still believes.

82.12   *Decimus Brutus*: although Seneca was hostile to all the killers of Julius Caesar, he is not speaking of M. Junius Brutus, who committed an honourable suicide, but the unrelated Decimus Brutus.

82.16   *gatekeeper of Hell*: Cerberus, in *Aeneid*, VI.400–1 (with a line added from VIII.297).

82.18   *your fortune will allow you*: more advice from the Sibyl to Aeneas, *Aeneid*, VI.95–6.

82.20   *the Fabii*: the Roman *gens Fabii* marched out as a private army to defend Roman territory against the Etruscans of Veii and were ambushed, leaving only one child below fighting age to continue the clan. This legendary self-sacrifice, dated to 487 BCE, corresponds to the sacrifice of King Leonidas and his Spartans at Thermopylae in 480 BCE; the details of Leonidas' exhortation come from Herodotus.

82.22   *not necessary to return*: this echoes the story of Caedicius' suicide mission told by Cato the Censor in his *Origines*.

82.24   *savage serpent in Africa*: this monster confronted the Roman force in its African expedition during the First Punic War. The following reference to Pythian Apollo is most probably an allusion to a Roman artillery machine named after the archer god, rather than to the god himself as slayer of the monster Pytho.

83.5   *the Aqua Virgo . . . the Tiber*: besides substituting a sun-warmed bath for natural cold water, Seneca had abandoned swimming in the mountain chill of Rome's Aqua Virgo for the warmer Tiber. On his strength as a (cold-water) swimmer compare letter 53.4.

83.7   *the din of the chariot races*: where was Seneca's house at Rome? If it is in earshot of the Circus Maximus it must have been on the part of the Palatine facing the Aventine across the Circus.

83.10   *Posidonius defends Zeno's position*: in this and subsequent letters Seneca frequently cites Posidonius: he might be using a doxography, but it is far more likely that he is consulting his own texts of at least some of Posidonius' works. Here (fr. 175, in I.4. Kidd, *Posidonius*, Vol. 3, *The Translations of the Fragments* (Cambridge: Cambridge UP, 1999), 240–1). Seneca acknowledges but is not satisfied by Posidonius' attempt to distinguish between a drunkard and a man actually drunk.

83.12   *Tillius Cimber as much as Gaius Cassius*: Cimber was a lesser member of the conspiracy against Julius Caesar led by Junius Brutus and Cassius. It was Cimber who triggered the attack by approaching Caesar with a petition on behalf of his brother.

83.14   *Lucius Piso*: according to Suetonius, *Tiberius* 42, Piso was a drinking companion of Tiberius: after a two-day binge Tiberius spontaneously made him prefect of the city, calling him and Pomponius Flaccus the sweetest of companions at all hours.

83.19   *the example of Alexander of Macedon*: Seneca abominated Alexander, whose drunken murder of Clitus shocked and shamed him but did not sober him up; drink would bring on the fatal fever which killed him at Babylon, when he allegedly drained the huge 'Goblet of Hercules'. These stories are in Plutarch's life, but were already reported in many other sources to which Seneca had access. Compare his thumbnail sketch at 94.61–3 (not in this selection).

83.23   *goblet of Hercules*: a huge bumper: Alexander allegedly died of alcohol poisoning.

83.25   *love for Cleopatra . . . wine*: Mark Antony took the wine-god Dionysus as his patron and model, and waged a campaign of words as well as war against Octavius, composing a defence of his own drunkenness.

84.3   *nectar sweet*: Seneca invokes Virgil's portrait of the bee-community, but draws on the bee-simile of *Aeneid*, I.432–3, not his earlier treatment of the bee community in *Georgics*, Book IV.

84.12   *men striving to greet them*: Roman custom required clients to attend the houses of their patrons early in the morning in order to greet them: intimates were invited into the bedroom, but most clients only reached the entrance hall.

84.13 *high pediment of rank*: Seneca implicitly compares the high peak of a hill to the honorific gable ornament called *fastigium*, awarded to triumphant generals like Caesar. Greeks and Romans alike learned from Hesiod that reaching the summit of virtue required sweat and toil.

86.1 *Cambyses*: according to Herodotus, the Persian king Cambyses, son of Cyrus, was both mad and alcoholic but conquered Egypt. Seneca introduces him as a heavy drinker and quotes a horrendous anecdote of his murderous skill in *On Anger*, III.14.1–4.

Scipio was to be at Rome . . . Rome at liberty: Seneca echoes the narrative and comments of Livy (Book XXXIX), who admits that he was confused by conflicting stories of the attempts to prosecute Scipio (or his brother Lucius) after they returned victorious from the campaign against Antiochus of Syria and the Peace of Apamea. Scipio had probably made private concessions to the king, and refused to show the senate his accounts, but the chief issue was the senate's fear of any one man becoming dominant in the state and making himself tyrant—a threat to the senate's liberty to govern in its own way. It is clear that Scipio withdrew to the family villa at Liternum in 183 before he could be prosecuted, and died in the following year.

86.4 *Liternum . . . big enough for an army*: Liternum was one of the maritime colonies founded to garrison the coast of Italy against pirates; hence this villa was fortified and equipped to withstand a siege.

86.5 *Dread of Carthage*: this is the name given to Scipio by Lucretius, *On the Nature of the Universe*, III.1034. Seneca quotes Lucretius again at 95.11, 106.8, and 110.6 below.

86.10 *blended with his own hand*: Seneca is surely confusing the duties of aediles, supervising public bath establishments at Rome, with the situation in this private bath in Campania. Fabius Maximus was Scipio's oldest and most revered political opponent, dying just before Scipio's victory. The thrifty and puritanical Cato the censor would be Scipio's opponent until his death.

86.13 *smells of breath-sweetener*: this echoes Horace, *Satires*, I.2.27 (cf. I.4.92).

86.14 *Aegialus*: this man was no ordinary farmer, but is mentioned with as much respect for his expertise in vine-growing by the elder Pliny (*Natural History*, XIV.49–50) as Pliny awards to Seneca himself in the same discussion. Pliny reports that Seneca was famous for the superior quality of the vineyards he purchased from Remmius Palaemon at Nomentum. The letter shows that he was highly observant, in his description of long-term renewal of vine and olive stocks, and the criticism he will offer of Virgil's instructions on when to plant various pulse.

another generation: the text that follows is corrupt: I have inserted a stopgap.

86.15 *late-born grandsons*: Virgil, *Georgics*, II.58.

86.16 *yearly millet crop*: Georgics, I.215–16.

87.2 *my friend Maximus*: Caesennius Maximus, a close friend in private life.

87.3 *a New Year*: Romans exchanged gifts of dried figs and dates on New Year's day.

87.8 *between their teeth*: these are the luxury riding horses sent by Latinus to Aeneas as a guest gift in *Aeneid*, VII.277–9.

87.9 *Cato the censor*: (see the previous letter). Consul in 196 BCE and censor in 184, Cato left fragments of political speeches proclaiming his economy as governor of Hither Spain and denouncing the extravagance of elite politicians, many of whom he prosecuted.

  to the sword or the knife: the typical profligate after losing his family property had to sell his own skills in the arena, either as a gladiator or a *bestiarius* (fighter of wild beasts).

87.11 *hampering*: Seneca is punning on Latin *impedimenta* (burdens) and *impedire* (hinder, hamper).

87.12 *The Peripatetics*: these followers of the school of Aristotle were the principal adversaries of Stoic moral teaching, making their claims relative (e.g. a little anger can be useful and a good thing!), where the Stoics were absolute.

87.16 *Chelidon . . . Natalis*: these contemptible persons are put beneath contempt by accusing them of sexual perversions. But Antonius Natalis would betray first Scaevinus, then Piso and Seneca himself (Tacitus, *Annals*, XV.55 f.) within two years of this letter.

  hairs: illegitimate children.

87.20 *rough iron*: why does Seneca cite Virgil, *Georgics*, I.53–8? Surely because of the context, warning that nature's laws limit what can be produced from each terrain. The highest good, virtue, cannot come from purely material sources.

87.23 *carried in triumphal processions*: this is an echo of Cato's dictum that small thieves were punished but great thieves rode in triumph.

87.31 *Posidonius*: fr. 170 (Kidd). Seneca quotes the philosopher, historian, and contemporary of Cicero fifteen times in these later letters. Here he credits him with two arguments against wealth: first that it was a cause of evil not because of its own actions but because it provoked men to commit evil, and secondly (§35: apparently a direct quotation) that it could not be a good thing because it did not confer courage or confidence or freedom from care; Seneca extends this to imply that in not giving these good states of mind wealth was actually an evil.

87.38 *Posidonius says*: the other direct Posidonius citation, adopting the argument of the second century Antipater, is more complex and tries to answer the sociological criticism of wealth as the product of many men's poverty by the logical reclassification of poverty as defined by its lack of possessions. Kidd questions the extent that this later argument

is taken from Posidonius rather than Seneca's own contribution. For a
serious analysis of Seneca's informal method of syllogism see Inwood,
Senca's Philosophical Letters, ad loc.

88.4   *from knowing everything else*: Seneca puts the ability to avoid fear and desire
        ahead of any intellectual expertise. But the text seems to be damaged, and
        Reynolds argues for a substantial lacuna after 'everything else'.

88.5   *Homer was a philosopher*: Homer was so important to Greek thought that
        each of the philosophical schools attributed to him their fundamental
        doctrines, even the Academics, who were sceptical that any knowledge was
        possible. In the next sections Seneca puts to scorn typical schoolmasters'
        questions about the dramatis personae of the *Iliad* and *Odyssey*.

        unknowable: the sceptical branch of the Academy held that nothing
        could actually be known.

88.8   *found out*: Ulysses appeared to Penelope in Odessey, Book XIX dis-
        guised as a beggar.

88.10   *lend my fingers*: Romans calculated digitally (with their fingers).

88.14   . . . *fire explores*: the quotation is from Virgil's adaptation of Aratus'
        Prognostica in *Georgics*, I.336–7, followed (in §16) by ll. 424–6.

88.21   *four kinds of art*: Posidonius, fr. 90 (Kidd). As we shall see in letter
        90 (§§7, 11, 20), Posidonius attributed the invention of various crafts
        to the wise men of old, but Seneca would not extend this dignity to
        the work of everyday craftsmen. Here his four kinds of *technai* include
        with these everyday crafts the arts of entertainment, whose appeal to
        the people led Seneca to despise them, and *pueriles artes*, the educative
        arts taught to children, the *enkuklioi*, which the Romans call 'liberal'.
        Seneca himself distinguishes these from the only true liberal arts, those
        which concern themselves with developing virtue.

88.34   *about the mind*: Seneca is evoking Pythagorean and Platonic ideas about
        metempsychosis, the mobility of the soul (here *animus* stands for *anima*
        = *psyche*), which Seneca does not claim to believe outright.

88.37   *real mother of Aeneas*: so the Alexandrian Didymus is concerning him-
        self with trivia: Hellenistic scepticism rejected the legend that Aeneas
        was the son of Aphrodite. The questions about the vices of lyric poets
        such as Sappho and Anacreon are pure vulgarity. Apion the grammar-
        ian, a slightly older contemporary of Seneca, is also treated (§39 below)
        as a learned fool or charlatan.

88.39   *Aristarchus . . . life on syllables*: Aristarchus of Alexandria edited Homer,
        developing a code of signs to indicate lines he thought not genuine.

        dust of geometry: geometrical problems were usually illustrated by being
        scratched on the ground in dust or sand.

88.43   *Protagoras . . .* : losing patience, Seneca belittles the pre-Socratics
        Protagoras and Parmenides by stressing their scepticism and crowd-
        ing them into an accelerating catalogue (44–5) of latter-day Sceptics,

followers of Pyrrho. (Cicero had used the same technique to belittle these latter-day schismatics of the Socratic school in *On Oratory*, III.62, which may even be Seneca's inspiration here.)

88.46   *Keep well*: the early manuscript tradition of our letters is divided between texts containing Books I–XIII (letters 1–88) and Books XIV–XX (letters 89–124). While this division seems to have arisen some centuries after the letters were first made public, and so need not represent separate publication by Seneca or his survivors, the first letter of Book XIV (letter 89, not in this selection) does seem to be framed as a new start: it offers a useful recapitulation of the nature and parts of philosophy, especially of moral philosophy which Seneca regards as the essential, to which natural philosophy (cosmology) and logic or dialectics are subordinate. It ends by arming Lucilius with a highly rhetorical (and philosophically irrelevant) retort to the imaginary interlocutors who have protested: 'How long will you persist in the same studies?'

90.1   *gifts of Philosophy*: since this letter opens with a kind of hymn to Philosophy, making it the giver of so many benefits, like a god, I have marked the personification by capitalizing the name.

90.5   *Posidonius*: although this is the first reference to Posidonius in the letter, we can assume that Seneca was following Posidonius' anthropology throughout, singling out only his chief objections (cf. §§11, 13, 20–3, 30, and 31). Unfortunately Seneca's conception of the wise man is much more ethically preoccupied than Posidonius', and he is not concerned with tracing the growth of civilization, as is e.g. Lucretius in *On the Nature of the Universe*, Book V, so that he brushes aside material of real interest to students of ancient anthropology. For a full discussion of Posidonius' account see note on fr. 284 in Kidd's edition, comparing the argument of Seneca's letter with what can be inferred about Posidonius' representation of the golden Age (Kidd treats 90.5–13, 20–5, and 30–2 as reflecting the views of Posidonius).

90.6   *seven men known for wisdom*: the Greek tradition marked seven statesmen of the seventh–sixth centuries BCE as sages, attributing to them wise political precepts. Their identities vary. Plutarch (in 'The Banquet of the Seven Sages') groups Solon of Athens with Periander of Corinth, Thales of Miletus, Bias of Priene, Pittacus of Mytilene, Cleobulus of Rhodes, and Chilon of Sparta adding one token barbarian, the Scythian Anacharsis (mentioned in §31 below). But the great founder of the Spartan constitution, Lycurgus, was more than a century earlier. Charondas and Zaleucus were lawgivers for Catania in Sicily and Locri in South Italy in the seventh century, before Pythagoras established his utopian community there, but came to be associated with him.

jurisconsults: at Rome expertise in private law originated as a privilege or service of the elite in the second century BCE, but had become professionalized by the time of Seneca.

90.7   *fishponds*: these were the artificial pools used by Roman gourmets as breeding-troughs for luxury fish—a favourite target of Senecan denunciation.

90.8   *lock and key*: the Latin actually names bolt and key: symbols of private property, a recognized stage in human degeneration from the innocence of the Golden Age.

90.9   . . . *with wedges*: from Virgil's account of the evolution of human skills in *Georgics*, I.144. The two lines of verse in §11 are from the same passage, I.139–40.

90.13   *towards the ground*: ancient philosophers claimed that men had been created standing upright to gaze at the sky (or gods), superior to quadrupeds forced to look at the earth.

90.14   *Diogenes and Daedalus*: according to legend, Daedalus invented many things such as wings and statues that seemed to walk; the fourth-century BCE Diogenes, in contrast, practised and taught doing without equipment. He founded the Cynic school, which advocated going without all but absolute essentials like bread and water.

90.15   *pipes*: Roman luxury sprayed saffron vapour through pipes onto the theatre audience.

90.17   *Scythians . . . people of the Syrtis*: these barbarian peoples lived in extreme climates, and are contrasted by Virgil in *Georgics*, III.349–83. The Scythians north of the Black Sea experienced bitter winters and resorted to living in dugouts; so did the African tribes of the desert inland from the treacherous sandbanks called Syrtis/Syrtes, but in order to escape the burning sun.

90.19   *for a master*: an interesting paradox. Both masters and slaves had their food and clothing provided, but slaves had no choice.

90.20   *smooth far and wide*: the description of the loom comes from Ovid, *Metamorphoses*, VI.55–8.

90.22   *into the mill*: this plays on the practice of using the flour-mill as a slave punishment; the millstones were turned either by slaves or donkeys.

90.25   *warmed . . . equally*: Romans used hypocausts (underfloor heating) especially to diversify the temperature in the hot and warm baths. On the luxury of baths see letter 86.

90.28   *secondary form of divinity*: this is an unusually explicit source for the Greek notion of *daemones*: Seneca equates three Roman forms of deity with *daemones*: the personal protective *genius* (cf. letters 9.1, 12.2, and 101). Many Greeks, like Socrates, believed in a personal guardian spirit which would prevent them from error. Greek thought also believed noble families originated with *heroes*, worshipped in family cult (the Roman equivalent was the Lar or household god). The last form of *daimōn* mentioned here seems to have developed later. Plutarch, writing fifty years after Seneca, speaks of these mediating spirits hovering in the air (like Christian angels, or later demons). Is this passage Seneca's own thinking or is he trying to provide an equivalent for something in Posidonius?

90.32 *Democritus*: the fifth-century atomist who also wrote on the evolution of human civilization.

90.35 *present of virtue to pleasure*: a hostile allusion to the followers of Epicurus, for whom pleasure was the highest good.

90.37 *without any man's demand*: from an earlier passage in *Georgics*, I.125–8, describing the Golden Age before Jupiter made life difficult for mankind to stimulate their initiative.

91.1 *Liberalis*: Aebutius Liberalis, the dedicatee of Seneca's seven books *On Benefits*, was clearly a native of Lyons, a city founded in 43 BCE and made into the capital of the three Gauls by Augustus in 12 BCE.

91.9 *the cities of Asia . . . Paphos*: the most famous instance of earthquake known at this time was the disappearance of two Achaean cities Helice and Buris in 373 BCE, reported by Ovid, *Metamorphoses*, XV.293–5, Seneca, *Natural Questions*, VI.23, Pliny, *Natural History*, II.225, VI.127–30. For Paphos in Cyprus cf. *Natural Questions*, VI.26.

91.13 *Timagenes*: a Greek historian who lived at Rome under Augustus and wrote contemporary history critical of the emperor.

91.16 *Ardea was captured, just like Rome*: a paradoxical way of putting it. As Ovid reports (*Metamorphoses*, XIV.572–80), after the death of Turnus, Ardea fell and the site was uninhabited.

91.17 *Alexander . . . over the Ocean itself*: Seneca (and his nephew Lucan) speak of Alexander as driven by vicious ambition to reach the Ocean in the East, and by his wild drinking to murder his best-friend Clitus and bring on his own death of fever (so letter 94.61–3, not in this selection). He was already the subject of a mass of anecdotes. Although the Greek Alexander-historians before Seneca's time may have been lost, the histories of the Roman Quintus Curtius may have been composed as early as this generation.

91.19 *Our Demetrius*: for Demetrius the Cynic see note on letter 67.

95.9 *Hippocrates . . . again*: the fifth-century Hippocrates of Cos (called the 'greatest of doctors' at 20 below) founded the first school of Greek medicine. Seneca would know the so-called Hippocratic Corpus of some forty treatises on health and disease attributed to his followers. Asclepiades and Themison came to Rome in the last century BCE and introduced new medical methods (hence they are associated with the so-called 'Methodist' school).

95.11 *to dissolution*: from Lucretius, *On the Nature of the Universe*, I.51–4.

95.16 *the rot of internal decay*: it is not clear whether Seneca is talking about foods decaying inside the body or the body's own decay.

95.21 *born to be penetrated*: the phrase is not Seneca's. Roman popular thought saw sexual penetration as conquest, and being penetrated as the duty of wives and humiliation of gay males. I have no suggestion for the reference in the next sentence about depraved women who 'penetrate men'.

95.24 *unhappy boy slaves*: the Latin says 'boys', but only slaves could legally be abused by this kind of pederastic exploitation (*puer* was also often used to designate a slave).

95.25 *Company's relish*: *garum*, a kind of sauce made from rotting fish (it has been compared with Worcestershire sauce); the best varieties supposedly came from Spain, and the same name is used by Pliny, suggesting that this was a recognized brand-name.

95.33 *now your masterful art*: Seneca fuses here *Aeneid*, VI.261 (to Aeneas) and VIII.442 (to the Cyclopian blacksmiths). See also letter 82.7.

naked: without clothing or defensive armour.

95.41 *dinners*: banquets held to honour new priests or magistrates.

95.45 *Marcus Brutus*: this is the Brutus who killed Caesar. He wrote a Stoically inspired treatise *On Obligations*, and another, *On Virtue*, addressed to Cicero.

95.47 *lamps on the Sabbath*: there were many thousands of Jews living in Rome in Seneca's time and the influence of their code had spread to gentiles, as Horace's *Satires* attest. Some of Seneca's knowledge of and attitude to Judaism comes through in the surviving fragments of his *On Superstition*.

does not look for servants: Augustine (*City of God*, VI.10) has preserved a powerful passage from Seneca's lost *On Superstition* denouncing the folly of Romans who performed personal grooming, etc., on the statues of the gods.

95.53 *foreign to me*: the quotation is from the Latin playwright Terence's adaptation of Menander's *Self-punisher*, but in the play the speaker is not philanthropic, just a busybody.

95.65 *Posidonius . . . characterismos*: for Posidonius' recommendation of precepts and the rhetorical techniques of persuasion, consolation, and exhortation as well as aitiologia (the tracing of causes or origins) and *ethologia*, the portrayal of character through physical description, glossed by Seneca as *characterismos*, see fr. 176 (Kidd).

95.68 *whorls of fire*: Seneca quotes Virgil, *Georgics*, III.71–83 and 85–7: the poet himself was assimilating the thoroughbred warhorse to a human hero.

95.69 *down from the Alps*: Seneca (and Lucan too) treat Caesar's army which came from his transalpine province as though it was composed of native Gauls. Caesar had in fact enlisted Gauls from some of the most trusted tribes in the legions as well as the allied *auxilia*.

95.72   *wooden couches of Tubero*: the Aelii Tuberones were notoriously poor,
         but Tubero provided only cheap benches and earthenware for the
         public feast at which most politicians displayed their generosity in lav-
         ish equipment and food. His banquet 'was a censorship' because he
         was making a moral statement about personal thrift.

97.3   *Cicero's actual words*: Seneca quotes from *Letters to Atticus*, I.16.5.
         Clodius was found disguised as a flute-girl at the women's ceremony
         presided over by Caesar's wife. It seems unlikely he expected to make
         love to her in those circumstances; more probably he was both curi-
         ous and eager to show his contempt for the goddess of chastity. He
         even provided a false alibi, which Cicero himself disproved, and was
         brought to trial, but the jury was bribed to acquit him, and bribed, as
         this letter reports, with sexual favours.

97.6   *unless they were going to condemn*: had the jurors found Clodius guilty
         his thugs would have beaten them up.

97.8   *Games of Flora*: the games were marked by mimes with female
         actresses, who dropped their clothes at a given signal. According to
         the poet Martial, Cato of Utica actually left the games to avoid sham-
         ing the audience.

97.13   . . . *staying unnoticed*: Epicurus, fr. 532 (Usener).

99.25   *words of Metrodorus*: the italicized text of Metrodorus is quoted by
         Seneca in the original Greek (although he has already referred to it in
         Latin in 98.9). This is exceptional in Senecan prose.

101.3   *as was his custom*: Seneca does not say so, but the prosperous business-
         man Senecio will have been a superior client, bound by etiquette to
         make morning calls on his patron.

101.4   *set out your vines*: these are the ironic words of Meliboeus, newly dis-
         possessed and cheated of his plans for the land in Virgil, *Eclogues*, I.73.

101.10   *the sharpened stake*: this *crux* is not the usual cross made from two
         stakes, but a single stake used as an instrument of torture to impale the
         victim.

101.13   *to so great a degree*: these are the words with which Turnus goads him-
         self to face his fatal duel with Aeneas in *Aeneid*, XII.646.

104.1   *milord Gallio*: this is either the orator Junius Gallio who adopted Sen-
         eca's brother Novatus (but he would surely be dead by now?), or Nova-
         tus himself. *Dominus* was often used respectfully among peers, even
         within Augustus' family, though Suetonius says he prohibited its use.

104.6   *Released into pasture*: Seneca borrows the famous simile used twice
         by Homer, for Paris and for Hector joining battle with the zest of a
         warhorse.

104.10   *thick of the enemy*: *Aeneid*, III.282–3, of Aeneas as a refugee. Many of
         Seneca's quotations compare the quest of the *proficiens*, or aspiring
         Stoic wise man, to the hero Aeneas.

104.15   *Nile . . . Tigris . . . Meander . . . sport of all poets*: Seneca uses his own
research into rivers for *Natural Questions*, the Nile in 4a, and the Tigris
(*Natural Questions*, III.26.4), also quoted by the poetry of Lucan and
Nero for disappearing below ground and resurfacing), along with the
Meander. Ovid in particular made poetic sport with the oxbow bends
of this river in *Metamorphoses*, VIII.162–6, and at II.246. Seneca's
Latin here plays games with sound and word order which cannot be
reproduced in English: *antequam sibi influit flectitur*.

104.21   *with Tubero*: cf. 95.72 above. 'The Catos' oddly combines the censor (praised in letters 83 and 86) with his Stoic descendant. Laelius
'*Sapiens*' is the consul of 140 and intimate of Scipio Aemilianus. The
list of Greeks is canonical, proceeding from Socrates to Zeno (founder
of the school), Chrysippus (its third leader), and Posidonius (cf. 108.38
and Kidd: 'Seneca groups Chrysippus and Posidonius together;
he sees no opposition between them. They are the two Stoic writers
to study').

104.24   *both Death and Toil*: this quotation, *Aeneid*, VI.277, is repeated almost
immediately to lead into the distinction between what looks dreadful
and what actually should be dreaded.

104.27   *his wife*: Socrates' wife Xanthippe was notoriously bad-tempered.

104.28   *twenty-seven years*: the war between Athens and the Peloponnesian
coalition led by Sparta lasted from 431 to 404, when the victorious
Spartans imposed an oligarchical government led by some of Socrates'
former aristocratic pupils (the 'Thirty Tyrants'): he resisted their
pressure to arbitrary executions, but the restored democracy punished
him for his own pupils' offences by condemning him to death for corrupting the youth in 399.

104.30   *in his province*: Cato of Utica was praetor in 54 BCE, but defeated in his
candidacy for the consulship of 51. (He would have been a disaster!)
He never had a province in the strict sense, but was sent to take over
the administration of Cyprus in 58–56, and charged by Pompey with
garrisoning Sicily during the Civil War.

104.31   *Achilles raging at both*: Seneca quotes *Aeneid*, I.458, which implies that
Cato was a hero like Achilles (and justified in his opposition to both
leaders?).

107.1   *more shamefully*: the text of this letter is damaged here and below. I
have adopted and translated the supplements of Reynolds and used
stop-gaps where he rightly obelizes the text as beyond restoration.

107.3   *grim old age*: from Aeneas' approach to the underworld, *Aeneid*,
VI.274–5; it will be repeated at 108.29 below.

107.11   *drag behind the laggard*: Seneca has made his own translation in iambic
trimeters of Cleanthes' 'Hymn to Zeus', and justifies his daring by
the precedent of Cicero, who made similar Latin verse translations of
Greek tragic verse.

108.1   *whole . . . of moral philosophy*: Seneca's treatise on moral philosophy is
first mentioned in 106.1: 'but you know I want to cover moral philosophy
and explain all the questions related to it', and mentioned again in 109.4,
but there is no other evidence for it; presumably it was never completed.

108.3   *Attalus*: his views dominate this letter, but see also letters 9 and 63.

108.7   *Phrygian piper*: the eunuchs are the *Galli*, priests of Cybele in the
Roman version of her cult, which was associated with the emotional
Phrygian mode of her native region.

108.9   *worst for himself*: Seneca is quoting separate one-liners, probably
originating in mime like the sayings of Publilius Syrus, but used as
school exercises; so also in §11.

108.13 *a king . . . censorship of the ruling class*: one of the Stoic paradoxes
claimed that the truly wise man was a king; Seneca subordinates
mere temporal kings to the moral rule exercised by the old republican
censors, who had the power to demote senators and citizens for moral
laxity.

108.15 *life of the community*: this probably means nothing more than abandoning private study of philosophy to resume a conventional public
career, but Seneca withdrew three times from the life of the city for
longer periods; once as a young man, when he went to Egypt for his
health; once when exiled in Corsica; and now in retreat from Nero.

108.17 *Sotion*: Seneca's older contemporary (cf. letter 49.2) and pupil of
Sextius; both followed the ascetic vegetarianism (and abstention from
beans) of Pythagoras, associated with the theory of metempsychosis
(cf. Ovid, *Metamorphoses*, XV.75–142 and 453–78), which meant that
a human soul could pass into any creature.

108.22 *evidence of superstition*: according to Tacitus, Tiberius was hostile to
Oriental cults with restrictions on diet, like Judaism, or animal fibres,
like the cult of Isis.

108.24 *Time flees beyond recall*: from *Georgics*, III.284.

        death unmerciful: again from *Georgics*, III.66–8.

108.26 *first to flee*: *Georgics*, III.67.

108.29 *grim old age*: *Aeneid*, VI.275, just quoted in letter 107.3.

        the stork a lizard: Ennius, *Varia*, 19–20.

108.30 *against justice*: Seneca treats Cicero's *On the Republic* as canonical in
the same way as Virgil's poetry, but this work was lost for centuries
(apart from excerpts quoted by Christian writers) and only partially
recovered during the nineteenth century. The most controversial
aspect of this work was probably Cicero's adaptation of Carneades'
notorious 'case against justice', spoken by Philus and answered on
behalf of justice by Laelius in the now largely lost Book III. What
survives of Philus' speech argues that Rome's empire succeeded by
violating conventional justice.

108.30   *grandson of Numa*: Cicero provided in Book II the first surviving history of early Rome up to the lawcode of the Decemvirs in 451–450 BCE.
He represents the first kings as coopted by the senate and people because
the deceased king had no sons. Thus the second king, Numa, was not a
child of Romulus, and was followed by the unrelated Tullus Hostilius.
'Master of the People' was another name for the dictators appointed
as commanders of the army (= People) in military emergencies, and
his second-in-command was 'Master of the Cavalry', as Antony would
later be for Caesar. Appeal was the precious right of *provocatio* from
summary condemnation by a magistrate to a court consisting of the
Roman people, more recently taken over by the emperor.

108.31   *Fenestella*: this historian of Roman antiquities writing under Augustus
has not survived except in quotation.

108.33   *service for his deeds*: Ennius enjoyed the patronage of Scipio Africanus,
and composed a poem (*Scipio*) in his honour, now lost. The lines
quoted use the form *opis*, from *ops*, help, resources, instead of the conventional *opera*.

108.34   *the mighty gate of heaven thunders*: impersonating the grammarian,
Seneca imagines him accusing Virgil of borrowing these lines (*Georgics*, III.261–2) from Ennius, as Ennius had borrowed from Homer: in
support he cites a similar phrase in two lines of Ennius' epitaph for
Scipio from a part of *On the Republic* (probably in Book V) which has
not been preserved.

108.38   *Chrysippus and Posidonius*: the same litany of predecessors quoted in
104.21.

110.1   *the common crowd*: Seneca quotes *Metamorphoses*, I.595, cf. I.173,
where Jupiter summons a docile assembly of gods, clearly resembling
the senate but including lesser gods. The 'divine escort' is the Roman
genius (Greek *daimōn*) discussed in letter 90.28, and Seneca's main
argument is for evidence of belief in divine concern for individuals.

       to each individual: this passage is one of the earliest pieces of evidence
for the allocation of a Juno to women corresponding to that of the
genius to men.

110.6   *in Lucretius*: Lucretius, *On the Nature of the Universe*, II.55–6, aims
to relieve adults of fears of death and the underworld as foolish as
children's fear of the dark.

110.14   *all the wealth of a city*: Attalus' example seems to be a triumph parading the wealth of newly conquered peoples, and the various snatches
of dialogue he quotes come from the watching crowd, those who can
survive on water and porridge.

112.2   *any random graft*: for Seneca's professional interest in grafting and
developing vine-stocks see letter 86, introduction and §20.

114.3   *style and his spirit*: it is tricky to convey the nuances of *animus*, which
includes a person's moral and intellectual aspects: I have used 'spirit'

to distinguish moral resolve from its intellectual manifestation in *ingenium*. *Ingenium*, however, is both the quality of a person's intellect and of his speech, hence it overlaps with 'style'.

114.4   *full of licence*: Reynolds brackets as an interpolation the following words in the manuscripts: 'Maecenas on his own lifestyle' (*Maecenas de cultu suo*), and editors have differed over the status of the excerpts.

114.6   *in the mime*: mimes commonly involved a scheming slave who cheated his master and tried to run away: he would be portrayed as furtive and suspiciously wrapped in his cloak.

    only one wife: Suetonius and others depict Maecenas as a slave to his imperious wife Terentia, who was supposedly the mistress of Augustus.

114.10   *unknown words*: the text is uncertain, but some phrase is needed to designate coined vocabulary as opposed to the archaisms associated in §13 below not with the generation of Gaius Gracchus (*flor.* 125 BCE) or L. Crassus, Cicero's teacher, or the elder Curio, but with the fourth- and early third-century Appius Claudius Caecus and Coruncanius, or worse the Twelve Tables, Rome's oldest-known text, dated to 451–450 BCE. Two generations after Seneca archaic literature and archaizing style would take over as a literary fashion.

114.13   *Coruncanius*: early Roman consul (280 BCE), defeated Etruscans and fought Pyrrhus.

114.16   *clausula*: a rhythmic pattern, associated with completing a periodic sentence.

    like that of Cicero: Tacitus, *Dialogue on the Orators*, shows that the new predominant fashion rejected Cicero's periodic style as too slow and elaborate as early as 75 CE. In the next sentence I have provided a paraphrase, 'being finicky', of what seems to be needed.

114.17   *passed for elegance*: in reaction against the periodic style of Cicero, the historian Sallust introduced a new, abrupt, asymmetrical style of writing. We know nothing about the lost histories of the Punic Wars by L. Arruntius (probably the consul of 22 BCE rather than his son) beyond what Seneca tells us. Regulus (§19) was the Roman commander made famous by Cicero, *On Obligations*, Horace (*Odes*, III.5), and Seneca himself (letter 67.7 and 12) for keeping his word by returning to the enemy and enduring terrible tortures.

114.23   *. . . they break faith*: from Virgil's anthropomorphizing description of the bee community, *Georgics*, IV.212–13.

114.24   *glutted with a bounty*: on festive occasions and at triumphs emperors threw edible treats to the crowd.

114.25   *other men's indulgences*: Seneca sees voyeurism as a more extreme form of depravity than ordinary debauchery; compare his denunciation of Hostius Quadra's mirrored bedroom ceiling in *Natural Questions*, I.16–17—but Hostius was a voyeur of his own indulgences.

115.2   *Patterning*: from rhetorical '*compositio*' (cf. 114.15 above), the art of arranging words in harmonious order, Seneca plays on its wider meaning in life: the state of being calm and composed. Grooming was a common source of rhetorical analogy, hence the affectations of smart hairstyles leads to the fancy patterning of *concinnitas* (neatness, symmetry) acknowledged by e.g. Cicero in *Orator* as a stylistic merit.

115.5   *whoever you be*: Aeneas addresses his disguised mother Venus (*Aeneid*, I.327–8, 330). It is such a challenge to describe the divine appearance of the truly virtuous man that Seneca resorts for an analogy to the appearance of a divinity, Venus, when she comes disguised to her son. But he does not finesse the gender-switch from male saint to female deity to the countenance (*facies*, f.) of this saint. I have imposed a translation.

115.13   . . . *with brilliant gold* . . . *its spokes*: both palace and chariot come from Ovid, *Metamorphoses*, II.1–2 and 107–8. But Seneca's denunciation of the modern valuation of precious metals in §§10–11 is also Ovidian, found in a similar diatribe in *Fasti*, Book I.

115.14   . . . *a good death* . . . *gods and men*: Seneca cites eight separate tragic sayings, no doubt found in an anthology. The group of five lines that follow come from Euripides' lost *Danae* (fr. 324, Nauck), and are spoken by Bellerophon, no doubt as comment on the imprisoned girl's seduction by Zeus in the form of a shower of gold. The scene was common in ancient wall-painting. The theatre episode must derive from Seneca's reading of a Hellenistic moralist; there is no reason, however, why this should come from Ariston of Cios cited in §8.

116.5   *Panaetius*: the Stoic teacher and friend of Scipio Aemilianus. His work on the duties of social behaviour was used by Cicero in *On Obligations*. This is fr. 114 (Van Straaten).

118.1   *comes into his mouth*: quoted from Cicero's *Letters to Atticus*, I.12.4 (cf. letter 97 above).

118.2   *Caecilius . . . at less than 1 per cent interest*: this is Atticus' uncle, whose bequest would soon make him rich. Loans to friends and kinsmen were usually interest-free; 1 per cent interest is actually by the month, so 12 per cent on our annual reckoning. But the subject-matter rejected by Seneca is taken from both the first book, and from the letters of the 50s when Caesar and Pompey backed various candidates.

118.4   *How much greater happiness*: this message is common to Stoics and Epicureans; compare Lucretius's image of the unambitious man delighted to watch the struggles of political careerists, like someone watching a dangerous sea-storm from a safe height on land (*On the Nature of the Universe*, II.1–13).

118.16   *makes an arch*: this letter is full of physical analogies, probably derived from Seneca's Greek reading.

121.1   *Posidonius and Archidemus*: this reference is pretty much all we know about Archidemus; it is more helpful that Posidonius is summoned to defend as part of ethics the question whether all animals are conscious of their own natural constitution. Kidd notes that we cannot tell how much of Seneca's argument is owed to Posidonius and how much is his own.

121.4 *can easily transform*: that is, by turning *felicitas*, happiness or lucki-ness, into *infelicitas*, unhappiness, unluckiness. But Seneca's whole argument here and elsewhere is that worldly success, so-called luck, is really unhappy.

121.5 *with easy gaze and hand*: ancient painters burnt their colours in with wax.

121.10 *most citizens in their togas*: Seneca's Latin uses *togati*, 'toga-wearing', to denote the better sort of Roman citizens, just as Virgil and Augustus himself spoke of Romans as the toga-wearing race.

122.1 *The daylight is now suffering some loss*: this opening phrase sets the letter some time after midsummer. Seneca probably associated the decreasing days with the approach of the autumn equinox described in *Georgics*, I.208.

122.2 *tardy lights for them*: from *Georgics*, I.250–1, Virgil's adaptation of Era-tosthenes' explanation of the relationship between the northern and southern hemispheres. But it is the seasons, not the time of day and night, which are reversed in the southern hemisphere.

122.3 *birds of night*: owls (*noctuae*) and other night-birds were ill-omened.

122.4 *in the arrogant shade*: the first of several phrases damaged in the text, which will be marked by angle-brackets and stopgap translation or paraphrase.

122.13 *give Butas the day's greetings*: Seneca groups two different sets of anecdotes, those about Butas and the jest of Pinarius Natta at Julius Montanus' addiction to descriptions of dawn and dusk reported in father Seneca's reminiscences, *Contr.* VII.1.27–8. (The excerpts from Montanus are otherwise unknown.) The link between the texts is made by Geminus Varus' two witticisms.

122.15 *Albinovanus Pedo*: a poet and declaimer, contemporary with Ovid. Sen-eca's father quotes an excerpt from Pedo's hexameters about Drusus' exploration of the Baltic.

123.7 *a squad of Numidian horsemen*: cf. letter 87.4–7 on the display of wealthy men when travelling; imported slaves, prized for their dark skins, were at a premium; so, it seems, were fancy household pages whose boyish skins needed protecting. The fuss, then, is about exteriors.

medication: to protect the page-boys' girlish complexions from suntan.

123.10 *your girlfriend's envy*: an interesting sidelight of casual sex relation-ships. This man has a mistress (and no doubt a wife somewhere), but can provoke her jealousy by flirting with slave-boys, who have no option but to suffer their master's attentions.

123.12   *unless he was bound*: Ulysses was a heroic model to the Stoics (compare Horace's outline of his adventures in *Epistles*, I.2), and bears out Stoic rejection of pleasure by having his men block their ears, and then bind him so he could hear the enchanting songs of the Sirens without yielding to temptation and following them.

123.12   *. . . is shameful*: the text is damaged after 'and in hope' and my translation is a stopgap.

123.16   *Superstition*: used here and elsewhere of false beliefs about real gods. By fearing them this worshipper wrongs them.

124.1   *. . . to know small cares*: from *Georgics*, I.176–7.

124.6   *The objector says*: (cf. §13). Seneca is representing an Epicurean and materialist adversary who measures everything against the goal of pleasure (§2) and bases all judgements on the evidence of the senses.

INDEX OF PERSONS

References are by letter and section; names in small capitals are philosophers and literary sources. Contemporary and historical Romans and Greeks are lower case. Romans are cited by the form of name used by Seneca.

INDEX OF PLACES AND THINGS

Some topics, such as death and Fortune, the wise man, heroic self-sacrifice, and luxury are so widespread that it would be impossible to list them; only a minimal selection is offered.

Bhagavad Gita

The Bible Authorized King James Version
  With Apocrypha

Dhammapada

Dharmasūtras

The Koran

The Pañcatantra

The Sauptikaparvan (from the
  Mahabharata)

The Tale of Sinuhe and Other Ancient
  Egyptian Poems

The Qur'an

Upaniṣads